B
Finance
27

P9-CSF-285

Financial Planning for the Entrepreneur

Notes, Profiles, Cases

Donald E. Vaughn

Professor of Finance
Southern Illinois University
Carbondale, Illinois

Prentice Hall
Upper Saddle River, New Jersey 07458

Library of Congress Cataloging-in-Publication Data

Vaughn, Donald E.
    Financial planning for the entrepreneur : notes, profiles, cases /
  by Donald E. Vaughn.
      p.   cm.
    Includes bibliographical references and index.
    ISBN 0-13-362906-6
    1. Small business—United States—Finance. 2. Small business—
  United States—Finance—Case studies.   I. Title.
  HG4027.7.V38   1997
  658.15'92—dc20   96-8288
                                                  CIP

Acquisitions Editor: Elizabeth Sugg
Editorial/Production Services and Interior Design: Laura Cleveland,
WordCrafters Editorial Services, Inc.
Cover Director: Jayne Conte
Prepress/Manufacturing Buyer: Ed O'Dougherty
Managing Editor: Mary Carnis
Director of Production and Manufacturing: Bruce Johnson

© 1997 by Prentice-Hall, Inc.
A Simon & Schuster Company
Upper Saddle River, NJ 07458

All rights reserved. No part of this book may be reproduced, in any form or by
any means, without permission in writing from the publisher.

Printed in the United States of America
10 9 8 7 6 5 4 3 2 1

ISBN 0-13-362906-6

Prentice-Hall International (UK) Limited, *London*
Prentice-Hall of Australia Pty., Limited, *Sydney*
Prentice-Hall Canada Inc., *Toronto*
Prentice-Hall Hispanoamericana, S.A., *Mexico*
Prentice-Hall of India Private Limited, *New Delhi*
Prentice-Hall of Japan, Inc., *Tokyo*
Simon & Schuster Asia Pte. Ltd., *Singapore*
Editora Prentice-Hall do Brasil, Ltda., *Rio de Janeiro*

Contents

Preface

Ten years ago, few colleges and universities offered a curriculum in small business management. Today, many universities have added this series of courses to their business curriculum. The reason for this becomes apparent when one analyzes the number of jobs created by small business concerns. Over the 1980s and into the 1990s, large businesses tended to consolidate and to eliminate unneeded jobs. The manufacturing sector in the nation, especially, lost jobs from about 1975 through 1984. Since that time, the sector has begun to expand slightly, but with downsizing in many industries. In the early 1990s, large firms began to streamline their operations by layoffs and early retirement incentive programs. Contributions to health-care plans that had previously been provided by the firms were now often required by the employees. The percentage of small business firms grew by a large ratio, creating a million or more jobs in most years. Special strength was noted in the finance and services sectors, although job growth continued to be moderate in retail trade organizations.

A typical small business management curriculum requires the normal business core courses in accounting, economics, management, marketing, mathematics, quantitative analysis in business, legal environment, international trade, business ethics, business communications, business policy, and the like. Other courses are usually added in the functional areas of business most needed by the business entrepreneur. These include a standard business law course covering form of organization, contracts, negotiable instruments, and sales; a course on small business marketing; a course on small business management; and one on small business financing. Other courses might involve some coverage of taxation of the partnership and S corporation and a capstone course on small business policy or an internship on small business problem solving.

The number of quality texts available on small business planning is woefully small. Few have been designed specifically to deal with marketing or financial problem issues faced by the small business person. Cases on small business finance are scarce. Business and industry profile data are ancient, if one depends on the start-up series published by the Small Business Administration in the 1970s with only a moderate amount of updates since that time.

This book-series, *Financial Planning for the Entrepreneur,* attempts to provide three types of information. First of all, teaching notes on the problem areas most often present in the area of finance to a new business person have been developed. Next, business and industry profiles have been developed which provide detailed information about the types of companies covered in the cases. Last of all, two or more cases have been developed that involve problem solving by the student about those topics previously covered in the teaching notes. More materials are provided in this teaching volume on financial planning for the entrepreneur than can probably be covered in one semester. First of all, the teaching note (consisting of one chapter of Part I) should probably be covered in class for about one hour. This might be followed the second day by an industry profile on the first case. The teacher might interview students interested in beginning a business in the chosen area. The case on the same industry might then be assigned and discussed in class the next day. Tear-out assignments are provided in a *Student Guide* designed to accompany this text. Another profile and case might cover other topics presented in the first teaching note, and so forth. Some 12 teaching notes, 18 business and industry profiles, and 18 cases are included in the volume. In total, perhaps 40 to 42 of these would be covered in a semester-length course. The students, in teams of one for a single proprietorship or two for a partnership or corporation, might be asked to develop the financial section of a business plan as a term project. The teaching notes and several of the profiles might be used in a two- or three-day workshop with emphasis on business plan development.

Prospective business persons, or those who may wish to upgrade their skills in financial planning, should find the contents of this volume informative and helpful.

Thanks are expressed to the reviewers of the text for their valid suggestions on the text and especially for the preparation of the teaching aids: Michael Cicero, Highline Community College; Richard J. Stanish, Tulsa Junior College; and David Wiley, Anne Arundel Community College. Thanks are also made to Mrs. Shari Garnett, SIUC, for the final manuscript preparation.

Donald E. Vaughn

Introduction

The two most often stated reasons for business failures in the nation are management and financial problems. That is, beginning business persons do not know enough about the problems and pitfalls in certain management areas. Moreover, they are undercapitalized and are unable to convince creditors of their worthiness to borrow funds needed for operating the firm. Interestingly enough, some four out of five business firms that are begun fail within five years of initiation. Those that are franchise operations under the direction of a franchiser have been able to reverse that ratio. That is, only about one in five of such firms fail. This is because a company that is franchising another, even though it charges an up-front fee of several thousand dollars and a periodic assessment fee for ongoing management, use of trade name, or joint advertising, has been in the business and has developed successful approaches to management. Moreover, it requires that a minimum capital be available to the prospective business person before a franchise will be issued to begin operations. The second problem area is that of financial management.

This combination book of teaching notes, business and industry profiles, and cases has attempted to draw together materials that are thought to be useful to the prospective entrepreneur or to one who is considering expanding his or her business. The profiles themselves have been developed around nine areas of possible interest to the new or expanding entrepreneur. These include industry characteristics and prospects, cost and types of assets needed to start a business, typical business ratios, site selection and facilities considerations, market opportunities in various-sized communities, experience and training required, legal considerations, keys to successful business, and sources of other information about the industry/type of business.

Since about 1972, the U.S. Department of Commerce has been classifying business firms by a standard industrial classification code (SIC code) of up to four digits. Several thousand different classifications are prescribed by the federal agency, and certainly only a few of these may be covered in case analysis in any one course. The SIC designations have been revised two times since 1972, with the addition of some separate SIC codes in 1989. For example, video rental was added as a separate category in that year. In earlier years, it was not very important, but by 1989, there were close to 100,000 firms in the nation that leased videotapes for home viewing. Since that time, some have failed while others have been initiated.

An effort has been made with the development of this teaching package to include one or more business profiles from most sectors of the economy. The ones on landscape firms and fruit farming are representative of those in the agricultural area. Homebuilding represents contract construction, and two are selected from the manufacturing sector. These are garment manufacturing and desktop publishing. Wholesale durable and nondurable goods are covered in a single profile. Most of the profiles are selected from retail trade and service industries, but these are the two that are the most widely represented by small firms. In the retail trade area, profiles are provided on restaurants, mail-order houses, and apparel and accessory stores. Service industries selected include such things as travel agencies, real estate offices, business services (janitorial), temporary help service firms, retirement centers and homes, and management consulting firms. The primary reasons for making these selections are two-fold. First of all, most can be started with a minimum of capital and often on a part-time basis. Second, most offer above-average opportunity for growth if operated efficiently.

Before a business firm is begun or expanded into another geographic area, it is wise for the planner to examine the degree of competition already existing in the area. The annual government document published by the Department of Commerce, *County Business Patterns*, is especially useful in this approach. One can determine on a national basis the average population and personal income needed (or actually existing) for the average of such SIC-coded businesses. An examination of those operating in a given territory, such as a county or adjacent counties, can then be compared with the personal income and population therein. Thus one can deduce, on average, whether or not the firm is over- or underrepresented in that geographical area. The retail, wholesale, and service volumes of the five-year *Business Census* might be used in similar fashion for a city of greater than about 2,500 population. Where the information is available, community profiles might be available from electric utility or telecommunications firms. Donneley Marketing Service, for a fee, will provide an analysis of certain types of firms within a given locale and does provide certain demographic data within a certain radius of a given city, such as 10, 20, or 30 miles. This type of information, of course, should be factored into one's thinking about the likelihood of success, or lack of it, that might occur if beginning a certain type of business in a given location.

Certainly a business firm should not be started unless the owner/manager has had some relevant experience. This might be gained from being an employee in a similar type of operation or from having worked in a family-owned business. However, engineers or marketing specialists frequently conceive ideas for marketing or manufacturing novel types of services and products. Steps needed to develop a business plan involve most functional areas of business, such as manufacturing (or buying) the product, marketing the product, financing the product, controlling the cost of the product, and so on. Problems exist in the legal areas, including need for proper zoning of the organization, carrying adequate insurance, proper income recognition and tax payment, and so on. These related areas are covered to a degree in the business and industry profiles, and some are mentioned as side issues in the teaching notes and short cases. An outline on important market analysis considerations and one for general management and financing factors, thought to be helpful in developing a business plan, appear in the *Student Guide*. An example of a business plan often required by banks or other lenders has been designed to aid the reader in such development. Certainly before a business firm is begun, a business plan should be developed by the managers/owners of the firm. Moreover, many bankers or other government program lenders require a business plan as an integral part of a loan application.

The business plan should provide a well-thought-out approach to beginning the operation, including such financial topics as selecting the form of business (a proprietorship, a partnership, or a regular or S corporation); the approximate assets needed by the firm (ratio analysis and projected statement preparation are important here); cash flow analysis; capital budgeting; working capital management (such as inventory, receivables, and cash); liability management; capital structure planning; and evaluating a closely held firm. The latter might be needed in buyouts and sellouts, in fixing the value of assets in legal suits, for estate tax purposes, and so on. Thus these areas have been included in the coverage due to their importance to small and intermediate-sized business firms and their management.

Ideally, a course in financial management for the small firm would have between 20 and 30 students. This would provide a class large enough to develop a good discussion of relevant case, profile, and problem areas while permitting sufficient time for each student to express opinions about materials being covered. It is suggested that for each of the 12 major topics covered, about one-half to one hour of class time be spent on the teaching note (consisting of one chapter in Part I), another hour on the discussion of major points for a given industry profile, and another half hour to one hour on each of the cases. A few of the longer cases might be appropriate for comprehensive written examination exercises.

Most of the cases are reasonably short, as they probably should be for undergraduate students or business persons in a management development class. The readers of the cases are directed to do certain things. Full-blown cases often provide industry and company information. Instead, this book takes the approach of developing rather extensive industry and business profiles with short cases developed to illustrate limited financial problems for a company in the industry already described in a business profile.

Other profiles are published in other sources, such as by the Small Business Administration, and some financial management teachers might find it desirable to team up the industry profile books with a casebook containing cases of greater length for graduate students. This combination book, however, is thought to contain a desirable mix of textual material, industry description, and case problem exercises for students in an undergraduate course in small business finance or students in a management executive program learning about financial management problems.

In this brief treatise on financial planning for the small business, however, only limited coverage is possible. Effort was made to concentrate on those issues thought to be of significant importance in the financial management area to entrepreneurship, including the following:

- The legal form of organization, including tax implications
- The importance of ratio analysis in planning
- Techniques and uses of projected financial statements
- Techniques and approaches for designing a cash flow schedule
- Reasons and approaches for developing a business plan
- Techniques and approaches for evaluating the capital budget
- Inventory management considerations
- Accounts receivable management considerations
- Cash and temporary investment management issues
- Liability management considerations
- Capital structure planning approaches
- Evaluating a closely held firm
- Business plan outline

As stated previously, a teaching note on one of the above 12 problem areas of financial management should probably be followed in class with one or two business and industry profiles. Two or three case problems might then be discussed which attempt to illustrate the concepts described in the teaching notes.

The executive development instructor would likely concentrate on the teaching notes and the industry profiles with limited time spent on the case problems.

PART I
Major Topics

1 *Selecting the Form of Business*

About 15 million business firms operate in the United States. Roughly 60% of them operate as single proprietorships, about 20% as partnerships, and about 20% as corporations. Some of the latter that qualify are S corporations while the others are regular corporations and are taxed as a separate entity.

The Proprietorship

The single proprietorship does not legally have to operate independently and apart from the personal affairs of the single owner. For example, a person may operate a family-owned business from within the home. Some examples include a person who works as a maid or painter for another, but works from her or his own home; a person who does home typing for others; a professional who does management consulting from a bedroom/office of the home; and so on.

Some communities require that an operating permit be obtained, but the Internal Revenue Service requires only that operating expenses be properly accounted for and reported on Schedule C of the federal Form 1040 (long form) income tax return. Where employees exist, social security taxes equal to 7.65% of wages (up to the maximum tax base of $60,600 in 1994) must be deducted from wages paid, along with appropriate deductions for state and federal income taxes, and paid into a depository financial institution at required intervals, such as monthly. Each employee must file with his or her employer an IRS W-4 tax withholding statement showing the number of exemptions claimed. The owner must then withhold the appropriate amount of taxes from earnings, accumulating the total, and report it to the IRS and the taxpayer on a W-2 statement the following year before January 31. Failure to make timely deposits of the withheld taxes with a depository bank is viewed by the IRS as embezzlement of government funds.

In a single proprietorship, the owner does not have to maintain separately the business and personal assets; but neither is there separation of them for business purposes. That is, a creditor may look toward business or personal assets in settlement of a claim of a business or personal nature. Thus, the owner should acquire certain types of insurance covering assets, professional action, and the like.

The Partnership

A partnership (an association between two or more co-owners of a business firm operated with the intention of earning a profit) may be operated on a formal or informal basis. Two persons may jointly buy a lottery ticket weekly, for example, agreeing to split the winnings of any lucky draw. Each should sign on the back of the ticket as co-owners. In a regular business situation, it is best to develop a formal agreement covering important points of the association of the two or more persons. The articles of copartnership, as they are called, should contain all or most of the following items:

1. The nature of the business operation, with any limits imposed
2. The name and business address of the firm and its owners
3. The beginning and ending dates of the partnership
4. The initial capital contribution of each partner
5. The bank(s) of deposit, drawers of checks, number of signatures required on checks, borrowing rights of owners, etc.
6. The treatment of additional advances to/from the partners
7. The right to cash withdrawals from the firm, with rate of interest charged (if any)
8. The amount of time that each partner is to devote to business
9. Limits on incurring contractual obligations in the firm's name (though not always binding on unknowing third parties)
10. The division of profits and losses (i.e., allocation of wages, return on equity, division of the balance, etc.)
11. Plans for accumulating additional capital in the firm
12. Any insurance coverage (property, liability, professional)
13. Limits upon the conduct of one or more partners (e.g., in the areas of hiring/firing employees, leasing/buying assets, or making certain important business decisions)
14. Plans for liquidating or continuing the business in the event of death or incapacity of one partner (e.g., buyout terms)
15. Plans for disposing of business properties in the event that the firm is dissolved
16. Treatment of other differences that may arise among the surviving partners or beneficiaries of a deceased partner
17. Execution of the contract with duly recognized witnesses

Of the preceding items, those that cause the most dispute are usually the amount of time spent in the business, other nonbusiness activities undertaken by one or more of the partners, and withdrawals of large amounts of funds from the firm for personal reasons.

A partnership should be operated with an organizational chart. That is, the partners and employees of the firm should have specifically assigned duties, such as the following:

Partner A, for example, might be in charge of buying inventory items, advertising, and developing selling strategies. He or she might make direct contact with the customers of the firm. The second partner might be in charge of operations, supervising the employees in their daily assigned duties. For example, the above organization might be appropriate for a janitorial or house-cleaning firm with two partners and several employees. One partner might concentrate on marketing their goods or services while the second one supervises the employees in their daily tasks. One of the partners, a spouse to one of them, or a hired person might handle office reception duties and record keeping.

While a partnership does not have to pay federal or state income taxes in its own name, the taxing authorities do require that an informational tax return be filed, allocating certain expenses and profits and losses to the partners. For example, interest, ad valorem taxes, and charitable contributions are allocated to the partners and claimed on their personal returns for actual deductions. Most other business deductions are subtracted from revenues in arriving at partnership profits. This (or the loss) is then allocated to each partner on the basis of a prearranged division, and this portion is recognized by each partner on his or her own income tax return. Income earned from a partnership or a proprietorship is considered to be self-employment income, and the person pays old-age, survivors', disability, and health insurance (OASDHI) taxes equal to two times the social security tax rate, with one-half of the amount being a deductible business expense.

The Corporation

A corporation is said to be an intangible being, existing only under contemplation of law. The statutes of a state govern how a corporate form of organization is to be set up and operated. Many states mandate that at least three shareholders and directors exist. Some permit as few as one. Most also require that articles of incorporation be filed with the secretary of state covering such things as the following:

1. The name of the corporation
2. The names and addresses of registered agents of the firm
3. The purpose(s) for which the firm is organized
4. The class(es), number, and par value of shares authorized
5. The number of shares to be issued initially
6. The names of the initial directors to serve on the board
7. An estimate as to the value of property owned by the firm, its location, gross receipts expected within the state, etc.
8. Other important provisions (preemptive rights, cumulative voting, duration of the charter, etc.)
9. Signature and address block for incorporators

The cost of incorporation may be very small if the amount of stock to be issued is not large. In many states, it is only about $50, plus perhaps a filing fee. In other states it may be several thousand. A not-for-profit corporation usually is issued an operating permit on a yearly basis and may have to renew this from year-to-year, perhaps paying a $5 annual filing fee. Many states issue a 50-year temporary charter to regular corporations.

Beginning in about 1958, federal tax laws permitted the formation of *S corporations* where certain conditions exist. Up to 35 owners are permitted, if all individual owners elect this treatment; all must be citizens (businesses are not permitted such holdings); and the election must be made within 90 days of the beginning of each tax year. The form for election must be filed with the federal IRS. Rather than the firm being taxed as a separate firm (as is a regular or *C corporation*), earnings are apportioned to the owners on the basis of their shareholding. Profits earned by the firm may be retained in the business for expansion purposes or withdrawn, but wages paid to the shareholders for services rendered are treated in the same way as for other employees. That is, the firm pays its 7.65% of wages, up to the OASDHI base, as social security (deducting a similar amount from the wages of the employee), withholds an appropriate amount for state and federal income taxes (depending on the W-4 exemptions claimed), and transmits the collected taxes to a depository financial institution monthly or more often. W-2 statements are then issued to employees soon after the close of each operating year. Extra taxable income is taxed the same as it is to self-employed persons (i.e., partners).

It is advisable for the incorporators of a corporation to draft a set of bylaws (containing somewhat similar items as the copartnership agreement above) that spell out certain aspects of business. For a small corporation, this might include the following items:

1. Location and address of the principal office of the firm
2. Location and time of annual (or special) meetings of shareholders of the firm
3. The number of directors and the duration of their terms
4. The officers of the firm to be appointed by the directors
5. The type of corporate seal used with stock certificates and other negotiable instruments
6. The types and locations of company books to be maintained
7. The fiscal year of the firm
8. The form and content of the stock certificates to be issued, along with the signatures required on each
9. The nature of dividends (cumulative on preferred shares) to be declared
10. Techniques for amending the bylaws of the firm

The organization chart for a corporation might be somewhat similar to the one for a partnership, except that it usually has several additional layers of management. These include:

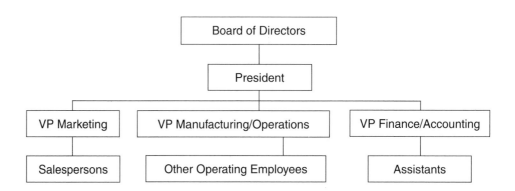

While the IRS requires that a corporation file a federal income tax return in its own name and recognize business expenses as offsets against operating income, a special chapter of the law, as stated above, does permit certain corporations to elect the S corporation treatment. Most firms pay out a portion of earnings as dividends and retain the balance for expanding working capital and long-term assets of the firm, to pay off contractual debt arrangements, and so on. The primary advantage of this form of organization, at some cost in taxes, is the separation of the business debts of the firm from personal debts of its owners.

Making a Choice

Whether a firm operates as a partnership, a regular corporation, or an S corporation depends on the desires of the owners. Tax considerations, the desire to limit liabilities to the owners, and financial leverage are some important motives for electing the corporate (versus the partnership) form of business. The ease in raising equity and debt by a corporation is a strong motivator. Having limited liabilities for corporate owners is another. Taxes are often higher for the C corporation than for individual taxpayers.

QUESTIONS/PROBLEMS

1. List five usual characteristics of the single proprietorship, the general partnership, the regular corporation, and the S corporation.
2. List ten problem areas that should be addressed by the articles of copartnership.
3. Suggest ten items that should be covered by the bylaws of a small corporation.
4. Suggest tax differences and similarities of a general partnership and a regular corporation.
5. Develop an organizational chart for two brothers who jointly operate a lawnmower sales and repair shop. Assume two employees: an office person and a sales/repair handyman.
6. Indicate the pros and cons of operating a firm as a proprietorship, a general partnership, a C corporation, and an S corporation.

2 *Financial Ratio Analysis*

Several types of financial analysts are interested in ratio analysis. Shareholders and bondholders are interested in the long-term financial strength of a firm, creditors are interested in the short-term credit repayment ability of a borrower, and managers are interested in keeping their firm financially viable so that it has potential borrowing power and is able to sell new expansion shares in the marketplace should the need arise.

Common-Sized Statements

Benchmark financial statements, balance sheets and income statements, are provided by a number of sources, such as: Robert L. Morris Associates (RLM) *Statement Studies*, the annual *Corporate Income* and *Unincorporated Income* publications by the Internal Revenue Service, and the annual updated comparative statements and ratios on 800 lines of business published by Dun & Bradstreet, Inc. (D & B). Such industrywide financial statements are sometimes published by trade journals and security investment services such as *Value Line Investment Survey* and Standard & Poor's *Industry Survey*.

Key Financial Ratios

Financial ratios are computed from balance sheets and income statements for a firm and for its representative industry, and then the ratios are compared. This is referred to as comparative analysis. As an alternative, the ratios may be compared between two, three, or more similar companies rather than for the industry and one company. Trend ratio analysis is sometimes done for a firm using financial statements for several years. Thus the trends in growing or waning financial strength can be seen.

The arithmetic mean (average) balance sheet and skeleton income statement for SIC 5651 (family clothing stores) are provided below for study. This statement was provided by the 1992–1993 D & B comparison of ratios for 800 lines of business. Some 1,464 stores from this SIC designation were used in computing the average financial statements. The statements are sometimes presented in dollar form with percentages shown parallel so that easy comparisons may be made by the financial analyst. The average statement for this designation is as follows:

Account	Dollars	Percentages
ASSETS		
Cash	$42,304	15.9%
Accounts receivable	19,157	7.2
Notes receivable	1,064	0.4
Inventory	133,565	50.2
Other current assets	10,377	3.9
Total current assets	206,466	77.6
Fixed assets	35,653	13.4
Other noncurrent assets	23,946	9.0
Total assets	266,065	100.0
LIABILITIES AND CAPITAL		
Accounts payable	23,414	8.8
Bank loans	1,064	0.4
Notes payable (other)	11,175	4.2
Other current debts	21,817	8.2
Total current debts	57,470	21.6
Other long-term debts	23,414	8.8
Net worth (equity of owners)	185,181	69.6
Total debts and net worth	266,065	100.0
Net sales	415,505	100.0
Gross profit	145,427	35.0
Net profit after taxes	22,853	5.5

The financial analyst may compute several dozen financial ratios from the above balance sheet and income statement. For example, the current ratio, or current assets/current debts would be $206,466/$57,470 or 3.6 to 1. This may then be compared to the similar ratio for a particular company. However, much work in the computations has been done by D & B, plus they have added another feature.

One might be interested in knowing whether or not certain ratios for their firm are in the top 25% of the industry's array, in the second quartile, in the third quartile, or in the lower 25%. This placement is facilitied by D & B in reporting upper quartile (UQ), median, and lower quartile (LQ) ratios for each of the 800 industry groups. For the SIC 5651 designation, 14 frequently used financial ratios, grouped as solvency ratios, efficiency ratios, and profitability ratios, are provided with these three point values. For family clothing stores, these in 1992–1993 were as follows:

Ratio	UQ	Median	LQ
Solvency ratios:			
Quick ratio (times)	3.4	1.1	0.4
Current ratio (times)	11.3	4.8	2.5
Current liabilities to net worth (%)	7.5	19.3	52.2
Current liabilities to inventory (%)	14.1	32.3	63.6
Total liabilities to net worth (%)	9.5	26.3	71.3
Fixed assets to net worth (%)	5.8	16.3	41.9
Efficiency ratios:			
Collection period (days)	3.7	12.4	35.8
Sales to inventory (times)	5.9	3.7	2.5
Assets to sales (%)	34.5	52.7	81.6
Sales to net working capital (times)	5.9	3.4	2.0
Accounts payable to sales (%)	2.1	4.3	7.2
Profitability ratios:			
Return on sales (%)	10.6	4.1	0.8
Return on assets (%)	16.0	6.1	1.3
Return on net worth (%)	24.0	9.2	2.0

We shall now review a few of the above ratios in the industry. The quick ratio is the relationship between quick assets (all current assets except for inventory) and current liabilities. For this industry, some 25% had quick ratios of 3.4 times or greater, 50% had such ratios falling between 3.4 and 0.4 times, and 25% had such ratios of 0.4 or lower. The median ratios (or the center company in the array of 1,464 firms) are shown in the center column. Debt to net worth ratios were from 9.5% to 71.3% for the inner-quartile range. That is, the center 50% of the firms had debt/equity ratios within these bounds. Some quarters fell above or below this range.

Mean Versus Median Ratios

Mean ratios and median ratios are not always equal. If the distribution of ratios is about symmetrical, they are identical or very close, but if the ratios are skewed to the right, the mean ratio will exceed the median ratio. This is usually the case in financial analysis. For example, the mean net profit after taxes (on sales) was shown above as 5.5%. The median ratio was only 4.1%. Thus, the above average return on sales was assumed to be on larger firms that weighed more heavily in computing the arithmetic mean. However, both of these comparisons are important for different reasons.

Mean ratios are unbiased estimates and may be used in computing estimated financial statements, while the use of medians may produce some inconsistencies. However, in judging whether a firm falls into the upper quartile, the upper median, the lower median, or the lower quartile (for credit evaluation, perhaps), the quartile figures and median figures are used.

Some of the above ratios, plus some additional ones for small firms, medium-sized firms, and large firms for about 400 lines of business (primarily retail trade and service firms), are reported in the annual update of RLM's *Statement Studies*. Should the financial analyst wish, for example, to know the percentage of sales paid as officers' salaries, this would be an excellent source. Moreover, bank loan officers in their credit analysis usually compare a firm's ratios to the RLM database. D & B ratios are easy to use and available on a larger group of firms, but the analyst might find some SIC designations provided in one of these sources that are not provided in the other. Thus both sources should be consulted where appropriate.

Interpreting Financial Ratios

The financial analyst should not be unduly alarmed if one or two financial ratios appear to be out of line for a company. The ratios should instead be viewed as a group. An out-of-line ratio should be investigated, however, as to the reason for its variance from the norm. For example, current liabilities may have risen to two times the previous level caused by tax liabilities owed due to a 500% gain in net profits. While this current debt must be paid, it also points toward a very attractive profit picture for the firm.

In the business and industry profiles that follow, only eight or nine of the key ratios described above are reported, selected from solvency ratios, efficiency ratios, and profitability ratios. The reader, of course, is encouraged to check out the above-referenced ratios at a nearby college or public library for more up-to-date information on his or her industry under review.

The short-term creditor is mainly concerned with the current debt-paying ability of the borrower. The bondholders or mortgage holders want security for their loans, as a rule, and are interested in the long-term viability of the firm. The equity owner prefers an above-average return on the owner's equity of the firm, but wishes to avoid so much financial and operating leverage (i.e., debt/equity mix and fixed versus variable expenses) that the firm might fall into bankruptcy or liquidation proceedings.

QUESTIONS/PROBLEMS

1. List five items on a balance sheet that are usually shown as current assets.

2. List five items that are classified as current debts.
3. List five solvency ratios provided by Dun & Bradstreet.
4. List five efficiency ratios provided by Dun & Bradstreet.
5. List five ways that profits or returns may be reported for a business firm. Refer to the above financial statements for your responses.

3 Forecasting Financial Statements

One of the major tools used by the financial specialist in a firm is forecasted financial statements. These balance sheets and income statements are prepared from either historical ones or from assumptions about the level of assets and operations (i.e., revenues and expenses) for the firm.

Illustration

Let us illustrate the techniques for forecasting income statements and balance sheets for a small firm that operates as a beauty shop in the setting of a retirement village. First of all, we must make some assumptions about the beginning level of clients or potential clients, how they are expected to grow, and the level of expected revenues anticipated. Then we need to assume (or know) the initial level of assets/equity committed to the establishment.

In this illustration, we shall assume that the beauty shop is to be operated in a retirement village with an average of 400 first-year citizens, 600 second-year members, and 800 third-year members. Let us assume that 55% of the community citizens are females and have need for beauty shop treatment at our small firm. Let us also assume that sale of beauty aids at two times their cost will average 20% of service revenues, and that the average charge per customer will be $10 in year 1, $10.50 in year 2, $11 in year 3, and so on, in order to keep pace with anticipated inflation.

Next, we need to make assumptions about the beginning level of assets for the firm. Let us assume that Mrs. Mary Smith, sole owner of the small corporation, plans to invest $15,000 of her savings in the business. She agrees to pay the owner of a commercial building 10% of revenues for rent and utilities; plans to pay 50% of service revenues as salary/commissions; expects fixed costs other than depreciation and amortization of leasehold improvement to be $200 monthly; expects payroll taxes of 10% of total payroll; and expects other variable costs to run 10% of gross receipts.

During the first year of operation, Mrs. Smith anticipates that 15% of the ladies in the community will desire weekly beauty treatment. This ratio is anticipated to rise by 1% yearly. Of the $10,000 to be spent for equipment in the shop, some $9,000 of it will have a 20-year life while $1,000 will have a 5-year life. A $6,000 note with no interest will be given in partial payment for the equipment with the balance to be repaid over 30 months. Each note payment is expected to be $200 monthly. The $9,000 expenditure for equipment is only enough to install two beauty chairs, with sinks appropriately located, and two sets of hair-drying equipment. The $1,000 is to pay for small electrical devices and hand-held equipment needed by each operator. As operators are added, they are expected to provide their own hand-held equipment. Mrs. Smith believes this level of equipment should be adequate for the first five years of operations. At that time, she may seek larger quarters and add another chair or two.

Initial Balance Sheet

The initial balance sheet for the Smith Beauty Salon, Inc., should appear about as follows:

Balance Sheet 1/1/X1
Smith Beauty Salon, Inc.

Cash in bank	$10,000	Trade payables (beauty aids)	$3,000
Inventories	3,000	Notes payable	6,000
Equipment:		Total debt	9,000
20-year life	9,000	Net worth	15,000
Miscellaneous (5-year life)	1,000	Total debt and net worth	24,000
Leasehold improvement	1,000		
Total assets	24,000		

Forecasting Revenues and Expenses

The next step in the procedure is to forecast the level of anticipated revenues to the shop. For year 1, this is expected to be about as follows:

patrons × average weekly spending × weeks open during year =
$400 \times (.55 \times .15 \times \$10.00) \times 50 = \$16,500$

Sales of beauty aids to patrons were estimated as 20% of this level (or $3,300). Thus, total anticipated revenues are $19,800 ($16,500 plus $3,300).

Anticipated expenses are about as follows for the Smith Beauty Salon:

Salary paid to Mrs. Smith, manager	$8,500
Payroll taxes: 10% of payroll	850
Fixed costs: $200 monthly × 12 months	2,400
Depreciation at 5% and 20%; amortization at 10%	750
Variable cost for rent and utilities: 10% of revenues	
(Revenues = $16,500 + $3,300 sale of beauty aids)	1,980
Cost of beauty aids used in operation (.10 × $16,500)	1,650
Cost of beauty aids sold to patrons (.50 × $3,300)	1,650
Other variable costs: Advertising, insurance, etc.	1,980
Total expenses	$19,760

Net income, then, is projected to be $40 ($19,800 less $19,760).

Forecasting an Income Statement

Now let us recast the income statement into the usual format used for such statements by most service-type organizations.

Income Statement for Year 1
Smith Beauty Salon, Inc.

Revenues:		
From services		$16,500
From sale of beauty aids		3,300
Total revenues		19,800
Expenses:		
Rent (including utilities)	$1,980	
Other variable expenses:		
Cost of beauty aids used	1,650	
Cost of beauty aids sold	1,650	
Payroll taxes	850	
Other variable expenses: 10%	1,980	8,110
Fixed costs:		
Salary to manager	8,500	
Other: $200/mo.	2,400	
Depreciation: $450 + $200	650	
Amortization of leasehold	100	11,650
Total expenses		19,760
Net income or loss		40

While the above suggests that the level of operation for the small firm is only about break-even the first year, this is about as good as is usually realized by a start-up firm. In the second year, if fixed and variable costs can be controlled and revenues improve, then some greater level of profits is anticipated.

Later Statements

Let us now recast the balance sheet as it should appear at the end of year 1 (or the beginning of year 2):

Balance Sheet 1/1/X2
Smith Beauty Salon, Inc.

Cash (squeeze to balance)		$7,190	Trade payables	$1,000
Inventories		3,000	Bank note	3,600
Equipment	$10,000		Accruals	1,200
Less depreciation	650	9,350	Total current debt	5,800
Leasehold improvement	1,000			
Less amortization	100	900	Net worth	15,040
Miscellaneous assets (assumed)		400	Total debt and net worth	20,840
Total assets		20,840		

We would continue this operation for a year or two. We might set the level of inventory, which we could probably buy on net 30- or 60-day terms, at several months of anticipated needs. We would, of course, need to stock a supply of beauty aids for sale to interested patrons as well as those needed in the beauty shop service.

Practice Exercise

As a practice exercise, assume that the number of women in the village increases to 330 during year 2, that 16% of them seek weekly service at the beauty salon; that prices charged rise by 5%; and that all other variable costs and fixed costs remain similar to the above schedule. Now construct the income statement for year 2 and the expected balance sheet at the end of that period.

QUESTIONS/PROBLEMS

1. Complete the practice exercise as suggested in the text.

2. Suggest assumptions needed for making projected financial statements by a start-up service firm.

3. Assume equity of $50,000 for each of two partners. Select a profile in this text and project sales for 5 years with a rate of growth in sales of 1/2, 1/3, 1/4, and 1/5 for years 2 through 5. Use common-sized ratios for your estimates. Project a balance sheet at zero time, after one year, and after three years. Comment on the reasonableness of your esti-

mates. Suggest amounts of funds needed from outside sources and some possible sources, by years.

4. For your firm in Problem 3, design an appropriate organizational chart and comment on personnel needs and availability in your geographic area of intended operation.

4 Projecting Cash Inflows and Outflows

Assumptions

This teaching note is a continuation of the one on the Smith Beauty Salon in Chapter 3, Forecasting Financial Statements, and the same facts or assumptions outlined in that situation will be applied in this analysis. The beauty salon has been in operation in a retirement village for three years, and the number of customers has averaged 220 in year 1, 330 in year 2, and 440 in year 3. Of these, some 15%, 16%, and 17% were weekly customers, spending an average of $10, $10.50, and $11.00 at each trip to the beauty salon, respectively. Tips go directly to the operator, so they are not reflected in the revenues earned by the Smith Beauty Salon.

Mrs. Smith had had prior experience with operating a beauty salon, and with the above number of clients, she felt that she could perform all needed services during years 1 and 2. She planned to hire a part-time beautician in year 3, and perhaps after that time expand the equipment in the plant to accommodate at least three or four operators. Sales of products (beauty aids) at two times their cost were estimated to amount to 20% of the collection from service revenues.

Expenses of operating the beauty salon (repeated from the previous chapter) were estimated to be as follows: salary for Mrs. Smith was $8,500 yearly (but other operators would earn 50% of the shop revenues generated and 5% of sales of products); rent and utilities were set at 10% of service revenues; fixed costs (such as insurance, advertising, and other items) were estimated to be $200 monthly; variable expenses, other than those drawn from the inventory of beauty aids, were 10% of service revenues; payroll taxes were 10% of wages or commissions paid; depreciation ran about $750 yearly; and beauty aid costs were 10% of service revenues and 50% of sales of beauty aid products.

Comparative Statements

Mrs. Smith invested $15,000 in cash in the firm, but investment into long-life equipment was to be paid for over 30 months with no charge for interest from the equipment supplier. The income statements and balance sheets for the first three years of operations are shown below.

Comparative Income Statement for Smith Beauty Salon, Inc.

	Year 1	Year 2	Year 3
Facts:			
Number of customers	220	330	440
Average weekly sales per customer	$.15 \times \$10$	$.16 \times \$10.50$	$.17 \times \$11$
Weekly revenues	$ 330	$ 554	$ 823
Weeks open per year	50	50	50
Revenues:			
Services (R)	$16,500	$27,700	$41,150
Beauty aid sales (Y)	3,300	5,540	8,230
Total	$19,800	$33,240	$49,380
Expenses:			
Labor (wages)	8,500	8,500	15,360
Payroll tax: 10% of wages	850	850	1,536
Rent: $.1(R+Y)$	1,980	3,324	4,938
Fixed expenses: $200/mo.	2,400	2,400	2,400
Other variable: $.1(R+Y)$	1,980	3,324	4,938
Depreciation and amortization	750	750	750
Beauty aids: $.1R + .5Y$	3,300	5,540	8,230
Total	$19,760	$24,688	$38,152
Net income	$ 40	$ 8,552	$11,228

With input from these projected income statements and her known initial investment, Mrs. Smith pulled together the expected balance sheets for the ends of years 1 through 3. These appeared as follows:

Balance Sheets for Smith Beauty Salon, Inc.

	Year 1	Year 2	Year 3
Cash	$7,190	$12,430	$23,408
Inventories	3,000	3,600	4,200
Equipment	9,350	8,600	7,950
Leasehold improvement	900	800	700
Miscellaneous assets	400	400	400
Total assets	20,840	25,830	36,658
Trade payables	1,000	1,200	1,400
Notes payable (equipment)	3,600	1,200	—
Accruals (taxes, etc.)	1,200	1,200	1,800
Net worth	15,040	22,230	33,458

Opportunity Knocks

In January of the fourth year of operation, Mrs. Smith was contacted by the retirement village real estate developer. He had been contacted by a franchiser of beauty shops who also acted as an agent for providing internships for advanced students from the nearby community college beautician's program. He felt that it was in the best interest of the firm to become a franchisee of the parent, and he offered to reduce the rent and utilities to 7% of revenues generated from the growing operation. Mrs. Smith explored the opportunity, discovering that she would need to pay a front-end franchise fee of $15,000 and 5% of combined service revenues and sale of products, with quarterly payments. She knew that this would squeeze her profits for a time, but she felt that she would be needing to expand. She therefore decided to equip her shop with three additional beauty stations, at a total cost of $18,000, and to make quarterly payments with no assessed interest over the next 30 months, payable to the equipment supplier. She felt that she would need to hire three full-time operators and employ some of the advanced students on a part-time basis. She decided that she would continue to handle the administrative chores of the firm and to provide beauty service to some of her better clients. She guessed that commissions would run 40% of revenues generated, as she would be drawing a salary rather than a commission on the work that she did. Moreover, the students were paid only minimum wage, so they would be generating some additional income for the firm. She decided to explore the possibility by pulling together projected statements for another three years and to prepare a cash receipts and disbursements statement for the fourth year. For planning purposes, she assumed that the fixed and variable cost components would continue about in line with those for year 3.

Estimating Sales

Since the number of clients was increasing, Mrs. Smith decided that sales during quarters 1, 2, 3, and 4 would likely be about 20%, 23%, 27%, and 30% of the annual total in year 4. The projected income statements are as follows:

Projected Income Statements for Smith Beauty Salon, Inc.

	Year 1	Year 2	Year 3
Facts:			
Number of customers	550	660	770
Average weekly sales per customer	.18 × $11.50	.19 × $12.00	.20 × $12.50
Weekly revenues	$1,139	$1,505	$1,925
Weeks open per year	50	50	50

	Year 1	Year 2	Year 3
Revenues:			
Services (R)	$56,950	$75,250	$96,250
Merchandise sales (Y=.20R)	11,390	15,050	19,250
Total	$68,340	$90,300	$115,500
Expenses:			
Labor (Mrs. Smith's wages)	9,000	10,000	11,000
Commissions: .4R	22,784	30,100	38,500
Payroll tax: 10% of above	3,178	4,010	4,950
Rent: .07(R+Y)	4,784	6,321	8,085
Fixed expenses: $200/mo.	2,400	2,400	2,400
Other variable: .1(R+Y)	6,834	9,030	11,550
Depreciation and amortization	2,595	2,595	2,595
Beauty aids: .1R + .5Y	11,390	15,050	19,250
Franchise fee: .05(R+Y)	3,417	4,515	5,775
Total	$66,382	$84,021	$104,105
Net income	$ 1,958	$ 6,279	$ 11,395

Cash Flow Statements

The next step in the analysis is to develop quarterly statements of cash inflows and outflows, assuming that most items would be paid on a cash basis as they arose. Exceptions would be the payments on the equipment and a small amount of payables equal to about one-third of the inventory on hand.

	Qtr. 1	Qtr. 2	Qtr. 3	Qtr. 4	Annual Total
	INFLOWS				
Percentage of revenues	20%	23%	27%	30%	100%
Revenues	$13,668	$15,718	$18,452	$20,502	$68,340
	OUTFLOWS				
Wages	2,250	2,250	2,250	2,250	9,000
Commissions	4,557	5,240	6,152	6,835	22,784
Payroll tax	681	749	840	908	3,178
Rent	957	1,100	1,292	1,435	4,784
Fixed	600	600	600	600	2,400
Other variable	1,367	1,572	1,845	2,050	6,834
Beauty aids	2,278	2,620	3,075	3,417	11,390
Franchise fee	683	786	923	1,025	3,417
Franchise cost	15,000	—	—	—	15,000
Equipment payment	1,800	1,800	1,800	1,800	7,200
Total outflows	$30,173	$16,717	$18,777	$20,320	$85,987
Net inflows (outflows)	($16,505)	($999)	($325)	$182	($17,647)

Projecting the Balance Sheet

The last step in the analysis is to prepare projected balance sheets for the ends of years 4 through 6. Key items that can be computed from the above income statements include the balance in the leasehold improvement account, the balance in the equipment account, the balance in the notes payable—equipment account, and the balance in the capital account. Let us begin with the capital account. The balance at the end of the third year would be changed to reflect reported profits in years 4, 5, and 6, as the small corporation is assumed to be an S corporation and to pay no taxes in its own name. Instead, Mrs. Smith (or she and other shareholders) would be taxed on the firm's income at a 15% rate. As income for the firm increases, it may be necessary for Mrs. Smith to withdraw more funds from the firm in order to service the income tax indebtedness. Cash in year 4 is obtained from the cash inflow/outflow statement. Some of the miscellaneous items are estimated in years 5 and 6, so the cash account becomes a squeeze figure in those years.

The balance sheets for year-end 4, 5, and 6 for the firm are as follows:

Balance Sheets for Smith Beauty Salon, Inc.

	Year 5	Year 6	Year 7
ASSETS			
Cash (squeeze)	$ 5,756	$6,674	$16,464
Inventories	4,200	4,800	6,000
Equipment (net)	23,455	20,960	18,465
Leasehold improvement	600	500	400
Other: Franchise fee and misc.	15,400	15,400	15,400
Total assets	$49,411	$48,334	$56,729
DEBT AND NET WORTH			
Trade payables	1,396	1,600	2,000
Notes payable (0% interest)	10,800	3,600	—
Accruals	1,400	1,600	1,800
Net worth	34,815	41,534	52,929
Total debt and net worth	$48,411	$48,334	$56,729

Analysis

A review of the above financial statements shows that the beauty shop will be set back about two years in its growth in profits by franchising, but hiring one or two operators and spending funds for several other sets of beauty operators' equipment might contribute to this situation if franchising is not done.

In the face of the threat of bringing in another franchised beauty shop (if Mrs. Smith decides against this route for her firm), what approach would you as owner of the firm take? Justify your answer with discussion.

QUESTIONS/PROBLEMS

1. Why is it critical before preparing pro forma statements to have a close estimate of (a) sales or revenues for the forecasted period(s)? (b) fixed expenses and variable expense ratio?

2. What does the term "sensitivity analysis" suggest (when applied to forecasts)? How can it be applied to preparing the forecasted statements for a firm such as Smith Beauty Salon?

3. Assume that all facts other than the number of patrons held true in the text example but that they grew by only one-half of the estimated rate for years 4, 5, and 6 (due to a slowdown in the economy). Reconstruct projected statements and comment on the differences from those shown in the text.

5 *Formulating Business Objectives and Plans*

Long-Term Objectives

The first logical step in financial planning is the formulation of long-term business objectives. The firm should have a ranking or hierarchy of objectives ranging from a grand design to limited, short-term programs. The grand design might be to grow to national or international scope and to become dominant in the industry. Short-term goals might include a 15% growth rate in sales in the coming year, the introduction of a new product line, and the successful operation of a new sales territory.

Need for Objectives

The development of corporate objectives is important for a number of reasons. First of all, financial plans, organization plans, and total corporate planning are designed around the corporate objectives. Second, formalized corporate objectives can help avoid such conflicts as short-term profit maximization versus customer satisfaction. Clearly stated objectives can also enhance efficiency on the part of corporate decision makers, and thus improve the development of corporate managers. Last of all, alternate courses of action may be evaluated in terms of broad capital objectives.

Input into Objective Development

These objectives may be formulated by one individual, such as the corporate promoter or president, or by rank-and-file employees. In the latter case, suggestions might be solicited from all employees, the ideas sifted by an appointed committee, and broad objectives formulated from them. The goals should be tempered by reality and amended from time to time. They should require some effort by the management of the firm, but they should be attainable when the whole organization works toward them. They should be shaped by the availability of internal resources and by environmental conditions.

Quantitative Objectives

A starting point in developing business objectives might be to define corporate objectives in quantitative terms, such as sales, profits, corporate assets, and capital components. The validity of corporate objectives should be tested in a number of ways. They should suggest a guide to action; they should suggest tools for measuring and controlling the effectiveness of corporate management; they should offer a challenge but be achievable within the constraints of available financial resources; and they should be related to both the broader and the more specific objectives of the firm.

Long-Term Assets

Capital budgeting is an integral part of overall corporate objectives, since the objectives provide a framework within which capital budgets must be developed. A capital budget is a plan to achieve corporate objectives. Capital budgets may embrace such projects as increasing plant capacity, modernizing equipment, gaining control of a supplier or competitor, expanding a product line, or implementing other cost-saving programs. Capital budgeting is concerned with allocating funds among alternate investment proposals so as to optimize long-term profits to the shareholders. The term is sometimes defined to include the design of an efficient capitalization structure that minimizes the overall cost of capital to the firm. The term is sometimes limited to decisions about the permanent asset management of the firm.

A Capital Expenditure

A capital expenditure differs from a current expense in that the former is expected to benefit more than one fiscal period, while the latter is expected to benefit only the current fiscal period or the amount is so small as to make capitalization and amortization unfeasible. Normally, capital expenditures are associated with items such as land, buildings, machinery, and equipment, while the cost of labor, materials, overhead, general and administrative expenses, and small tools are ordinarily charged to current operations when incurred.

Range of Projects

The managers of all types of firms (construction, manufacturing, trade, or service, for example) continually encounter capital budgeting problems. Some of the more common ones include decisions on whether to buy or lease a truck or auto, whether to rent or lease space in a building versus building a structure, whether to buy longer versus intermediate life assets, whether to invest in more automated production lines so as to save on labor, and whether to extend the length of salesperson and delivery routes versus setting up regional offices or satellite warehouses, and the like.

A growing business firm frequently spends a significant amount of each sales dollar for research and development of new, potentially profitable items, projects, or processes. This R & D, if successful, may reveal more potentially profitable projects than the firm is able to finance. The financial management team or budgeting committee must then decide which proposals to accept and which to defer or to reject. It must also carefully screen projects that offer relatively low returns and those that bear significant risk of loss.

System for Evaluation

A good capital budgeting system should provide for the development of new projects; provide the efficient, unbiased evaluation of potentially profitable proposals; and provide for timely implementation of the projects. The accounting, cash budgeting, and capital budgeting systems should be coordinated. Members of top management should combine their efforts in order to achieve maximum growth in profits consistent with an acceptable risk of loss on principal investment.

Capital projects are frequently recommended by research, engineering, production, sales, transportation, or the finance and accounting department, but they should be evaluated and studied by an unbiased capital budgeting committee, perhaps with membership from the several divisions of the firm. Thus the committee should be able to apply evaluation concepts to replacement planning, market expansion, new product development, and cost-savings programs and to prioritize them so as to keep a healthy operating balance in the firm and to maximize profits in line with willingness to assume risks of losses.

Capital Budgeting Committee

The capital budgeting committee should be familiar with the capitalization mix acceptable by its industry. Dun & Bradstreet, Inc., Robert L. Morris Associates, and other sources make this information readily available with yearly updates. The committee should also remain informed about the current and long-term cost of short-term debt, long-term debt, and equity funds and, over the long haul, attempt to minimize the cost of capital to the firm.

Determining a Hurdle Rate

The weighted average cost of capital is frequently suggested as the hurdle rate of achievement in returns from projects of average riskiness in order to maximize the long-term profits to the firm. The computation of the weighted average cost of capital for a firm with a projected capital structure of 30% debt, 10% preferred stock, and 60% common equity is illustrated.

Computing a Weighted Average Cost of Capital

Type of Issue	Proportion	After-Tax Cost	Weight
Bonds/bank borrowing	.30	.07	.021
Preferred stock	.10	.10	.010
Common equity	.60	.14	.084
Totals	1.00	—	.115

This firm might set a hurdle rate of 12%, after taxes, on replacement planning, 14% on area expansion in the United States, 16% on new product development (which carries more risk of uncertain cash flows), and 18% to 20% on international expansion (since normal risks plus monetary value risk are present in such endeavors).

Capital Rationing

Where more capital projects are available than can be financed with available funds, the capital budgeting committee is confronted with having to allocate available (or scarce) funds to worthy projects. Such projects, in keeping with their risk-adjusted costs of capital, are frequently ranked as to expected return on investment, with those showing the highest ROI having the greatest priority. Unfunded ones might be postponed to the following year and compared to newly developed projects at that time. Chapter 6 will illustrate techniques for making these rankings.

Follow-Up and Control

Last of all, in order to gain experience and accuracy in making long-term forecasts of revenues (or other benefits), the needed investment of assets, and the periodic expenses associated with a project, a process of follow-up and control should be developed at appropriate time intervals, such as at the end of the first year, the end of the second year, the end of the fifth year, the end of the economic life of the project, and so on. In the process, estimates should be compared to actual costs, expenses, returns, and the like. Mistakes should be corrected, as appropriate.

Many of the above suggestions are incorporated into quantitative models in Chapter 6, Capital Budgeting Project Evaluation Approaches.

QUESTIONS/PROBLEMS

1. In outline form, propose a quality system for implementing an operational capital project evaluation system for a fast-growth firm. Select an industry previously studied.

2. With the use of D & B's *Key Ratios for 800 Business Lines*, assume that you start a firm with a 75th percentile size of capital. Plan for the firm to grow to *mean* average size in five years, and develop projected income statements and annual balance sheets. Use an industry previously studied in this course. Suggest sources of funds for meeting growth objectives (i.e., prepare a sources/uses of funds statement by year).

6 *Capital Budgeting Project Evaluation Approaches*

Financial analysts, economists, and business advisors sometimes use one or more approaches to evaluating a capital budgeting project. Remember that we defined in Chapter 5 a capital budgeting project as a long-term investment in order to (a) increase profits over the long term or (b) achieve a cost savings over an extended time period. The most frequently applied techniques to evaluate the economic worthiness of such proposals include: (a) payback, or the number of years required for the anticipated cash inflows to equal the outflows; (b) the average return promised on the committed funds; (c) the discounted cash flow rate of return, or DCF ROR (or the determination of that rate of discount that equates cash outflows and inflows); and (d) the profitability index method, or PI, whereby a discount factor (such as the weighted average cost of capital, or the risk-adjusted cost of capital) is applied against anticipated cash inflows to see if the index between present value inflows and outflows exceeds 1 or 100%.

Capital budgeting projects may be divided roughly into five different categories. These are:

1. Replacement projects
2. Marketing expansion project
3. New product development projects
4. Cost-savings projects
5. Projects required by law that might or might not provide a profit

Examples of the latter might be required on-premises restrooms, hot lunch facilities, fire escapes, storage space for dangerous commodities, and so on. Of the above, categories 1 and 4 are somewhat less risky than average, and the firm's weighted average cost of capital might be an appropriate hurdle rate or discount rate. Marketing expansion plans and the development of new products are even more risky types of expansions and should return a premium over the weighted average cost of capital, perhaps plus 2% to 4%. Category 5 projects must, by law, be accomplished regardless of their cost or benefits, so their discount is hardly relevant.

The cost of capital may be computed for a given firm or for the industry in which it operates. Let us assume that managers of the firm are satisfied with the approximate industry average of permanent capital mix of 40% debt and 60% stock equity. Let us also assume that market cost of long-term bonds (for the grade issued by the firm) is 10%. Further assume that the cost of equity to the firm is 3% dividend yield and a recent growth rate in book value per share and earnings per share of 9%. The marginal tax rate to the firm is assumed to be 36% (as bond interest is shielded from taxes to this extent).

To compute the weighted average cost of capital for a firm, set up a worksheet with headings for types of securities, ratios, after-tax costs, and the product of the latter two; then find the total of column 4. For the above example, the schedule will be as follows:

Type of Issue	Proportion	After-Tax Cost	WACC
Long-term bonds	.40	$.10 \times .64 = .064$	.0256
Common stock equity	.60	$.03 + .09 = .12$	.072
Total WACC			.0976

For discount purposes, it is expedient to assume that the above weighted average cost of capital is 10%, but it probably should be computed once a year or so by the firm, as market conditions change. This 10% is then used as our discount rate for cash inflows and outflows for projects of average or below-average riskiness. We might decide to use 12% as a discount rate in the more risky area expansion, 14% for new product development, and perhaps 16% for international operations. Choice of the above is a matter of risk assessment of these types of projects, but greater uncertainties for success exist for categories 2 and 3 than for the others. Examples of these major types of projects will now be illustrated.

Replacement Planning Projects

Assume that the transportation unit of a firm is considering the addition of a delivery truck to replace shipment by a common carrier. The investment in the vehicle will be $30,000; the tax (and economic) life of the project is five years; the scrap (trade-in) value of the truck is estimated at $5,000 at the end of five years; and annual benefits before depreciation and income taxes are expected to be $8,000. Management wishes the above types of evaluation approaches to be applied to these estimates.

Thus, payback = $30,000/$8,000 = 3.75$ years, which exceeds the life of the project, which points to buying the truck. Note, however, that this payback method disregards scrap value of the project and the time value of money. Let us try another method.

The average return on the average investment is sometimes referred to as the accounting method, as it employs historical accounting values. Thus, by the average return method:

$8,000 – $5,000 depr. – $1,080 tax/[($30,000 + $10,000)/2] =
$1,920/$20,000 = 9.6% after taxes

This is slightly below our hurdle rate of 10%, so we would decide to continue to use the common carrier based on this analysis alone. However, this method does not fully incorporate the value of the scrap into the equation, so we will employ the time value of money, PI or DCF ROR.

For the PI method, let us set up a schedule of anticipated cash flow savings from owning the truck and compare its present value with our initial outflow of $30,000. This is done in the following manner:

Year	Computation	Amount
1	$8,000 – $1,080 = $6,920 × PV of .909	= $6,290
2	6,920 × .826	= 5,716
3	6,920 × .751	= 5,197
4	6,920 × .683	= 4,726
5	$6,920 + $5,000 = 11,920 × .621	= 7,402

The total present value of the above expected cash inflows equals $29,331.

Again, the present value of the cash inflow is slightly lower than the initial outflow of $30,000 (weighted with 1), so the decision is to continue with the common carrier. However, if we were to use an accelerated method of depreciation rather than straight line, or if the firm were in a lower income tax bracket, the firm might very well determine that ownership of the delivery vehicle is preferred to use of a common carrier. During times of economic weakness, investment tax credit for equipment purchases is sometimes provided by the U.S. Congress. In such instances, the investment would be reduced by the investment tax credit, and some marginal projects might prove to be economically acceptable that would not otherwise be.

The above analysis could be extended with another worksheet using a 9% discount rate. The actual DCF ROR would then be linearly interpolated between 9% and 10%. The only significant difference between the PI and the DCF ROR is that the discount rate implicit in each is the assumed reinvestment rate for periodic cash inflows. Thus, the PI is somewhat easier to apply, and this rate appears to be a more defensible reinvestment rate than a different one computed for each project being evaluated.

Geographic Market Expansion Projects

Suppose that a marketing research study suggests that if $13 million is invested into additional resources, growth in sales in years 1 through 5 would be as follows: $15 million, $20 million, $15 million, $10 million, and $5 million. The gross profit margin before depreciation on the new sales of products is expected to be 50%. Variable distribution costs are expected to be 10%. The tax rate for the firm is 36%. Determine the profitability index for the above using a discount rate of 12%.

Present Value Calculations (millions)

Item	Year 1	Year 2	Year 3	Year 4	Year 5
Gross sales	$15.0	$20.0	$15.0	$10.0	$5.0
Less: Cost @ 50%	7.5	10.0	7.5	5.0	2.5
Less: Depreciation (units method)	3.0	4.0	3.0	1.5	1.0
Less: Distribution costs @ 10%	1.5	2.0	1.5	1.0	.5
Pretax profits	3.0	4.0	3.0	2.0	1.0
Less: Tax at 36%	1.08	1.44	1.08	.72	.36
After-tax profits (ATP)	1.92	2.56	1.92	1.28	.64
Cash flows:					
Depreciation +ATP	4.92	6.56	4.92	2.78	1.64
Times: PV factor @ .12	.893	.797	.712	.636	.567
PV amount	4.39	5.23	3.50	1.77	.93
PV amount, total					$15.82

Since this is above the cost of $13 million for the investment, and using a discount rate of 12%, the PI then becomes $15.82M/$13M = 1.22 or 122%. This project would compete with others for available funds, and those with the highest PI rankings would be chosen.

New Product Development Projects

Assume that our research and development staff has determined that a new product can be manufactured and marketed with an investment of $15 million in five-year assets, zero scrap, and $5 million in working capital. Assume that benefits before depreciation and income taxes on the new product will be $8 million yearly for each of five years. Working capital will be recaptured at the end of the fifth year. Determine the profitability index for the proposal using a 14% discount rate. We shall use the present value of 1 per period table as a shortcut in this problem.

The PV of the periodic cash flows is the same in years 1 through 5; thus the value = $8M – $1.8M taxes = $6.20M. We now multiply this by the PV factor at 14% for 5 years, or 3.433; the product is $21.285 million. The recapture of working capital at the end of year 5 is $5 million times the PV of 1 at the end of five years, or $5M × .519 = $2.595M. The sum of these two values is $23.88 million, and the PI = $23.88M/$20M or about 1.19. Thus, our marketing expansion project described above would slightly outrank our new product development, although each surpasses our risk-adjusted hurdle rate by a very nice margin of safety. If funds are available, we would undertake both of these projects.

Cost-Savings Projects

The calling of a bond issue, or perhaps the replacement of a manufacturing process with a less expensive one, are examples of long-term projects that call for minimizing cash outflows. We shall now formulate such a project and illustrate its analysis.

Suppose that the XYZ Corporation has a $10 million, 15-year bond issue outstanding that carries a 13% interest rate. Assume further that the bonds are callable at a 10% premium. New bonds that carry a market yield of 10% can be issued with a 15-year maturity. Assume further that fixed flotation costs (legal, printing, accounting, etc.) will run $200,000. In this proposal, some $1,200,000 for refunding call and flotation costs will be the investment. The annual savings will be .03 × $10M or about $300,000 yearly. The present value of this stream of savings will be 7.606 (PV factor for 1 per period for 15 years at 0.10) times the $300,000 yearly, or $2,281,800; and since this is far greater than the investment of $1,200,000, we make the bond call. The refunding call expenses, $1,200,000, would be amortized over the remaining life of the called issue, for tax purposes, which we have assumed is the same as the life of the replacement issue. Thus, we have computed benefits and costs on a before-tax basis. We should be consistent in our calculations, however, comparing before-tax figures or after-tax figures.

Range Estimates

Some evaluators select their most likely estimates for costs, life of the project, periodic benefits, and scrap values. They then vary this by 10% or 20% above and below these figures for one of the variables, holding the others constant. This is referred to as sensitivity analysis. Still others might use a range of estimates for these four variables, using a table of random numbers and expected frequency of occurrence and simulate the results by computer for, perhaps, one thousand computations. The average and standard deviation of this set of iterations can then be computed so as to make a more informed risk/reward decision. This type of approach has been referred to as Monte Carlo simulation.

Selecting a Method

The payback shows how rapidly cash is returned to the business, thus having its merits. The average return method is good for evaluating the performance of a corporation's division. The PI method is somewhat easier to apply than the ROR DCF and does consider the time value of money. Since the long-term affairs of a firm depend so much on capital investment decisions, a few extra minutes should be spent in applying each of these methods to a project under review before making a decision.

QUESTIONS/PROBLEMS

1. Discuss briefly, including the variables that go into each calculation, the four most-often-used methods for contrasting and selecting mutually exclusive capital budgeting projects (e.g., the payback).

2. Indicate five categories/classifications for capital budgeting (e.g., replacement planning), and suggest an example of each not given in the teaching note.

3. Select an industry previously studied in this course. Use *Value Line Investment Survey* and other current sources to estimate the weighted average cost of capital to the firm. Disregard the current debt in your calculation but use only permanent capital. Suggest reasons for using or omitting current debts from the calculation.

4. For the replacement truck example, assume that sales targets were accurate through year 5, but that the equipment deteriorated thereafter and was sold for zero scrap (but a tax write-off). Recompute the actual rate of return on the project at the end of its life as a budget follow-up analysis.

7 *Inventory Management*

Why Bother?

For some firms, the size of the inventory is significant compared to total assets. For example, in a retail trade or wholesale trade firm that leases building space, the size of the inventory may exceed one-half of total assets. It is necessary for wholesale firms to buy large quantities of merchandise so as to gain price advantages, and some items (such as canned goods) may be available only for certain months of the year. For other types of firms, such as transportation, engineering construction, or utilities, the commitment to inventories may be small in amount. For the manufacturing firm, about 20% to 30% of total assets, customarily, will be invested into inventories, with holdings of raw materials, work-in-process, finished goods awaiting sale or delivery, and packing supplies.

Cost to Hold

There is no explicit return from the items held in inventory; however, certain factors are relevant in computing the cost of holding inventory. These include the initial purchase price of the delivered items (which varies with the price paid and the quantity held), the per-transaction ordering cost (which is largely fixed in nature and is made up of such things as the value of the time for the person making out or placing the order, the cost of receiving and checking the order, the cost of placing the order in storage, and the cost of accounting for and issuing the check), the carrying cost (which is largely variable and consists largely of the value of money, rent on the space taken by the merchandise, ad valorem taxes, insurance, and obsolescence for the goods), and last of all, the shortage cost (or forgone contribution to profits if merchandise is out of stock when needed to fill orders).

Safety Stock

Many business firms, in their management of inventories, will attempt to set aside a safety stock of each major type of inventory. This is mainly done for two reasons: to avoid stockout cost and to avoid production shutdowns when out of stock of a critical item. Some firms use a small safety bin and a larger bin for storing the items to be placed into work-in-process. When the large bin is depleted, it is time to place an order for the item. The items in the small bin are then used during the delivery period. Still other firms set the level of safety stock depending on the consequences of running out of the item. If it is so critical as to shut down production, then a long supply of this item may be kept on hand at all times. Other factors include the variability in demand for the item, the nearness to suppliers, and the variability of lead time in receiving items once an order has been placed. Other firms computerize their inventory holdings, reducing the level of withdrawals and increasing it by new arrivals. The problem with this system, aside from possible theft, is that a worker who withdraws the items might forget to punch in the withdrawals (or fill out the appropriate withdrawal slip). Shortages then occur, cost of goods sold is overstated, and profits and income taxes are overstated as the records are in error.

Controlling Amounts

Many firms stock several dozen or even thousands of different items in their inventory of materials. The ABC approach has been developed whereby class A applies to a few items whose value in total is a significant proportion of total value of inventory. Class B consists of average items with average usage rates, and class C consists of a large number of items that are not used in total to a significant degree. Certainly more time and effort should be placed in optimizing the size of order (and inventory stocking) for items in class A than in class C. Some attention is directed to items in class B.

Inventory Models

Inventory models have been developed that minimize the total cost of ordering and carrying the merchandise, including a built-in penalty for stockout. These models apply to both merchandise items that are manufactured and those that are ordered and resold in smaller units; thus the model might apply equally to retail, wholesale, and manufacturing firms. The information needed to develop an inventory model includes (1) knowing the demand, which should be at a reasonably constant rate; (2) knowing the lead time for placing and receipt of orders; (3) developing a safety stock; and (4) being able to buy units at a constant price for all sizes of orders. Economies of scale for large purchases might be factored into the model, but additional calculations would be needed.

The next step in our analysis is to assign letters to each factor important in the decision model. The following values are used:

D = units demanded during the period (year, month, week, etc.)
F = fixed cost to place the order, in dollars (see definition above)
P = purchase price, in dollars per unit
C = carrying cost per period, expressed as a ratio of P
Q = quantity of each order, in units (size of order)
$\overline{EOQ}$ = economic order quantity, in units
N = number of orders per period, or $D/\overline{EOQ}$ rounded to units of Q
T = total inventory cost per period, in dollars

The EOQ Model

In the EOQ model, $\overline{EOQ}$ can be expressed as the square root of $2DF/PC$, or

$$\overline{EOQ} = \sqrt{[(2)(20{,}000)(\$8)/(\$8)(.20)]} = 447$$

where D = 20,000 units, F = \$50, P = \$8 per unit, and C = 20%. Now if Q = 100 items, we could order either 400 or 500 units without substantially affecting the total cost of carrying/ordering the items. If Q = 144 (a gross), we might order 3 gross, or 432 items. We would place the order about 20,000/400 = 50 times yearly, or about once a week. If the order were slightly larger, we might order every 8 calendar days.

Suppose, however, that our demand is about constant at 5,000 units monthly from January through April; falls to 3,000 monthly from May through August; and slides further to 2,000 monthly for the balance of the year before returning to this pattern. We need to divide the year into three planning periods and recompute the $\overline{EOQ}$ and N for each of these subperiods. Let us assume in this problem that F = \$50, P = \$20 per unit, and C = 30%. Our equation for the first four months then becomes

$$\overline{EOQ} = \sqrt{[(2)(5{,}000)(\$50)/(\$20)(.30)]} = 288$$

Now, assuming that each order size Q is a gross, or 144 items, then we should order 2 gross each (288/5,000) × 30 days in the month, or about every 1.72 days (perhaps three or four times per week). Suppose that our average time between placing an order and receiving it is 14 days; then we might have eight orders outstanding at any point in time, with arrival expected about every two days. Coffee-roasting companies often follow this procedure, placing orders with foreign shippers with the orders spaced so as to arrive every few days. Shipping time (from African or South American shippers) runs from three to five weeks, so having a dozen or so orders outstanding is customary for such a firm. When a dock-workers' strike (Gulf stevedore union strike, for example) is expected, stockpiling of inventory or buying from a secondary supplier in the United States with rail hauling is sometimes done in order to safeguard against shortages of green coffee beans.

The similar calculation provides an $\overline{EOQ}$ of 224 for the second four-month period and 183 for the third portion of the year. Of course, if units of purchase were something other than a gross, it might be possible to have an order size very close to the $\overline{EOQ}$. The total cost function is a very flat-bottomed curve, however, which could be verified by computing the total costs (fixed and variable) of orders with sizes varying from about one-half times to perhaps two times the computed $\overline{EOQ}$ and plotting the results.

Production Run Sizes

While the graph of the inventory held differs for the purchase and the manufacture of goods, a similar EOQ model may be used in determining the ideal length of production run (or number of units to produce in a given production run) before converting the general-purpose machinery to another usage. Let us assume the same cost pattern as in the above exercise, but let us assume the cost of machinery setup and stocking the items from the run to be $4,000. The equation for the first period of the year becomes as follows:

$$\overline{EOQ} = \sqrt{[(2)(5,000)(\$4,000)/(\$20)(.30)]} = 2,581$$

Solving for the other two periods yields 2,000 units in the middle period and 1,632 units in the last period. Since sales are presumably continuing as inventory is built, the inventory holding rises and then falls when production of this item is no longer taking place. Suppose that it is possible to produce 500 units per day of the item; we would set up the equipment (probably on the weekend when the plant is closed to the production workers), produce for five days, and then reconvert the equipment the next weekend to another usage during January through April. During the second four-month period, the strategy might be to produce the items for three or four days, paying overtime to the equipment setup crew for evening work and so forth. Thus, from January through April, the strategy might be to produce the items about each alternate week with the equipment used for other purposes during the other weeks.

The EOQ Model and Bond Issue Size

The EOQ model can be applied with similar results to determine the optimum order size (or issue size) of a bond issue where demand for outside funds is constant. The variable cost is the cost of bond interest reduced by the short-term investment return, such as from a temporary investment in

Treasury bills returning 5%, for example, when the bond issue costs 9% to the firm. Fixed flotation costs per order might be $200,000; constant demand might call for $10 million dollars per year. The optimum bond issue size then becomes the square root of (2)($.2M)($10M)/[.09 − .05 = .04] or $10M, so the strategy would be to make one bond issue yearly, investing surplus funds into T-bills. As an alternative, some firms establish lines of credit with banks and deplete such drawdowns before "funding" the debt (i.e., converting it from short term to long term). However, the bank loan rate is ordinarily higher than the T-bill rate, so the initial strategy suggested is usually optimal from an economic standpoint.

QUESTIONS/PROBLEMS

1. Suggest types of firms with which you are familiar that have unique sets of inventory control problems.

2. Suggest ways for avoiding stockouts and discuss their potential for decreasing profit contributions on the immediate and future sales.

3. Explain each term that goes into the EOQ model.

4. For one of the EOQ examples in the text, make a graph with units on the x axis and cost on the y axis. Estimate optimum order size from the graph (i.e., the low point on the curve).

5. Suppose in the text expansion example that demand for funds doubled, the yield on bonds fell to 8%, and the T-bill rate declined to 4%. Compute the revised optimum bond issue size and suggest the frequency of an issue of this size.

8 Receivables Management

Relative Importance

For firms that sell on credit terms, the accounts receivable account is usually the second largest item in the current assets section of the balance sheet, following inventories in importance. For example, if all sales of a wholesale firm are on credit, there is a receivables turnover of ten times yearly, and assets are 25% of sales, then the receivables amount to about 36 days' outstanding sales (average age) and come to about 40% of total assets. For the average manufacturing firm, receivables usually run about 12% to 20% of total assets. The figure is even less for some retail trade firms, as some sell largely on a cash-and-carry basis. Still others permit charges or accept major credit cards, requiring a few days to collect on the credit card slips. In an auto dealership, accounts receivable run about 12% to 13% of assets, while the figure is about 3% to 4% for women's accessory stores. The balance in notes receivable is small for most types of firms other than those in installment financing. Typically, operating firms have less than 0.5% in notes receivable.

Important Considerations

Several factors determine the level of receivables held by a firm. The most important one, of course, is whether sales are made on credit terms or for cash. Just as important is the terms of credit granted. That is, if a company offers its customers the terms of net 30 days, the customers have 30 days after the purchase to pay the net amount. Few will offer to pay until the end of the prompt payment period. In order to encourage them to pay earlier, firms in the industry may offer terms of, say, 1%/10, net/30. This means that a 1% cash discount may be taken if the invoice is paid within 10 days of the shipment (or arrival) date. Otherwise, the entire amount is owed at the end of 30 days. Since there are 360/20 days or 18 such periods in the year for which the 1% applies, this is analogous to offering an 18% annual rate (approximately) for the early payment. Similarly, 2%/10, net/60 means that the imputed cost of the credit of 60 days – 10 days = 50 days costs 2% credit in forgone discounts. This is analogous to $7.2\% \times 2 = 14.4\%$ on an annual basis, a slightly higher rate than commercial banks usually assess on secured business loans.

Competitive Forces

Competition influences companies in an industry to set about the same credit terms as their competitors. Other popular credit terms include 1%/10 EOM, net/30. This means that a 1% cash discount may be taken if paid within the first to tenth days of the month following purchase; otherwise, the net amount is owed by the end of the next month. Textile firms and suppliers of jewelry offer even more generous terms, with 8%/10, net/60 or 90 being common. The imputed interest of the latter discount forgone would be $360/80 = 4.5 \times 8\% = 36\%$, so the customer should borrow from a bank or other lender in order to pay its trade suppliers. If the credit reputation of the buyer is very poor, it may be asked to pay COD or CBD, meaning cash on delivery or cash before delivery of the items. Some firms are willing to place their own inventory in an outlet on a consignment basis (retaining title to the merchandise) and collect monthly for the billing price of merchandise sold to the ultimate customer. In the event that the firm (with the consigned goods) should go into bankruptcy, the supplier of the consigned items still has title to the inventory and (presumably) can repossess the goods.

Customer Risk Evaluation

Techniques for evaluating the credit worthiness of a client are gained with experience. Several books (McGraw-Hill, Inc., usually has one or more such books in print) suggest effective ways for managing credit or accounts receivable. The firm may wish to subscribe to a service provided by Dun & Bradstreet, Inc., which about six times a year publishes regional and national directories of credit evaluations on about half of the business firms in the United States and Canada. The books are arranged by geographical region, by state, and then by city. The type of information carried by these *Reference Books* includes the size of the capital of the firm, its SIC designation, the address of its home office, and a composite credit rating. All of this information is condensed, but a user soon learns to interpret strengths and weaknesses of the (prospective) client from a review of this information.

D & B also publishes credit reports in several versions on the business firms that they monitor. The basic subscription to the credit service provides a reference book some two times yearly with perhaps 50 credit reports. More can be added to the service by paying a higher fee. Some communities have their own credit information gathering agency that competes with the service provided by D & B. These credit reports usually have a historical section showing such things as the name and address of the firm, its four-digit SIC code, the approximate level of sales, assets, and capital, and any past bankruptcy action of the firm. The average workforce is sometimes shown for the firm. A section showing outstanding credit to suppliers and the amounts past due is generally followed by some comparative financial statement data. A few paragraphs of text describe recent activities and financial affairs of the firm. These credit reports are usually one or two pages on most firms, and they are updated one or two times yearly as requested by the subscribing customer of the service.

Assessing an Account

It is difficult to evaluate the merits of selling credit on a single account other than to test it against preset guidelines for creditworthiness. For example, the decision might be reached that we will sell on credit unlimited amounts of goods to those that D & B rated as "high" or "good." These are the top two of four ratings and usually have excellent or good debt-paying histories. "Fair" and "limited" are the bottom two grades. We might be willing to extend up to 5% of expected annual sales to a customer with a fair credit rating, but watch this group of accounts carefully to safeguard against their aging several months. We might offer little or no credit to those accounts judged to be of limited credit rating. Over a period of time, the manager of accounts receivable might monitor the payments of these graded accounts and determine that one-half percent is the average loss on the high-grade accounts, that it runs 2% on the good accounts, that it averages 5% on the fair accounts, and that it runs 15% on the limited accounts (before they are turned over to a credit collection agency). When this latter step is taken, the collecting agency may make the collections it can and remit to us a fraction of the account, such as one-half, keeping the balance for its expenses. Delinquent trade creditors are sometimes taken to court, or even forced into bankruptcy by several distraught suppliers of merchandise that press for payment. Still other firms recognize that some accounts will go sour and write them off against the reserve for doubtful accounts, and refuse to sell additional merchandise to the firm except on a COD or CBD basis. Some firms do return to profitable status and clean up doubtful (aged) accounts, but this is more rare than customary in most lines of business.

Setting Lines of Credit

Whether a firm should supply credit to customers with a fair or limited credit rating should depend upon the gross profit margin of the goods supplied and the period of adequate servicing of the account expected from the customer. For example, if the merchandise carries a markup of 10% (such as might be customary for a jobber providing candies, tobacco, and personal items to grocery stores or drug stores), then little or no credit might be the rule. If the supplier is a manufacturer attempting to offer a new line of products in a given territory and the gross profit margin is 20% or 25%, then the firm might be willing to assume some greater risk and sell to the low-credit-rated firm with a limited line of credit. A method that might promote the credit supplied from that of a general creditor to that of a secured creditor might be to sell the goods on consignment, checking on the inventory level monthly, replenishing sold items, and collecting a share of the sales on items actually sold.

Selling on Consignment

For example, let us assume that a paint distributor that offers a line of paint that retails for $14.99 per gallon offers to place $30,000 of the inventory in a store on consignment, providing that the store displays the wares, keeps one-third of the selling price, and remits the other two-thirds to the distributor. As sales are made, funds might have to be escrowed to pay for the portion owed to the distributor. Once each month an inventory is taken and the paint inventory is brought back to its original level, probably rotating the older stock to the front of the display area and the newer items to the rear. The distributor must make enough on the sale to cover the cost of delivering the merchandise and designing the display area and the time value of money. With this line of merchandise, and the value of credit at 10% yearly, the average collection period might be the 30 days in a month plus another 10 days to collect the cash. Thus, interest on the $20,000 of inventory (our assumed cost) × 40 days at 10% amounts to $2,600 monthly. Adding to this an assessment of perhaps $100 to cover delivery cost of the new inventory, then monthly sales must be about $2,700 × 3 or $8,100, which is equivalent to a merchandise turnover of almost four times per year. We might have an agreement that we would commit this size consignment for one year and see whether or not it proves profitable. If not, we might seek other outlets.

Extended Credit Terms

As an alternative to keeping an old account on the books, a supplier of credit might accept an interest-bearing note receivable. The notes receivable might be discounted at a bank. Still other holders of accounts receivable sell them to factoring firms or pledge them as collateral on a loan at a commercial bank. These two types of transactions will be explained briefly.

Open Book Account Loans

A commercial bank that is unwilling to make a business loan to a client on an unsecured basis might be willing to grant the loan if secured by a pledge of 125% of quality receivables or field warehouse receipts. As the receivables are collected by the firm, either 80% of the amount is paid to the bank or the amount is replaced by another account of about equal value. The cost of the bank loan is usually set by the prime rate charged by large money-market banks, but might be 1% or 2% higher at smaller banks. The bank loan officer might insist that only receivables from high- and good-credit-rated firms are acceptable as pledged credit, so that the sales to lower-quality accounts, while not prohibited, would not be acceptable as collateral for a receivables-secured loan.

Factoring Receivables

The factoring of accounts receivable is their outright sale to a factoring company. Again, the factoring company might be willing to accept only those accounts rated as high or good by D & B, and might assess an interest rate of 2% to 4% above that charged by banks and apply the rate to the general credit terms (prompt payment period) plus about 10 days. A reserve of perhaps 5% is retained to cover any returns and allowances. Over a period of time, these funds might be made available. This type of credit is somewhat more costly than bank credit, and some business persons view the factoring of receivables as only one step away from bankruptcy. Still, it is done in several lines of business with long mercantile credit terms, such as textiles, jewelry, and so on, and some of the firms in these industries have been in business for decades.

Summary

It is not necessarily the optimum strategy of the financial manager of a firm to minimize the amount of funds allocated to receivables. Instead, it is more important to monitor the amounts in such accounts that are slow or delinquent in payment. "Slow" is usually from prompt payment date to plus 30 days, while delinquent accounts are over 60 or 90 days in age. It should be the objective of the firm to send forceful collection letters to the slow and delinquent clients on a monthly basis. Threats of lawsuit or turning the account over to a collection agency should be followed up with such action. Needless to say, all clients should be evaluated one or two times yearly with some reasonable line of credit established (depending on their size in sales and credit paying record). This line of credit might be amended if the firm begins to fall into a slow-paying category.

QUESTIONS/PROBLEMS

1. Discuss the relative importance of trade receivables to one of the industry groups that you have previously studied.
2. Suggest usual credit terms for one of these industries.
3. Suggest reasons why accounts receivable vary over the business cycle.
4. Suggest ways for reducing holdings in receivables.
5. Mention factors that influence credit terms set by merchants.

9 *Cash Management*

Amounts Needed

Cash or near-cash items are carried in varying amounts by business firms, but usually amount to between 5% and 12% of total assets. Cash is defined as currency, coin, and demand deposits; but in recent years, near cash might be used as a substitute for cash. For example, although banks are not permitted to pay interest on demand deposit accounts, many do permit a depositor to set up a negotiable order withdrawal (NOW) account whereby a draft is drawn and funds are transferred out of a savings account and into a withdrawal fund. Similarly, money-market funds, savings banks, savings and loan associations, and credit unions have begun to use drafting accounts on which they pay an interest return. An alternative to holding funds in a financial institution is to make a short-term investment into Treasury bills or other money-market securities (such as prime paper or sales finance company paper sold by large companies that purchase automobile notes and notes on other large consumer purchases).

Reasons to Carry

Cash is held for three main reasons. One of these, and often the most important one, is the transaction motive. For example, the management of a firm, church, or the like might set as a minimum the holding of not less than two weeks of operating funds in a cash account. If demand is about constant and most items are paid for with cash (rather than with credit), this might amount to about 2/50, or roughly 4%, of the annual sales or budgeted expenditures.

The precautionary motive is the second reason, so additional funds might be stored in an interest-bearing account until needed in the operation. An individual, and perhaps a business firm, should have a secondary line of defense, perhaps running about three months' usual expenses. For a business firm, this might be an unused line of credit rather than a savings account.

The third reason for holding cash is for making speculative, but potentially profitable, investments. For example, bargain purchases might be made at certain times of the year if funds are available. Of course, storage costs for the items are a factor. The reader might wish to refer to Chapter 7, Inventory Management.

Penalty for Excess or Insufficient Cash on Hand

The penalty for carrying excess amounts of cash is the forgone interest on the account. Excessive amounts of cash carried by a closely held corporation might also subject the firm to an excessive retention of earnings tax imposed by the Internal Revenue Service. However, if cash is being accumulated with a plan toward using it in the normal work of the business later in the year, no tax penalty is usually assessed.

The penalty for carrying insufficient cash might be the unplanned slowdown in the activities of the firm due to insufficient cash. That is, workers expect to be paid at frequent intervals, trade suppliers of credit expect to be paid for merchandise bought, utility firms expect to be paid on time for utilities provided, and the like. Certainly the taxing authorities demand that funds be placed into tax depository accounts at appropriate time periods, or the IRS might bring a foreclosure action against the nonpaying firm—seizing its assets and selling them at auction to pay the deficient taxes owed.

Conserving Cash Inflows

A growing business firm usually borrows funds in the long-term debt market and leaves a portion of its earned profits in the firm to build up its net worth (owners' equity). For example, suppose that an all-equity firm is earning 15% on its net worth, on average, but has an opportunity to grow (in terms of asset expansion) by 20% yearly. The decision might be made to pay out 3 of the 15 percentage points in cash dividends, to reinvest the balance of 12%, and to borrow the additional (20 – 12 percentage points or 8%) funds needed in the mortgage or bond market. This implies a trend toward a debt/long-term capital ratio of about 40%, as 40% of needed funds is coming from long-term debt and 60% from a buildup of equity. This is the approximate mix of capital for many manufacturing firms and large ones in wholesale or retail trade. Smaller firms, and those in finance, service, and utilities sectors frequently use 50% to 60% debt.

Cash may be conserved in at least two other major ways. Some firms encourage deferred income savings accounts from their highly paid employees to be invested in their own securities. Corporate 401K plans, however, must not be highly discriminatory, and those earning over $66,000 yearly (in 1994) could not defer a ratio of income more than 2% greater than those with lower earnings levels. In addition, some firms have significant amounts of noncash expenses, such as depreciation charges, amortization of intangibles, and depletion allowances that are expensed against income but require no immediate cash outlay. Thus, internally generated funds might be conserved by this means. Since federal tax laws change frequently, the reader should check on current IRS requirements in these areas.

Optimizing Cash Holdings

Cash is a type of inventory, so the economic order quantity (EOQ) inventory model introduced in Chapter 7 can be applied to determine an appropriate bond issue size. The information needed to determine the bond issue size, which should probably be recomputed each time a bond issue is made, is as follows:

1. The borrowing rate on long-term bonds; assume 10%.
2. The Treasury bill or money-market return rate; assume 6%.
3. The annual amount of long-term bond funds needed; assume $4 million yearly.
4. The fixed flotation costs; assume $100,000 per bond issue.

Using the EOQ equation introduced in Chapter 7, the optimum bond issue size (BIS) is equal to the square root of (2)($.1M)($4M needed)/(.10 less .06 savings rate), or $4.47 million. This suggests that such a firm would minimize total borrowing costs by floating a bond issue about every 14 months (as the amount needed would grow by 20% yearly), invest the surplus funds at 6%, and draw upon the account as funds are needed. An alternative might be to borrow from a bank at a rate of, say, 12%, and to sell a bond issue periodically and use the funds to repay the bank. Utility firms that are undergoing an almost constant construction program often follow the latter technique.

Since Treasury bill issues are made weekly on an almost continuous basis by the Treasury Department (through the facilities of the Federal Reserve System), this type of temporary investment has gained favor during recent years over those that have less of a continuous or secondary market.

Accelerating Cash Collection

Prudent financial management attempts to speed up the collection of cash. This might be done by pressing customers that buy on credit to pay promptly. Prompt payment might be solicited by offering some cash discount. For example, if the normal terms are 1% discount if payment is received within 10 days of delivery and net amount due in 30 days, this rate of discount is equivalent to 1% savings for 30 − 10 days of credit, or about 360/20 = 18% yearly. This is generally above the bank lending rate, so our customers (presumably) would borrow from a bank or in the long-term debt market in order to take their discounts on goods we sell to them.

Another technique for speeding up the collection of cash is to have our trade creditors mail their payments directly to a post office box (i.e., a lock box system) that is managed by the depository bank. A bank employee daily receives the checks, credits them to our account, and sends our book-keeper a list of the credited checks so that proper credits may be entered for the cash transmission on our records.

Some business firms use centralized management of cash, having the trade accounts collected at the home office, and set up a separate payroll account for payroll purchases, pay all trade payables centrally (so as to benefit from all cash discounts possible), and so on, and decentralize the operating divisions (i.e., the sales, purchases, manufacturing, etc. portions) of the firm.

The Cash Budget as a Tool of Management

A tool frequently used in cash management is the cash budget. This is a listing of expected cash inflows and outflows by short time periods so as to determine overages and underages of cash flows. Deficiencies might be covered with bank loans, while excessive amounts of cash might be invested on a temporary basis. Some handlers of large amounts of cash, such as telephone companies or banks, might budget cash on a daily basis. Weekly budgets might be adequate for wholesale firms, while retailing or service companies might use monthly budgets.

Inasmuch as about 20% of total assets is financed with trade payables and miscellaneous debts (such as payroll taxes payable, interest and ad valorem taxes payable, etc.), their management is important to the optimization of the holding of cash. The management of these items, however, is considered in the discussion of the management of short-term debts in the following chapter.

QUESTIONS/PROBLEMS

1. Suggest reasons, with examples, for a firm's need to carry cash.
2. Suggest reasons why some firms carry more cash than others, relative to total assets.
3. Suggest penalties for carrying inadequate/excessive cash.
4. Describe several ways used for optimizing cash holdings.
5. Suggest approaches that might be used for accelerating cash collection of receivables.
6. Outline techniques for developing a budgeting system for one of the industries that you have previously studied. Include accounting statements, cash budgets, and capital budget systems.

10 *Liability Management*

Debt/Equity Mix

Most business firms maintain some preset balance between the debts of the corporation and its equity account. This is usually set in accordance with what is generally accepted in the industry, plus or minus perhaps 10%. For example, it is not unusual to discover that farming operations that have been in existence for many years may have 80% or 85% equity with little debt. On the other extreme will be found banks and savings and loan associations that may have as little as 6% to 8% equity, with the balance of the assets financed with liabilities. Most manufacturing firms use 15% to 20% financing with each of short-term and long-term liabilities and 60% to 70% financing of assets with net worth. Retail trade and service companies ordinarily use about 40% to 55% debt with the balance in equity. A review of the breakdown of assets and credits for a wide range of business firms is provided by Dun & Bradstreet, Inc., in its annual review of 800 business firms. Robert L. Morris Associates in its annual publication *Statement Studies* provides similar information on about 400 different lines of business, broken down by size of firms. The IRS publishes information from tax returns on unincorporated and corporate forms of business, designed along SIC classifications.

Synchronizing Assets and Liabilities

One rule of thumb that offers some safeguard against risks is that short-term assets should be financed with short-term debt and that long-term assets might be financed with long-term debt and equity. The definition of short-term assets is generally those assets that are cash or expected to be converted to cash within one year of the date of the balance sheet. Short-term assets include such things as cash and near-cash items, accounts receivable, inventories, and miscellaneous accruals such as prepaid taxes or insurance. Short-term debts include such things as accounts payable to trade creditors (for financing purchases of inventories or supplies, predominantly), bank loans, notes payable to other lenders, and miscellaneous current debts. Longer-term liabilities include mortgages payable on the purchase of land or structures; bonds payable; or term loans owed to the bank, the Small Business Administration, insurance company lenders, and the like. The average trade firm has about 150% to 250% of the total of current debts invested in current assets. Very small firms often use more debt, as a percentage of assets, than do the more mature firms.

Self-Generating Debt

Some types of current liabilities are said to be self-generating. That is, as business is done, certain liabilities arise. For example, as goods (inventories) are bought on credit terms, there arises the asset of merchandise inventory and the trade payable debt account simultaneously. Perhaps one-half to one-third of the inventory account can be financed (at any point in time) with trade payables. The balance, of course, would be paid for with longer-term liabilities or equity ownership. Another significant amount of current liability would be included in the other current debt account for such things as wages accrued, payroll taxes owed, ad valorem taxes that are accruing, and the like. Accounts payable to the buyer of the goods gives rise to the accounts receivable account on the books of the seller, so that the cost of accounts payable becomes approximately analogous to the cost of the capital to the supplying firm.

The Cost of Trade Credit

One way to compute the cost of trade payables is to determine the discount given up if not paid in time to take the cash discount. For example, terms of 1%/10, net/30 mean that it costs 1% for the use of credit from the 11th to the 30th day, and since there are $360/20 = 18$ such periods in a year, this is analogous to saying that the annualized cost is 18% for forgoing the discount. Since we have 30 (rather than 20) days of credit for a total cost of 1%, we might assume the cost to be 12% on an annualized credit. This is usually close to the bank lending rate during a period of inflation of 3% to 5% such as generally prevailed from the mid-1980s through 1995 in the United States.

The Cost of Bank Loans

The cost of bank loans may exceed the one expressed in the lending agreement if the bank insists on a compensating balance. That is, if the bank is charging 11% interest on a loan but insists that our cash account not fall below 15% of our loan balance, then we are permitted to use only 85% of the credit extended. This causes the real rate of credit to become about 13%, computed as follows: .11/(1 – compensating balance) or .11/.85 = 12.94%. We might also have to provide quarterly audited financial statements to the lender, thus increasing the cost of funds to a higher level. Credit might be available from alternative suppliers of credit at a lower cost than bank credit. Guaranteed bank/SBA loans, for example, that are described subsequently, might carry favorable rates to small firms.

Other Short-Term Credit

Certain other types of short-term debt will be mentioned. As a buyer of permanent life insurance builds equity in the policy, he or she usually also has a borrowing right against the cash surrender value of the policy. The rate may be about 5% to 7.5%, depending on the rate of return built into the policy. For the purchase of automobiles or trucks (for personal or business usage), some dealers (through the manufacturing firm's captive finance company, such as GMAC) offer discount rates of installment credit. That is, the large finance companies may be able to sell high-grade notes or bonds in the capital market that yield about 8.0% to 9.0%. This rate, or sometimes even lower for incentive vehicle selling, may be passed along to the buyer of the product. The rates usually only apply to the first-time sale of products (new products, or perhaps demos or executive vehicles). Such bargain financing, however, might save the buyer several hundred dollars in interest payments over the repayment period of three or four years. Some dealers also offer to lease vehicles rather than to sell them outright. The imputed rate of interest may be low, but the lessee should be aware of three things. First of all, he or she builds no equity as payments are made. The vehicle must be returned to the lessor at the expiration of the lease (or perhaps bought at some contracted price). Secondly, the terms of the lease may call for certain maintenance scheduling at frequent intervals. This cost should be compared to what would be owed to an independent auto service firm (rather than the dealer). Moreover, sales taxes, ad valorem taxes, licensing, and insurance costs ordinarily have to be paid by the lessee, so these costs should be considered. They would probably be about the same as for the vehicle bought on an installment payment contract, however. Last of all, vehicle leasing contracts usually specify some maximum number of miles that are covered under the leasing terms. Extra miles are usually billed at an additional cost of $0.10 to $0.15 per mile. Some additional 10,000 miles might cause a lease closeout fee of $1,000 to $1,500. Open-end mortgages might require the lessee to make up any difference in the estimated buyout price and the wholesale price of the vehicle at the time of lease expiration. Thus leases of vehicles are not without risk.

When vehicles are leased, the lessee should carry adequate insurance on the vehicle, as the lessor looks to the contractor for fulfillment of the lease contract payments plus the preset buyout price. This may exceed the insured (or market) value of the vehicle as determined by the insuring firm. Thus gap financing by an insurance firm for this contingency might be considered.

Since 1986, the home equity loan, due to the interest deductibility for income tax purposes, has become an important source of credit to the entrepreneur. Loan origination fees, title insurance, a survey and/or appraisal, and so on, are somewhat more expensive than the origination of a bank business loan, but the interest rate might be about the same as on a 15-year fixed rate, purchase money mortgage when the loan is adequately secured (i.e., the first and second mortgage/home equity loan do not exceed about 75% of the appraised value of the structure).

Finance Company Credit

Finance companies, such as small loan companies and sales finance companies, have most of their portfolio of loans invested into installment notes receivable. Having a large fraction of these assets financed with short-term credit, such as their own notes sold in the money markets or short-term borrowing from several banks, provides them with a high degree of financial flexibility. That is, as their business becomes slow, they are able to retire a portion of their short-term liabilities and thus keep their interest cost to a manageable level. Firms in other industries should also be able to reduce debts and current assets when business becomes slow during a recession. This is why the rule of financing a substantial portion of current assets with current debt is important. Independent finance companies that finance installment notes for equipment purchase or for factoring receivables usually charge upwards of 18% yearly interest, but they often make higher-risk loans than will be approved by a commercial bank.

Longer-Term Debt

Small business firms do not have much access to the bond market. The large investment banking firms (underwriters) are not interested in underwriting bond issues of much below $10 million. Unless a firm has upwards of $50 million in assets, it would not likely be selling a bond issue of $10 million or more. Thus the small firms might have to look to large commercial banks, life insurance companies, or the Small Business Administration for term credit of 5 to about 15 years' maturity. Such loans would probably carry a rate of interest slightly higher than the rate charged on short-term credit, but the compensating balance (described previously) usually would not apply. When using longer-term credit, some flexibility should be built into the contract that might permit early repayment of the debt (especially if the interest rate is high) with little or no penalty for early repayment. Again, some flexibility for financing or refinancing has been preserved by the user of the debt.

Small Business Administration Loans

The SBA was created in 1952 to provide (or guarantee) long-term loans to small concerns. Virtually 99% of U.S. firms qualify, as the definitions may be based on the workforce or the level of sales of the applying company.

The most popular type of SBA loan is referred to as the 7–A loan, whereby a bank makes a loan up to the approved amount (generally less than $750,000 with 125% or more collateral) for the financing of working capital expansion, equipment purchase, or purchase of real estate. The maturity of the loan depends on its intended purpose, and the SBA usually guarantees up to 90% of the amount of the outstanding loan. The rate charged is usually not more than 2.75% above the prime loan rate, and the rate is adjusted quarterly to market rates. A business plan, personal financial statements, and past tax returns of the applicant are required with this type of loan. Repayments are usually monthly or quarterly over the life of the loan.

Beginning in 1994, the SBA implemented several other types of loans that might be appropriate for very small concerns. Two of these, the Green-Line Revolving Line-of-Credit and the LowDoc loan will be discussed briefly. The former is an asset-based loan by an approving bank with an SBA deferred guarantee of up to 85% of the outstanding loan. Under this loan, no annual cleanup of the loan is required (as is customary with a regular bank line-of-credit-type loan). The SBA guarantees up to 75% on the maximum-size line of credit of $750,000, with a maximum maturity of five years. Origination fees of the loan are fairly steep, including a 2% SBA origination fee, filing fees, lien title searches, legal fees, and so on; but the lending institution must provide a statement of estimated fees to the credit applicant. When loans turn sour, the pledged assets are liquidated and offset against the outstanding loan before the guarantee (up to 85%) is paid by the SBA. The lending institution and the SBA use care in monitoring operations of the borrowers, especially required payroll tax deposits, as the lender(s) might find themselves targets of the IRS in such collection proceedings. The Low-Doc requires only a two-page loan application, with one page completed by the potential borrower and the second page by the participating bank. The loan limit in 1995 was $50,000. Tax returns and personal finance statements are also required as supporting documents with this type of loan (where loan application is between $50,000 and $100,000). Maturities of repayments depend on the intended usage of the funds. Only certain banks participate in these "trial-type" SBA loans, and information on them should be sought from the Washington, D.C., office of the SBA by an interested applicant.

Debt with Sweeteners

Some growth-oriented small and intermediate-sized business firms are able to market debt with sweeteners attached. That is, bonds or preferred shares (with lower-than-market yields) might be marketed with stock purchase warrants attached. For example, each $1,000 bond might have 50 stock purchase warrants attached that permit the purchase (over a period of, say, five years) of shares at $10 each. On issue date, let us assume that a fair value of the shares was between $8 and $9. Suppose that the value of the shares climbs to $20 over the life of the warrants. The value of the warrants, then, is about equal to the value of the underlying bonds. The bonds themselves might be convertible into shares of stock, perhaps at the rate of one share for each $10 face amount of bond in years 1 through 3; for each $12.50 during years 4 through 6; and so forth; until the expiration of the bond. Such bonds should also be callable in order to permit the issuer the degree of flexibility of perhaps calling the bond for retirement and replacing it with a larger issue or one with more favorable terms once the growth of the issuing firm is well established and it becomes well known in financial markets.

Why Finance with Debt?

The major reasons for using debt by the issuing corporation are threefold. First of all, debt costs less than equity, as interest is recognized by the IRS as a business expense payable from pretax profits, while dividends on preferred or common shares are paid from after-tax profits. Thus, market cost of debt to a firm in the 36% federal and state income tax bracket is its market cost $\times$ (1 – the tax rate), or perhaps about 64% of the stated market cost. A second reason for debt usage is favorable usage of leverage. When the firm is earning a higher rate on total capital than it pays on debt, the debt's lower cost increases the return on owners' equity. The third reason is to preserve the voting control of the equity owners. That is, the managers of the firm (directors) are elected by the shareholders of the firm. Creditors are protected by law, of course, so contracts for debt and their servicing should be reviewed carefully by corporate management and their attorneys for fairness and flexibility in servicing (including extinguishment). Most bond issues are callable at a premium so as to provide the issuer with some flexibility in refinancing.

Lease Financing

Some business firms are able to use off-balance-sheet financing of certain types of assets. Leasing arrangements require a periodic payment of rent, but the value of such assets and their underlying debts usually do not appear on the balance sheet itself. Leasing of buildings, offices in commercial buildings, and equipment has grown in importance in the nation in the post–World War II era. The assets are usually owned by life insurance companies, pension funds, and individual investors that may themselves use significant amounts of debt (with some equity) in financing the structures or equipment. Still, the cost of capital to the long-term asset owners may be less than the cost of capital to a small or growing firm; thus their usage may be cheaper than attempting to buy all assets used. Moreover, the leasing of operating facilities under a one- to three-year lease may be less risky to a retail or service firm than buying the structure outright, even with financing. Assets can thus be preserved for working capital with a minimum of investment into long-term assets.

Preserving Some Borrowing Power

A prudent financial manager of a business firm should not exhaust its borrowing ability during a boom period but should preserve some additional borrowing ability for a "rainy day," such as a business depression. This preservation might be in the pledging of assets for asset-based loans, such as borrowing against receivables or the outright sale of receivables (called factoring). This type of credit is usually more expensive than other types, but might be considered as a stop-gap measure. Last of all, when the firm attempts to grow more rapidly than the ratio of retained earnings for the year to book value of common stock, either it must finance more heavily (than is prudent) with debt, or be willing to give up some equity ownership. Going public, or selling some share of stock to a wide range of stockholders, might be the answer, and a separate teaching note (Chapter 12) has been developed on this topic.

QUESTIONS/PROBLEMS

1. Suggest inputs that influence the debt/equity mix of a firm.
2. How could a firm synchronize asset and debt lives? Why is it desirable to do so?
3. How can a small firm tap the long-term debt market?
4. Contrast types and costs of debt arrangements to small firms.
5. Describe types of debt sweeteners.
6. Why preserve debt for a "rainy day" if its cost is less than equity?

11 *Capitalization Management*

Meaning

The term *capital* is generally used to refer to the equity of a business firm. The term *capitalization* is somewhat more embracive and includes both long-term debt and equity financing. Equity financing, for some firms, includes both preferred and common stock, as well as other paid-in-capital and retained profits. The capital account is treated somewhat differently for a partnership and a corporation, so both will be illustrated in this teaching note.

A partnership does not pay taxes in its own name, but the federal income tax law requires that a partnership file an informational income tax return, prorating the earned income (and certain types of expenses) among the partners. Each would then recognize his or her portion of such income on their respective personal income tax returns. Partners are treated as being self-employed for federal social security tax purposes; thus the firm does not pay social security taxes for them.

Let us assume that a merchandising firm, BWB Merchandising Mart, is formed by three partners: Mr. Black, who is to be a full-time officer in the firm and receive $2,000 monthly as general manager; Ms. White, who is also full-time and will be the buyer and training officer in the firm and receive $1,750 monthly for her services; and Mr. Brown, who agrees to work half-time for $1,000 monthly and serve as controller and treasurer of the firm. Further assume that the capital contributions of the above persons, respectively, are $50,000, $40,000, and $110,000, for a total of $200,000. The division of profits, beyond the monthly drawing for salary compensation, is to be 3% quarterly for return on investment. Any additional profits will be divided equally among the three partners. Assume that the profits in the firm amount to the following for the four quarters of last year (before allowances for partners' salaries): $21,000, $44,000, $51,000, and $48,000. The object is to allocate the funds to the three partners. For the present, assume that all funds will be withdrawn from the partnership at the end of quarter 4 so as to leave the initial capital in effect.

For the first quarter, the division of profits will be as follows:

	Total	To Black	To White	To Brown
Salary	$14,250	$6,000	$5,250	$3,000
Return on investment	6,000	1,500	1,200	3,300
Balance (equally)	750	250	250	250
Total allocated	$21,000	$7,750	$6,700	$6,550
Less: Funds drawn		6,000	5,250	3,000
In drawing account		$1,750	$1,450	$3,550

The capital account for the BWB Merchandising Mart at the end of the first quarter would, accordingly, be as follows:

Capital: Mr. B. B. Black	$ 50,000	
Drawing account	1,750	$ 51,750
Capital: Ms. I. A. White	40,000	
Drawing account	1,450	41,450
Capital: Mr. C. B. Brown	110,000	
Drawing account	3,550	113,550
Total for the firm		206,750

The process would continue until the end of quarter 4, with each person quarterly receiving credit for his or her salary (time input into the firm), the value of his or her investment (3% quarterly), and the balance divided equally.

Most business expenses of a partnership are written off against income in arriving at net income for the partners. However, three types of expenses are not expenses but are instead prorated to the partners in proportion to their net income from the firm. These are: ad valorem taxes, charitable contribution gifts, and interest expenses. Let us assume these to be, respectively, $3,000, $1,000, and $3,200, for a total of $7,200. It would be necessary to compute the allocation of the earnings during the last three quarters of the year to the three partners and total such allocations for the year in order to determine the total division of these expenses. As an exercise, the reader is asked to perform these allocations. Assume constant profits for the four quarters.

Tax Return Preparation

Each partner must keep his or her own set of books and file a quarterly declaration of estimated taxes. In addition, social security must be paid on the division of profits from the partnership (up to the base amount of $61,200 in 1995), as must Medicare (which has no base limit), which is increased each year about in line with the inflation rate. We will assume that Mr. Black and Ms. White had no other income on which Social Security taxes were paid but that Mr. Brown had taxable income of $36,000 from another source. The latter would owe self-employment taxes of 7.65% × 2 = 15.30% of the self-employment income, with one-half of the amount being a business expense. Each would also have paid into a declaration tax account an amount to cover federal income taxes for the year on anticipated taxable income. In 1995, the first $39,000 for a married person filing jointly is taxed at 15%, while the amount from this level to about $94,250 is taxed at 28%. Only one-half of Social Security taxes paid by the partners is deducted from gross income in arriving at adjusted income, so their tax burden may be about 35% of their gross incomes.

Incorporation

Let us assume that the firm decides to incorporate at inception rather than to operate as a partnership. It issues shares of stock to the owners/employees at an assumed price per share of $10 and distributes the same salary level to the employees as above. However, some changes must be made in accounting for expenses. First of all, the ad valorem taxes, the charitable contributions (not to exceed 5% of taxable income), and the interest expenses are business deductions and are not prorated to the capital contributors/managers of the firm. Next, the firm pays OASDHI taxes of 7.65% times the salaries of each partner and deducts a similar amount from the salaries of these persons. Thus, salaries to the three persons amount to $4,750 monthly or about $57,000 yearly, and net income (after the $7,200 expense and $4,361 in OASDHI taxes) is $164,000 – $11,561 = $152,439. After distributing the salaries and paying these expenses, some $95, 439 would be left in the profits before federal income taxes. This is taxed at a sliding scale running from 15% to 34%, but might average about 25% to this size firm. Thus, the retained earnings account at the end of the year would be about $95,439 × .75 = $71,579. The capital account for the firm at the end of the year should be as follows:

Capital Account for BWB Merchandising Mart, Inc.

Capital stock:	
Authorized: 100,000 shares at $4 par	
Outstanding: 20,000 shares at $4 per share	$ 80,000
Additional paid-in capital	120,000
Undivided profits (retained earnings)	71,579
Total capital, December 31, 199x	$271,579

Capital Distributions

The board of directors, which would logically consist of the three owners of the firm, might meet and decide to distribute another fraction of the retained profits as dividends. Let us assume this to be $1.00 per share of stock held. Mr. Black should receive $5,000 in dividends, Ms. White should receive $4,000, and Mr. Brown should receive $11,000. The other $51,579 would be retained in the firm to promote growth in assets. Cash dividends are taxed to the recipient, but stock dividends (those paid as additional shares of common stock) merely adjust downward the cost basis per share on the shares held by each owner.

As a firm grows in size, it might attempt to maintain a balance among current debts, long-term liabilities, and net worth of the firm. Let us assume that a 20%, 20%, 60% relationship is acceptable to the owners and to their major creditors. As capital grows, then, and as sales increase, the current debts such as trade payables and accrued items (wages and taxes, primarily) will also increase about in proportion to sales. Long-term assets might be bought with installment notes, a structure might be bought with a mortgage payable to a bank or insurance company, the firm might borrow from the Small Business Administration or some other federal financing program in order to promote growth, or an intermediate-sized firm might sell bonds.

Raising Capital

Ultimately, it might be in the best interest of the growing corporation to sell stock to selected stockholders and attempt to establish some market for the shares. That is, some trading in outstanding shares might be encouraged so as to develop greater interest in the firm. Shares might be sold (at about book value) to selected key employees, suppliers, or major customers. A regional over-the-counter dealer might be encouraged to buy some shares in the firm and promote trading in the shares. Let us assume that this is done, but the original owners might wish to retain over one-half of the total outstanding shares so as to ensure continuity of voting control.

Some growing firms issue preferred shares, pledging a certain dividend rate on the shares about equal to the rate paid on bonds. In 1995, preferred stock was yielding about 7.5% to 8% in the market, depending on the financial strength of the issuer. Most preferred issues carry cumulative dividends, which must be paid before dividends may be paid on common stock. Suppose that the firm wishes to buy another smaller firm in its industry with stock. It might agree to pay $100 par, 6% cumulative preferred shares, each convertible to 3 shares of common in the parent corporation at the time its own shares are trading from $29 to $31 per share. The receiver of the shares receives a tax-free transfer of shares (no taxes are owed until the shares are sold by the holder), receives some assurance of dividend payments, and is freed from the daily management chores associated with common stock ownership. Moreover, if the common stock in the acquiring firm continues to rise, the value of the convertible shares goes up about in proportion. The shares probably are denied voting rights unless dividends are in arrears a certain number of quarters, such as six.

Convertible Bonds

Some firms sell bonds which may be converted to common shares or bonds with stock purchase warrants attached. They usually do this in a market with high interest rates and relatively low stock prices, making the bonds callable at a premium, and hoping that the holders of the hybrid-type issues will convert to common within a few years. In most years, convertible bonds amount to only about 5% as much as straight debt issues.

Listing

A large firm usually lists most of its outstanding publicly held security issues on one of the major exchanges, such as the New York Stock Exchange, the American Stock Exchange, the Midwest Stock Exchange, the Pacific Coast Stock Exchange, and so on; or some merely promote the trading of their shares in the over-the-counter markets. Studies have shown that stock with good trading and marketability usually trades at about a 25% premium over stocks or bonds with limited marketability.

Institutional Stockholders

By the mid-1990s, large pension funds, mutual funds, and common trust funds in total accounted for about one-half the ownership of U.S. corporate equities and about 80% of their trading. Thus, vast amounts of capital can be raised and traded through the corporate form of organization.

QUESTIONS/PROBLEMS

1. Assume that partners A, B, and C contribute $50,000, $50,000, and $25,000. All work full-time for $2,000 monthly, withdrawing these amounts. After receiving 10% return on equity, the remaining profits and losses are divided equally. Annual profits run $100,000. Show the annual division of profits and the balance sheet capital section if only monthly salaries are withdrawn.

2. Use the same facts as in Problem 1, and do the same for an S corporation.

3. For one of the industries that you have studied to date, design an appropriate capital plan, assuming that assets and debts are mean averages but that profits run at the upper quartile level for three years. Assume that half of the earnings are retained. Project and update the capital structure for the three-year period.

12 *Valuation of a Closely Held Firm*

Defining Value

The term *value* carries different connotations to different people. What is the value of a used auto, a 10-year-old home, a going concern? There are several published guides as to the value of a used auto, such as by National Auto Dealers Association or another referred to as the *Blue Book*. Real estate appraisers use several techniques for appraising a home, such as comparing its value to others that have sold in that region and that have several similar characteristics. Rental income property might be evaluated so as to return 16%, 18%, or 20% gross rent on the value placed on the project, depending on the level of ad valorem taxes paid in the region, the prevailing interest rates, and other factors such as normal maintenance costs and insurance expenses.

Valuing a Going Concern

Placing a value on a going concern business may be even more difficult than on one of the above-mentioned items, inasmuch as it is made up of some current assets, some long-term assets, and some intangible assets such as going concern value or goodwill. Nevertheless, having a reasonably close estimate of the value of a single proprietorship, a partnership, or a closely held corporation might be needed for a number of reasons. A proprietor might wish to admit a partner in order to promote growth; one partner may have died and the estate is willing to sell his or her equity to the surviving partners at a fair and just price; the estate must evaluate all assets for estate tax purposes; the owner of a business property may be obtaining a divorce from his or her spouse and there is a court-ordered division of assets; a large minority interest holder is bringing suit for a share of the business assets to be paid in cash; the entire firm may be on the market for sale or merger into another; the management of the firm may be spinning off one of its divisions (selling it to another firm) and needs to place a value on it; and the like. The reasons for needing such a valuation are almost endless.

Two methods of valuing a firm are readily ascertainable. These are book value and market value, and these will be defined briefly and illustrated with an example. Then other, and perhaps more useful, methods will be suggested and illustrated.

The book value is merely the owners' equity in a business firm. The value of the assets less the outstanding debts provides the evaluator with this figure; but what are the values of the assets and debts? Realizable value or liquidation value might be one approach. Cash and near cash (with up-to-date posting of accrued interest) are evaluated readily. Accounts receivable are not all collectible, but perhaps a reserve for doubtful accounts, such as 1% of current accounts and 5% of aging accounts, might be deducted to provide a fair estimate of collectible value for them. But what would it cost to collect the items? Inventories might include some obsolete items (rusty items that have been on hand for several years) that are still carried on the books at cost. Still other items might be worth more than when acquired if prices have risen. What could the land and structures be sold for? A real estate appraiser might be hired to place a value on this. But what of lease-holds and leasehold improvements? It might be difficult to obtain our intangible investment from this type of asset even though our terms of lease might permit its being assigned/sold to another firm. Is the trade name or going concern value worth anything? Liabilities are often measured at book or recorded value, but the evaluator should ascertain that all debts are recorded. Is the firm accruing ad valorem taxes on a monthly basis that will be billed by the taxing authority at a later date; are past tax burdens paid in full; are there any outstanding bills for commercial insurance charges; are there any contingent liabilities that might become real for such things as warranties on past work or items sold? Subtracting the total of debts from the value of the assets should produce a revised net worth figure, and in a closely held firm, this might be used.

Market Price Versus Value

If the common shares are traded in the over-the-counter market or through the facilities of one of the stock exchanges, the most recently traded price times the number of shares provides us with a market value; but this varies between trades and from day to day. In an acquisition, the average closing prices for the 30 days before and after merger announcement are sometimes used as the indicated value of the selling firm and the buying company.

Capitalizing Earnings

The capitalization of earnings, such as that illustrated for an income-producing real estate venture above, might be applied to the pretax or after-tax income of a going business concern. But should one use last year's earnings, this year's expected earnings, or forecasted earnings for several years? In reality, this becomes a bargaining point in the selling of business firms. Some would look at the usual multiple in the marketplace of after-tax income and the market price of shares, or the earnings yield, and apply this to a closely held firm. In reality, the marketability of shares probably gives them a premium value of perhaps 25% to 35%. The complement to the earnings yield is the price/earnings ratio, or the P-E ratio. Suppose that this is 12 times for a listed firm in the same industry. This would be analogous to an earnings yield of 1/.12 or 8.333%. But rather than using 12 as the multiplier, perhaps it should be reduced to 9 or 10 due to the lack of marketability of the firm being acquired. Moreover, the fringe benefit program for the larger firm might be better than that of the one being acquired, so stated earnings (or reported past earnings) might have to be developed on a pro forma (or reconciled) basis, handling depreciation expenses and fringes in a similar fashion for the two companies. Thus, finding an appropriate capitalization rate for earnings becomes a chore. The most appropriate approach might be to analyze several listed companies operating in the same industry, determine their capitalization rate for current earnings, discount it by about 25% for lack of liquidity in the firm being acquired, and offer that indicated amount. For example, if current after-tax earnings are running at the $200,000 level, the average P-E ratio in the industry is 12 times, and we perceive marketability as being worth 25% of the total, then a multiplier of 9 provides an indicated value of $1,800,000. The sellers might want it in cash or might be willing to accept it in equities of the acquiring firm so as to be viewed by the IRS as having a tax-free transfer of like assets. In a tax-free transfer, the tax basis of the shares acquired becomes the tax basis of the assets given up, and no income taxes are owed at the point of exchange. It is only when the assets are later sold (or disposed of in some other manner) that taxes must be considered.

Buyout-Workout Agreements

When a firm is bought for cash, it is sometimes acquired on a conditional sales contract. For tax purposes, in order to prorate the amount of profits to the years in which cash payments are received, it is important not to receive more than 30% of the total price in the initial year. Otherwise, the profits on the entire transaction will be owed immediately (in that tax year). Instead, 29% might be accepted in November and 31% (for example) in January, and the other 40% (plus interest at a fair rate not below the government's borrowing rate) might be payable in years 3 and 4. Thus the seller would prorate his or her cost into the four income tax paying years and probably end up with a smaller tax burden than if all profits are lumped into one year. The seller of a business, upon retirement, may seek this type of sellout. He or she should, however, stay on with the firm in a consultant capacity in order to provide for an orderly transfer of assets and continue to service the past clients of the firm without loss of goodwill or past customers.

When earnings after taxes are erratic from year to year, or they are substantially influenced by the weakness or strength of the business cycle, average past earnings for about three years, and perhaps anticipated earnings for the next three years, are sometimes used rather than just last year's earnings or the current year's anticipated profits. In a buyout situation, the buying firm might offer a premium price 25% to 50% over the apparent value of the firm to be acquired in order to obtain early entrance into appealing markets for their products. The price might be payable in inflated shares, however, such as those trading at an above-average P-E level, so the seller should be aware of the possibility of such prices sometime declining back to more normal levels.

Some acquisitions are made on a conditional performance level. For example, the offered price (in terms of shares based on average closing price for 30 days before the merger consummation) might be something like 10 times after-tax earnings; plus a bonus of 4 times earnings in year 1 in excess of 112% of the previous year's earnings; plus a bonus of 3 times earnings in year 2 in excess of 112% of year 1's actual earnings, and so forth. This causes the management to continue to work diligently in building up the earnings of the sold organization. Key employees that are not already shareholders in the old (or new) firm might be given stock options so as to feel that they will have a share in benefits from an above-average future performance of the firm. Letter stock or investment stock, with limited marketability for a year or two, might be exchanged for the equity in the sellout firm.

Sellout Concessions

Owners selling their firm and not continuing with the acquiring firm are usually asked to sign a noncompetitive contract whereby they will not work for or develop a competing firm located within a certain radius of the one being sold for a stipulated period of time, such as five years. The reason is obvious, as a firm might be sold only to see its initial owner set up a competing firm and steal away valued customers, thus leaving the buying concern with a faltering division.

Holders of bonds and preferred shares of a firm being acquired also have a vested interest in whether or not to sell. They might be obtaining securities with greater marketability, or they might merely have their bonds guaranteed by the acquiring firm, making their assurance of being serviced somewhat greater. Still others will hold out for cash for the debt instruments or preferred stock interest. This becomes a negotiating point, so the manager of a firm should preserve as much flexibility as possible by making bond issues and preferred stock issues callable at some price, perhaps at a premium of about a year's interest or dividends.

Factors Influencing Share Prices

The shares of some firms tend to trade very close to book value per share; others trade at close to sales per share; and still others tend to move in relationship to reported earnings or cash flow per share. The reasons for these relationships will be explored briefly. The assets of financial institutions are mobile, and their earnings largely depend on the level of interest rates and the spread between the rate earned and that paid for funds. The shares of financial institutions tend to trade from about 75% to perhaps 125% of the book value for the shares. An extracting firm that receives a depletion write-off based on a percentage of revenues, or a firm taking accelerated depreciation write-offs on large amounts of assets, usually has a closer relationship between cash flow per share and market price than between reported after-tax earnings per share and market price. Where cash flow per share (net income plus the write-offs divided by the outstanding shares) is approximately equal to the reported earnings, the latter is more often used as the evaluator for the shares. An accounting firm, a management consulting firm, a temporary help firm, a travel agency, and the like, have little invested in assets compared to the revenues generated. These firms often sell for about one or two times average annual revenues.

Reasons for Valuing Firms

The valuation of firms may be important for several reasons; thus, we have explored several ways that going concern value might be made for a division of or the entire business firm. In reality, these estimates of value are merely that, and the final price depends upon the desire to sell or the urgency to acquire the firm. However, one or more of these techniques should be applied so as to determine a ball-park figure of evaluation for such a going concern where there is no readily determinable market price for the shares of the company.

QUESTIONS/PROBLEMS

1. Suggest five possible reasons for evaluating a firm.
2. Suggest and describe four frequently used firm evaluation methods.
3. Develop an appropriate workout-sellout plan for an average firm in a profile that you have studied to date. Consider tax laws.
4. Determine P-E ratios for several publicly traded firms in Problem 3 above, and use current quotation sources to set a fair price.

PART II
Business Profiles

Fruit Farms

Fruit farms have been assigned the Standard Industrial Classification (SIC) code 0171 through 0175 by several governmental agencies. Those studied for this profile include the following: berry crops (SIC 0171), grapes (SIC 0172), citrus fruits (SIC 0174), and deciduous tree fruits (SIC 0175). SIC code 0173, for nut trees, is not covered by this industry and business profile.

Many people are interested in the supply and demand for foods, as the average family of four in mid-1993 was spending about $110 weekly at the supermarket. Add to this an amount for other food expenditures (i.e., for such things as eating out, spending at farmers' markets, and items bought in bulk and stored in freezers for later usage) and the total may be an additional 20% to 25%. Younger adults, those age 20 to 44, spend about 50% more in eating out than do older adults, while singles spend about two times the average for eating away from home. A part of the reason is purchasing power, but a single person finds it inconvenient and excessively time-consuming to prepare a single meal at home. Older adults may be on special diets (weight control, low salt, bland foods, few spices, etc.) that reduce their frequency of eating out.

An increase in the cost of food items by more than the gain in disposable personal income (DPI) for a family begins to erode the family budget. As DPI increases, spending on food items, except for fruit juices, rises, but by hardly the same rate. As inflation rate exceeds the increase in DPI, the sale of fruit juices is one of the first items that suffers sales reductions.

Food weighs heavily in the consumer price index (CPI), with vegetables and fruits in 1993 being weighted at slightly above 3% each. According to published data, food prices sometimes rise by 10% in droughty years and then adjust back to about half of this unusually high gain. The increase is usually about the same as for the general level of inflation as measured by CPI changes.

Some fruits, especially strawberries, are very susceptible to severe production declines during a drought. About one inch of rainfall (or irrigation equivalent) per week is needed before and during harvest season of strawberries in order to produce a good crop. Most other fruit crops can stand a few weeks of little or no rainfall, but long droughts and above-average temperatures may severely reduce the harvest and even damage the trees, vines, or bushes on which the fruits are grown.

The sale of fruits has been increasing as a snack food, especially for adults past the age of 45 or for nutrition-minded families with children. Bananas, apples, grapes, and oranges are becoming increasingly popular snack foods. Strawberries, blueberries, blackberries, apples, peaches, and nectarines are popular fruits that are picked and canned or frozen during harvest seasons by numerous families in fruit-growing regions.

Many supermarkets have expanded their offerings from about 75 to about 225 different products, with several varieties of apples, peaches, oranges, grapes, exotic fruits, in-season strawberries, blackberries, blueberries, plums, cherries, and so on, carried in their vegetable/fruit display cases. Some of these are bought from distant shippers, while some, when available, are bought from local growers.

Propagation of Plants

The fruit trees are the result of grafting the appropriate bud on hardy rootstock, but unless a person has such skill and knowledge, the time used in this grafting process might be better spent in buying trees from a nursery. Various types of fruit plants are propagated somewhat differently, usually by large, regional nurseries. Most trees (citrus trees, deciduous fruit trees, and nut trees) are started from base stock (or rootstock). Seeds are planted to produce the seedlings, and then budding or grafting of the desired species is made to the rootstock. A very hardy rootstock is used which is not very susceptible to severe weather or disease. Once growth begins from the bud or graft, branches above this level are removed (cut away), leaving only the top portion of the tree being the variety desired. Cold weather frequently kills the desired variety, causing the plant to put out branches from the rootstock. The plant should be rebudded to some other desirable strain of fruit, as most rootstock varieties produce native fruit of poor quality and size.

The buds must (for good results) be placed on rootstocks that are compatible to them. That is, citrus budding or grafting would be done on base stocks of that major plant type; apple seeds might be planted and the rootstocks used to graft (or bud) pears. The seedstone varieties (i.e., cherries, plums, peaches, nectarines, apricots, etc.) may be budded on the seedstocks from one another, but uncooked peach seeds are frequently acquired by a nursery from a cannery of the fruit, planted in the late winter or very early spring, perhaps two to three inches apart, and budded in June to August. The bud from a desired variety is inserted in a slit on the trunk of the small seedling tree and held in place for about a week with light cotton string or masking tape, and growth is forced by clipping back about half the top on the tree. The bud is usually placed about an inch above ground level. As it begins to put out growth of its own, more of the top of the plant is removed so that additional nutrients are fed to the new plantlife. Tops of undesirable native stock are removed, as many fruit plants do not produce true from their own seeds but revert back to the rootstock base.

There is some tendency to bud (or graft) nectarine, peach, and apricot buds onto peach rootstocks, while cherries and plums are often grafted onto the rootstocks of one or the other. The latter two are smaller in size and more of a dwarf, and a smaller, but more hardy tree develops from using cherry or plum rootstocks than grafting them onto rootstocks of small peach trees.

Either 2-year-old or 3-year-old trees are reset from the nursery to the fruit farm fields (when about 3 to 6 feet in height). Planting is usually done in the early spring or late fall, and young plants should be watered well when set out and again at weekly intervals unless rainfall is adequate. The hole should be large enough to permit stretching out the roots, which should be about one-half to one-third as long as the tree is tall. Roots should not be permitted to dry out, or the tree is likely to die. A good book on gardening should be followed on soil testing, types of nutrients to apply, and periodic care of the plants. The advice of a regional nursery expert or a county agricultural agent should be sought before and during such activities until experience is gained, as certain varieties are raised for different purposes. For example, the Alberta peach is a good canning variety. Certain types of apples are more appealing for cooking than for fresh consumption. Some types are early and still others are mid- or late-season varieties.

Grapes are propagated from an about-8-inch cane of dormant wood (a small branch from the plant, removed in the fall of the year so as to promote better fruiting of the mature plant the following year). Three-year-old grape vines are probably producing some grapes. From 20 to 60 buds, on about four to six branches, are usually left to produce the crop for the following years. This may mean leaving six current year's growth limbs, each of which contains about eight to ten buds. These will send out runners which will bear next year's crop. Leaving an excessive number of buds will produce a large plant filled with very beautiful leaves but bearing little fruit. The removed branches, about the diameter of a pencil and containing four buds, should be bundled, heeled out in soil to keep them moist until the following spring, and set in half-way, vertically, in soft, loamy soil for rooting and branching into new plants. Grapes produce true and do not need to be budded. They must be watered from time to time, and two sets of roots will grow from the two buds underground. Vines will grow from the two buds left above ground. In $1\frac{1}{2}$ to 2 years, the vines should be transplanted to the field, spacing them about 8 feet apart in the row, with perhaps 10 feet between the rows to permit space for cultivation, admission of sunlight, and the passage of air currents. The Concord variety appears to be a uniform-type grape popular for making grape juice and jellies and can be grown almost anywhere in the United States. Small, white seedless grapes, grown widely in California, and other red and black seedless varieties are more popular as eating grapes. Most grape crops are harvested in the late summer or early fall, except in southern California (where wine and raisin grapes are grown) and in Florida where crops may be forced to yield fruit at other times.

Blueberries are started from cuttings from the parent plants. However, most varieties of blueberries are not self-pollinating, so a grower usually must have at least three varieties. Since blueberries provide a crop over about a three- to four-week time period, with some ripening every few days, many commercial growers will alternate rows of early, midseason, and late-season blueberries to extend the harvest season over about 10 weeks. Moreover, the midseason variety will usually pollinate the early and late varieties. To get good pollination, a good bee population is needed, and this may mean the placement of a few beehives around the periphery of the fields. About half the crop of honey may be taken by the beekeeper, providing another source of income, and still leave enough honey for the bees during winter months. Beehives are sometimes leased by fruit farmers who have an inadequate supply to pollinate their trees during the blooming stage.

Very short blueberry plants are popular in the New England and Atlantic seaboard states. Bush varieties, growing to 6 or 8 feet in height, are more popular in the midwestern states (Michigan, Illinois, Indiana, Ohio, Wisconsin, etc.) where blueberries are raised commercially. Special care in planting, cultivating, regular watering, and fertilizing is needed with blueberries, so an experienced nursery expert or other knowledgable person should be consulted on their special care. Due to the difficulty of propagating blueberry plants, most are imported from the Pacific states and reset in the midwestern states.

Most berry plants are produced by taking up young suckers, or canes, that have sprouted from the roots of the parent plants. Most varieties are self-pollinating. The second-year plant produces the berries and then dies. These dead canes should be removed during the winter, or the berry row will become thick with thorny, dead berry canes and become a menace to the would-be harvesters of the fruit. Blackberries and raspberries do not always do well when grown in the same field.

Strawberry plants are set out in the early spring from young plants that have been harvested (as runners) from parent plants and kept in cold storage (at nurseries) for a few months. They may be transplanted from one row to another by the farmer, but strawberries are profuse feeders and need a great deal of water at regular intervals during the harvest season (requiring irrigation to ensure a bumper crop), and soon send out excessive numbers of runners. In cold climates, the field rows must be protected with straw (wheat straw is often used to minimize the introduction of weeds into the rows of strawberries). Suckers might be pulled off the parent plants, but after about three or four years of production, suckers are often picked for starting new rows in the middles between the rows, and the old beds are turned under as green fertilizer. Thus, a strawberry farmer might have four fields of strawberries with only three of them in production. The fourth would be the first-year planting of new sucker vines that should not be permitted to bear the first year (i.e., small, green berries should be removed and discarded).

Over the 1960 to 1990 period, a great deal of experimental work went into the development of miniature fruit trees, genetically size-reduced, (peach, nectarine, cherry, apple, plum, almond, etc.) that promise a much faster yield than standard varieties. Moreover, the miniature trees appear to have lives of 18 to 25 years, as much as most standard varieties of fruits, exceeding the expected 8- to 10-year lives of dwarf varieties (i.e., large type with small rootstocks). Regular-sized trees usually get into full production in about their sixth to eighth year (or even later for pears), while the miniature trees begin to produce fruit their second or third year. Any fruit should be removed and discarded during the second year, however, in order to give the plant a chance to develop its growth of branches and roots.

Harvest per acre on the miniature varieties may be greater than on the standard varieties, as the trees are planted much closer together. The fruit farmer is interested in the number of tons of fruit (of salable quality) that can be harvested per acre. For peaches or apples, this may be about 12 to 16 tons per acre, beginning in about the sixth to eighth year after transplanting the trees to the fruit fields. By the fourth year, the miniature variety has largely reached its full growth of 8 feet in diameter and 6 feet in height and has more fruits than the tree can support (meaning that the fruit should be thinned by hand to eliminate the misshaped, injured, small fruit), and the yield per acre is equal to or above that of the 12- to 20-foot-high trees. For the regular, full-sized varieties of peaches or apples, trees are often set about 20 feet apart in rows that are often 25 feet apart. The miniature plants could be set 8 to 10 feet apart with some greater space between rows. Thus, about four times the number of miniature trees are planted per acre than for the large varieties. A regional nursery expert and county agricultural agent should be consulted for varieties proven to do well in a given region. For small fruit farmers who want an early harvest (three versus six years in the future), the miniature fruit trees may be the desired choice.

Prospects Department of Agriculture estimates suggest that fruit as a food will grow somewhat more rapidly than average food sales over the next 20 years. Older adults (aged 55 and over) are increasing in number about four times as rapidly as the general population and consume more fruit than in past years. Health-minded parents have increased the purchase of fruits as snacks (rather than cookies that cause cavities and snack chips that sometimes promote skin problems from excessive cooking oil). Thus, a larger share of the family income is likely to go toward the purchase of fresh, frozen, or processed fruits in future years. Families with home freezers often pick their own at local fruit farms (orchards, berry fields, vineyards, etc.), and some vegetable growers offer in-season fruit as well as organically raised vegetables to nearby patrons.

A word of caution is in order, however, as certain types of fruits do not do well if planted on land recently used for certain vegetable crops. The raising of peppers, tomatoes, eggplants, and potatoes may infest the soil with a certain type of virus harmful to most varieties of fruit trees. The land should be used for some other purpose for several years (four or five). A small vegetable farm may be separated from the fruit farm with a hay-raising or animal-raising operation. Waste from one of the operations might be useful to another (e.g., hogs relish spoiling fruits and vegetables).

One of the greatest debates now going on in agricultural research is the optimum treatment of the floor in orchards. Should it be short grasses, legumes, bare (mulched) soil throughout the orchard, bare soil near the trees but short vegetation away from the trees? Each has some advantages and disadvantages, but this is a decision that must be made by the would-be fruit farmer. Varieties to plant, marketing techniques, annual care needed, sources of temporary labor, and supplemental sources of income in the event of crop failure are other problem areas.

Market Opportunities in Various-Sized Communities

Before initiating a new business firm, the (prospective) owner should develop a business plan. An integral part of the business plan is the market analysis, or a study of the demographics of business and individual clients, supply for the product considered, demand for the product, and other information about competition and other areas needed to make the business a success.

Information helpful in developing a market analysis can be obtained from many sources, some free and others at a small cost. Local libraries (for government documents, especially), the local chamber of commerce, large public utility firms, the nearby small-business development center, commercial research firms, and state agencies designed to provide aid to small business firms may provide useful information.

Large fruit farms usually market their products to food companies that can, freeze, or process them into jellies, juices, or confectionary products. Some small fruit farms attempt to market their products directly to local supermarkets (or regional cooperatives) and restaurants. Some fruit farmers develop several thousand repeat patrons who pick their own fresh fruit, notifying previous years' customers with mailouts of postcards or using field signs or newspaper ads to alert interested patrons. The financial backing, available markets, and probable level of profits should influence the size of the fruit farm.

Someone intending to combine a fruit farm and a vegetable farm may wish to do extra reading on vegetable farming.

Franchising

Franchising is not important in most types of fruit farming. Instead, the owner of the land may sharecrop the venture. That is, a tenant does the work and the owner and tenant split the revenues after allowing for out-of-pocket costs. The ratio varies, depending on the worth of labor versus capital.

Development and Site Requirements

Most fruit farms are developed on agriculturally zoned acreage. Ad valorem taxes, in most locations, are much lower on farm property than on some other classes of zoning (residential, industrial, and commercial, for example).

Most types of fruits must be grown on average or above-average fertile farms with gentle slopes and adequate moisture. Some, such as citrus fruits, are very susceptible to frosts or freezing weather and must be grown in the states where cool or cold weather is the exception. Thus, California on the Pacific Ocean and south Texas and the lower half of Florida have become the areas where the bulk of the commercial citrus crops are grown. Oranges and grapefruits are sold in vast amounts for fresh fruit consumption, while lemons and limes are shipped more to the soft drink bottling companies that use their extracts in making lemon-lime sodas. To a degree, each is sold to canneries or firms that freeze extracts for frozen juices; but over the past 20 years, canned food sales have declined as frozen juices and other fruit-bearing products have increased in popularity. Apples and peaches generally need two or three months of cool weather (but not below about 15 degrees below 0, Fahrenheit) during the year in order to yield good crops. Bananas are not native to the United States but are instead bought from wholesale vegetable and fruit sellers that import them from Central or South American countries.

Certain of the major fruit crops are grown in very large fields for commercial marketing, such as apples in the state of Washington; citrus in the lower half of Florida, the lower valleys of Texas, and California; and grapes (eating, raisin, or wine) in California.

Many types of fruit are grown over a wide range of climates and in most geographic locations of the United States. The following types of fruit are widely grown in the United States (and abroad) and are covered in a general way in this industry and business profile: grapes (eating, raisin, wine, or jelly and juice grapes); berries (strawberries, blueberries, blackberries, boysenberries, and raspberries); citrus (oranges, grapefruit, tangerines, lemons, and limes); and deciduous tree fruits (apples, peaches, plums, nectarines, apricots, pears, and cherries). While many of these may be raised on fruit farms that have been in the family for five or more generations, some people have in recent years developed the urge to begin a vegetable or fruit farm as a way of life and as a means of creating income to cover family expenses.

Fruit farms are usually developed on the sides of very gently rolling hills. Slow runoff of water and cool air during frosty weather are important to fruit growing. The soils should be reasonably fertile or nutrients should be added. Blueberries love an acid soil while other fruits grow in most places suitable for vegetables. Strawberries are exceedingly thirsty, and in order to obtain a good stand of strawberries with a good crop yield, a source of water for irrigation is needed. A drought of more than a week during May or June (in most locations) will reduce the crop of strawberries. Other types of fruit are less adversely affected by lack of rainfall, as their root systems are deeper than those of strawberries that draw surface moisture.

Rodents, such as mice, field rats, or rabbits, and deer sometimes become a problem in chewing the bark on young fruit trees. Certain types of poison baits may be helpful in eliminating the pests, or a few cats and some rabbit hounds may keep the population reduced. Using miniature trees, planted about 8 to 10 feet apart, may cost slightly more in developing an orchard, but production is usually begun in three rather than about six to seven years, and yields and life expectancy of many miniature varieties of fruit trees equal that of standard-sized trees.

Cost and Types of
Assets Needed to
Start a Business

Most types of fruit farms are labor intensive, but annual income from each acre of ground devoted to a fruit farm should approximate the value of the acre after improvement. Add to this the amount invested into other assets (i.e., working capital, sorting sheds, storage facilities, transportation vehicles, etc.), and income must be substantial to cover expenses and offer a reasonable return on invested net worth. During years of slight over-supply, the forces of supply and demand cause the per-unit selling prices of the products (sold to large canneries, fruit packers, etc.) to decline to about a break-even level.

A small vegetable/fruit farmer could likely make about $100,000 in annual revenues with 18 to 20 acres. One-third of this acreage might be devoted to a fruit farm, another one-third might be devoted to organic, and intensely cultivated vegetables, and the balance might be an area used for raising hay (for mulch) or for rotation of certain crops. The small farm would likely require two around-the-year workers, with about four additional workers hired on a seasonal basis. The produce might be sold to nearby consumers who enjoy picking their own produce and fruits. The price charged should be about 67% to 75% of retail market price, but some patrons are willing to pay such a price and invest some of their own (leisure time) labor in harvesting the produce.

Each year, Dun & Bradstreet, Inc., provides financial profiles in *Industry Norms and Key Business Ratios* for about 800 industry lines. The IRS likewise provides key financial ratio studies on many industry lines. These industry benchmark statements and ratios are useful to the owner/operator in developing a business plan of his or her anticipated operations.

A small fruit (or fruit/vegetable) farmer should start on a much smaller scale than those suggested by D & B for these intermediate- to large-scale companies, but the IRS does not provide data separately for each SIC code in its *Statistics of Income Source Book*. It simply shows breakdowns for agricultural firms by size of firm and not by SIC designation. Thus, D & B data are thought to be more meaningful to a specialty firm in agriculture.

The approximate averages of percentage financial statements and key ratios for four types of fruit farms are reflected in the following schedules. These include berry, grape, citrus, and deciduous fruit farms. For the average of 1992–1993 data provided by D & B, the common-sized financial statements for the four types of fruit farms are as follows:

	Berries	Grapes	Citrus	Deciduous
Assets				
Cash and near-cash	10.1%	7.1%	11.4%	11.0%
Accounts receivable	9.5	9.4	11.7	7.7
Notes receivable	.5	.3	1.2	.6
Inventories	5.2	20.0	3.3	8.4
Other current assets	7.5	3.8	4.8	3.9
Total current assets	31.2	41.6	39.6	29.8
Fixed assets	47.5	40.6	32.4	31.6
Other noncurrent assets	20.7	27.4	32.7	25.3
Total assets	100.0	100.0	100.0	100.0
Debts and Net Worth				
Accounts payable	1.7	2.7	7.5	4.9
Bank and other notes payable	3.7	4.1	5.7	7.0
Other current debts	7.0	8.6	9.4	9.7
Total current debts	12.4	15.4	22.6	21.6
Long-term debts	18.5	23.6	18.4	24.4
Deferred credits	2.3	—	3.3	.2
Net worth	66.8	61.0	55.7	53.8
Total debts and net worth	100.0	100.0	100.0	100.0
Assets (thousands)	$2,517	$2,330	$4,886	$ 977
Sales (thousands)	1,815	1,574	3,900	1,219
Gross profit	37.0%	39.9%	26.8%	43.4%
Net after-tax profit	5.6	13.1	4.7	5.7

Average assets for the farms in this D & B array of companies were from about $975,000 for deciduous tree fruits to about $5 million for citrus fruits. Sales are usually about 50% to 75% of assets for berry and grape farms and perhaps about 85% to 90% of assets for citrus and deciduous tree fruit farms. Net worth amounts to about 54% to 66% of total assets, on average, for the four types of farms. Some individual farms have very little debt while others might finance with half debt.

The above statements suggest that the grape farms were most profitable, but this level changes over time. Thus, one undertaking such an operation should make marketing studies and gain some assurance that items grown and harvested might then be sold for prices adequate to cover expenses and to provide a reasonable return on net worth.

Typical Business Ratios
Each year, Prentice-Hall, Inc., in its *Almanac of Business and Industry Financial Ratios* provides common-sized income statements for major SIC groups broken down by size of firm. For the smallest two size categories, the following expense breakdowns are provided for the SIC 0400 group (agricultural production) from the 1992–1993 issue:

	Under $100,000 Assets	$100,000–$250,000 Assets
Cost of operations	73.0%	50.8%
Compensation of officers	1.8	4.8
Repairs	2.1	2.6
Bad debts	—	—
Rent on business property	6.5	9.7
Taxes (excluding federal tax)	2.2	3.7
Interest	2.6	4.0
Depreciation/depletion/amortization	4.0	6.9
Advertising	—	.1
Pension and benefits	.1	1.0
Other expenses (mostly labor)	11.7	22.2
Profit or loss	Loss	Loss

Each year, D & B, in its study on *Industry Norms and Key Business Ratios*, provides certain solvency ratios, efficiency ratios, and profitability ratios. D & B shows these key ratios for the upper quartile (25th percentile of the array), median quartile (50th percentile), and lower quartile (75th percentile). The approximate averages of the median ratios for 1992–1993 were calculated as approximations in the subindustries for fruit farming. (A reader wanting greater detail should review D & B information.)

Key Ratio	Berries	Grapes	Citrus	Deciduous
Solvency ratios:				
Quick ratio	.9:1	1.0:1	1.0:1	.9:1
Current ratio	1.6:1	3.7:1	1.9:1	1.9:1
Total debts to net worth (percent)	40.3	54.6	61.4	61.4
Efficiency ratios:				
Collection period (days)	42.3	104.4	42.4	28.8
Sales to inventory (times)	10.1	1.2	5.7	8.6
Assets to sales (percent)	91.2	153.6	109.1	89.2
Profitability ratios:				
Return on sales (percent)	3.8	9.5	3.4	4.1
Return on net worth (percent)	6.4	13.4	6.4	9.7

Grapes are grown for drying into raisins as well as for marketing fresh or selling to wine presses, thus accounting for the large inventory level relative to sales.

Legal Considerations   Persons buying real estate, whether it be for developing a fruit farm, a vegetable farm, or a fish farm, should use the skills of an attorney in doing a title search and in drawing up the legal documents. Forming a corporation or partnership also requires the use of an attorney. Most small farms are operated as single proprietorships, being operated by an individual or a husband/wife team, with little separation between personal and business assets. One of a husband/wife team may have a part-time or seasonal job away from the farm, such as teaching during the academic year and available to work on the farm during the summer months of greatest need, to earn some cash income.

Most labor-intensive vegetable and fruit farms hire seasonal workers, beginning in mid-spring and extending through the harvest season. The capital-intensive grain farms, requiring vast acreage and expensive farm equipment, may hire seasonal workers to aid in the harvest of the grain (perhaps lasting two or three weeks), but family members may do the bulk of the other work, such as plowing, disking, harrowing, seeding, thinning, application of herbicides or fertilizers, irrigating, and safeguarding against natural disasters (birds, insects, excessive flooding, frost damage, etc.). Some knowledge about federal laws in the areas of minimum wage requirements, child labor laws, payroll tax deductions and payments, health-care laws (covering such things as in-field restrooms or portable potties, hand-washing facilities, drinking water, medical care after an insecticide or injury incident, etc.), and need for various types of insurance is needed for the manager (or owner) of a farm.

The fruit farm manager should have the proper licenses to operate and sell fresh fruits, be aware of federal and state laws that require certain things, especially in hiring and work practices, and have some standby financing available for use during years when crops are poor. The federal government and certain states issue marketing orders and agreements that must be followed by fruit and vegetable farmers.

A fruit farmer should have a suitable insurance program. This includes property insurance, insurance against hail and other crop perils, coverage on vehicles, a general liability insurance policy, and workers' compensation insurance. The aid of an insurance evaluator might be engaged to design a program for a given firm.

Experience and Training Required

A person should not undertake the development of a fruit farm or vineyard unless he or she has had some training and/or experience in the product. Hours are long, income is usually low, and the farmers are at the mercy of the elements and nature (frost, freezes, rainfall, hail, birds, various types of fungi, etc.). For those who have some land and the fortitude to begin a fruit farm, however, the following pages may prove to be of some value.

The owner/operator of a fruit farm must enjoy the rigors and discipline of this profession. It means an around-the-calendar working environment from daylight to dark. Any size farm operation requires one or more on-premises workers. This may be a hired manager who has been with the business for many years and whose family may live in a sharecropper's cabin on the premises. Some experienced older adults make very good managers of such operations. Most fruit farm operations require some seasonal employees to take care of grass cutting, tree pruning, insect and disease spraying, planting, watering, harvesting, crating, shipping the product, protection of the trees or bushes from inclement winter weather and rodents, and the removal and replenishment of old or dead plants. Birds are usually pests against fruit crops, striking about one day before planned harvest, eating large amounts of bush crops and pecking holes into peaches, pears, and apples.

The owner or manager must be trained in agriculture, whether through agriculture programs at colleges and universities, working on a nursery, growing up on a farm and participating in such activities as a teenager/young adult, or years of on-the-job training and observation. Most techniques used by vegetable and fruit farmers have been learned by trial-and-error during past years. A new operator, however, should spend months in studying about such techniques, pitfalls, and possible benefits before undertaking such a venture.

Many seasonal farm workers have finished less than the eighth grade of public school. Many are Mexican-Americans, living in California but performing seasonal harvest jobs along the Pacific seacoast; being domiciled in Texas but working seasonally in the grain belt or the central vegetable and fruit farm belt; or living in Florida and moving seasonally along the Atlantic seacoast states.

Training in the use of equipment and insecticides should be given to adult and younger workers to safeguard against environmental hazard, injury, and illness. Attention is needed to the upgrading of substandard housing facilities provided by the large grain, vegetable, and fruit farmers or processors to workers and their families.

Keys to Successful Management

Keys to successful operation of a fruit farm and a vegetable farm are similar. One of the major differences is that fruit farming produces little income for the first few years of operations, whereas vegetable farming may produce cash revenues the first year. Other keys to a profitable fruit-farming operation are as follows:

1. The owner must attempt to reduce the cost of the mid-marketing channel of distribution. The grower, if possible, should handle his or her own grading, sorting, and transport to nearby markets. If this is not possible, more than one possible buyer of the product should be investigated, granting the business to the highest, most reliable bidding firm.

2. The operation requires about three or four years to develop revenues from tree-type fruits, with berry crops coming on in the second year after planting. Blueberries begin to bear about the same time as miniature fruit trees (after the second or third year). Harvest usually increases while the trees are growing and then levels out about the sixth to eighth year. For the tree-type fruits, about 15 or more tons of fruit should be harvested per acre of orchard.

3. Financing is required to cover living expenses for the family and to meet operating expenses of the business during the period of small income. Thus, many fruit farmers will operate small vegetable farms until production of fruit comes on-stream.

4. The commercial fruit farmer may have a limited number of crop types, such as a well-known variety of peaches (Alberta is a popular freestone variety) and apples (red delicious is popular). One who seeks to sell directly to residents of a nearby city (or to deliver to restaurants and regional supermarkets) should have more diversity. Different varieties of a fruit may be used for different purposes. For example, Alberta is a better peach for processing than for the fresh market. Some apples are better for cooking than others. Different varieties of fruits have different harvest dates and storage life.

5. An acre devoted to each of apples, peaches, blueberries, and strawberries and another two acres divided among other types of fruit crops such as nectarines, plums, cherries, grapes, and blackberries should, with good weather and adequate care from the owner/operator or hired assistants, supply fresh and frozen fruit to 300 to 500 families. Keep in mind that a good harvest from an acre of peaches is about 15 tons. This would be 30,000 pounds, or 100 pounds per family, on average. About 48 to 50 pounds of fruit equals a bushel, the measurement generally used for selling peaches, apples, and nectarines. Few families would buy more than two bushels of each of the popular fruits for fresh consumption or freezing. Berries and grapes are frequently sold by the pound, bringing about 60% to 75% of retail price at nearby supermarkets.

6. The fruit farm operator must vigorously market the produce from his or her farm. Raising the trees/bushes/vines/canes to productive age is one of three major activities. The second is producing a bountiful harvest. The third is effectively marketing the product at the appropriate time. Since other farmers will be competing for customers and will have harvests at about the same time, it is essential that repeat clients be developed for a pick-your-own operation. Spot TV and radio commercials supplement mailout of cards to past customers for pick-your-own farms.

7. The owner should consider joining or forming an association for marketing surplus fruit harvest, perhaps receiving more favorable consideration from regional canneries or companies that freeze or otherwise process fresh fruits.

Information Sources   Several sources of information are available to the (prospective) fruit farmer. In addition to word-of-mouth suggestions from retired farmers, the advice of local or regional nursery experts should be sought. The advice and written pamphlets from a nearby agricultural college, the county agricultural agent, or a large public library are usually beneficial. Written sources of information about fruit farming that may prove useful include a listing of associations, books, journals and magazines, industry government reports, ratio studies, investment services, and general U.S. government publications.

Selected industry sources of information are updated each few years in *Encyclopedia of Business Information Sources*, Gale Research, Inc., Detroit, Mich.

Franchising (Any Industry)

Business Types, Industry Characteristics and Prospects

Close to one-half of retail sales and a growing share of service firms' sales were being made by franchising operations in the mid-1990s. The total was about $800 billion and expected to grow by about 8.5% annually for several additional years. One estimate placed the number of franchisees at about one-half million, the number of franchisors at close to 2,500, and the total of persons being employed by franchised businesses at about 9 million.

Franchising is the granting of certain rights to others. It usually grants, for the payment of an initial fee and usually some periodic royalty, the use of a trade name, a patent, a secret recipe, a logo on the uniforms, employee training, management assistance, financial assistance, and so forth, to one firm from another.

Franchising is not a new innovation, as the concept has been used by Singer Sewing Machine Company since the mid-1800s. Major petroleum companies franchise their service station operators, the larger auto manufacturing companies franchise auto dealers, and soft drink companies franchise local bottlers. In more recent years, many of the national food-franchising chains, such as McDonald's, Hardee's, Kentucky Fried Chicken, Pizza Hut, Bonanza, and so on, have shown substantial growth in terms of outlets and total revenues.

Franchising differs from private ownership and operation of a business firm in the same industry in a number of respects. For a fee payment and additional private investment, the franchisee obtains a distributorship in a nationally advertised chain, with the right to sell a proven, recognized product. The franchising firm provides help in locating a site, constructing a suitable building, and equipping the facility with fixed assets, supplies, and inventories, and offers training to management staff and support personnel. Revisits to the site are usually made periodically in order to aid the owner/manager in problem troubleshooting, setting reasonable sales targets, and reaching preset goals.

The franchisee has certain obligations to the franchisor. The outlet is expected to offer a preset good or service that meets quality control standards. Supplies and inventory of items may have to be bought from certain suppliers. Restrictions may be placed on relocation, expansion of territories, or reduction in services. Last of all, the terms of the contract may call for operation of the contract for a lengthy time period, such as 10 or 15 years, with an option to renew for 5, 10, or 15 additional years. While some of the restrictions placed on a franchisee by the franchisor's operating policies may seem harsh, the parent organization does have several tools that normally lead to successful operation by their franchisees.

It is interesting to note that the failure rate of new franchised businesses is only about 5% per year, compared to that of new independent businesses at start-up of about five times this level. The two predominant causes of failure in a small firm are:

1. Inadequate management skills and knowledge about the operation of the firm
2. Inadequate financing

The franchisors have attempted to overcome these two weaknesses. That is, many work closely with the would-be franchisee and train them in directions proven to be effective in other locations by other managers. Second, there is almost always a minimum financial commitment required by a franchisee that is adequate to begin such a business. If not, the franchisor may help to locate venture capital, or some will accept a deferred payout of the franchise fee for a period of time.

The franchisor offers some benefits not afforded a single proprietorship working independently. Some of these include brand names, trademarks, copyrights, uniform logos, recognizable signs or storefronts, uniform layout of the sales floor, proven recipes, economy-of-scale purchasing of supplies and inventory of items, national advertising, training programs for managers and other key employees, and aid in site location and preparation. Aid may also be given for the grand opening and the design of a simple, but workable, accounting system for the firm. The investor in a franchise obtains a well-recognized name and the ability to get started a year of two before an independent business person could reach a break-even level. Group purchasing, research and development, and national advertising may save about as much to the firm as the cost of the royalty payment. The independent business person, on the other hand, would have to learn by trial and error and cover the franchisee's shared expenses alone, but would have more independence than the franchise operator.

Prospects in the franchising area during the next twenty years are excellent, according to most forecasters. Many expanding retail and service lines, even electronic banking, are moving in this direction. As franchisors develop good track records of rapidly expanding outlets, sales base, and profits, they increasingly will become targets of takeover firms that wish to acquire them at substantial prices above their book values. Moreover, such acquiring firms usually insist that the driving forces on the management team of an acquired firm continue with the parent firm for several years and oversee its continued growth and development. Thus, opportunities abound for the small entrepreneur to begin and see a small firm grow to an economically feasible size, and those with vision about a business opportunity should be able to prosper by expanding their dreams through the infusion of capital and management skills of others through the franchising approach. Some economists forecast that franchised operations should expand by 6% to 8% annually for the balance of the century, which is about three times as rapid as total anticipated expansion in commerce in the United States.

Personal Characteristics Needed by a Potential Franchisee

Before deciding to pursue the route of a franchisee, a good hard look should be taken at oneself by the prospective owner/manager of such a firm. One should ask oneself, "Am I willing to work hard? Are my dreams supported by my spouse and other family members? Is my formal training and experience background suited for pursuing the life of an entrepreneur? Do I have some management and marketing skills? Am I enthusiastic about developing the business? Will I stick to the business for ten or fifteen years into the future?" These are some questions that should be answered in the positive before a person seriously appraises several franchising opportunities.

Ideally, a business person should know something about the product, but a successful middle management executive in one line can usually learn about a different product if knowledgable in management, marketing, and promotional skills. An honest evaluation should be made of oneself and the potential for the franchised operation. Such questions should be asked as, "Do I have sales potential? Will the product likely sell this year, next year, and five years from now? What emerging competition can I expect? How much protected operating territory will I have? If my sales do not reach expectation, can I be forced out of business at a financial loss? Are there opportunities to make additional investments in nearby franchised operations if the first one is a success? Are there sources of venture capital that may be available for start-up financing?"

An enterprising business person should spend time in doing research into the background and normal contract terms for several franchisors in areas of interest. On several possible acceptable lines of business, initial contact should be made with franchising firms. Information about franchising opportunities with their chains should be sought. This is usually provided at no cost to the interested party, as franchisors are continually seeking to bring in new outlets for their product or service in areas not already being covered adequately. Information should be sought about the type of product/service sold, the level of investment required, restrictions on full-time management employment with the franchised operation, the franchising fee and licensing royalty arrangement, the duration of the contract, the ownership/risk assumed with the fixed asset facilities, training assistance provided by the franchising firm, and protection afforded the franchisee in the event that the business is not a success. Since the late 1970s, the Federal Trade Commission has required that franchising firms provide prospective clients with a "disclosure statement" setting forth information in many of the above-mentioned areas. Any estimates of capital needs or expected rates of return on investments should be compared to those being earned by large, national firms in similar areas of operation.

Sponsored Training Programs

Most expansion-minded franchisors provide a period of initial training for the manager/owner of the franchised operation and some key employees. This usually involves a training program at the home office of the franchising firm, often embracing most phases of operation of the business, and may last from one to several weeks. The franchise fee may cover the cost of tuition, room, and board, or the cost may be out-of-pocket to the franchisee. This point should be clarified before an expensive commitment is made. Some on-site training of rank-and-file employees is usually made a few days before the facility is to have its "grand opening." A member of the management team may remain on board for the grand opening, making suggestions as to types of services to offer, portion and quality control, and problem solving.

Sales goals are usually set, certain advertising campaigns are made by the franchisor and other ads of a local nature may be required of the franchisee. For example, 1.2% to 2.5% of revenues may have to be spent for local advertising as a part of the franchise agreement. If sales goals are not reached, a management specialist from the franchisor's firm makes a site visit and attempts to make recommendations for overcoming the problems.

The selection of a franchisor partner should not be based only on the size of the franchise fee and the royalty ratio. The apparent desire of the franchisor's management to see successful operations from their franchisees and the willingness to work with them through their period of start-up difficulties may be of greater importance to the ultimate success or failure of the new facility.

Market Opportunities in Various-Sized Communities

It is suggested that a study be made of the demographics of the community in which the franchise will be located. The shopping patterns for the patrons living in the community should then be studied. If many citizens are traveling several miles to do a substantial amount of their shopping, then a nearby supplier of such goods and services would likely meet with financial success. A comparison of the number of firms and employees in each SIC designation might be determined for the county of interest from a recent state issue of *County Business Patterns* and the figures compared to national averages. If it is thus determined that the region appears to be underrepresented with such firms, a well-located and -managed one should prove to have a good chance for financial success. Should statistics show that there is already an oversupply of such firms by 10% or more, it is likely that profits would be small, and the entrance of more firms into the competitive arena will only drive out present operators or result in failure of the new ones after a short operating period of disappointing revenues and profits.

Development and Site Requirements

A franchisor is likely to have certain requirements about an acceptable site for an enterprise to be operated under its trademark or trade name. Management of the franchisor is usually helpful in locating a site that meets several preset tests of traffic density, adequate space, and appropriate zoning for the establishment. Prepared building plans, placement of signs, and interior layout are usually also standard, which expedites preparing the site for operation. The franchisor will usually have catalogs of several suppliers of equipment needed by the firm, as well as uniforms, supplies, and inventories.

The franchisee usually buys the fixed assets with some downpayment and a long-term financial arrangement for making monthly payments to a bank, life insurance company, the Small Business Administration, or a venture capital firm such as a small-business development company, for a number of years. A ten- to twenty-year payout of debt on the structure, with a shorter payout, such as seven years, on equipment, is customary.

Cost and Types of Assets Needed to Start a Business

Some of the franchised operations require a very small payment of a franchise fee while others are very large. For example, some chains of weight-watching salons charge only $1,000 in initial fee. Some large hotels charge about $1 million. Many service chains charge from $5,000 to $20,000 as an initial franchise fee plus some ratio of sales, such as 2% to about 7.5%. This up-front franchise fee is only a small portion of total asset needs, however, which may run six to ten times this level in the typical small business concern.

Some capital is self-generating, however, which means that some credit is supplied by sellers of inventory and supply items, by accrued wages and taxes, and so on. Benchmark ratios should be sought for privately owned firms operating in a line of business similar to the franchising one. Four sources of widely used sets of financial ratios are suggested in the last section of this text, along with mailing addresses, so these will not be repeated at this point.

Each annual issue of *Franchise Annual*, published by Info Press, Inc., provides key financial statistics on widely franchised operations. For the lines of business covered in the profiles in this volume, the initial single-unit franchise fees in 1991, provided by the above reference, were as follows:

Category	Lower Quartile	Median	Upper Quartile	Provides Financing
Restaurants	$15,000	$20,000	$25,000	10.2%
Hotels/motels	20,000	30,000	45,000	—
Recreation/travel	12,380	22,500	30,150	28.6
Printing/copying	17,880	23,000	38,000	33.3
Employment services	10,000	15,000	25,000	30.0
Maintenance/cleaning	8,500	15,000	18,500	57.1
Construction/home improvement	13,300	17,250	25,000	34.4
Retailing: Nonfood	15,000	20,000	32,750	9.5
Retailing: Food	15,000	20,000	25,000	24.1
Health/beauty aids	12,500	19,500	25,000	36.8
Real estate services	N/A	20,000	N/A	60.0
Miscellaneous services	11,500	16,500	24,920	29.6

Of the above, each category had 80% or more of units formed over the past 5 years that were still in operation by early 1992. Of these lines of business, the greatest dropout rates were for employment services (18.2%, 5-year dropout rate) and real estate service firms (13.4%, 5-year dropout rate).

The 5-year survival rate, to 1992, was greater than 98% in each of restaurants, hotels/motels, construction/home improvement, and health and beauty aids. Few franchising firms reacquired the licenses issued to franchisees over this period.

In order to go into a franchised operation, some capital investment funds should be available. For an in-house operation of a babysitting service, little capital investment is needed. A contracting firm for home repair would be intermediate in financing needs. For a franchised McDonald's operation, financing of close to $300,000 would be needed. To franchise a large hotel, the fee might be even larger. Most lines of retail and service companies, in which franchising has recently become very popular, generally have average equity capital about 50% to 70% of total assets. In a financial institution, such as a bank, this ratio is very small. For personal loan companies, the ratio is about 25% to 30%. In a service firm, the commitment to fixed assets is small in many of the labor-intensive firms (such as supply typists, janitorial services to businesses and the home, housecleaning, babysitting, grannysitting, lawncare, swimming pool care, etc.). In a food chain, substantial investments are needed in fixed asset investments, such as land, building, and equipment. An existing facility might be obtained on a 1- or 2-year lease, thus limiting the potential loss to an unsuccessful start-up business person. Additional funds are needed for cash and near-cash items, receivables, inventories, supplies, and miscellaneous assets. Dun & Bradstreet, Inc., in *Industry Norms and Key Business Ratios*, and Robert L. Morris Associates, in *Statement Studies*, provide useful financial statements on large groups of firms for several hundred companies in each of their covered industries. The annual edition of *U.S. Industrial Outlook*, published by the Bureau of Domestic Commerce, Department of Commerce, Washington, D.C., provides insights and forecasts into the operation of most sectors other than agriculture, financing, and service.

Legal Considerations

Several areas of the precontract and contract should be reviewed by an accountant and/or an attorney before being signed by a prospective franchisee. Remember that a desirable client (a new franchisee) is in a strong bargaining position, while someone already operating and under contract to do certain things is in a poor bargaining posture. The following are legal or quasi-legal areas that call for review by a professional.

1. Ask that the copy of the precontract be reviewed by an experienced accountant or attorney. Many of the general standards stated in the document are negotiated with certain of the new franchisees, so most franchisors expect to make concessions on some of the points.

2. If financing is somewhat of a problem, the franchisor may be asked to accept one-third of the franchise fee immediately upon signing the contract, another one-third at the end of 6 moths, and the last one-third at the end of a year. About 16% of the franchisors provide some financing to their franchisee firms. Fairness of the contracts should be reviewed by an attorney.

3. The protective measures for the franchisor should not be exceedingly harsh on the franchisee. If they seem so, then some adjustment needs to be made to them. Attempt to learn what operating terms competing franchisors are offering and make counterproposals to the prospective franchisor along similar lines.

4. The prospective manager/franchisee and his or her attorney or accountant should be alert in reviewing the proposed contract to spot hidden investment costs, such as mandatory: attendance of training programs at franchisee's expense; annual audit of records of franchisee at his or her own expense; purchase of inventory and supplies from a company under the control of the franchising firm; and ability of the franchisor to void the franchise (with substantial financial loss to the franchisee) if a certain sales quota is not met within a certain time period.

5. The prospective franchisee should make sure that the formula for computing the weekly, monthly, or quarterly licensing fee is clear.

6. The prospective franchisee should review the planned insurance coverage for adequacy in the areas of property coverage, liability, and fidelity insurance on employees that handle large sums of funds. Life insurance on the manager/franchisee and key employees may be desirable.

Keys to Successful Franchising   The following are suggested as some steps in the overall process for evaluating the merits and shortfalls of franchising, rather than individual ownership, in a line of business.

1. One must evaluate one's own strengths in selling, management, and willingness to devote long hours and years of endeavor to the franchising business.

2. If the thought of having another team draw up the set of playing rules, with little room for suggestions, is troublesome, then franchising may lead to a stormy marriage between the franchisor and the franchisee firm.

3. One must assess the likelihood of a growing demand for the product or service offered in the operating territory of the planned franchisee firm over the terms of the proposed lease. If demand does not appear to be expanding nationally or regionally, the possibility of expanding the territory or types of goods/services offered should be written into the franchise contract before it is signed.

4. One should review the franchisor's profile for any shady business practices in the past, such as past bankruptcies, lawsuits brought or defended, and so on, and evaluate their merits. One should also evaluate the chances that problems could be on the horizon that would involve the prospective franchisee and its ability to operate profitably.

5. One should evaluate the level of support services for reasonableness in light of the size of the franchise fee, and determine with several personal interviews how other managers/franchisees view their past relationships with the managers of the franchisor.

6. One should review the cost estimates and estimates of return on investment or equity capital suggested by the franchisors for reasonableness in comparison to independently operated firms in the industry.

7. One should determine outside sources of venture or credit capital available in the event that equity funds are not adequate to meet asset and expense needs.

8. One should review provisions for protecting the operating territory of the franchisee from other franchised operations. Is there any provision for relocation in the event that a major competitor locates a similar firm nearby?

9. One should assess the likelihood of an open line of communication between the management staff of the franchisor and the manager/franchisee during the future.

10. Is there a strong, long-term commitment to invested funds and human endeavor by the would-be franchisee? If not, one should probably seek another line of business.

Information Sources Several sources of information are helpful to a business person investigating the advisability of pursuing a career in franchising. These include associations, books and periodicals, ratio studies for key industry lines, investment advisory services, and government documents and reports. A suggested list appears in each update of *Encyclopedia of Business Information Sources,* by Gale Research, Inc., Detroit, Mich.

Landscaping and Lawncare Firms

Business Types, Industry Characteristics and Prospects

Landscaping firms and lawncare service centers are classified as SIC code 0781 from the broader classification of SIC 078 (landscape and horticultural service). Lawn and garden services have been assigned the SIC code 0782. The former group deals largely with garden and landscape planning, landscape architecture, and landscape counseling. The second group of firms includes the installation of lawns (except artificial turf), lawn care (fertilizing, mowing, mulching, seeding, spraying, sprigging, sod laying, turf installation, except artificial, etc.), garden maintenance, cemetery upkeep, and highway mowing. Since many firms that operate in this subindustry undertake a wide range of such activities, both landscaping and lawncare firms will be covered in this business and industry profile.

The lawncare business is cyclical and seasonal in nature, but it is often fast-growth during periods when residential construction is booming (i.e., during a period of pent-up demand following two or three years of below-average housing starts and when mortgage interest rates are reasonably low—say 9% or less). During other periods, substitute housing arrangements are pursued, with increased purchases of mobile homes (as temporary housing), greater use of apartment dwellings, and purchases of older homes with the idea of remodeling and enlarging the structure. With these types of housing situations, spending on landscaping is much less than with new single-unit dwellings or homes bought for refurbishment of the structure and upgrade of the grounds.

Landscaping firms are often involved in four distinctly different but related activities. These include (1) landscape architectural design; (2) landscaping and planting of trees, shrubs, ground cover, and decorative structures such as patios, walkways, walls, and so on; (3) the production, or at least wholesale buying and preservation, of plants to be used in landscaping and planting activities (SIC 0783); and (4) the provision of complete (contractual) lawncare service to residential and commercial accounts.

After several years of lackluster housing sales in 1978 to 1983 due to very high interest rates, a strong resurgence in the industry began in 1984. This continued through the 1980s until interest rates again began to rise.

This strong residential housing growth was paralleled by strong growth in the landscaping business, as packaged lawncare revenues grew from $1.9 billion in 1985 to $2.3 billion in 1986. A growth of 15% was shown from 1985 to 1986, while 1987 revenues were about 111% of those for 1986. Growth was less but positive for a year or two, and then the revenues for the firms began to decline along with a soft real estate market. It has been estimated that over six million homes are using complete packaged lawncare services. Roughly the same patterns were shown in the early 1990s, with substantial year-to-year growth shown in years of strong housing starts and some reductions in years when housing starts declined.

The exact value of landscaping to a home is open to debate, but most surveys tend to support the idea that $1,000 spent for landscaping will usually return a home seller from $800 to $1,200 in additional price for the home. Some real estate persons feel that the return is even higher, especially for the better-groomed, expensive homes. On average for a new home, about 10% of the value of the land and structure is spent on landscaping.

Spending on home landscaping projects is not limited to newly acquired residences or those intended for sale. About 25% of homeowners have some annual spending on landscaping and grounds beautification, with an average of $150 to $200 as the annual expenditure. New homeowners usually spend about $1,500 on landscaping projects, with 80% of them planning to do it themselves. Popular landscaping projects and items preferred by the do-it-yourselfers include the following (in order of popularity):

Landscaping Projects	*Items Preferred*
Landscaping along driveways, walkways	Annuals, perennials
Adding deck, plant containers	Ornamental, flowering trees and shrubs
Replacing existing trees, plants	Specialty plants
Renovating existing landscapes	Shade trees
Planting a privacy hedge	Ground cover
Installing a plant island	Evergreen shrubs
Landscaping/energy conservation	Deciduous trees

Since landscape designing and planting are so highly cyclical and geared to a strong housing market, some landscaping firms have begun to promote contract lawncare work for (1) upper-income-level, management-type persons, (2) retired individuals, (3) public projects (i.e., schools, playgrounds, parks, golf courses, country clubs, churches, municipal facilities, etc.), and (4) commercial office buildings, malls, downtown beautification projects, and so on.

Providing continuous lawncare service does spread the work over the calendar months as the heavy landscape planting takes place during the late winter/early spring months and again in the late fall/early winter months. Contract lawncare work is heaviest during the late spring, summer, and early fall months when little planting is involved. The two snowy winter months might be heavy with vacationing by employees, or certain clients might be interested in contracting for grounds care, snow removal, and so on, during such months. Protection of plants from rodents (rabbits, mice, and rats) requires more snow-time activity, so such endeavors do tend to level out the work assignments around the calendar (smoothing income).

Some landscape design and complete lawncare business firms contract with nearby nurseries for the plants that they plan to use on their projects. Some landscaping firms have extensive displays of such plants surrounding their showcase business office and displayed in an enclosed greenhouse or fenced nursery area to the rear of their office building. Others attempt to combine the production of popular plants with their architectural design/lawncare services, and the extent of the success of such diversification depends heavily on competition in the region, available financing, and management talent available to the firm.

The level of activities for landscape and lawncare firms is likely to remain strong for the balance of the century as family formations should continue at a rate two times the general growth in U.S. population. This is influenced substantially by the large number of post–World War II babies ("baby boomers") reaching the ages of 30 to 55, the ages when more money is spent on these types of services. In addition, the number of U.S. working wives almost equals the number of working males, so less time is available for do-it-yourself projects. More contract work is hired out due to higher income levels for the two-wage-earner families.

Market Opportunities in Various-Sized Communities
A part of every business venture is the business plan. A part of the business plan, the market analysis, is of primary importance. Doing a market analysis will tell the prospective entrepreneur if the neighborhood can reasonably expect to support the proposed venture, the expected level of revenue, types and level of competition, and other information necessary to make it as a successful business.

Conducting a market analysis can be simple or exhaustive. Sources of information about local demographics can be obtained from the local chamber of commerce, local governments (city or county offices), U.S. Census Bureau, some state agencies, some not-for-profit community groups (development commissions, for example), large utility firms, such as electric and telecommunications companies), commercial research companies, small-business development centers, public libraries, and the like.

The nursery portion of the landscape operation may be located in a rural area, probably several miles away from the nearest city. The landscape design office, ideally, should be on the outskirts of a medium-sized, expanding city, preferably in the direction of expansion of residents from the city. More clients and potential customers will, therefore, be traveling by the landscape office and stop to browse or to receive a bid on a proposed project.

On average in the United States, one combination firm in the nursery/garden store/landscape business operates for about every 30,000 persons in population. Thus, the degree of competition already serving the area should be analyzed by a prospective entrepreneur in the landscape counseling and lawncare area.

Franchising

Several of the larger (often franchised) companies such as Scott & Sons, ChemLawn, Tru-Green, and Lawn Doctor do a large portion of the contract lawncare work.

The franchisors often promote their products by developing a nursery/plant store in a certain operating territory that uses, sells, and distributes their line of chemical products (i.e., insecticides, herbicides, fertilizers, etc.), and offers complete lawncare services.

The cost of distributing direct mailouts to potential clients for the service/products is sometimes shared by the franchisors and the franchisees (or other independent plant shops that may stock the product brand). The descriptive literature may have valuable coupons for redemption at the merchant's place of business, such as $1.00 off each bag of "weed-green" (a combination of weed control and fertilizer), for example. Another promotional idea may be to offer five bags for the price of four (called "bundling"). The supplier of the product would share in the cost of the promotion by offering supplies to be used in the promotional campaign at reduced prices.

A popular method for starting a lawncare firm is for a well-trained landscape architect to work for a similar firm, gaining experience and saving funds, and later to begin a franchise operation. In such instances, one or more franchising companies should be contacted and asked to provide information on the services they offer, the cost of the franchise and required amount of financial backing, the franchise percentage fee and advertising budget contribution, financing aid available through the franchising firm, and other important information. The interested reader may wish to consult the business and industry profile on Franchising.

*Development and
Site Requirements*

Before developing a landscape architecture or lawncare firm, the owner should make sure that his or her location is properly zoned. Some communities (such as rural areas zoned by the county highway board) will permit a home office and business to be operated from a homesite. This is especially true if the area is zoned agricultural. Those located within a city should be zoned commercial.

A modern landscaping office should be on a well-traveled street or major thoroughfare. It should be set back from the street or highway enough to allow for off-street parking of several customers' vehicles. Service vehicles, or those owned by employees, should be parked away from the attractively landscaped front and side views of the office. Plants offered for sale, including trees, flowering trees, evergreen plants and hedges, and groundcover plants, should be generously used to decorate the exterior of the landscaping office. Several types of bed gravel can be effectively used in different areas of the landscape (i.e., in plant beds adjacent to the front or sides of the structure or around the base of flowering trees). Shopping customers may see first-hand the choice of items available to purchase.

The inside of the landscaping office should be well lighted and provide other landscape scenes in photograph form, three-dimensional models, or video presentations. A friendly, helpful receptionist/secretary should be on hand to greet the patrons and make them feel at home. Colorful brochures are useful to show an array of plant offerings with approximate price ranges.

A landscape/design architect should meet with serious patrons, perhaps gaining some insight into the type of project under consideration and with program-designed software, provide a sketch in three dimensions that illustrates his or her concept of the desired landscape design. Changes made in the plan to meet the tastes of the client can then be added. Once the design has been finalized, a printout of it, along with a spreadsheet of cost data, should be run. About thirty minutes spent with each client should be sufficient to give them a fair estimate of what can be accomplished and at what price.

The landscape firm's structure is likely to be divided into several different rooms. The front one is spacious and offers the browsing area. One office houses the design architect. Another houses the accountant/bookkeeper/billing/credit functions. A walkway into the rear of the facilities should permit the patrons to browse an area where a selection of plants is housed.

Other well-ventilated rooms should be reserved for (1) an inventory of insecticide chemicals maintained for use on the company's nearby plants or intended for use on clients' contracts and (2) a storage room for other digging equipment and supplies such as fertilizers, bags of mulch, bales of peat moss, containers of decorative gravel or tree bark, and so forth, which should be located near the rear and to one side of the store.

Trucks should have ready access to the inventory storage room in order to discharge and load plants and supplies. Browsing customers in the plant area should be warned (either by signs or in person by a floor sales employee) that the plant foliage has been treated with chemical insecticides and handling should be minimized.

One or more washrooms should be provided, with soap and towels, for employees or patrons who come in contact with the treated plants or bottles of insecticides.

If an adequate inventory of plants is available, the firm may wish to promote cash-and-carry sales of plants and lawncare supplies in addition to doing landscaping and contract lawncare.

Cost and Types of
Assets Needed to
Start a Business

A landscaping and lawncare business may be started in one of several ways, and the method selected will have a large influence on the amount of funds needed. A son or daughter of a nursery owner, for example, may attend an outstanding program in landscape architecture (such as that offered at the University of Illinois) where students develop skills in such subjects as architectural engineering, plant selection and preservation, the use of electronic data processing (EDP) programs and equipment in designing the grounds layout project, the safe use of agricultural chemicals, and so on. The family-owned nursery business may be adequate to provide needed capital for funding the landscaping business, along with hiring some experienced nursery workers.

Other landscape firms are begun either as privately owned firms or as franchised operations, requiring upwards of $50,000 in invested capital by the owner(s).

Each year, updates are made on several hundred lines of business by Dun & Bradstreet, Inc., and by Robert L. Morris Associates on common-sized financial statements and key financial ratios. The D & B study *Industry Norms and Key Business Ratios* for 1992–1993 for these firms suggests the following mean average asset, debt, and net worth breakdown of such firms:

Assets		Debts and Net Worth	
Cash and near-cash	14.0%	Accounts payable	10.8%
Accounts receivable	28.0	Bank loans	.4
Notes receivable	.8	Other notes payable	7.6
Inventory	7.0	Other current debts	15.9
Other current assets	6.0		
Total current assets	55.8	Total current debts	34.7
Fixed assets	33.2	Long-term debts	15.9
		Deferred credits	0.2
Other noncurrent assets	11.0	Net worth	49.2
Total assets	100.0	Total debt and net worth	100.0
Total assets	$198,000		

During 1992–1993, the mean average gross profit margin for landscape counseling firms was about 41%, and the net profit margin after income taxes amounted to 5.2% of revenues. As the size of the firm grows in terms of the sales level, gross profits, and financial assets, there is a trend toward computerizing the landscape design, spreadsheet cost analysis of the project, and certain other inventories or record-keeping chores of the firm.

Computerization of the landscape design requires about a $20,000 to $30,000 expenditure for one or two office computers, software packages, and other landscaping equipment and supplies. Some enterprising landscape firms are able to incorporate video cassette messages into computerized drawings and make subsequent changes desired by the patrons. A final, three-dimensional drawing can then be formulated on the EDP equipment, along with a spreadsheet showing cost estimates for each phase of the project. As a job is in progress, step-by-step reports may be monitored comparing actual costs with estimated costs in order to improve expense control and facilitate the updating of information on bids for other potential contracts.

Typical Business Ratios The average landscape counseling firm had 1992–1993 revenues of about $670,000; some 3,000 average-sized jobs at $2,200 or 1,000 larger jobs averaging a charge of $6,700 would be necessary to reach this level. Expenditures for plants and other inventory items should run about 59% of revenues, while labor should take another 20%. A payroll of $150,000, for example, only pays for one landscape designer (about $30,000), one office bookkeeper/accountant/correspondence secretary (about $15,000 to $20,000), a receptionist (perhaps $10,000 to $12,000), a nursery/foreperson (perhaps earning $22,000), and several hourly employees (averaging $8,000 to $12,000 on a full-time basis). Thus, the total number of employees for such an operation would/should equal about 9 to 11.

It is doubtful that one small community could sustain such an enterprise, but it might serve the communities in several nearby growing towns. Thus, landscape counseling firms usually locate in medium-sized, growth cities where demand for their products and services is adequate to cover expenses and provide a generous return on invested capital.

Knowledge about expense breakdown is helpful in designing the financial statement projections, usually a part of the business plan and required by most bank loan officers and government lending agencies. Prentice-Hall, Inc., provides each year in *Almanac of Business and Industry Financial Ratios* a breakdown of major expenses on about 400 lines of businesses. For the corporations that operate in the agricultural services sector, the following were provided in the 1993 edition:

	Under $250,000 Assets	$250,000–$500,000 Assets
Cost of operations	59.0%	78.9%
Compensation of officers	6.8	2.6
Repairs	2.6	1.3
Bad debts	—	.1
Rent on business property	.8	.9
Taxes (excluding federal tax)	2.1	1.6
Interest	1.1	.6
Depreciation/depletion/amortization	3.5	1.7
Advertising	.6	.5
Pension and benefits	.7	.2
Other expenses	18.7	10.0
Net before-tax profit	4.3	1.6

Inasmuch as the agricultural services, forestry, and fishing classification includes many types of firms, some with a very small net profit margin and rapid inventory turnover, the above expense categories might not be indicative of a lawncare establishment. However, this is the closest that can be obtained by use of the Internal Revenue Service data, taken from corporate income tax returns.

The use of industry benchmark ratios on a large number of similar firms is sometimes helpful in making financial comparisons with a subject firm's operations. The preparation of projected financial statements is also enhanced. Certain median ratios for the 1992–1993 D & B studies for landscape counseling firms are as follows:

Solvency ratios:

Quick ratio (cash + accounts receivable/current liabilities)	1.2:1
Current ratio (current assets/current liabilities)	1.7:1
Total debts to net worth	85%

Efficiency ratios:

Collection period (accounts receivable sales × 365)	38 days
Sales to inventory (net sales/inventory)	30.1 times
Assets to sales (total assets/annual net sales)	32.2%

Profitability ratios:

Return on sales (net after-tax profit/annual net sales)	3.8%
Return on net worth (net after-tax profit/net worth)	15.3%

Legal Considerations

The owner/manager must ascertain that the business has the proper retail sales, service, and chemical use licenses. The latter may be controlled by the state's environmental protection agency or a regional office.

Attorneys should be engaged to aid in the drafting and/or submission of articles of copartnership, articles of incorporation, franchising contracts, land purchase contracts, long-term leasing arrangements, customer/client contracts for jobs, and similar transactions.

An accounting firm may be engaged to aid in developing a suitable system of accounting or in setting up a computerized approach to expense monitoring and control. A knowledgable tax accountant should be consulted on changing tax laws or decisions made where tax consequences are thought to be important.

The owner/manager should be familiar with federal and state income tax withholding reporting and subsequent depository rules for payroll taxes. The services of an accounting or bookkeeping firm might be appropriate in maintaining the accounting records and filing the tax returns for a small concern. As the firm grows in size, a staff person might be added to undertake the duties, along with estimating costs of jobs to be bid.

Small firms operating in the lawncare area might operate as a single proprietorship, merely collecting information adequate to show revenues and expenses on Schedule C of the federal Form 1040 tax return. A partnership or an S corporation does not pay federal income taxes, but the partners (or shareholders) instead are taxed on their proportionate share of income at their own individual rates.

A landscape management and lawncare service firm should carry workers' compensation on its employees (as required in most states). Otherwise, the firm is assumed by the courts to be self-insured and may have to pay the same benefits (sometimes for years) that have been established by the state legislature in case of on-the-job injury or incapacitation (for example, the breathing of a toxic chemical).

The firm should have an adequate insurance program on (1) the premises, (2) valuable inventory items, (3) transportation vehicles (especially liability insurance), and (4) if affordable, coverage against work-related lawsuits (such as the death of a pet or sickness of a child) from excessive application of a certain type of chemical (herbicide, insecticide, or fertilizer) to the customer's yard. The manufacturer of the chemicals may have certain product liability, but some firms attempt to disclaim liability on the basis of negligence on the part of the landscape and lawncare service company. Thus, incorporation of the firm to safeguard other personal assets might be of prime importance to the manager/owner of the firm.

Risk of lawsuits by work-injured employees (such as for chemical exposure), clients, neighbors of clients, and so forth, dictate that the larger of these firms should be incorporated to offer some protection by limiting liabilities to an owner's personal assets.

The manager/owner should be aware of the possible civil and criminal penalties and loss of licenses for using chemicals not in accordance with their labeling instructions (from $5,000 to $50,000) and should train the employees in strict adherence to their safe use. Disposal of the containers, after careful triple rinsing with water, should be practiced. Provisions of safety equipment (coveralls, respirator, rubber gloves, and boots) may be required for use with certain types of chemical applications either in the greenhouses, on the firm's inventory of plants to use on service contracts, or at the sites of clients.

Experience and Training Required
The owner/manager should be an experienced design architect specialist with general management and marketing skills. At least one other office person, perhaps the computer design person and combination bookkeeper/accountant should have some landscape design ability and serve in this capacity during the absence of the owner/manager.

As a minimum, the foreperson of the planting crew should be an experienced nurseryperson. Workers may be trained and supervised on the job, but each should be required to read a safety manual on the application of and health hazards involved in using certain types of farm herbicides/pesticides and chemical fertilizers. Overuse and misuse must be avoided. Old chemicals should be properly disposed of (in keeping with environmental protection laws) rather than applied after their expiration date. Use of them would probably be futile and a waste of employed labor, so billing on a job might be in whole units of containers with the partially used ones given to the client or properly disposed of.

It is usually necessary for the landscape design person to visit the site of the proposed landscaping in order to (1) color-coordinate the plants and flowering shrubs to the colors of the home or neighboring structures/ landscaping, (2) determine the degree of sunshine ordinarily available to certain portions of the space to be landscaped, (3) evaluate the condition of the soil and need for fertilizers, mulches, drainage additions, and so forth, and (4) determine any needed terracing, erection of earth support walls, and similar improvements.

The preliminary estimate of the landscape job, in terms of plant arrangement and costs, may need to be modified upon closer inspection of the work assignment area. It is better to reach an agreement between the firm and the client before work begins than after it is partially or completely finished. Weekly progress reports may be run on the computer, thus keeping track of the work in process and costs of plants, labor, and supplies.

Office workers and sales personnel are likely to be hired with requisite skills, but a monthly planning meeting where employees are permitted to air their grievances or make suggestions for a smoother operation may lead to high employee morale. A profit-sharing arrangement, such as 20% of the profits after a certain return on invested equity (such as 12%), might encourage the rank-and-file employees to be more conscious of waste in labor and supplies.

Periodic training sessions are needed to teach the employees the proper use of newly acquired equipment and the desired methods and rates of application for new brands of chemical fertilizers, insecticides, and herbicides.

Key to Successful Management The owner/manager of a landscape service establishment should be well trained and experienced in several areas, including (1) landscape designing, (2) computerizing the design and cost estimate, (3) proper techniques for propagating, planting, and care for plants, and (4) safeguards needed when working with farm chemicals.

General management, marketing, and office skills are needed, but staff persons are often hired who may be proficient in these areas. The top-level management should promote a friendly atmosphere from its employees when dealing with clients.

In dealing with contract customers, the landscape design specialist should develop the following procedure:

1. Sketch the yard and plant arrangement.
2. Evaluate the soil condition as to the degree of swampiness, drainage or lack of drainage, rocky, sandy, excessive clay, chemical content of potash, nitrogen, and so on.
3. Evaluate the light and exposure of the planting area.
4. Determine the color of plants, flower blossoms, and so on, that would blend in well with the structures and the neighborhood.
5. Decide with the client whether to use evergreen or deciduous plants, considering their attraction to deer and other pests.

6. Come to agreement with the client as to continuing service and the guarantee on the plants.

7. Reach an agreement as to the amount of the contract and the payment terms.

Employees should be adequately trained, especially in the application of insecticide/herbicide chemicals. A high standard of business ethics should be adopted by corporate management, and protection of employees and clients should be of paramount importance to the firm.

Information Sources

Several sources of information are helpful to a person considering the development or expansion of a landscaping and lawncare service firm. These include associations, books, directories, periodicals, franchising firms, ratio studies, investment services, and government documents. One excellent reference source, updated every few years, is *Encyclopedia of Business Information Sources*, by Gale Research, Inc., Detroit, Mich. Some state agencies also provide information hotlines and provide information useful to the entrepreneur.

Construction: Residential Housing

Residential housing construction has been assigned the SIC code 1521 from the group 152. SIC 1521 refers to general contractors of single-family houses, while SIC 1522 refers to general contractors of residential buildings other than single-family dwellings.

Home ownership by a majority of the citizens was adopted as the goal of the nation in the early 1930s. The Federal Housing Act provided for the Federal Housing Administration, and the act was designed to promote (1) minimum standards in residential housing, (2) affordable housing for the masses with small downpayments and long payouts that approach the cost of rent, and (3) flexible terms that permit early payoff of the mortgages with little or no penalty. By the early 1990s, some 64% of the families in the nation were living in owner-occupied housing, with the balance in rented facilities. The ratio declined slightly from about 66% that was reached in the late 1970s. Home ownership is encouraged by permitting taxpayers who itemize for federal tax filing purposes to deduct the ad valorem taxes and mortgage interest on one or two homes and through the practice of building equity in the home as the mortgage is paid down.

The construction sector of the economy accounts for about 9% of the total gross domestic product (or the final round of sales) of the nation. This sector may be divided into the three broad categories of industrial and commercial construction, residential construction, and home repair. The SIC designations of 1521 and 1522 are used for the residential housing industry. Many firms in the residential housing industry are flexible enough that they build single-unit dwellings, duplexes, triplexes, four-plexes, multi-unit (over-four-unit) apartment buildings, condominium buildings, commercial buildings, industrial structures, and so on.

Civil construction firms usually engage in paving, roadwork, road repair, bridge construction and repair, and so on.

In 1993, about $400 billion was spent for new construction, and another $103 billion (approximately) was spent for home repair and modernization. In times of low interest rates on home mortgages (ranging from 7.5% to 9.5%), the sale of new homes and existing homes appears to be strong. When the mortgage rates on 15-, 25-, or 30-year fixed-rate mortgages climb much above the 10.0% hurdle, many homeowners that need more space or amenities in housing may decide to add another room (bedroom, den, or bathroom, for example) rather than shop for a larger home. Thus the sale of new and used houses suffers.

The building of utility plants and manufacturing plants (referred to as industrial construction) was much more rapid in the 1970s than in the 1980s in the United States. However, the operation of U.S. manufacturing plants at close to 82% of capacity (as was true in 1993) influences some business firms to design more manufacturing facilities. The electric utility industry, needing a lead time of about 6 to 10 years from the time that plans are made until a fossil fuel or nuclear powerplant comes on line for production, misjudged the rate of growth in demand for electric power and overbuilt in the late 1970s and early 1980s. Many, by about 1985, when most of the plants under construction came on line, had standby generating capacity of 30% or more of base load needs. Thus, few new ones were begun from 1985 to 1993. Electric power demand seems to be growing by about 2% yearly, however, so by the turn of the century, more electric power generating plants will be needed. In fast population growth areas, the need will likely be felt even sooner. Growth in new hospitals should be rapid so as to keep pace with an aging population in the United States and their greater need for health care.

Commercial buildings, such as shopping malls, downtown stores, motels/hotels/inns, wholesale warehouses, stand-alone retail and service firms, residential apartment buildings, condo complexes, and so forth, are frequently overbuilt in one business cycle and suffer for the next few years from excessive unused space (referred to as vacancy rate). A vacancy rate of about 5% is standard in residential rental property and commercial property, but when interest rates are extremely low or the current federal income tax laws favor ownership of real estate properties (rapid depreciation guidelines, for example), there is some tendency to see overbuilding in commercial real estate projects. Due to high 1993 vacancy rate and commercial properties held in bankruptcies of financial institutions, this segment of the building industry should witness little growth before the late 1990s.

As stated above, a residential construction firm with adequate funds may at times concentrate on single-unit dwellings but may at other times undertake the development of multi-unit structures. Some also concentrate on commercial structures, when demand is adequate, or switch among industrial, commercial, and residential housing projects. During a period of high interest rates, when demand for new housing is light, many concentrate on home repair (expansion of existing homes or modernization of older homes). Their workforce and equipment are generally multi-purpose and can be used in most of these types of projects. Many undertake renovations during periods of low housing demand, adding bathrooms, bedrooms, garages, or dens to existing homes.

The past and future demands for residential construction depend not only on the strength of the overall national (and state) economy and the level of interest rate, but also on the demographics of population, such as ages and household types. For example, young married adults usually prefer relatively carefree apartment living for a few years. Those with children usually desire more space (inside the dwelling, and a fenced yard for the children). Older couples with teenage children may wish to live in a location near a swimming pool, tennis courts, and the like, or own them on their own land if space and income levels are adequate. Mature adults, say those above the age of about 55, may wish (for the favorable tax reason of once-in-a-lifetime profit forgiveness of up to $125,000 on the residence if certain conditions are met) to dispose of the large family residence and either live in a relatively maintenance-free apartment or condo. With these two types of living arrangements, the tenant of the apartment or the owner of the condo may be provided, for some monthly assessment, with lawncare and snow removal from sidewalks and driveways.

The years 1946 to 1964 in the United States have been dubbed as the "baby boom" years, meaning years of high birth rate. From 1965 to 1973, birth rates declined, and the years were dubbed as the years of the "baby bust." Since about 1974, the national birth rate has been about average. The so-called "baby boomers" are (in 1995) between the ages of 30 and 48, and their needs for housing will impact on the total needs during the balance of the century. For example, single-unit residential sales are likely to have reasonably strong demand, if interest rates are low enough to make housing affordable to the masses. The need for housing (smaller homes or apartments) by the over-55 population is likely to be strong over the next several decades as the ratio of senior adults (above age 65) expands from about 11% in 1988 to perhaps 20% by about the year 2028.

Many first-time homebuyers are unable to afford the downpayment or monthly payments on principal and interest, ad valorem taxes, insurance, and utilities needed to live in a single-unit dwelling. Thus, many states have instituted a program of low-interest-rate loans to first-time homebuyers and have coupled it with a forced savings program for a few years by the prospective homebuyers. While many retired persons remain at the poverty level (this is especially true for surviving widows who must live largely on survivors' pension benefits), others have built up supplemental retirement programs and deferred income benefits. The pressing need in residential housing, as felt by some state planners and economists, is likely to be for the construction of affordable housing for the aged in retirement villages or in other locations over the next 20 to 30 years.

Trade literature, along with the Bureau of Economic Analysis, Standard & Poors, and other forecasters, attempts to track recent operating levels in the residential construction industry and to forecast expected future levels of activity. An astute manager/owner of such a firm should attempt to stay abreast of such trends so as to avoid unwise speculative home-building and overcommitment of resources. In 1994, the *U.S. Industrial Outlook* was relatively pessimistic about the intermediate trend for activity in commercial construction, due to recent overbuilding and above-average vacancy rates in many large cities. Residential construction had shown about a 15% increase from recent comparisons, but this depends very much on the level of mortgage rates (as explained above). When rates fall to about 8.0% or below on 15-year, fixed-rate mortgages, then annual demand for new housing units averages about 2 million. When rates rise much above 10%, then demand declines to about 1.2 million units. Demand declined to below 1 million units in about 1979 to 1982 (when mortgage rates rose to the 15% to 17% range on fixed-rate mortgages). The affordability of the monthly payment, along with the need for a downpayment of about 10% of the property value, sets the effective demand for new houses. Thus, the demand for residential housing is very much influenced by the level of interest rates. Roughly 60% to 70% of unit sales of newly constructed residential property are single units (1- to 4-family dwellings), about 10% are mobile homes, and roughly 20% are multi-unit construction; but the ratio varies from year to year.

Since the passage of the 1986 Tax Revision Act, which lengthened the depreciable life on residential rental housing to $27\frac{1}{2}$ years and on other commercial property to $31\frac{1}{2}$ years (from about 19 to 21 years) and mandated the usage of straight-line depreciation, commercial and industrial construction levels began to decline. While lower depreciation write-offs on commercial property may serve to increase reported taxes (accelerate their payments), it reduces cash flows in early years.

The U.S. Department of Commerce expects about 2% annual increases in real terms in residential construction, moderate declines in office space, but vigorous building in health-care and manufacturing facilities in the 1990s, fueled by demand and low interest rates (*U.S. Industrial Outlook*, 1994, Chapter 5).

Market Opportunities in Various-Sized Communities

Before starting a residential construction firm, the owner should develop a business plan. A business plan is basically a blueprint for the business and should include important information about the venture. Topics that should be addressed include: whether demand in the region could support another firm; the current population base and need for new housing (or modernization of existing housing); the effective buying and borrowing power of the residents; the availability of bank lending to residential construction firms; job expansion in the region; the availability of materials and construction labor in the region at reasonable costs; and other facets of the business that the owner/manager must know in order to develop a viable and profitable business.

Assistance in developing a business plan may be obtained by a small business person from several sources, such as the chamber of commerce, local bankers, accounting firms, governments (such as city hall and business-promoting state agencies), regional development groups, small-business development centers, public libraries, and the like.

The number of firms in the building construction industry rises and falls with the level of interest rates (and its stimulation or depressing impact on sale of new homes) and with the extent of natural disasters such as hurricanes in Florida or earthquakes in California. The number averages about one firm for every 2,000 population or one for about every 700 family units. There are many unincorporated firms in the construction industry, but many of the smaller ones with limited capital concentrate on home repair and modernization rather than on residential construction.

The size of a community is not so important toward determining the need for one or several construction firms as is its rate of growth. For example, if a retirement village to house 2,500 persons in a mixture of single-unit, multi-unit, and apartment dwellings is planned in a small city of about 5,000, several residential construction firms would be engaged during the building activity. It is typical that certain types of work be subcontracted, such as cement work, electric wiring, heating and air conditioning, and roofing. The basic layout, framing, and finishing work might be done by the prime residential construction firm. A painting crew would likely be hired, along with another subcontractor to lay the flooring and carpets, tile the bathrooms, and so forth.

Since the demand for residential construction activity rises and falls dramatically over the business cycle, and since this oscillation is greater in small than in large cities, the owner of such a firm must remain vigilant in order to note trends of declining demand for his or her speculative home-building. Otherwise, the firm will be left with unsold houses, having to carry them at bank rates of interest approximately two times the inflation rate until they can ultimately be sold. As the strength of the economy begins to wane, certainly the contract construction firm manager/owner should reduce his or her risk as far as possible by turning to other avenues. At the very least, he or she might switch to building only when permanent financing is assured to the buyer. Related work that might be undertaken includes repair of existing structures or bidding as subcontractor on some large projects, such as the development of shopping mall properties or commercial buildings already begun.

Franchising Franchising opportunities exist for the residential building industry. In many instances, this franchise opportunity is for subcontractors that do only a portion of the building activity rather than for the prime building contractor. Some of these, including the approximate capital required and length of training period, are shown in the following schedule:

Name of Firm	Primary Service	Minimum Capital	Training
ABC Seamless, Inc.	Guttering/siding	$ 30,000	Sales/installations
Acrysyl Intl. Corp.	Roofing, siding	35,000	Technical
Bathcrest Inc.	Porcelain resurfacing	20,000	On-the-job
B-Dry System	Basement waterproofing	40,000+	Initial +
California Closet Co.	Custom design	51,000	Initial +
College Pro Painters	Residential painting	65,000	Initial +
Eldorado Stone Corp.	Manufacturing stone	46,000	Initial +
Eureka Log Homes	Wholesale of log kits	20,000	Manual +
Four Seasons GH	Solariums	50,000+	Initial +
Heritage Log Homes	Sale of log kits	50,000+	Initial +
The Linc Corp.	HVAC	35,000	Management training
Lindal Cedar Homes	Manufacture/sale of homes	3,000	4 days
Mr. Build Intl.	Residential/commercial remodeling	4,000+	Continuous
New England Log Homes	Sale of 40 log kits	100,000+	HO and site
Northern Products Log Homes	Sale of 23 log models	20,000+	5 days +
Perma-Glaze, Inc.	Kitchen, bathroom remodeling	17,000+	5 days +
Ryan Homes, Inc.	Residential single units	150,000+	Field support
Timbermill Barns	Prefab storage	18,000	5 days +
Wall Fill WW, Inc.	Siding/gutters +	31,000	Start-up

Franchising gives the entrepreneur an opportunity to use the mass buying power, training programs, specific territory, experience, and name recognition of the franchisor to build a viable and profitable business.

Most franchising firms provide training at their home office for key officers of franchisee businesses. Video cassettes and training manuals may be provided which illustrate correct selling and operating/installation techniques for products being sold. Ongoing training is also provided, especially as new products, installation techniques, or new equipment becomes available.

Whereas the general failure rate of a new independent firm is about 80% in its first five years of operation, the failure rate of franchised operations is about 20%. This is due to the better training of management and insistence upon adequate financial backing before letting a franchise contract.

The cost to the franchisee firm is usually a few thousand dollars up front plus a small percentage of revenues to pay for the use of the franchisor's name and management know-how, group advertising, ongoing management assistance, and so on.

Development and Site Location
When selecting a location and a specific site for the business, consideration must be given to local zoning requirements. Some local zoning commissions will not permit a home-operated business, so it is a good idea to ascertain that the planned rented space or constructed building will meet zoning as a commercial contract construction firm.

Other considerations in locating a business are the need for adequate storage space with proper ventilation, proper fire-extinguishing equipment in place, adequate parking for workers and customers, attractive office space and signage, and so on.

A very small builder may, if local zoning ordinances permit this, operate out of a home office and store tools and supplies in his or her garage. A larger builder that employs more than about two office workers and several crews of construction workers might want to have an attractive office along a busily traveled street and another fenced location nearer the building sites for storing a trailer holding tools and lumber and other products for the construction itself.

A single proprietorship is frequently operated by a husband and wife. A larger firm might be operated as a partnership and might involve, say, two husbands doing the construction supervision, buying of materials, and engaging/shepherding subcontracting work, while the wives may meet with the residential clients and offer them selections of finishing, kitchen appliances, bathroom fixtures, lighting, and so on. An attorney is usually hired in most states to handle the closing of the real estate transaction.

Larger firms are usually operated as corporations, with the main office including the president, a chief financial officer (who may bid on the contracts), a buyer of materials and subcontracted work, a chief salesperson for the organization, and perhaps an attorney who handles the legal work. The financial officer is often a cost accountant or a construction engineer (often referred to as an estimator) and is often second in command to the firm's president. Crews of workers include forepersons, carpenters, assistant carpenters, laborers, and so on, depending on the extent of the work provided and that obtained from subcontracting firms [heating, ventilation, and air conditioning (HVAC), roofing, cement, finishing, cabinet installation, etc.]. The main office of a construction corporation is often located in a commercial building away from the building site. The building superintendents and forepersons attempt to obtain the maximum work from the carpenters and other workers and to promote safety at the site.

Cost and Types of Assets Needed to Start a Business

While some small construction firms operate with little capital and assets, a rule of thumb is that assets should be about one-third as great as anticipated annual sales. Grading of the lot through laying of the foundation, erection of the frame and roof, installation of the HVAC systems, and finishing the home requires about two to four months. A small crew of two or three carpenters might undertake the building of a smaller home and subcontract some of the work on the structure. The owner is usually able to borrow from 75% to 90% of the value of the lot and home, and progress payments for materials and labor might be made by the lending institution, such as a bank or savings and loan.

During a 12-month period, a small builder might construct a home about every 2 months, using his or her crew of carpenters on the basic construction and subcontracting much of the finishing work. The severe winters in some locations might dictate the cement work and framing to be done in the late fall on one or two structures, with their completion during the cold months. Construction is somewhat seasonal, being highest in the spring and summer in most years.

A common-sized income statement and balance sheet for residential construction firms is available from two sources. Dun & Bradstreet, Inc., in *Industry Norms and Key Business Ratios* and Robert L. Morris Associates in *Statement Studies* provide them.

The mean income statement, according to D & B, was about as follows in 1992–1993:

	One-Family	Other Residential
Net sales per firm	$850,000	$1,400,000
Gross profits	24.9%	22.9%
Net after-tax profit	5.1%	4.4%

In 1992, the average balance sheet provided for SIC 1521 and 1522 by D & B was as follows:

	One-Family	Other Residential
ASSETS		
Cash and near-cash	18.2%	17.3%
Accounts receivable	19.2	29.9
Notes receivable	1.2	1.5
Inventory	10.7	4.8
Other current assets	15.7	15.0
Total current assets	65.0	68.5
Fixed assets	23.2	17.0
Other noncurrent assets	11.8	14.5
Total assets	100.0	100.0
DEBTS AND NET WORTH		
Accounts payable	12.6	17.2
Bank loans	.5	.5
Notes payable	7.5	5.0
Other current debts	18.3	16.0
Total current debts	38.9	38.7
Long-term debts	14.6	13.1
Deferred credits	.3	.4
Net worth	46.2	47.8
Total debts and net worth	100.0	100.0

A review of the above common-sized financial statements tends to show that single-unit construction firms, on average, are smaller than those that concentrate on multi-unit dwellings. Account breakdowns are similar except that the single-unit firms tend to have more invested into inventory but less in trade payables than do the larger firms. Other current debts are for such things as wages payable, payroll taxes payable, and other accruals. The capital structures of the firms are similar.

Having an average breakdown of expenses for an industry is helpful in controlling expenses for a firm. Prentice-Hall, Inc., provides an annual update in *Almanac of Business and Industry Financial Ratios*. These, from the 1993 edition (taken from IRS tax returns filed for mid-1989 through mid-1990), were:

	Under $100,000 Assets	$100,000–$250,000 Assets
Cost of operations	68.2%	72.2%
Compensation of officers	5.0	4.3
Repairs	.4	.4
Bad debts	—	—
Rent on business property	1.0	1.3
Taxes (excluding federal tax)	2.0	1.9
Interest	.6	1.1
Depreciation/depletion/amortization	1.4	1.5
Advertising	.5	.2
Pension and benefits	.7	1.0
Other expenses (mostly labor)	16.7	11.8
Net before-tax profit	3.6	4.2

Knowledge of the typical financial ratios is sometimes helpful for business owners for expansion and for lending officers in appraising the financial strength of the loan application. The D & B study reports the following for SIC 1521 and 1522 for 1992–1993:

	One-Family	Other Residential
Solvency ratios:		
Quick ratio	1.1:1	1.3:1
Current ratio	1.7:1	1.8:1
Total debts to net worth	91.0%	105.6%
Efficiency ratios:		
Collection period	22 days	37 days
Sales to inventory	25 times	33 times
Assets to sales	28.4%	33.7%
Profitability ratios:		
Return on sales (median)	4.2%	3.4%
Return on net worth (median)	23.0%	15.1%

Since the mean ratios from the D & B study are greater than the median ratios, one would conclude that the larger firms are generally more profitable than the smaller ones. The larger firms also tend to work on larger projects and projects that are under construction longer than do the single-unit builders—thus accounting for the differences in collection period and assets-to-sales ratios.

Legal Considerations A firm that designs and builds residential structures may be operated as a single proprietorship, a partnership, or a corporation. The Bureau of Economic Analysis of the U.S. Bureau of the Census and the IRS estimate that over 1.5 million firms operate in the construction industry, with over 90% of them being unincorporated firms. Thus, the industry is one in which a large number of small firms operate and a small number of large firms exist. A handful of companies in contract construction are large enough to list on the major exchanges.

There is a slight tax advantage to operating a firm as a single proprietorship or as a partnership. The sole proprietor only has to keep enough records so as to report revenues and expenses on Schedule C of the federal Form 1040 tax return for income tax purposes. A federal employer identification number is obtained so as to properly deduct and remit payroll taxes. The partnership must file a partnership return and each partner must recognize his or her proportionate share of profits on his or her own respective tax return. Such business profits are considered to be self-employment income, however, and subject to the 15.3% social security tax on the tax base up to $60,600 (or even higher on Medicare payments) per person (in 1994), with one-half of this being a taxable expense. The primary disadvantage of operating as an unincorporated firm is that the private assets of the owner(s) are at risk to the business creditors.

The shareholders in a corporation have liabilities limited to their investments in the firm, but the firm must file a corporate income tax return. The S corporation, with fewer than 35 shareholders and with consent from them, may elect not to be taxed as a separate firm, but the shareholders instead are taxed on their own share of net income. This IRS filing generally must be done within 90 days of incorporation. A regular corporation is taxed at a rate of 15% on the first $50,000 of profit, at 25% on the next $25,000, and at higher rates thereafter. Due to the complexity of the federal income tax laws, with frequent changes, it is wise for a business firm to hire the aid of a tax attorney or accountant in preparing or reviewing tax returns. An informed tax person can usually save the client several times as much in taxes as his or her charges.

The legal considerations are greater for the contract construction firm than for most businesses, other than utilities and communications firms. The use of an accountant might be helpful in setting up a system of general accounting, in cost control, in tax planning, and in budgeting. The treasurer of such a firm is usually an industrial engineer or cost accountant and bids on the projects. A public accounting firm might be engaged for some of the other assistance, such as tax return preparation.

Attorneys are used in real estate purchases and development, lien filing, notary public work, contract drafting, and the like. Lawsuits brought by or against the construction firm should be handled by an experienced attorney.

It is important that the owner of a construction firm account properly for taxes owed, not discriminate in its hiring practices, and not discriminate against buyers of the properties. Otherwise, several federal laws might be broken. The laws and rules imposed by the federal agencies involved in housing and real estate loans must be known and followed. Thus, some of the larger real estate development firms employ one or more attorneys on their staff of officers.

Many local and state laws apply to real estate development. Local zoning laws control the usage of property, but the developer must make sure that the firm is adhering to proper setbacks, insets, percentage of land usage for structure, heights of the structure, sewage disposal, and other utility requirements. One person in a construction firm may devote most of his or her time to legal work.

A proper insurance program for a residential construction firm includes a commercial policy providing fire and extended coverage on real assets, liability insurance on third persons (injuries at the site by other than the workers), workers' compensation for job-related injuries for workers, liability insurance on vehicles, fidelity insurance on persons handling significant amounts of liquid funds, life insurance on key officers/managers of the firm, and perhaps group health insurance as a fringe benefit to the full-time employees. An insurance planner might be helpful in assessing the insurance needs of the individual firm.

Experience and Training Required

Most persons, other than laborers who work for residential construction firms, are experienced in construction work. Since several areas of planning and activities are involved with residential construction, the employees of such a firm usually have diverse backgrounds. Market analysis as to demand for homes and whether or not they will sell (Are they affordable? Are loans available at reasonable terms?) involves studying the availability and cost of mortgage credit and the willingness to assist potential home buyers in this endeavor. Small firms sometimes hire a real estate office to handle the sale and closing of their real estate transactions and concentrate on the building activities. Larger firms often have their own selling staff.

Obtaining appropriate zoning permits, buying materials in adequate amounts and of high quality, and having materials and working equipment at the correct site on time are important. One or more persons would be in charge of these activities.

The building crew usually consists of at least one job foreperson and several carpenters. Hourly paid laborers might earn about 40% to 50% as much as the skilled carpenters. Union workers usually are paid at a higher scale than nonunion workers, but a federal law (Allyn-Bacon) prescribes that where federal funds are involved, union-scale wages in the region must be paid whether or not the workers are unionized.

Since the demand for residential construction moves from about 1 million units in a very poor year to perhaps two times this level in a very strong year, the owner/manager of the firm must maintain enough flexibility in the workforce so as to effectively control expenses. Interest rates sometimes move very quickly on mortgages, so gauging future demand for the finished homes is often difficult, leaving the building firm with unsold inventory of completed homes. Knowledge about this area, and constant vigilance, are required by the manager of a residential home building firm if the company is to survive several business cycles. The bankruptcy rate is higher in contract construction than in most other lines of activity.

Some residential housing firms depend on outside architects and interior design persons, while the larger ones sometimes hire these trained specialists. It is helpful if such persons keep abreast of the latest in home features in order to make the homes more appealing to potential clients. Attendance at trade fairs and conventions should be strongly encouraged.

Keys to Successful Management A firm that operates in residential construction for a lengthy time period usually adopts a set of guiding principles, such as the following:

1. Managers/owners of construction firms must be realistic. They must be able to judge the effective demand for their product, the purchase of completed residential structures. This may vary at times from very strong sales of single units to the purchase of condo units or factory-built homes.

2. Successful managers/owners of construction firms must have imagination, gaining a feel for what is likely to be the near-term trend in real estate demanded by persons in the area of operation. They should be able to assess what types of homes are likely to sell and which ones are likely to remain unsold. They must, thus, become judges of human nature and its longings. Also they must advertise their goods and present them in an appealing light to potential buyers.

3. The managers/owners of such a firm should build strong business relationships with local/regional lumber companies, subcontracting firms, the city planning commission, bankers that are willing to advance interim financing, other lending institutions that provide long-term mortgage credit to buyers, and the current or potential crew of construction workers. They must show that they care for more than just their own profit generated on a project if they are to be given favors so desperately needed at times in the building industry.

4. Construction firms must place quality of construction and pride in workmanship at the top of the list of important things. Quality construction with quality materials builds a good reputation for a firm, while a firm that cuts corners may find itself embroiled in legal battles or with an unenviable reputation of distrust in the community (citizens, government officials, bankers, trade credit suppliers, and the like).

5. The management structure of the firm should be kept to as few layers as possible. Top-level managers should be known by the working level, and periodic visits to the construction site are generally worthwhile. Otherwise, wastage of materials and labor (excessive downtime or inefficient operations) and having inadequate supplies and equipment where needed will follow. The depth of management should be adequate to carry on the project during an illness or absence of a key person.

Information Sources   A prospective entrant into the field of residential construction should have a general knowledge of the facets of the industry, but he or she should also be familiar with several sources of information. These include trade associations, general works, periodicals, ratio studies, investment services, and government sources. The periodic update of *Encyclopedia of Business Information Sources*, by Gale Research, Inc., provides this and other information on most industry groups.

Garment Manufacturers: Women's, Misses', and Juniors' Dresses

Manufacture of women's, misses', and juniors' dresses has been assigned SIC code 2335 from the broader classification of 233 for women's, misses', and juniors' outerwear clothing.

Sewing centers, or garment manufacturers, suffered losses of sales to foreign imports over the 1970s and 1980s. As sales dried up, so did the number of jobs in the industry. During the 1950s and early 1960s, some garment manufacturers that were located in the New England and Atlantic seaboard states began to relocate to cheaper labor cities of the South. This continued for a few years, but then imports from Korea, Taiwan, and other oriental nations of low-labor costs began to intensify competition. Some restriction on imports, however, coupled with the declining value of the dollar abroad; computer-aided technology in design, cutting, and other mechanical portions of the job; and better inventory control have combined to bring about some vitality in the industry, with sales of U.S.-made products gaining about 1% yearly in the 1990s but with production jobs declining about 1% to 2% yearly due to greater productivity.

In this profile, we shall look at the wide array of clothing manufacturers and then inspect the financial statements for SIC 2335 for women's, misses', and juniors' dresses. Actual SIC numbers ranging from 2300 to 2399 have been assigned to the various textile subgroups.

The range of fabric products made include the following:

Men's and boys' suits	Men's and boys' nightwear
Men's and boys' trousers	Women's and misses' blouses
Men's and boys' clothing	Women's and misses' suits
Women's and misses' dresses	Women's and misses' underwear
Women's and misses' outerwear	Women's and children's underwear

Corsets and garments	Millinery
Hats and caps	Children's dresses
Fur goods	Children's coats
Fabric dresses and gloves	Children's outerwear
Robes and dress gloves	Waterproof garments
Leather-lined clothing	Apparel belts
Apparel and accessories	Curtains and draperies
House furnishings, NEC	Textile bags
Canvas products	Pleating, stitching
Apparel bindings	Fabric textile products, NEC

As orders are received, apparel companies are usually equipped to make a wide variety of the various types of garments that can be made with their range of sewing machines. For example, a firm might hold itself out to accept orders for the following: women's, misses', and children's dresses and underwear, uniforms, nightwear, blouses, and so on.

Garment manufacturers are usually small to medium-sized and are located around medium-sized cities or near the perimeter of large cities where an abundant supply of relatively inexpensive labor may be found. According to Department of Commerce estimates for 1993, some 75% of apparel sales were made by diversified, large firms, while small firms accounted for the balance. Such business firms were operating with about 11 million production workers, earning an average hourly wage of $7.10, some 2% above 1992 wage levels. Another 1 million had nonproductive-type jobs in the industry. This provided a mean annual wage of $15,000 for the production workers, with higher levels for supervisory staff. While workers in Korea, Taiwan, and other garment-exporting countries earn a small fraction of this wage level, import competition intensified during the 1970s and early 1980s. By 1987, roughly one-half of the $125 billion garment sales in the United States was being manufactured abroad. This persuaded U.S. manufacturing firms to set up overseas sewing factories, causing garment imports to expand by 10% or more per year during the 1970s and early 1980s.

By 1993, these statistics had changed somewhat. Employment in the industry was estimated at 986,000, with production workers making up about 85% of the total. Value of shipments in the United States was about $68 billion, and imports were about 51% of this level. Imports had gained close to 40% from 1989 to 1993, while domestic shipments were up by only about 8%. Men's clothing was showing much stronger growth than was women's wear. Canada, Mexico, Europe, and Japan were heavy importers of U.S.-made goods, while our imports were heaviest from Hong Kong, China, Korea, and Taiwan.

Beginning in the 1980s, several trends seemed to be occurring that could breathe more life into the declining U.S. garment industry. Facilities began to utilize computer-aided technology that would facilitate the mechanical jobs of making patterns of different sizes by use of computer software, the layout of material to minimize material wastage, and mechanical cutting of a stack of material with lasers or other methods. Consequently, as fashions changed during the year, several national firms became overstocked with large inventories of trendy clothing articles in recent years. Thus, many of the distribution firms, such as K-Mart, Wal-Mart, and other department or specialty stores, began to shift their orders back to U.S. firms where shorter lead times (from about four weeks to as short as a few days) between order placing and receipt of inventory could be guaranteed.

Ordering from overseas suppliers requires an average of at least 13 weeks compared to a few days or weeks from U.S. garment makers. Some U.S. firms, such as Cluett Peabody Company Arrow Shirt Division and Haggar Slacks, pride themselves on receiving an order on Sunday evening and shipping it out on Tuesday. So, in response, close to 2,400 retail organizations have set up inventory-monitoring barcode systems through their cash registers that record the size and type of garments being sold. Orders may then be placed electronically by telephone or faxed to suppliers and filled mechanically from inventory stock almost immediately. Also, to coincide with the ordering procedures, mechanized order filling has been created to cut down on employee costs and time.

Not only are firms beginning to reopen or expand some of their U.S. locations; some foreign garment manufacturers have begun to locate within this country. For example, offshore work at some international firms has declined from 40% to about 20% of their total. In the late 1980s and early 1990s, some U.S. firms were diversifying their production; others were adding to their level of production facilities; but most were reducing their nonproduction workers. The reason, of course, is that many U.S. apparel distributors have begun to seek out suppliers with shorter delivery times, despite some cost spread that tends to favor imported garments.

Federal grants have been let to develop technology transfer ideas from defense-oriented industry to peacetime goods. Some of the technology ideas used in space travel, for example, are being tested for usage in the apparel industry.

It is likely that implementation of computer-aided technology in cutting and inventory control and the desire to minimize inventory stocking and decrease the lead time from order placing to receipt of items will continue into the later 1990s for apparel.

Future trends in the industry are likely to be toward (1) the development of smaller, but more efficient, operations; (2) the use of computers in certain aspects of the firms, such as developing size of patterns, laying out cloth so as to minimize wastage, and the cutting of the materials; (3) semi-automation of the sewing process; (4) inspections through cameras rather than by traveling persons; and (5) greater automation in sizing, labeling, boxing, crating, and shipping the finished products.

Japan is likely to become a major target of exporters in the 1990s, as discount stores there are springing up and American styles are becoming more popular. Some manufacturing output malls are being added, as well as discount stores such as Toys R' Us. It is likely that the 1990s will see globalization and consolidation of many of the smaller and intermediate-sized garment manufacturers.

Market Opportunities in Various-Sized Communities

Before starting a sewing factory, the owner should develop a business plan. In developing a business plan, several important types of information are needed, including whether or not the market could support the proposed venture, the existence of an unidentified market niche that may be exploited, the level of competition in the area, the customer base population, competitive pricing strategies, and a variety of other facets of the business that owners or managers need to know to develop a viable and profitable business.

Assistance in developing these business plans may be obtained from many sources—some free and others at a small cost. A few sources available for assistance are the local chamber of commerce, banks, accounting firms, local and state government bodies such as city hall, business promoting state agencies, management departments at colleges and universities, small-business development centers, and public libraries.

Many sewing factories are large in size and tend to locate in the low-rent districts of large cities. In more recent times, there have been smaller facilities erected with less than 2,500 square feet of floor space to be used as satellite operations by the large apparel firms. These small facilities are usually highly automated. Whether or not these small satellite plants can operate profitably has not as yet been tested during an economic recession.

Some home-based sewing firms offer custom garment making such as wedding dresses (brides' and bridesmaids'), garment alterations, and so on, and some are located around small cities. Some of these firms do major alterations of previously worn wedding dresses (perhaps by an older sister, mother, or aunt); tailor outer garments, such as coats that no longer fit the owner; and do minor maintenance on clothing for patrons who do not have the time or inclination to do their own sewing. Some of these firms offer very short lead time from receipt of order, for bridesmaids' dresses, for example, as compared to bridal retailers that may have to order them from a garment manufacturer.

Import quotas levied against certain textile-exporting countries into the United States have slowed down the rate of growth in these imports. Some large chains of department stores are apparently beginning to merchandise a larger ratio of American-made garments than in past years, with much of this rising popularity being attributable to (1) faster promised deliveries, (2) smaller stocking of inventories (meaning less risk of unsold garments), and (3) rising labor costs abroad that bring the prices of imports and domestically made garments closer together. Garment makers should stay abreast of such import quota changes and assess the likelihood of such changes in demands for their products.

Development and Site Requirements

Before beginning a sewing center, consideration should be given to local zoning requirements. Many communities forbid, through zoning ordinances, the establishment of home-based businesses. A sewing center is classed as a manufacturing firm, so it is a good idea to check with the approving zoning authority before spending money on such an operation.

Often sewing factories are located at the outskirts of large cities where there is an abundant supply of inexpensive labor. The sewing factory is usually built as a multi-floored building, with the cutting room and inventory storage facility on the ground level. Upper floors will be equipped with rows of sewing machines where a production-line type of sewing is utilized. For example, one line of workers might do nothing but make sleeves, with others making collars, assembling the garment, or adding zippers, buttons, or decorations. The last two stations would be inspection, tagging, and boxing; and crating and shipment.

The parking space should be adequate for the employees' vehicles, and unloading and loading docks need to be located in an appropriate area for the delivery of raw materials inventory and the pickup of finished products, respectively. Most factories are equipped with one or more service elevators for moving boxes of inventory from floor to floor for the incoming and outgoing shipments.

Space should be provided for office workers, such as pattern and cutting planners, accountants, and general managers. Break rooms and restrooms should be made available to employees for lunch and other break periods, and storage areas are needed.

Many national firms have mechanized the inventory ordering of products. The receipt of cash register sales information from the approximate 2,500 retail customers assists the manufacturers in developing orders and shipping out the items needed every three days rather than the customary seven weeks. Thus, inventory stocking is minimized for the retail establishments, and the manufacturing firm is able to develop optimum-order-size runs and to optimize its own commitment to finished goods inventories.

Gerber Garment Technology (CN) supplies computer-directed cloth-cutting machines to the apparel industry. It is possible to acquire equipment that will grade the material, handle the cloth layout, position patterns for minimum wastage, and actually cut the bolts of materials. The firm apparently began its operation by automating the cutting of seat covers for General Motors but has extended the idea to cutting machines for the garment industry. This would permit semi-automation of the receiving and cutting rooms of the apparel factory.

Cost and Types of Assets Needed to Start a Business

Initial investment factors to consider for a start-up firm include: How much capital is required to operate the business until the break-even point is reached? How much would be needed for materials, wages, other expenses, equipment, renovation of the plant, and unforeseen expenses?

Developing a sound business plan would enable the entrepreneur to target these and other areas effectively.

Financing the business usually means a combination of owner-supplied funds, borrowed funds, and public sources of monies. In many lines of manufacturing, owners' equity amounts to 50% to 60%. Some debt is self-generating, meaning that as inventories are bought, trade payables occur. Wages are paid on a weekly or twice-monthly basis in most industries, so wages payable and payroll taxes payable are other sources of short-term debt. Bank loans and loans from other lending institutions are common sources of borrowed funds. Public monies might come from regional development groups, the Small Business Administration, or one of several loan programs sponsored by state lending agencies.

The usage of common-sized financial statements for companies operating in an industry are helpful in developing a business plan and in forecasting projected financial statements required by many lenders of funds, both private and public.

Robert L. Morris Associates, in *Statement Studies*, and Dun & Bradstreet, Inc., in *Industry Norms and Key Business Ratios*, provide composite financial statements on a large range of industries. For SIC 2335 (women's, misses', and juniors' dresses), a breakdown of assets, debts, and net worth accounts in 1993 was as follows (for about 450 of the firms in the survey):

Assets		Debts and Net Worth	
Cash and near-cash	12.9%	Accounts payable	20.9%
Accounts receivable	28.7	Bank and other loans payable	5.4
Notes receivable	.3	Other current debts	17.7
Inventory	33.5	Total current debts	44.0
Other current assets	9.8	Long-term debts	7.2
Total current assets	85.2	Deferred credit	.1
Fixed assets	9.3	Net worth	48.7
Other noncurrent assets	5.5	Total debts and net worth	100.0
Total assets	100.0	Total debts and net worth	$582,300

Significant amounts of funds are invested in accounts receivable and inventories. A manufacturing firm has three types of inventories: the raw materials (cloth, buttons, zippers, thread, etc.), work-in-process, and finished goods. About one-third of total assets are usually tied up in inventories. Roughly half of the assets are provided by equity owners, with the balance raised from various types of creditors. "Other noncurrent assets" refers largely to leaseholds and leasehold improvements. "Other current debts" is largely made up of accrued wages, taxes, interest, and the like.

Typical Business Ratios The two types of business ratios associated with women's and misses' dresses refer to common-sized income statements and balance sheets and to ratios between balance sheet and income statement items.

Let us analyze the cost of production of a typical garment that sells for $100 in the United States. Trade sources suggest about the following breakdown as a percentage of sales:

Cost	Domestic Dress	Imported Dress
Materials	45%	40%
Labor	30%	15%
Overhead/profit for manufacturer	25%	10%
Duty, shipping, quota charges	—	35%
Total wholesale cost	$50	$40
Costs of retailers (including markdowns)	$19	$35
Total wholesale and retail costs	$69	$75
Retail profit margin	31%	25%

Retail profit margins on imported clothing are reduced, as compared to domestically produced garments, by frequent markdowns, large inventories, longer lead times, and slower turnovers.

Each year, Prentice-Hall, Inc., in *Almanac of Business and Industry Financial Ratios*, provides a breakdown of operating expenses for most major lines of business. The 1993 edition of this source provides the following for the three smallest (of about 12 size categories) asset size categories for profitable manufacturers of women's and children's clothing:

	Under $100,000 Assets	$100,000–$250,000 Assets	$251,000–$500,000 Assets
Cost of operations	77.8%	73.0%	75.1%
Compensation of officers	—	2.0	1.1
Repairs	.1	—	.4
Bad debts	—	.4	—
Rent on business property	2.2	3.2	1.8
Taxes (excluding federal tax)	.5	.2	3.2
Interest	1.1	2.5	1.8
Depreciation/depletion/amortization	.9	1.3	1.6
Advertising	—	.2	.6
Pension and benefits	3.8	—	.2
Other expenses	9.1	15.3	13.2
Net before-tax profit	4.4	1.9	1.0

Small concerns are more likely to employ owners as workers in the business, thus paying out a larger amount of funds as compensation to officers than do larger firms. Some firms show direct manufacturing labor as a cost of operation, while others might classify it into other expenses; thus these two ratios tend to differ for very small and medium-sized firms.

The federal income tax law permits a business firm to expense up to $17,500 in depreciable equipment in the year acquired rather than to capitalize and depreciate it. Thus, depreciation rates would be smaller for the small firm as compared to larger ones.

Key financial ratios are sometimes helpful to a business person in forecasting financial statements or needs for funds. Certain solvency, efficiency, and profitability ratios for women's and misses' dress manufacturers, as suggested by D & B for 1993, are as follows:

Solvency ratios:
    Quick ratio (cash + accounts receivable current liabilities)   .9:1
    Current ratio (total current assets/current liabilities)   1.9:1
    Total debt to net worth (liabilities/net worth)   106.8%
Efficiency ratios:
    Collection period (accounts receivable/net sales × 365)   49.2 days
    Sales to inventory (net sales/inventory)   8.7 times
    Assets to sales (yearend assets/net sales)   31.8%
Profitability ratios:
    Return on sales   2.1%
    Return on net worth   10.1%

Legal Considerations

Professional legal assistance in the areas of accounting, information processing, and law is sometimes needed to design one of several information systems for a firm. These might include a payroll system, a general accounting system, an inventory control system, and pattern design and layout.

Also, assistance may be needed in certain activities of a business, such as drafting articles of copartnership, incorporating, reorganizing, liquidating, leasing or buying major facilities, or franchising.

As for most business firms, a sewing company should carry adequate insurance. This might be a commercial blanket insurance policy of property and liability insurance and workers' compensation. Extra insurance should be carried on business vehicles.

Experience and Training Required

Garment manufacturers have several different types of workers, requiring each to be experienced and trained with his or her division. The managers/owners should be experienced in production, marketing, and cost control within their industry. The assembly-line workers should be experienced at sewing, but not necessarily with the same type of equipment as that used by the firm. Cutting employees should be experienced or obtain training for operating the new generation of equipment.

Garment factories in the United States are becoming increasingly more automated in pattern development, cloth layout, cloth cutting, movement of components along assembly lines, boxing, and so on. The next step in automation in the industry appears to be in apparel warehousing that would reduce labor cost, inventory level, and response time for shipping out orders.

Top-level officers and other key employees are often provided half-day workshops and seminars at trade conferences that emphasize growing technology in garment manufacture, with the trend toward smaller but automated facilities.

Keys to Successful Management

Profitable operation in the garment manufacturing industry depends on a healthy blend of general management; efficient production in the areas of pattern development, cutting, and sewing of garments; cost control of materials and labor; the development of labor-saving approaches; and effective marketing of their product lines. Thus, top-level managers in the garment industry should embrace production, marketing, and accounting/finance staff persons.

Apparel manufacturers were able to increase their ability to compete more effectively with foreign suppliers beginning in the latter 1980s due to installing labor-saving devices. Automated pattern development and cutting and some semi-automation in the sewing process, inspection, packaging, and shipping led to labor cost reductions.

Promotion of sales has largely come about by promising shorter lead times from receipt of order to shipment. Filling of orders is largely being automated through tie-ins with the cash registers of the retailing customers. Thus, items needed to replenish the inventories can be shipped from telephone or faxed orders within a few days. Such automation is likely to reduce the imports of garments and to make American-made items more price competitive.

Finance and accounting assignments have largely been directed toward promoting greater efficiency in the operation of the production process and through expense control. Thus, the decline in the sale of American-made textiles appeared to be arrested in about 1985, with some upturn, especially in exports, underway in the latter 1980s and early 1990s. This two-digit growth of the latter 1980s slowed to a 1% to 3% level in the early 1990s.

Strategies for success in the 1990s appear to be the following: Develop appropriate strategies (target marketing), aim for a world-class manufacturing base, promote flexibility and speed in production and delivery, and develop a computer-aided system for engineering pattern layout and cost control.

Information Sources

Several sources of information are helpful to top-level management in the garment industry. These include the information and seminars at professional association meetings, general books and directories, periodicals, federal reports on imports and exports, and financial ratio studies. Local libraries, the chamber of commerce, community colleges, universities, and small-business development centers are possible sources of information. One periodic updated source is *Encyclopedia of Business Information Sources* (latest), by Gale Research, Inc., Detroit, Mich.

Desktop Publishing and Quick Printing

Business Types, Industry Characteristics and Prospects

Miscellaneous printers are listed as SIC code 2741. According to recent business census reports, one to four employees was the size classification of most small firms, although the mean was about nine laborers. Managerial staff earn two to three times the rate of the lower-level employees, who usually are part-timers that earn minimum wage with periodic increments. The desktop publishing industry is one of the most rapidly growing, with the number of outlets increasing by about 30% yearly in the early 1990s.

Business service-type print shops do speedy jobs for individuals, commercial accounts, and professionals (such as attorneys, accountants, architectural firms, engineering firms, land appraisers, real estate abstract companies, etc.). Over the years, print shop ventures have also been equipped to make blueprints from drawings by architects and to do other printing and duplication projects.

During the 1980s and early 1990s, there was a large number of quick duplication shops formed to cater to the steady growth in usage rates for individuals. Many such firms are located adjacent to colleges and universities, as professors and instructors have discovered the ease of delivering a finished document (class notes, workbook assignments, syllabus, etc.) to the quick-print shop and then telling the students to buy a copy. The reduction of support funds at colleges and universities has shifted some of this reproduction cost burden from the schools to the students. Students with term papers or class presentations are often asked to prepare copies of their papers (in outline form) to be distributed to their classmates.

Another major usage of desktop printing and quick-print duplication is by home office consultants who find it more convenient than to maintain such equipment on premises. A large percentage of retiring professional workers develop some clientele following in a home office environment after officially retiring.

The average family has witnessed an augmented need to duplicate important papers, and many find a quick-print shop less expensive and more convenient than using the Xerox or similar copy machine at the bank or post office. As the home computer has increased in sales and use, so has the duplicating of materials prepared on the PC (personal computer). Many of these copy machines are self-service. Some are coin-operated, while others operate automatically by indicating the size of paper, the number of copies, and whether or not to collate multiple copies of a run. A cashier collects the posted charge on the number of copies made by the self-service patron. For a somewhat higher charge, many quick-print shops prepare copies for the customer.

The owner/operator of a quick-print shop must be aware of all the operating expenses of the business and charge enough to cover cost of paper, toner (or blown carbon), the service charge on the equipment, the depreciation of the equipment, rent, utilities, labor cost of the operators, insurance, taxes, and other business expenses. In recent years, many aggressively managed firms have offered copying for $.05 to $.06 per copy near colleges and universities, but this is probably less than the actual cost for small lots. A more realistic charge is two sheets for $.15, or about $.075 per copy. If labor is supplied by the shop, the charge on standard $8\frac{1}{2} \times 11$ inch sheets should probably be $.10 and legal-sized paper about 25% higher, or $.125 each. If sheets are wasted by the patrons, they should be paid for. If paper is wasted by the store employees, the business should absorb the loss. Direct cost to duplicate a sheet is about $.04, as paper costs almost $.01 per sheet, toner costs another $.01 per page, the charge (maintenance and usage) on many of the nicer printing equipment models is about $.02 per page, and rental or repair of machines averages $.01 per page. Thus, this direct cost of about $.04 per page should be literally doubled to cover other operating costs and leave a reasonable profit to the owner/operator.

While some quick-print shops are located in dingy stores on back streets of cities where rent and taxes are low, the trend during the 1980s and 1990s has been to relocate to high customer traffic areas in stores with large windows and good lighting, and to provide adequate off-street parking. Many of the well-established print shops with a good list of repeat commercial clients have become targets for acquisition during the mid- and late-1980s.

The prospects for future sales in the quick-print shop industry are generally toward growth over the next 20 years, although certain types of services will grow very rapidly while others will shrink. Many forecasters expect a real shakeout (weaker firms going out of business) in the printing industry until about the year 2006, as desktop publishing of many of the small printing runs replaces conventional approaches. Desktop publishing, SIC code 2741, has been aided by the development of more powerful computers, better software aids, and color printers that provide very glamorous outputs. Many catalogs, advertising inserts, and some magazines by 1995 were being published by desktop means rather than with offset printing. In total, quick-print shops are expected (data from the Department of Labor) to increase employment by about 2.4% yearly until the year 2000, with a 4.1% yearly increase in productivity (due primarily to equipment improvement and technological advances in the industry). Desktop publishing was increasing even more rapidly, with gains of 25% to 30% yearly from about 1986 through 1993.

Cost and Types of Assets Needed to Start a Business

Dun & Bradstreet, Inc., annually provides common-sized income statements in *Industry Norms and Key Business Ratios*. For SIC 2741 (miscellaneous printing) and 2752 (commercial printing) during 1993, average total assets were about $419,000 per firm. Home office operations, of course, may expense purchases and report very few operating assets. Net worth averaged 51% of this level, while working capital (or current assets) amounted to 66% of assets. Fixed tangible and intangible assets represented a smaller total. According to D & B statements, the following breakdown was average for the 276 firms in their sample of miscellaneous publishing, with some growth coming through consolidations of smaller firms:

Assets		Debts and Net Worth	
Cash and near-cash	16.8%	Accounts payable	11.8%
Accounts and notes receivable	29.6	Bank loans and notes payable	4.7
Inventories	10.2	Other current debts	17.8
Other current assets	9.1	Total current debts	34.3
Total current assets	65.7	Long-term debts	13.4
Fixed assets (net)	16.7	Deferred credit	.9
Other noncurrent assets	16.7	Net worth (equity)	51.4
Total assets	100.0	Total debts and net worth	100.0
Total average of assets		$418,736	
Net sales per establishment		$910,404	
Gross (operating) profit		49.9%	
Net after-tax profit		7.2%	

Other noncurrent assets consist primarily of intangible items such as leaseholds and leasehold improvements. Other current debts could be represented by items such as taxes payable and other business accruals.

A new quick-print shop could conceivably open with a very limited amount of capital. Space might be rented in a desirable location that requires very little fix-up costs. The equipment might be acquired on a leasing arrangement whereby the operator pays a certain fee per copy produced. This is often enough to pay for the equipment in about three years, including the carrying cost of interest. The fee charged is about $.02 per copy on many duplication models, including a maintenance contract. At the termination of the three-year contractual period, the equipment can usually be bought by the user for a small fee. The wisdom of buying the equipment depends on its adequacy to meet the present needs of the firm and whether the machine is up to date technologically. Funds would also be essential to buy the inventory of paper and toner, the cash register, a small calculator, a paper cutter, and so forth. Even the paper and toner might be bought on terms of net 30 days from some commercial suppliers, so a minimum expenditure in this type of firm may be all that is required.

Typical Business Ratios Business ratios are sometimes helpful to a potential entrepreneur in preparing forecasted balance sheets and income statements for a planned business (often required on a loan application). Upper quartile, median, and lower quartile ratios on 800 lines of business are provided yearly by Dun & Bradstreet, Inc. Several median figures of the 1993 published data are shown for SIC 2741. Half the companies in the array had ratios falling between the UQ and LQ figures. The median is the center company, or the average between the 138th and 139th firm in the sample of 276 establishments in this study.

Solvency ratios:

Quick ratio (cash + accounts receivable/current liabilities)	1.4:1
Current ratio (current assets/current liabilities)	2.1:1
Total liabilities to net worth	75.2%

Efficiency ratios:

Collection period (accounts receivable/sales × 365)	40 days
Sales to inventory (net sales/inventory)	14.3 times
Assets to sales (total assets/annual net sales)	44.5%

Profitability ratios:

Return on sales (net after-tax profit/annual net sales)	6.2%
Return on net worth (net after-tax profit/net worth)	25.6%

Since these common-size financial statements and the key ratios computed from them change from year to year, a recent publication by D & B or other alternate source shown in the last section of this report should be sought for more up-to-date information. A standard business finance textbook usually provides one concise chapter on developing and understanding financial ratios.

The IRS compiles expense breakdown ratios on many lines of business. These are published by Prentice-Hall, Inc., on a preliminary basis. For SIC 2735 (printing and publishing), the following were provided in 1993 for the tax filing year of 1990.

	Under $100,000 Assets	$100,000–$250,000 Assets
Cost of operations	46.0%	27.1%
Compensation to officers	27.3	20.3
Repairs	.3	—
Bad debts	.7	—
Rent on business property	.7	1.0
Taxes (excluding federal tax)	1.2	1.4

	Under $100,000 Assets	$100,000–$250,000 Assets
Interest	3.8	.9
Depreciation/depletion/amortization	2.9	11.5
Advertising	5.0	1.9
Pension and benefits	—	2.8
Other expenses	21.4	21.3
Net profits	—	11.8

The larger firms tend to capitalize and depreciate more of their assets, whereas the smaller firms may expense them as bought. Also, the larger firms tend to develop pension plans for their full-time employees.

Development and Site Requirements

Several factors should be considered by a prospective owner/operator of a quick-print shop before settling on a given location. These include the customers to be served, the labor market from which to attract workers, purveyors of equipment and supplies, transportation considerations, and potential site locations available. For this subindustry, we will comment briefly on each of the above five areas.

Customers served will likely be a mixture of business firms, professional office staff, and individuals. In a college or university town, large numbers of senior and graduate students are likely to provide a major part of the walk-in traffic. Larger jobs done by the owner/operator will probably originate from commercial businesses and professional offices (e.g., accounting firms, legal firms, engineering firms, research and development firms, marketing research organizations, and the like). Individual homeowners, churches, industrial accounts, and local governmental agencies are also possible patrons. The risk of losing business is lessened with a broad-based group of different types of accounts. Moreover, some of these accounts will have heavy paperwork at certain times of the year. The tax season precipitates a larger work load on an accounting firm, as does the end of a semester for college students when term papers are due. Adequate paper and toner supplies should be maintained during rush periods to meet the demand, or alternate service firms may be sought by current patrons. Repeat customers need to be cultivated by this service and retail business.

The owner/operator of such a small establishment may have several outlets in a good-sized city or in nearby towns. It would be necessary to decide on efficient hours of operation and maintain at least one worker in the facility during all operating hours. This might be from 7 a.m. to 11 p.m. in order to meet the needs of clients during periods other than the normal working hours. Some 16-hour days multiplied by six or seven operating days in a week would require three to four part- or full-time operators. Many of the hourly workers are senior or graduate students who must be paid the going wage for their level of training in order to avoid excessive employee turnover, recruitment problems, and a period of on-the-job training.

Equipment and inventory suppliers and sellers (or lessors) of duplicating equipment may be located in nearby cities. Office products suppliers are located in most cities of 10,000 or greater population, but mail order supplies of paper and ink (or toner for blown-carbon-type duplication equipment) are usually less expensive than buying from a local office supply firm. However, having a nearby firm to supply emergency needs is important, even though the cost might be 5% to 15% above the wholesale price usually available with large purchases.

Many of the commercial accounts will deliver the items to be duplicated, giving the owner/operator or a designated agent certain instructions. Off-street parking for such patrons is important. A small storage room for extra paper and toner should be adjacent to an area easily reached by trucking firms that usually deliver the supplies. The agent for the equipment normally provides delivery and setup of the equipment to the quick-print shop, but accessibility to nearby parking and unloading is important to such functions.

More than one suitable location should be reviewed by the prospective entrepreneur. Strong and weak features should be offset, such as density of pedestrian and motor traffic near the store, possible room for expansion, the expenditure needed to renovate the commercial space, terms offered on the lease (e.g., cost, duration, subleasing provisions, payment of taxes and insurance, ordinary maintenance, and the like), and how well the firm will be welcomed into the neighborhood.

Market Opportunities in Various-Sized Communities

For a small city, the services of duplication might be provided at a bank. A popular alternative is to offer such a coin-operated duplication service in a very small area of some other type firm, such as an office supply retailer or a convenience store. Location near a laundromat would likely generate heavy customer traffic, but high humidity from the washers and dryers would be harmful to the paper, toner, and the proper functioning of the equipment. An operator of such an establishment (part of another business) should strive to cooperate with compatible businesses as much as possible. Upon request, many banks or post offices place a coin-operated duplicating machine in their lobbies. Public libraries also sometimes offer this service, so most communities provide duplication service through privately owned firms or quasi-public institutions. Desktop publishing of quality work requires more-experienced PC operators and at least $10,000 in equipment. The Macintosh equipment and software, especially, seems designed to meet these needs.

Experience and Training Required

The owner/operator of a quick-print shop should have some general management skills. Such a person should have basic knowledge about the various functions of business such as marketing, personnel matters, accounting and income tax information, financing alternatives, and the ability to be flexible in decision making. Ideally, for a small shop, the owner/operator should be skilled at equipment maintenance, as printing equipment may malfunction several times weekly (or daily). Unless there is a nearby maintenance firm to service the equipment (on contract, if possible) the downtime can cost the firm a large fraction of its daily business. The average time to obtain an out-of-town service person for such equipment is often a day or two, so idle or standby equipment is routinely acquired just to provide adequate duplicating equipment when one or more pieces are not operational.

Most new models of duplication equipment are installed by a salesperson/representative of the equipment company. Typically, the representative will give a repair demonstration on how to use the equipment and how to recognize any common problems (improper paper feeding, need to refill paper trays or toner container, etc.). Other maintenance problems are best left to a professional repair person in most cases. The demonstration is usually free to lessees of the equipment, their staff, and perhaps employees of a nearby institutional user of the equipment. A new employee in a firm can usually grasp the operating techniques of the equipment and coach clients on the use of equipment designed for self-service. Correcting more serious problems, however, should be accomplished by a knowledgable operator. Severe burns or electrical shocks may be the result of servicing by an unskilled person.

The office manager needs to have cash register and computational skills in order to calculate charges on walk-in, self-service jobs (unless the machines are coin operated). Most small quick-print shops have only one or two operators as they strive for high-volume, low-profit-margin business and must minimize labor costs. More-skilled persons are needed to do blueprinting for commercial, architectural, or engineering firms. Preparing bound volumes of reports for research organizations, accounting firms, or attorneys requires cutting and binding equipment as well as some additional skills in product design and production.

Legal Considerations Every potential business person should decide whether to operate the firm as a single proprietorship, a partnership with two or more co-owners, or a corporation. The services of an attorney should be sought in drawing up an efficient set of articles of incorporation that will comply with state corporate statutes. Some knowledge of the federal securities laws (for intermediate to large firms) is needed.

Every business owner must be knowledgable about income tax laws, payroll tax requirements, business permits needed, and the zoning requirements for the possible properties involved. Many cities of 25,000 population or greater have developed their own set of ordinances on building setbacks, size of signs, noise level, off-street parking, and so on, which should be reviewed by the potential owner/operator.

Obtaining adequate insurance, even for leased facilities, can be crucial to a business person. Commercial insurance coverage on property in which the entrepreneur has an interest should include fire insurance, personal liability insurance, theft insurance, vandalism coverage, and perhaps several types of extended coverage. Fidelity insurance on employees handling substantial amounts of cash is prudent. Most states assume that workmans' compensation insurance is obtained by a business firm. If it is not, and an employee suffers a job-related injury, the firm will have to pay the state-set monthly benefit (possibly through the normal working life of the injured person). Thus, workmans' compensation insurance is a virtual necessity to protect business firms.

Print shops are covered by the provisions of Occupational Safety and Health Administration (OSHA) rules and guidelines. Inspections frequently are made unannounced, resulting in business stoppages until any problems are corrected. Fines are sometimes assessed for repeated violations. Certain safety areas usually giving problems to printing operations include lack of safety guards on operating equipment, poor grounding on electrical equipment that might result in electrical shock or electrocution of users, inadequate fire exits or fire extinguishers in the working area, and lack of safeguards from flash fires from cleaning solvents. Miscellaneous violations are frequently levied for storage of combustible materials too near electrical outlets or other possible sources of a flame (a gas space heater, for example). For multi-floor buildings, a nearby fire escape is required.

Keys to Successful Management

Some keys to successful management in the quick-printing shop industry might be remembered as PEP, referring to promotion, efficiency, and punctuality. Advertising is needed to reach and maintain a level of profitability for most such business firms. The media should include newspaper ads, a listing in the yellow pages of the local or regional telephone directory, spot radio advertising, notices placed on prominent bulletin boards frequented by large groups of potential clients (such as hallways of a student union or classroom buildings of nearby schools), and direct mailings to potential commercial and individual clients (such as professors with assignments to large numbers of students). About 5% to 10% of the revenue for the average quick-print shop is spent on promotion.

A business manager/owner should strive for an efficient operation. The layout of the facility should cut down on wasted steps. The limited number of workers should be able to see the entire store in order to minimize nonpaying customers, disturbances, and vandalism. An adequate level of supplies should be kept on hand to accommodate the expected volume of business. Such inventories should be secured in a storage room, but convenient for ready movement to the paper trays of the duplicating equipment. A convenient standby supplier of paper and ink (or toner) is needed in the event that ordered items are not delivered (but backordered for next week's delivery). Last of all, the more profitable jobs should be promoted rather than those that are only break-even in revenues versus costs. An attempt to maximize the usage of equipment and labor should be targeted. Attempts to promote good relationships between the store and its employees by paying a certain fraction of profits as a bonus (perhaps at Christmas) may promote longevity of trained employees.

Punctuality in delivering the contracted jobs is very important in the printing business. The clients are depending on delivery on a certain day, perhaps a day or two before a very important meeting with valued clients. A missed deadline on delivery, for whatever reason, will usually cost the business for the printer—conceivably forever if there are alternate suppliers of printing service nearby. Some small printing firms will arrange a rush order on a reciprocal agreement with another nearby printing firm that might have similar equipment and subcontract out certain portions of the work for fast completion.

Management and employees should treat the printing jobs done by them as confidential. Some federal securities laws could apply to the leakage of inside financial information through printing organizations; and the leakage of sensitive information could lead to the loss of business or bring about legal action. Employees should be trained in such business ethics.

Information Sources Information useful to a potential owner/operator of a quick-print shop includes trade associations, dictionaries and books, periodicals, directories, ratio studies, investment services, and government documents. The listings in the *Encyclopedia of Business Information Sources* are useful to one learning more about the operation of a small business concern.

Travel Agencies

Business Types,
Industry
Characteristics and
Prospects

Travel agencies are grouped into the broad classification of SIC 472. Passenger transportation arrangement companies, classified by federal agencies as SIC 4724, numbered about 23,000 in 1984 but were increasing, net of discontinuances, by about 4% to 6% yearly. The growth in number continued until about 1991, when the recession caused the number to decline. For the next few years, satellite ticket printer (STP) locations gained in popularity. By late 1992, some 40,000 agencies and STP locations were in place in the United States, with the latter growing by 28% in 1992. Some 32,000 travel agency locations were in place in that year, and revenues gained about 9% above the depressed earlier year's level. Department of Labor estimates suggest a continued growth in annual employment for the firms through the year 2005, averaging about two times the growth in population. The total number of firms is not likely to grow so rapidly in the 1990s as in the 1980s due to the trend toward consolidation of financially weaker or smaller firms into larger ones and the use by major airlines of STP locations.

The travel and pleasure industry in the United States is the third largest, ranking behind food and auto sales. The broader travel and pleasure industry boasted annual revenues of about $390 billion in 1993, with a 3% to 4% annual gain expected for the balance of the decade. This broad classification embraced transportation, lodging, food and beverages, entertainment, recreation, and the purchase of incidental items by travelers and vacationers. The broad classification includes U.S. airlines, intercity bus companies, auto services, commuter lodging, campground and trailer parks, eating and drinking places, amusement and recreation facilities, auto rentals without drivers, taxicab companies, travel agents, general merchandisers, and miscellaneous rentals. Travel agencies make up only one small fraction of the total of the travel and pleasure industry, but this segment comprises a large number of small firms with little invested capital, on balance (average of about $80,000).

Growth in the broader travel and pleasure industry can be seen from a study of the recent past level of revenues, employment, and travel price index changes over the 1982 to 1993 years. The figures were as follows (with dollars in billions and employment in millions):

Year	Expenditures	Employment	Travel Price Index
1982	$198	4.24	100.0
1983	209	4.30	104.0
1984	235	4.77	107.9
1985	255	5.01	113.1
1986	271	5.24	112.6
1987	290	5.4	118.2
1988	288	5.5	129.5
1989	309	5.7	125.8
1990	334	6.0	136.2
1991	344	5.95	145.0
1992	372	6.12	149.9
1993 (est.)	393	6.29	153.5

Estimated by *U.S. Industrial Outlook*, 1994, Chapter 41.

The reasons for the decline in the cost index in the travel service industry from 1985 to 1986 and from 1988 to 1989 were twofold. Gasoline prices declined by 10% to 15% from the previous year, and much of this cost reduction was passed through to the service users. Many of the airlines were vigorously following a promotional price-reduction policy. TWA, for example, advertised a "See the U.S. during the year" program in 1986 for only $1,199 per person. Many flights could be taken for the bargain fare, and thousands of retired persons signed up for the flights. Cut-rate fares were customary in many recent years.

While a major share of the spending for the travel and pleasure industry is done by U.S. business persons and vacationers, foreign travel in the United States accounts for about 15% of the total spending. On average, Japanese travelers spend more than any other nationality. Foreign travel has been growing by about 3 million travelers per year during recent years. European and Asian travelers increased by about 14% and 31%, respectively, in 1992 over 1991, Canadian travelers increased 3.5%, and travelers from Mexico gained about 7%. Canadian travelers amounted to about 42% to 44% of total foreign travelers in the United States in 1992.

In the broader travel and pleasure industry, price-war competition for ticket sales led to the reduction of U.S. air carriers from about 100 in 1984 to about 70 by 1987 (with stabilization thereafter) due to consolidations. The forecast in the 1990s is for further Chapter 11 restructuring and consolidations. Airlines suffered major losses in 1992, due partially to price wars, but profits were generated in 1993 and 1994. The load factor (or the ratio of seats occupied, on average, on flights) had risen to 62% to 63% by 1993 (from about 54% to 55% in the late 1970s). Competition was beginning to intensify somewhat, as ocean-going travel, the use of the private auto (especially for shorter trips of fewer days), and stable use of Amtrak continued.

A very large share of airline tickets are issued by travel agencies. Ticket-buying vacationers and business persons prefer to buy at convenient locations, to be assisted in planning their schedule, and to receive their tickets immediately or in about 24 hours rather than to stand in long waiting lines at major airports for ticketing. As compensation for this service, travel agencies receive a commission from the airlines or other transit companies. This commission may range from zero by companies that do not use agents for issuing their tickets (some of the bus companies, smaller airlines, and Amtrak, generally), while many of the U.S. and foreign-based airlines provide commissions averaging about 10% of the ticket price to the ticketing agents. According to surveys, several airlines were paying in excess of 10% agency commissions. These included: Aeromexico, Royal Jordanian, Thai International, and Varig. Other international and U.S. air transport companies were generally paying lesser rates of commissions for ticket writing.

The travel agencies should do more than issue tickets to business and vacation travelers in order to return a good profit on time committed by owners/managers of the firms and on the financial commitments of assets to the endeavor. Many travel agencies promote group vacation packages, including the cost of travel, lodging, and certain meals and entertainment; some provide services in obtaining passports for foreign travelers; and still others act as exclusive buying ticket agent for large corporate clients (or institutional clients, such as a nearby university) that spend a large share of total operating revenues on business travel.

The travel agency business is a glamorous one, witnessing many new openings during strong economic years and many closings during hard times. Many of the closing firms are losing money, often falling more than 60 days late in remitting funds to their airline customers and having their agency relationships cancelled. The deregulation of the airline industry has led to a reduction in the fares charged by many of them, thus reducing the dollar amount of commissions paid to the travel agencies certified to issue tickets for the airlines. This certification is done by a corporation that evaluates a new agency for adequacy of training of personnel, financial strength, and other factors. This certifying firm, an association owned by about 150 U.S. and foreign airlines, is referred to as Airline Reporting Corporation (ARC). Generally, travel agencies with tickets in stock must post a minimum performance bond of $20,000 to protect airlines against loss or theft of the tickets. Weekly activity reports have to be made to ARC by the ticketing agents.

As in any industry, there are strong points and weak points on the intermediate-term horizon for travel agency firms. Unemployment rates are likely to hover around current levels, interest rates are likely to oscillate a small amount, and departures of U.S. travelers are likely to rise by 4% to 5% yearly for the next five years or so, barring a major recession in the nation. Some storm clouds on the horizon could materialize from several changes in the industry. Expected changes include a growing usage of automatic ticketing machines by the major airlines, the increase of mail order and/or supermarket sale of tickets by national travel agency firms, the use of PC access software so that individual customers may, effectively, make their own flight reservations, the shift toward more large airline users writing their own tickets (rather than using agencies), and the worry of airlines over excessive usage of the agencies (with the possibility of the agents pushing traffic to a few airlines and away from others). Some airlines with current commission arrangements through travel agencies have begun installing a large number of automatic ticketing machines at strategic locations, such as busy shopping malls or supermarkets.

In future years, it is likely that the growth of new entrants into the arena may greatly exceed the growth in population, but discontinuations will likely run 60% of new formations. Dual-income families and the growing retired group are traveling more, and they prefer to use travel agencies rather than to pursue the slow, tedious job of working out their own travel plans. Productivity gains in the industry will largely be due to the speed of gathering EDP information on flight originations in a given city and terminating (or serving) another location. Many very fast and efficient operators, equipped with the interactive computer, can determine needed flight information, make a confirmed seating assignment, and write the ticket during a five-minute telephone conversation with a client. Tickets are often promised for pickup within two hours, if written in-house, or perhaps on the following day if written in a nearby home office from an agent's station in a supermarket, for example.

Market Opportunities in Various-Sized Communities

With over 40,000 travel agencies and STP locations in the United States, some 6,500 in population for each is about average. A small community of 5,000 might afford one agency of two to four employees. The community, ideally, should comprise several hundred travelers that prefer to buy tickets from a local agency rather than from the regional airport. Many small communities do not have a feeder airport, but the air travelers must instead drive a few hours to a regional airport.

The development of a client following is necessary in order to change the shopping habits of the occasional flyer, but a vigorously aggressive owner/operator could probably establish a travel agency in a community of 10,000 citizens of average or higher personal income. A few large business or institutional clients should also be developed. Many owners/managers of travel agencies are active in community organizations, such as Lions, Rotary, or Kiwanis clubs, enjoy meeting people, and promote their community (and travel to and from it) vigorously.

Franchising

In order to break into the black as soon as possible, a new entrepreneur ideally would have had some experience at writing tickets, and perhaps at managing a travel agency office for someone else (perhaps having bought out a retiring owner). Payment of about 25% of the selling price (usually about 10% of the previous year's revenues) is a common downpayment in a buyout, with the balance paid off over two to five years from earned profits.

Some travel agencies have merged with others in nearby cities, expanded their office sizes and employee base, and acquired more EDP equipment to speed up ticketing for clients. Some have gone public and sold stock, rather than continue operating alone as a single proprietorship. Being a member of a group does provide a chance to develop associations with other similar business executives and permits cooperative advertising and promotion of tours that are sponsored by the company, and gives some greater assurance of stability to clients.

Still other new owners buy franchises in order to gain a going concern. The business has already been developed to about, or somewhat above, the break-even level. With the office usually goes some experienced employees, valuable information on how to and how not to conduct the business, joint advertising, and continuing tips on management. The greatest hurdles are the initial franchise fee, sometimes running from $50,000 to $100,000, and the assessment of an annual fee equivalent to 2% or more of revenues.

Development and
Site Requirements

In order to generate a large volume of travel ticket sales, a travel agency should be visible to a large number of persons who travel several times yearly. Quick, accurate, efficient service is important. Most of the customers contact a travel agency from a listing in the yellow pages, but convenient auto parking near the office is important. A pleasant atmosphere that welcomes the client is likewise important. A bright, sunny interior, with wall decorations and well-cared-for plants, may brighten up the interior. Scenic pictures, brochures of vacation trips, and pleasant conversation with clients that frequent the office are all important.

Some travelers shop around at various agencies, not even being sure where they wish to travel on vacation. A business person merely wants travel accommodations that are dependable and contain the smallest amount of layover time. Reimbursement will usually be made by the employing firm, so price is of somewhat lesser importance than to the casual traveler. Efforts should be made to cultivate repeat business for each of the clients, but the business traveler will often make his or her reservations by phone rather than in person, wanting an efficient agency employee to expedite the ticket reservations, writing, and charge write-up.

Most new agency offices are small, perhaps about 12 by 40 feet in size (or equivalent), and contain about three to five desks, a safe for storing unwritten tickets, and other office equipment such as filing cabinets, a typewriter, and an interactive computer showing scheduled flights, seats still open to various locations, charges for first class and tourist, and so on. Reservations usually have to be made immediately, although some agencies agree to hold a travel slot for one day pending final approval by the patron.

Some agencies attempt to appeal to senior adults since they are growing in number much more rapidly than the average population base and spend more time in travel. Adults aged 50 to 65, with both spouses still working, should be promoted as clients; thus the owner of a new travel agency should consider locating in an area convenient to those frequented by such adults. A busy shopping center or the front area of a supermarket in a high-class neighborhood have sometimes proven to be good promotional locations. Since travel agencies write tickets at the same cost as charged by the airlines, a majority of airline passengers prefer to shop from a convenient agency rather than from the ticketing counter in a busy airport. Convenience for the traveler, then, is the key to a good location.

Cost and Types of Assets Needed to Start a Business

Many newly formed travel agencies occupy leased space on a well-traveled street, such as in a shopping center, near a university, or in a downtown hotel cluster. Many travel agencies lease office space or a booth at the front of large supermarkets frequented by above-average income earners. For space leased as a free-standing store, rent is usually a definite amount. Shopping center developers often charge from 5% to 7% of revenues generated by their space-leasing clients. Those that operate from a busy supermarket often pay a set amount for rent plus another amount, such as 1.5% of revenues.

The amount of needed funds to operate a travel agency is influenced by several factors, such as the number of customer service employees. For the typical beginning travel agency, these are likely to comprise an experienced owner/operator, another experienced office manager, and one or more persons who are learning the routine of the business (training on the job). The *U.S. Occupational Outlook Handbook* provided 1992 information showing that each such employee earned about $13,000 yearly at the entry level, growing to about $25,000 with 10 or more years of experience. The owner/operator and other full-time persons usually earn fringe benefits such as insurance coverage and vacation time.

The average newly formed travel agency will have about three trained employees to assist customers. Another may serve as telephone switchboard operator, office receptionist, and bookkeeper for the firm. Thus, revenues should be adequate to pay a going wage for about four persons.

Office furnishings, typewriting and computing equipment, display racks, and a reception area for clients are customary in an office measuring about 500 square feet, perhaps being about 12 by 40 feet in size. The office should be brightly lighted and have attractive carpeting and plant arrangements.

The start-up costs on a travel agency are substantial, with close to $10,000 being average for the grand opening. Another $35,000 to $50,000 is likely to be needed to meet expenses until the business reaches the break-even level, in about six to nine months on average. In order to reduce the long period of losses, some owners/operators buy out a going concern, usually paying about 100% of the previous year's revenues.

Typical Business Ratios

A recent Small Business Administration *Starting Out Series* (Number 202) indicated that salaries averaged 70% of revenues on about a $1 million annual volume of business, that advertising expenditures were about 6% to 8%, that rent amounted to about 7%, and that miscellaneous expenses brought the total to about 90% of revenues. This would provide 10% of revenues as pretax profits. On revenues of $100,000 and with an average commission on ticket writing of 10%, some $1,000,000 in tickets would have to be written in a year.

In the early 1990s, with the average cost of a ticket being about $200, an office might earn about $20 on each ticket written at that price, or need to write about 5,000 tickets during the year to earn about $100,000. With 250 working days in the year, such an office would need to write, on average, about 20 tickets daily. Two account executives might handle this volume of traffic. A larger office would need more employees.

Revenues charged by the hour for consulting services to certain clients or commissions earned on planned and/or promoted tours would be another possible source of revenue for the established travel agency. Some agencies promote traveling tours around the United States with a tour guide, but this introduces its own set of problems, covered below in the training for employees and legal sections.

Industry guides suggest that each account executive should be able to arrange travel of about $250,000 to $300,000 yearly. Another way of viewing this is to say that about 1,000 round-trip tickets yearly, averaging about $250 to $300 each, should be written by each agency employee. Dividing up this dollar volume of ticket revenues needed computes to about four round-trip ticket sales per day by each of the employees in order to cover labor costs and other business expenses.

The single proprietorship types of travel agencies are usually small in size, perhaps hiring one or two employees in addition to the owner/operator. On balance, according to published IRS data, the single proprietor earn profits, but far less than each experienced employed person in an agency with a good location.

A review of the common-sized balance sheet published yearly by Dun & Bradstreet, Inc.'s *Industry Norms and Key Business Ratios* shows about the average breakdown in assets and liabilities/capital for travel agencies. For the 1993 year, this was about as follows:

Assets		Debts and Net Worth	
Cash and near-cash	34.2%	Accounts payable	14.6%
Accounts receivable	24.8	Loans payable	4.6
Notes receivables	.8	Other current debts	17.1
Inventory	.6	Total current debts	36.3
Other current assets	8.7	Long-term debts	9.9
Total current assets	69.1	Deferred credit	.3
Fixed assets	15.6	Net worth	53.5
Other noncurrent assets	15.3	Total debts and net worth	100.0
Total assets	100.0	Total debts and net worth	$157,500

Typical Business Ratios Each year, the IRS publishes in *Corporate Income* and Prentice-Hall, Inc., estimates the expense breakdown for about 800 lines of business. For SIC 4700 in the most recent year, this was about as follows for very small and small firms:

	Under $100,000 Assets	$100,000–$250,000 Assets
Number of enterprises	11,104	3,757
Total receipts (thousands)	$4,585	$4,140
Cost of operations (percentage of sales)	74.4%	61.6%
Officers' compensation	4.0	3.5
Repairs	.5	1.0
Bad debts	.3	—
Rent on business property	2.8	1.6
Taxes (excluding federal tax)	1.6	1.6
Interest	.4	.4
Depreciation/depletion/amortization	.8	1.4
Advertising	.6	.8
Pension and benefits	.7	.3
Other expenses	14.0	26.6
Net before-tax profit	1.0	1.0

For the smallest of these categories, annual revenues were about $400,000 on average, but they increased to about $1,100,000 for the second category. Thus, revenues amounted to about six times the asset base, on average. In pricing an agency, the price is more often based on one to two years of revenues generated rather than on book equity.

D & B publishes 14 important ratios on 800 business lines. Certain of these, selected from the categories of Solvency, Efficiency, and Profitability ratios, are useful to the growing travel agency owner or a would-be entrepreneur. From the 1994 service, the following are average:

Solvency ratios:

Quick ratio	1.8 times
Current ratio	2.1 times
Liabilities to net worth	133.7%

Efficiency ratios:

Collection period	10.6 days
Assets to sales	150.3%
Sales to net working capital	21.8%

Profitability ratios:

Return on sales	1.4%
Return on net worth	15.5%

Experience and Training Required   The owner/manager of the new travel agency should have experience as an employee of a similar firm for at least two years. Ideally, he or she should have been manager of the similar-type firm for at least a year. At least one other person in the office should have had employee experience.

About this level of experience is required before the Airlines Reporting Corporation (ARC) will certify the agency to write tickets as an agent for the airlines in the membership corporation (ARC). Approval by ARC usually takes several weeks, so patience in breaking into the business is required. Certified Meeting Professional (CMP) designation requires about 18 months of part-time training in an advanced course through the Institute of Certified Travel Agents, according to the 1994–95 *Occupational Outlook Handbook*. Thus, such a business person needs to have supplemental income to support the business or a substantial store of cash.

The experienced owner/operator and one additional experienced employee should be able to train additional employees to handle flight scheduling, booking, and ticketing as the level of business grows. As revenues earned begin to cover all expenses and provide a generous return on assets invested in the firm, additional lines will likely be added, such as the promotion of ocean-going cruises, vacations at popular resort spots, and planned guided tours. Some agencies send an employee free of charge (expenses paid but without pay) on a tour then let the person be the tour guide on a subsequent tour to a similar location. This person, or another employee in the firm, might handle the mechanics of booking motel, entertainment, and restaurant accommodations for the passengers on the next tour.

Legal Considerations

The owner or prospective owner of a travel agency firm must be certain that it is operating and licensed appropriately. The owner must obtain a federal and state tax identification number and letter of clearance from the department of revenue within its state(s) of operation.

The new owner/manager of a travel agency may have to be licensed by a local governmental body. He or she should check with the local/regional chamber of commerce in order to determine such rules and regulations. Certainly the location of the firm should be commercially zoned.

Any business owner/manager is faced with a substantial number of other legal considerations. An attorney, an accountant, and perhaps a travel consultant should be consulted in making decisions about form of organization, financing alternatives, income tax considerations (i.e., payroll accounting, depreciation write-offs, installment buying or selling of a business, record systems needed, internal controls to install, etc.), and successful techniques for effectively promoting such a business.

Acquiring the proper types of insurance coverage on such a business is of extreme importance. Fire insurance and blanket liability insurance on patrons frequenting the firm are important. Fidelity insurance on employees handling large amounts of money, checks, and unwritten tickets is also needed. Theft insurance on theft of the same should be provided. Last of all, anti-fraud insurance and liability insurance covering clients on a tour are very important.

Courts usually construe that due care expected of a knowledgeable person must be used by the tour guide employee. Price might be important in planning a tour, leaving a reasonable profit for the firm, but care should be used in selecting the firm(s) to supply the travel, lodging, food, and entertainment. Advertising promotions should be honest, or some of the disgruntled travelers not only will criticize the agency to their friends (potential future clients) but may bring a lawsuit for injury sustained or fraud in advertising. Some insurance coverage to safeguard against such legal entanglements is highly desirable.

Keys to Successful Management

Several steps should be followed by the owner/manager of a newly established travel agency in order to make it profitable. The following are suggested for consideration:

1. The location should be on a heavily traveled street or in a small location within a busy shopping mall (preferably near a high-income neighborhood) or within a supermarket catering to above-average-income patrons.

2. Efficient, courteous phone service operators should be hired or trained. Business clients usually shop by phone rather than in person.

3. A vigorous attempt should be made to line up three or more large business customers that provide repeat business on a weekly basis.

4. The owner/manager should consider some diversifying into more than one type of business or in cultivating more than one type of client. Areas might include writing airline tickets, selling tickets for tours planned by others, or providing consulting or aid in obtaining passports as part of the regular ticketing service (or on a time-charge per diem basis).

5. A computer terminal linkage to nearby regional airlines should be used so that scheduling, seat assignments, and reservations may be completed in a minimum of time. An attempt should be made to write tickets while the client waits or delivery promised in 24 hours.

6. Some travel agencies deliver the tickets to the client's place of business or home, provided it is within a 5- to 10-mile radius of the travel agency's office. This may be an unnecessary expense, however, as many business travelers take lunch breaks to shopping centers or downtown areas. Extending the hours of business beyond those of other nearby firms may attract some clients. The courtesy of reminding a client that the ticket is ready to be picked up, and waiting a few minutes after normal closing, may develop a repeat client.

7. Inducements such as the gift of a travel atlas or a subscription to a travel magazine once a certain level of business is reached, or providing reading literature on a trip, should be considered. Free brochures of vacation trips should be freely displayed for clients who are shopping around. The gifts should promote future travel, if possible.

8. The demographics of the nearby population should be considered. Promotion should be developed to the type of client that has the financial ability to travel. Newspaper ads (not on the grocery page, however), spot radio announcements on stations listened to by the target clients, and direct mailouts to selected clients are sometimes effective promotional approaches.

Information Sources Several sources of information are available to the new owner/business manager of a travel agency. These include associations, books, magazines, directories, ratio studies, investment services, and government services. A list of these usually appears in the periodic updated _Encyclopedia of Business Information Sources_, published by Gale Research, Inc., Detroit, Mich. Annual information about this and other industry groups is published by _U.S. Industrial Outlook_ and _Occupational Outlook Handbook_, both being U.S. Department of Commerce publications.

Wholesaling: Durables and Nondurables

Business Types, Industry Characteristics and Prospects

Firms in the wholesale trade industry have been assigned SIC code 50xx for durable goods and 51xx for nondurable goods. This business and industry profile has been designed to provide some general operating and financial characteristics of these two broad types of firms. A more detailed breakdown of firms that operate predominantly in wholesaling, with some 1989–1992 statistics, appears in Table 1.

Wholesale firms include merchant wholesalers, manufacturing branch sales offices, manufacturing representatives, and commission brokers. The first category, merchant wholesalers, are the most numerous and dominate in most subindustries of wholesaling. In general, they buy goods from manufacturers, sort them, assemble and grade them, and store them for sale to professional firms, commercial retailers, farms, governments, and institutional users (such as schools, prisons, hospitals, and the like). Such firms also establish and promote markets for suppliers' products; provide delivery, labeling, and advertising; and extend credit.

Large firms tend to dominate the wholesale trade industry, with 2% of the largest firms accounting for about 22% of the total volume of sales. Some consolidation occurred during the 1980s so as to improve operating efficiency and to cut cost and be competitive with imported goods. Some of these labor-saving approaches included automating services, computerizing inventory order filling, barcoding control of inventory storage and retrieval, and telemarketing.

In Table 1, "sensitive" refers to the product's sensitivity to movements in the business cycle. The items marked "insensitive" are relatively insensitive to movements in the overall business cycle. A larger percentage of nondurable goods, naturally, are insensitive to general business strength than are durable goods. Many large contracts for structures or electric utilities are little impacted by business cycle strength; thus, electrical items are relatively insensitive to the cycle.

It was estimated that about 70% of U.S. manufactured goods moved through wholesale distributors in recent years while 30% moved directly to retailers or the ultimate consumer. Businesses were growing more rapidly on the east and west coasts than in other geographical areas of the nation. In order to maintain a healthy net profit margin, many of the larger firms were increasing their usage of EDP software. The several areas where this appeared to be effective were in designing custom packaging, in strategic business planning, in route scheduling for salespersons and delivery vehicles, in customer and product profit analysis, in internal and external marketing, and in sales analysis.

TABLE 1. Merchant Wholesale Sales, 1989–1992
(billion dollars)

Item	Sensitive (s)/ Insensitive (i)	1989	1990	1991	1992
Total	s	$1,728.5	$1,790.4	$1,741.6	$1,787.6
DURABLE GOODS					
Motor vehicles	s	164.7	169.7	154.4	154.5
Furniture	s	29.7	30.5	28.1	28.1
Lumber	s	57.6	55.8	52.6	58.5
Professional communications equipment	i	110.8	116.1	116.4	129.0
Metals and minerals	s	86.9	88.9	76.3	76.0
Electrical goods	i	110.5	113.1	113.7	117.0
Plumbing and heating equipment	s	44.0	45.1	41.3	41.5
Machinery and equipment	s	146.9	157.3	156.2	164.0
Miscellaneous	s	109.4	113.7	107.3	112.0
NONDURABLE GOODS					
Paper	s	50.0	50.7	48.6	49.5
Drugs	i	43.0	47.9	54.2	60.5
Apparel	s	59.0	60.8	60.7	65.5
Groceries	i	242.7	246.6	254.4	264.5
Farm materials	s	129.5	123.2	118.0	116.0
Chemicals	i	37.6	43.0	44.8	46.0
Petroleum	s	140.7	156.3	138.7	124.5
Alcoholic beverages	i	42.9	45.4	47.1	51.5
Miscellaneous	i	119.8	126.2	128.6	129.0

Exporters of goods were growing about 40% more rapidly than were nonexporting wholesalers. Of goods exported, some 73% of the cargo (in tons) was by ship, 28% by air, and 9% by land. It was estimated that half of the exporting firms were using domestic export brokers while about half dealt directly with foreign buyers. The total number of wholesale firms grew by about 1% yearly during the 1970s, but the growth rate in number of firms was about 2% yearly in the 1980s. This 2% annual increase (in tonnage) is expected to continue into the mid-1990s.

As stated above, the wholesale firms that are growing most rapidly, for a given subindustry, are those that emphasize the export of products. Faster-than-average growth rates have been reported for electronics, tools, and bio-engineering firms; but the trend in some industries has been to add retail establishments. This has been pronounced in the wholesale food industry (and many of them have added EDP, on-line order entry systems), with the firms employing more than 10,000 including the following national retail/wholesale chains: Super Value Stores (over 3,200 retail outlets), Fleming Companies (over 5,200 retail outlets), Sysco, Watterau, Inc., and Price Company. In recent years, the trend has been for the larger firms to buy up the smaller, less-profitable regional firms.

In future years, it is expected that wholesale firms, both in the durable and nondurable sectors, will continue to move toward greater emphasis on exporting and toward increasing cost efficiency. Their total sales are likely to gain about 2.2% yearly in real terms, or perhaps 5% to 6% yearly in dollar volume, as inflation is likely to run at 2% to 4% yearly during the 1990s. In total, the dollar amount of wholesaling is somewhat greater than the dollar volume of retail sales due to wholesale sales abroad, to manufacturing, to other wholesalers, and to institutional buyers. Wholesaling accounted for about 5.3% of the total output of the economy in the early 1990s.

Market Opportunities in Various-Sized Communities

Before a business firm is begun, its owner(s) should develop a business plan, which includes a marketing plan. The marketing plan is an analysis of potential clients and the level of sales that they might generate, the degree of competition already existing in the region, and the channels of distribution through which the goods or services might be effectively marketed.

Demographic data as to numbers and sizes of competitors and the approximate level of potential customers are important in developing a sales forecast and marketing plan. Some sources of information helpful in developing the plan include the regional chamber of commerce, government offices (city, county, or state), a small-business development center, banks, accounting offices, public or college libraries, and private research organizations.

Few wholesale firms locate in small communities. An exception to this exists in farm product gathering and petroleum product (crude oil) gathering and wholesaling, as each tends to concentrate near the source of raw materials or supply. Most other wholesale firms tend to locate on the outskirts of large cities that enjoy above-average transportation facilities (rail and trucking) into and out of the city.

Mail order wholesale firms can be exceptions to the tendency to locate in large cities, and some are begun in very small communities. Many of these, however, merely serve as manufacturing representatives for the makers of the products that are sold; accepting orders and processing them, and perhaps supplying credit to the buyers of the products. Some of the mail order firms do not actually perform physical delivery of the products they sell but merely process orders, having them shipped from the facilities of the manufacturers. (Note: The reader may wish to read the profile on Mail Order Firms.)

Development and Site Requirements

A wholesale firm is a commercial establishment, so it must be located where the property is already or can be zoned commercial. Wholesale firms are, more often than not, located near their source of supply or near the outlets that they service. For example, one would expect a heavier concentration of wholesale firms in motor vehicle and auto equipment near their manufacturing and assembly plants. The same is true for most consumer durable goods manufacturers. Thus, most SIC 50xx wholesale firms are located near manufacturing sectors. Electronics firms tend to locate more heavily in about four locations in the nation: around Massachusetts, Florida, Texas, and California. Paper and paper products firms tend to locate near their source of raw materials, which is across the soft-timber states of the eastern United States, in the western timber states (Oregon and Washington), and across the Gulf South.

Apparel firms, while once concentrated in the New England states, have diversified into southeastern states due to less unionization and lower wage rates. Oil and gas gathering and distribution firms tend to locate near sources of supply, with heavy concentrations in the Gulf South. The same is true for chemical firms, especially those that need large amounts of seawater in their operations.

Farm products firms tend to concentrate near growing regions, such as the midwestern farming states. Groceries and related products and beer, wine, and distilled beverage wholesalers are more widely located.

Wholesale firms have several characteristics in common with one another. First of all, they wish to minimize total transportation, storage, and distribution costs. Thus, they usually locate near railroad, barge, and highway terminals. Most have vast amounts of storage space so that volume buying and storage may be done, especially for items that may have a short production season but a sales season throughout the year. They also have substantial amounts of parking space and loading docks in order to accommodate truck transport vehicles. Most are located near railroad spurs so that shipments may be obtained or sent out by rail. Those that participate highly in exporting goods often seek a location that accommodates barge traffic.

Visibility is not important to most wholesale firms. Rather, they seek locations in the low-rent districts that are conducive to minimizing transportation and storage costs. When sales increases are difficult to obtain by growth-minded managements of wholesale firms, many enter other avenues.

Some wholesale firms diversify horizontally, meaning that they expand geographically. Still others seek to diversify vertically, perhaps buying into major suppliers of goods or into retail establishments. In the 1980s, this trend was especially noticeable in the retail grocery business.

Cost and Types of Assets Needed to Start a Wholesale Business

Before beginning a new wholesale operation, an estimate should be made of the level of sales probably achievable. The next step involves estimating needs for working capital assets such as cash, receivables, and inventory. Other funds are needed to buy operating equipment, renovate or build a structure, and acquire delivery equipment. Funds to pay salaries and other operating costs, including withdrawals by owners, until the firm reaches a break-even level are needed.

Funds are available to a small firm from a number of sources. The owner usually provides about 50% to 60% of total funds. Short-term credit such as trade payables, wages payable, and unpaid payroll taxes makes up a major portion of current debts. Bank loans or borrowing from a state lending program might be possible. Using a well-designed mix of short-term credit, intermediate term credit, and equity capital, if competition in a given industry/location is not excessively severe, should permit a well-run business to turn a modest profit.

In general, wholesale firms are less numerous but larger in size than are retail establishments. They tend to locate near transportation and manufacturing hubs, extending their distribution territories several hundred miles from their locations. Satellite warehousing (shipping terminals) are sometimes located in regional shipping centers.

Composite financial statements and key financial ratios are published in a number of sources, such as Dun & Bradstreet, Inc.'s *Industry Norms and Key Business Ratios*, Robert L. Morris Associates' annual update of *Statement Studies*, and SIC classifications of IRS publications. Comparison financial statements are provided below for major categories of wholesale items: durable and nondurable firms. While the breakdown of assets by these types of firms show some differences, they all show significant asset investment into accounts receivable and inventories and heavy reliance on debt.

	Durable Goods	Nondurable Goods
ASSETS		
Cash and near-cash	11.8%	12.8%
Accounts receivable	30.8	30.3
Notes receivable	.7	.6
Inventory	33.9	24.8
Other current assets	3.8	4.7
Total current assets	81.0	73.2
Fixed assets	11.5	15.7
Other noncurrent assets	7.5	11.1
Total assets	100.0	100.0

continued

	Durable Goods	Nondurable Goods
DEBTS AND NET WORTH		
Accounts payable	21.3	20.8
Bank and other notes payable	6.7	6.1
Other current debts	14.0	13.0
Total current debts	42.0	39.9
Long-term debts	10.7	11.2
Deferred credit	.2	.1
Net worth	47.1	48.8
Total debts and net worth	100.0	100.0
Net worth (thousands)	$251,454	$347,476
Sales (net) (thousands)	$1,609	$2,578
Gross profit	27.7%	21.0%
Net after-tax profit	3.4%	2.7%

The reader may wish to obtain detailed statistics on lines of business in the wholesale trade industries from the 1992 wholesale volume of the 5-year business census (published in spring of 1995).

The above ratios are mean averages of firms in the D & B breakdowns, that included over 2,000 establishments in each of the two major categories. D & B statistics differ somewhat from those published by Robert L. Morris Associates, inasmuch as they are drawn from different samples. The D & B study uses credit reports, while RLM uses bank credit application files at association member institutions.

Key Business Ratios Financial ratios are of two types. The first type of financial ratios is merely a statement of operating expenses as a percentage of net sales. The second type is the computation of industry ratios from composite balance sheets and income statements. The IRS compiles annual corporate income statement and balance sheet data. Such information is published by Prentice-Hall, Inc., in the *Almanac of Business and Industry Financial Ratios*. From the 1992 edition, expense breakdowns for three different types of wholesale firms, apparel, drugs and chemicals, and groceries, are illustrated, inasmuch as these are three very important types of goods that are sold through wholesale firms.

	Apparel	Drugs and Chemicals	Groceries
Cost of operations	73.3%	82.0%	86.8%
Compensation of officers	3.2	1.0	.9
Repairs	.1	.2	.3
Bad debts	.3	.2	.2
Rent on business property	1.1	.8	.7
Taxes (excluding federal tax)	1.8	1.1	.8
Interest	1.4	.7	.6
Depreciation/depletion/amortization	.7	1.0	.9

	Apparel	Drugs and Chemicals	Groceries
Advertising	.8	.8	.3
Pension and benefits	.7	.6	.6
Other expenses (wages, etc.)	13.3	10.4	8.1
Net before-tax profit	3.3	1.3	Nil–1.7

The above are for all sizes of business firms in the respective industries. Most industries have more wholesale firms with assets of $100,000 to $250,000 than with assets of under $100,000. In most wholesale industries, profit margins tend to narrow, as do most types of operating expenses, as the firms grow in size.

Financial ratios are useful in comparing the affairs of one firm to those of the average in its industry, and these are employed by financial planners and loan officers in making financial decisions. For SIC 50xx and 51xx, the 1993 key financial ratios were as follows:

	Durable Goods	Nondurable Goods
Solvency ratios:		
Quick ratio	1.0:1	1.1:1
Current ratio	2.0:1	1.8:1
Total debts to net worth	102.2%	95.5%
Efficiency ratios:		
Collection period (days)	36.9	26.3
Sales to inventory	8.2%	15.4%
Assets to sales	33.4%	27.2%
Profitability ratios:		
Return on sales (median)	2.1%	1.5%
Return on net worth	12.2%	10.7%

Legal Considerations

As with all firms, a wholesale firm should be in a properly zoned facility, have a valid local and state selling license, and have a tax identification number if workers are hired.

While a wholesale firm has the normal need for accountants to set up general accounting systems, systems of inventory control, and tax savings programs, many have a greater need for legal representation than do retailers. Product liability to wholesalers has become a major concern to them during recent years. In some instances, lawsuits are brought against wholesalers of imported goods rather than against the foreign manufacturers. Some states have enacted laws that unify liability exposure for wholesalers and make insurance coverage affordable to them. At times, wholesale firms are stuck with large amounts of inventory items that have been declared as unsafe for sale. They may have guaranteed to rebuy such merchandise from their retailing clients in order to make the sales. It is not always possible for them to effectively press their legal claims, especially against foreign sellers of the merchandise.

Certainly wholesale firms, as all firms, must be aware of required workers' compensation laws. This coverage is very expensive in some states, and wholesale firms that operate on slim gross profit margins may locate in states of lower workers' compensation costs rather than the more expensive, nearby ones.

Experience and Training Required

The functions performed by wholesale firms are diversified, and so are the required backgrounds of their employees. These firms promote wider distribution of products from a manufacturer than would perhaps be possible without wholesale firms; they provide a trained sales force for similar goods; they provide marketing and research assistance to both manufacturing and retailing customers; they carry assortments of items, purchasing and storing them in large quantities; they provide warehousing and delivery services; they offer financing to many retailing firms that would be unable to obtain such terms from fledgling sellers of the products; and they accept the risk of theft and obsolescence of the products that they stock.

In many instances, the wholesalers of merchandise are larger than either the manufacturers of the items they buy or their retailing or institutional clients. While most are full-service wholesalers, some merely operate as agents or brokers.

In some instances, wholesale firms have been family owned for several generations, but the trend in more recent decades has been toward more specialized, and sometimes professional, managers that may or may not be stockholders in the firm.

Since large amounts of capital and a large workforce are needed in large wholesale firms, attention must be given toward promoting a management staff with strengths in general management areas, marketing, and financing. In recent years, the trend has been toward computerizing many areas of wholesalers, including accepting orders via the computer from customers, filling such orders within three hours by using EDP barcoded identification tags, and shipping the orders the same day (or next day) as the receipt of orders. Linear programming models are being used to work out optimum routes for salespersons (when personal calls are made on suppliers or customers) and for fleet delivery by motor carrier.

Most large firms have their own training programs, devoting several hours weekly or monthly to the training/retraining of workers. Most large firms are highly automated so as to reduce the size of the labor force. While the workforce was reduced about 10% during the 1980s for the total of wholesale firms, the improved operating efficiency has more than offset this decline in number of workers. Salaries of wholesale firms run about 95%, generally, of those paid by manufacturing firms, which is close to two times the level paid by retailing establishments.

Keys to Successful Management

In order to be successful in its lines of endeavor (i.e., buying, taking title and possession of products, storing them, assembling an assortment of items, providing credit, promotion, and delivery of the items to their clients), a wholesale firm should develop operating goals and develop strategies for reaching them. Such goals might include such things as filling 90% or more of orders received within three hours of receipt of the order; filling orders with 99% or greater accuracy; and suffering less than 2% breakage of the delivered items.

Orderly receipt and filling of orders within a short time probably means the stocking of large amounts of inventory that can be easily retrieved. This suggests that the orders received should be automated with the withdrawal of goods from the physical inventory. Barcoding and automated retrieval have contributed to the speed of inventory shipping.

Where shortages of items exist, the decision must be made as to (1) making partial delivery, (2) holding up the order until the full amount can be shipped, or (3) providing a substitute (similar) product. A combination of these approaches may be used, as some clients prefer some delivery immediately and might be willing to wait a few days on a backorder of some of the products. Shipping the wrong items ties up the inventory for several days, and it may irritate some clients to the extent that they buy from another source. However, advising the client of the partial shipment with backorder promised in a few days is usually acceptable to most buyers of goods.

Broken items, if caught by the customer when inspecting the merchandise upon arrival, are usually returned to the shipper. This costs a good share of the profits to wholesalers, so they wish to minimize such breakage. Common carriers may carry insurance that would compensate the shippers for such breakage, but ill will might ensue if such occurrences become commonplace. Instead, alternate suppliers might be sought. Thus, prompt delivery of salable merchandise is a goal sought by wholesalers.

Another possible goal is to provide limited financing to the buying clients. Small manufacturers might be strapped for funds, and the wholesale firms might have enough financial strength to buy for cash from their suppliers and pass along 30 days (or more) of credit to their retail or institutional clients. They also may provide record keeping to certain clients, sometimes placing goods in stores on a consignment basis and charging only for those items that have been sold by the next delivery date.

In order to be successful, wholesale firms must constantly be upgrading their quality of service and efficiency. This means increasing their degree of automation and efficiency in accepting, storing, order filling, and delivery of goods being sold. Many statistical (optimization) models have been developed which aid the wholesaling firms in these endeavors. The reader is referred to a good book on linear programming which describes and illustrates these models.

Information Sources In order to remain abreast of changes in its areas of operation, the managers/owners of a wholesale firm should maintain membership in one or more professional organizations, subscribe to one or several trade publications, and have a small library of materials helpful in reaching informed decisions about the business. The *Encyclopedia of Business Information Sources*, with periodic updates by Gale Research, Inc., of Detroit, Mich., is especially helpful in this endeavor.

Apparel and Accessory Stores

Retail apparel stores have been assigned the SIC codes 5611–5659 from the broader classification of 56. These include men's and boys' clothing and accessory stores (5611), women's clothing stores (5621), women's accessory and specialty stores (5631), children's and infants' wear stores (5641), and family clothing stores (5651). The financials on several of these will be reviewed in this profile.

Retail apparel may be sold through certain departments of large, national department stores or through small specialty shops. The federal agencies assign one of several SIC codes to stores operating predominantly in retail trade of apparel and related items, including the following data from the 1991 Retail Trade Business Census from the 1994 edition of *County Business Patterns: United States.*

SIC	Types of Items Handled	No. of Stores	No. of Employees (thousands)	Payroll (millions)
561	Men's and boys' clothing and furnishings	13,979	100.6	$2,416.8
562	Women's ready-to-wear	48,845	444.6	4,043.8
563	Women's accessories and specialties	7,906	43.6	459.2
565	Family clothing	17,955	292.9	3,038.3

The 1991 edition of *County Business Patterns: Retail Trade* estimated that about 147,600 establishments operated in retail trade of apparel. The women's ready-to-wear stores outnumbered the three other types combined (those that handle apparel goods for males, infants and children, or the entire family).

The sales at the women's departments of large department stores dominate the sale of women's apparel and accessories. Such departments often carry a wide range of such merchandise, offer credit card sales, and have a generous return policy. Many keep a list of previous customers and send them postcard notices of approaching markdown sales of clearance merchandise. In the women's department of a large department store, two or more female clerks usually are available to aid customers in fittings, locating matching accessories, and ringing up sales.

A very large number of small firms make up this industry, with the mean number of employees averaging about four to nine in most of these SIC designations. However, the family clothing stores, with their wider range of merchandise, have about two times the number of employees as the single-line stores. The median number of employees is between four and five. The model number of employees in such a small store is four paid employees, with about half the clerks being similar in age and sex to the expected clients. That is, male clerks often work in men's stores and teenage or young adult females clerk in stores for young misses. Mothers and grandmothers are frequently hired to advise shoppers on buying for tots.

The retailers of apparel have had relatively static sales over the late 1980s and early 1990s, in terms of units, with a rising fraction of revenues coming from sales of foreign-sewn apparel items. For example, the number of U.S. textile workers declined from about 729,000 in 1988 to about 668,000 in 1991 and then began to rise by about 1.5% yearly. Earnings of the workers kept pace with changes in the consumer prices, growing from $303 weekly in 1988 to about $368 in 1993. Imports as a percentage of the total grew from 36% in 1988 to an estimated 45.7% by 1993. Countries that have increased exports of apparel more than average include many oriental countries, such as China, Taiwan, Hong Kong, South Korea, and the Philippines. In 1983, the exporting countries had a real price advantage when manufacturing textile goods for export, but the falling value of the U.S. dollar in international trade has begun to slow the growth rate in imports within this industry. Over the 1983 to 1985 period, for example, the quantity of such imports grew at about two-thirds of the rate of the value of imports, meaning that higher-priced goods were being sold. Over the latter 1980s, the U.S. garment manufacturers began to compete more effectively with foreign suppliers. (The reader may wish to read the profile on Garment Manufacturers.)

In the 1970s, many young adult women and teens were brand conscious and would only wear one or two favorite brands. Most firms that sold these brands did so at the recommended list price for the items. The trend during the last few years has been toward the sale of off-price merchandise some 10% to 12% below the nationally advertised price. Some malls have been created for the special purpose of marketing off-price apparel for various types of customers. Some suppliers are more than willing to discount their lines of products to off-price stores, but some will do so only with model closeouts, seconds, or slow-moving merchandise lines. Manufacturers' malls have become important for this group of industries, where the first item is usually sold for regular retail price and the second item may be sold for half price. Some such stores discount all items by up to one-half.

A large fraction of retail apparel imported into the United States comprises women's and misses' tops, textile goods not elsewhere classified, gloves, raincoats and other waterproof outer garments, and women's handbags and purses. Labor-intensive items, rather than capital-intensive items, have a tendency to be imported from countries with a large supply of workers and a low per-unit labor cost for such production.

Annual survey results of sales level, sales per square foot of space, usual markups, markdowns, and stock turnovers for various types of women's clothing items in large department stores are reported in *Seventeen* magazine. A prospective operator of a women's specialty shop selling a broad range or a specialized range of items could learn a great deal from studying the results of the annual survey. For example, the average markup on the items is about 51% to 52%, meaning that an item that cost $27 would be offered for about $55. Markdowns occurred on about 28% of the items, on balance, including sales to employees (where a 10% discount is not unusual), bringing the gross profit margin, on average, to 42%. The average stock turnover per year is about 3.6 times. Some aggressive companies do not wish to carry over from one year to another the lines of merchandise that might be replaced with other more fashionable items. Uniforms, however, do not usually change from year to year and might not be marked down during the year. An inventory reduction sale, near the end of a given selling season, will usually see most items marked down a certain rate of the initial offering price, such as 25% or 30% below nationally advertised price. Unsold lots, after a few days of the sale, may be reduced in price again. On balance, about one-fourth of the gross profit margin from original pricing erodes with markdowns. Some stores attempt to carry a wide array of offerings while others with more limited display space or available resources limit their offerings to the more rapidly moving items.

Prospects for the retail apparel stores are mixed for the 1993 to 2000 period, according to estimates made by the Bureau of Domestic Commerce (*U.S. Industrial Outlook*) and the Department of Labor. The latter federal agency estimates employment to gain about 1.5% yearly in SIC code 56 from 1993 to 2000, compared to a 1972 to 1986 annual growth rate of about 2.25%. The need for employees is not likely to be uniform across firms that cater to different age groups, however, as the ratio of women from 20 to 34 years of age should decline by about 15% over the years 1986 to 2005. Those from ages 35 to 64 should grow by close to 38%. In addition, more of the young females, ages 16 to 19, are likely to enter the labor force as the overall rate of unemployment hovers around current levels of about 5.6%.

Several negative trends have been present in the retail apparel industry for the years 1970 to 1993. More women have entered the labor force, but a large number of them wear pants rather than dresses. Thus a firm must keep abreast of the trend toward certain types of items growing in popularity while others decline. There was also a growing trend toward the casual lifestyle, with a smaller fraction of working women spending the extra funds to buy the latest fashion of clothing. Imports have continued to rise but at a decreasing rate, as prices on items manufactured abroad have lost some of their competitive advantage as the value of the dollar in foreign trade has declined over much of the past 15 years. Sales of bridalwear has declined about 2% yearly for several years, reflecting the smaller number of females moving into the prime marrying age (18 to 30).

Apparel sales were up about 5% in 1993 over 1992 levels. Some apparel manufacturers were carrying their items from city sources to rural outlets and providing van or trunk shows to sales representatives of the client firms. Some foreign investors, especially in Japan, have begun to buy into American retail outlets for clothing. Men's clothing sales were growing faster than those for females during the recent past.

Market Opportunities in Various-Sized Communities

Part of every business venture is the business plan. An integral part of the business plan, the market analysis, is of primary importance. Doing a market analysis will tell the prospective entrepreneur if the neighborhood to be served can logically support the proposed venture, the expected level of sales, types and level of competition, and other information necessary to make it as a successful business.

Conducting a market analysis can be simple or complex. Sources of information about local or regional demographics can be obtained from the local chamber of commerce, governing bodies, U.S. Census Bureau, state agencies, some not-for-profit groups, large utility firms, commercial research companies, small-business development centers, and public libraries.

A retail apparel store exists for about every 3,000 persons in the United States. Roughly 4,500 persons, or about 2,000 females, support each women's and misses' apparel store. Many small communities do not have a department store, but the residents must instead travel 30 to 100 miles to a regional shopping mall. A community of about 3,000 to 5,000 persons would not very well support more than one women's or family apparel retail store. Greater density of such stores will likely provide below-average profits on invested assets at the location. Some retail apparel stores operate a mail order business for patrons of other ages than those served by merchandise carried in the store's inventory.

In many communities, more retail apparel stores attempt to operate than can reasonably be supported by the demographics. It is important for the aggressive store manager to attempt to differentiate his or her establishment from others as much as possible. Market research into the demographics of the population within a radius of about 20 to 30 miles from the store may safeguard the firm from being stuck with excessive amounts of merchandise that are designed for other ages of patrons, or those of larger or smaller sizes. Some business persons owning similar stores located in various nearby communities are able to transfer off-sizes of merchandise to other communities and receive better response. Large utility firms (electric and telecommunication) may have community profiles containing this valuable information.

Advertising on a local radio station, a nearby television channel, or in the regional newspaper may attract shopping patrons to the store. Attractive displays and friendly, helpful sales clerks are needed to finalize the sale. More advertising dollars are spent in March (promoting Easter sales), in April and May (promoting prom or graduation apparel), and in August and September (promoting back-to-school wear) than in other months. January, February, and December, in that order, are months of lowest monthly spending of the advertising dollars. Mailers are often sent to prior customers and holders of department store credit cards.

Franchising

Franchising does not appear to be popular or very important in the retail apparel industry.

Development and Site Requirements

A retail store is a commercial establishment, and before a building to house one is leased or constructed, it is necessary that the owner ascertain that it is zoned properly and can meet the various rules and regulations of the local zoning commission and the fire department that enforces safety requirements.

Several factors are important in site selection. In order to minimize the risks of owning and operating a business, little should be invested in fixed assets until the firm is well established in the community. This means that most begin small and operate out of leased quarters from busy shopping centers.

The smaller of the independent retail apparel stores are located in busy shopping malls. Some of the larger ones are located on busily traveled streets in downtown shopping areas. A good location would be near some complementary-type firms, but not one that offers a nearly identical line of merchandise. Women tend to shop more for the merchandise they buy, checking out the items for fit, color, and quality of materials. Men tend to be less fussy about the items they buy, often shopping for color but paying less attention to fashion or price.

If a mall or strip center location is chosen, the tenant mix of the neighboring establishments is very important. Nearby clothing stores generate traffic and boost sales but preferably complementary rather than competing ones. A store that sells dresses and jackets is aided by a nearby store that sells fashionable shoes and purses, and vice versa.

Lighting, interior design, and creative displays of attractive merchandise are increasingly influential. The decor of the store, including background music, should fit the proposed clientele. Rock music might attract the younger patrons, but it would be avoided by older adults, for example. Classics would be enjoyed by most older adults.

Window displays are functional, and they serve as advertising as well as creating an awareness of what lines are currently being carried by the store. Window displays remind customers that fashions and seasons are changing and that their wardrobes may be slightly out of date. Developing such a response may lead to the promotion of in-season sales.

Evening and weekend hours are required in this business. A large percentage of families have two income earners that do their shopping on evenings and weekends. Location on well-lighted streets where other businesses are also open, or in shopping malls that keep evening hours until about 9:00 or 9:30 p.m., is typical. Monday through Saturday hours, as well as Sunday afternoons, are typical for this type of business. Location near a large department store or a large, heavily patronized supermarket is sometimes an aid in drawing a large crowd of shoppers into the apparel store. Some of the retail apparel stores have attempted to offer limited babysitting service to children of shopping patrons. While this could increase sales, a liability is assumed should the children become ill or injured while in the care of the store's employees.

Each square foot of space in the women's apparel section of department stores in the early 1990s should have had annual sales of about $150 to $160.

For the average of large department stores, annual sales of apparel departments averaged about $48,000 per employee in 1982. Adjusted for cost of living increases of 4% yearly, this approaches $75,000 per employee in terms of 1993 prices. Thus, a store with sales of $300,000 should be able to support one owner/manager plus about four additional employees. When applying a dollar figure of $150 in annual sales per square foot of display space, a store of 2,000 square feet would be justified. Thus, a store of 40 feet by 50 feet or equivalent should produce this level of sales.

Cost and Types of Assets Needed to Start a Business

Starting a business can be an expensive endeavor. The retail apparel business is somewhat capital intensive, as monies are needed to support daily activities (cash), to stock inventories, to carry receivables, and for investment into equipment, leasehold improvement, or building ownership.

Monies to operate a retail apparel business might be a mix of owners' equity (about 45% to 65% is common), short-term trade and other payables, bank borrowing, state or federal business funding programs, and the like. A prudent mix of owners' and borrowed funds should be sought.

Several sources of industry-wide common-sized financial statements and key financial ratios are available. Dun & Bradstreet, Inc., in *Industry Norms and Key Business Ratios*, Robert L. Morris Associates' *Statement Studies*, and the statements published for unincorporated and corporate firms by the Internal Revenue Service provide such insights. D & B data are based on firms on which D & B gathers credit information, including comparative financial statements. RLM bases its data collection on statements filed with association member commercial banks as a part of their loan requests. The IRS provides certain key information from unincorporated business persons based on Schedule C data or on corporate returns filed by incorporated businesses.

Common-sized financial statements are provided for SIC codes 5611, 5621, 5641, and 5651 with median data of more than 1,300 firms in each of the four SIC groups, based on 1993 and 1994 (as reported by D & B).

	SIC 5611 Men's	SIC 5621 Women's	SIC 5641 Children's	SIC 5651 Family
ASSETS				
Cash and near-cash	13.4%	16.6%	14.9%	15.9%
Accounts and notes receivable	7.1	7.3	3.5	7.5
Inventories	57.2	51.4	59.3	51.9
Other current assets	3.3	3.4	2.8	3.9
Total current assets	81.0	78.7	80.5	79.2
Fixed assets (net)	11.7	13.5	12.7	12.1
Intangible and other assets	7.3	7.8	6.8	8.7
Total assets	100.0	100.0	100.0	100.0
DEBTS AND NET WORTH				
Trade payables	13.1	10.2	10.4	9.1
Notes payable	4.4	4.5	5.4	3.6
Other current debts	10.5	11.1	11.3	8.6
Total current debts	28.0	25.8	27.1	21.3
Long-term debts	9.0	9.9	9.9	9.4
Deferred credit	—	—	—	.1
Net worth	63.0	64.3	63.0	69.2
Total debts and net worth	100.0	100.0	100.0	100.0
Total debts and net worth	$217,000	$135,000	$106,000	$291,000

A study of the above common-sized balance sheet items leads one to the following conclusions. For the median companies in the survey, current assets amount to about 79% to 81% of total assets, meaning that a large majority of the firms are operating from leased quarters. Fixed assets, net of depreciation, ranged from 11% to 13% of total assets, with the investments largely being in store fixtures, such as display racks and cash registers. Intangible assets, consisting of such items as capitalized organization costs, trade names, leaseholds or leasehold improvements, amounted to a slim percentage of total assets for this type of firm, suggesting that most were leasing the facilities on a continuing (year-to-year) basis and doing little remodeling to the facilities. Other noncurrent assets are often long-term investments in subsidiary firms. Some of the companies may own land on which a future building site is planned. Others may have had some investment in stocks of supplier firms or the like.

Let us assume that a prospective entrepreneur has $60,000 to invest in the equity of a women's clothing store. According to the common-sized financial statement, this should support about $100,000 in assets, as the $60,000 in inventories would be partially offset by about $18,000 in trade payables. Notes payable (bank or other current notes) would, on balance, provide close to $10,000 in funds. Another $10,000 might be a combination of wages, interest, and taxes payable. Long-term debts are small in this type of concern.

Business ratios are of several types. One type refers to a common-sized balance sheet (shown above), another to a common-sized (percentage) income statement of expenses. Still another usage of the term is key financial ratios, constructed from balance sheets and income statements, such as solvency, efficiency, and profitability ratios. The latter concept is illustrated in this section of the business profile.

Each year, Prentice-Hall, Inc., provides an update of the expense ratios for about 400 different types of businesses. This information is published in the *Almanac of Business and Industry Financial Ratios*. From the 1993 edition, the following were given for the smallest two size categories (of about 12) for apparel and accessory stores. The study is based on information collected by the Internal Revenue Service on corporate income tax returns.

	Under $100,000 Assets	$100,000–$250,000 Assets
Cost of operations	56.0%	59.6%
Compensation of officers	6.5	3.8
Repairs	.2	.2
Bad debts	.1	.1
Rent on business property	7.8	9.3
Taxes (excluding federal tax)	2.5	2.2
Interest	.8	.7
Depreciation/depletion/amortization	1.9	.9
Advertising	2.0	1.8
Pension and benefits	.6	—
Other expenses	18.3	15.9
Net before-tax profit	3.5	5.4

The cost of operations is equivalent to the cost of goods sold. This means that the average markup (on sales), net of markdowns on the items, is about 44% in the smallest category and 41% in the other category. The second-largest expenditure is for labor and payroll taxes, shown above in the "other expenses" category. Rent amounts to about 7% to 9% in many retail apparel stores. Most such stores are located in rented quarters. The depreciation would be on store shelves, office equipment, and so on.

Key financial ratios are sometimes helpful to the prospective entrepreneur in monitoring the financial health of the firm or in developing projected financial statements. The following were provided by the 1994 edition of D & B's *Industry Norms and Key Business Ratios*, for four types of apparel stores:

	Men's	Women's	Children's	Family
Solvency ratios:				
Quick ratio (median)	.7:1	1.0:1	.6:1	1.1:1
Current ratio (current assets/current liabilities)	3.4:1	3.8:1	3.9:1	5.2:1
Debt to net worth	43%	37%	41%	29%
Efficiency ratios:				
Collection period (days)	12.4	11.3	6.6	11.0
Sales to inventory (times)	3.7	5.0	4.1	3.9
Assets to sales	47.5%	39.2%	40.4%	50.8%
Profitability ratios:				
Gross profit on sales	38.4%	36.4%	35.2%	35.0%
Before-tax profit on sales	4.2%	4.0%	4.8%	4.3%
After-tax return on net worth	12.3%	12.9%	14.7%	10.4%

The investor of $60,000 in the women's apparel firm with assets of $100,000 should expect, on average, sales of $250,000 (i.e., sales 2.5 times as large as assets), and officers' compensation equivalent to 5% of $250,000 or $12,500. Return (before taxes) on the $60,000 equity of 12% should produce another $7,200 in profits. Thus, a store of this size might support one owner and about three other personnel, each earning an average of about $9,300 (in terms of 1993 dollars), according to *County Business Patterns* information. Such stores often pay about 6% to 8.5% of revenues as rent. The gross profit on sales of 41% means that the hypothetical firm with $250,000 in annual sales should pay $250,000 × 59% or about $147,000 for merchandise sold and have some $103,000 to cover all other expenses (including the compensation for the firm's officers) and generate $7,200 in profits for the owner. Thus, careful budgeting of expenses in this and any small firm is very important.

D & B's information suggests that children's apparel retail stores earn somewhat more profits, for each dollar invested by owners, than do men's or women's apparel stores. Family apparel stores are less profitable, stocking some items for each sex and age group family member and generally having a blend of these ratios for the other three groups of stores.

Legal Considerations The owner/operator of a retail establishment must make sure that it is operated in accordance with law. This means that local zoning requirements must be met, a selling license must be obtained (locally or at the state level), and a federal employer identification number (FEIN) must be obtained so that payroll taxes may be properly accounted for.

An owner/manager of a retail apparel store should seek professional help in several areas. The services of an accountant should be sought in determining an appropriate form of organization (i.e., in order to minimize the tax burden), and for the development of an effective system of merchandise management accounting. Payroll accounting records and inventory records are important for this type of concern.

Roughly 58% of the firms in this industry incorporate, about 7% operate as partnerships, and most of the balance are single proprietorships. The corporations tend to be several times as large as the single proprietorships, in terms of outlets, sales, and employees. For example, the corporations have an average paid workforce of 24 compared to 3 for the single proprietorship.

The advice of an attorney should be sought in certain areas, such as incorporating the firm, evaluating a franchise contract, buying real property, developing or reviewing the terms of important contracts, handling leases or sales of real property, handling liquidation or bankruptcy problems, and in bringing or defending a suit against a third party.

Adequate commercial insurance coverage is necessary for the manager/owner of a retail apparel store. Even in rented quarters, fire insurance on inventory and other fixed assets should be maintained. Coverage of theft, loss, or vandalism should be carried. If large amounts of cash are kept on hand, fidelity insurance to protect against embezzlement by employees is desirable. Liability insurance covering injury to patrons on the premises and lawsuits by, possibly, patrons falsely accused of shoplifting should be considered. Workers' compensation insurance for job-related injury to employees is required in many states. Last of all, care should be taken to ensure that advertising campaigns are not fraudulent.

Experience and Training Requirements

The owner/manager of a retail apparel store should have some experience in merchandising and buying product lines to be sold. An experienced owner should be able to train other assistants on the job.

Knowledge of fashions and particularly buying fashionable items is crucial, especially since many apparel lines are purchased two to three seasons ahead of intended sale. Thus, attendance at trade fairs is important for the buyers of merchandise. Accurate inventory and sales records should be maintained in order to document popular sizes, colors, styles, and so on, in order to avoid inventory buildup and forced markdowns of low-demand items.

Sales personnel should be friendly and knowledgeable about the products being sold. Preferably, they should be of the same gender and about the same age as usual patrons. Extra services are sometimes helpful in promoting increased sales by a retail apparel establishment. These may include free delivery, mail order at similar costs, free minor alterations, material repair, custom ordering, layaway, free coffee, or free child-care for shoppers.

Keys to Successful Management

As experience is gained, the owner/manager of a retail apparel store should develop strategies that tend to increase sales and promote return by previous patrons. The following list is suggested for consideration.

1. Consistency is important. The store should establish a certain style of clothing and stick with the plan that promotes a feeling of continuity and confidence in the prospective clientele. It is also helpful to target the

desired market before stocking a store (i.e., elderly fashions, teen fashions, upscale apparel, large-size apparel, off-price discounting, etc.). It is also advantageous to carry certain lines of apparel and advertise those brand names for recognition value and consistency. Breadth of choice is a plus, if space and capital of the owner permit this, as patrons prefer to shop at one store for several items rather than to shop from store to store.

2. Markup is often greater on accessories, such as jewelry, belts, shoes, socks, ties, purses, wallets, colognes, scarves, shoe polish, and so on, than on apparel items. Stocking a wide array of accessories may permit the sale of several items to one customer, thus increasing total sales to the firm.

3. Pricing is very important. The policy should be consistent from season to season. Most establishments drop prices about five cents below a dollar figure, such as $13.95. This figure sounds like a lower charge than $14.00. Sales taxes are added at the point of sale.

4. Acceptance of checks from well-known customers, or credit cards from strong underwriting organizations, is a must. Few women carry cash when shopping, but prefer to pay for purchases with charge cards or checks.

Information Sources   Several sources of information are helpful to the prospective entrepreneur in retail apparel. These include associations, directories of retail lines, magazines, ratio studies, investment services, and government documents. A representative list appears in each periodic update of *Encyclopedia of Business Information Sources*, published by Gale Research, Inc., Detroit, Mich.

Restaurants

Business Type,
Industry
Characteristics and
Prospects

Eating and drinking places are categorized under SIC code 581. Eating places, including restaurants, are assigned SIC code 5812. Many of these establishments serve both food and alcoholic beverages, although establishments that are exclusively drinking places fall under SIC code 5813. SIC 581 (eating and drinking places) is part of the retail trade sector and includes retail establishments that sell prepared foods and drinks on premise. Lunch counters and refreshment stands are also included in this group.

Restaurants, lunch counters, and drinking places operated as part of a service facility and leased by outside operators (e.g., eating or drinking places operated by hotels; eating places operated by department stores; mobile food and dairy wagons; and bars and restaurants owned and operated by civic, social, and fraternal associations) do not fall within the above industry group classification.

The industry may be further broken down into descriptive types of services and menus provided, such as family-style restaurants, cafeteria operations, hamburger chains and other fast-food vendors, specialty restaurants (such as seafood exclusively), ethnic restaurants (Greek, Chinese, Italian, soul), et al.

Estimated (National Restaurant Association) breakdowns of estimated restaurant food sales from 1991 through 1993 are shown in the following schedule, with amounts in billions of dollars:

	1991	1992	1993[P]
Fuller-service restaurants	$ 78.4	$ 80.3	$ 83.5
Limited menu restaurants	71.9	75.6	80.2
Commercial cafeterias	4.4	4.5	4.5
Social caterers	2.4	2.5	2.7
Ice cream/frozen custard stands	2.3	2.4	2.6
Bars/taverns	9.4	9.2	9.3
Subtotal commercial eating/drinking places	$168.7	$174.5	$182.9
Food contractors	N/A	15.5	16.4
Lodging places	N/A	15.2	16.0
Other commercial sales	N/A	20.3	21.3
Total commercial food services	$217.9	$225.5	$236.5

	1991	1992	1993ᵖ
Institutional food services	27.5	28.3	29.9
Military food services	1.1	1.2	1.2
Grand total U.S. food services	$246.5	$254.9	$267.6

Source: Standard & Poor's Industry Survey, 1993, L45. Reprinted by permission of Standard & Poor's, a division of McGraw-Hill, Inc.

ᵖPreliminary.

Fuller-service and limited menu restaurants were about 65% of the total.

The restaurant industry is noted for the large number of yearly start-ups with an almost equal number of closures. In many communities, market saturation (too many restaurants) leads to intense competition with corresponding pressures on promoting cut-rate pricing and thin profit margins. The 1% annual increase in U.S. population was much too small to support an increase in restaurant outlets by the major restaurant chains of approximately 10% annually during the 1980s. The rate of expansion in family-type restaurant chains (especially from 1986 to 1988) has been above this average. Hamburger chains have been expanding below this average in the United States and moving instead into various foreign countries. Independently owned and operated restaurants, of course, must compete with the franchised chains for the limited number of customers and a limited commitment of funds to eating out. A periodic Department of Commerce Study, *Franchise Opportunity Handbook*, lists more than 200 franchisers in the restaurant industry. In 1992, the top six franchisers in the industry, in terms of annual sales, appeared to be McDonald's, Burger King, Hardee's, Pizza Hut, Kentucky Fried Chicken, and Wendy's. The next six were Taco Bell, Domino's Pizza, Dairy Queen, Little Caesar's Pizza, Red Lobster, and Denny's. The reader may wish to refer to *Leisure Time*, Mar. 11, 1993.

Even though severe competition reigns in the industry, it is likely to continue to see new restaurants opened in most intermediate- to large-sized cities each year, with others simultaneously closed for lack of patronage or bad management. On a national basis, large chains or franchised restaurants have seen profit margins and returns on equity decline. In 1988, according to *Value Line*, such firms were earning about 14% to 15% on equity capital, down from 17.5% some five years earlier. Profits are much better than this level at many restaurants, though about 20% of the enterprises lose money in most years. It is likely that intense competition will continue in this line of business due to over-expansion. Another factor that squeezed profits in the industry were the increases in the minimum wage rate in 1990 and 1991. The industry is known for being labor intensive, with a majority of the part-time workers paid near minimum wage, with few fringes and having moderate to high employee turnover.

Essential to the start-up of any new business is an analysis of the market that will support the new venture. The prospective restauranteur should assess the community's potential to support his or her business by evaluating the size, lifestyle, income, education, age levels, and competition in the targeted community. Local utility companies (electric and telephone) and certain marketing services may have developed a recent community profile that will prove helpful in determining geographic areas with potential for profitable business additions. Prospective owners with financial resources may employ the services of a marketing research firm to conduct a market survey and analysis. However, many prospective owners are not able to contract for such services and will have to do the research themselves. Excellent sources to contact would include the local chamber of commerce, local small-business development centers, community colleges and universities, local or regional libraries, trade associations, local newspapers, the research and development units of city and county economic development departments, the U.S. Department of Commerce (census reports), and state agencies designed to promote a healthy business climate.

In addition to studying profile data, statistical reports, and research studies to obtain a better understanding of the community, client population, and competition, the prospective business owner might elect to conduct a mail, telephone, or direct contact survey. Many marketing consultants would caution against using a mail survey technique exclusively because of the low response rate. However, when used in conjunction with a follow-up telephone survey, the combined approach could yield valuable information. Direct contact might be in the form of visiting local business and commercial establishments in the general vicinity of the prospective restaurant site to discern perceived service gaps and listen to potential customer opinions. Visiting eating establishments in the area will also provide first-hand opportunity to critique the competition.

National figures suggest that an average, total personal income of about $10 million, an average population base of about 700 persons, and an employee force of 15 workers are average for a restaurant. Thus, a city of 70,000 population with average per capita personal income could reasonably be expected to support about 100 eating and drinking establishments.

Inexperience in these areas may dictate exploration of franchise opportunities where such policies are already well established. Training in personnel is handled differently for franchised and owner/manager businesses. The latter are likely to advertise and attempt to hire employees with some past relevant experience. On-the-job training is often given for part-time, previously inexperienced personnel, with wages paid very near the minimum wage scale for other than cooks. Cooks seem to justify a job premium of one-third to one-half above that earned by hostesses, waiters/waitresses, buspersons, dishwashers, and so forth. A planned opening for a franchise operation may require an on-site training period of a few days by the new workers for the jobs they will be doing when the firm opens for business. Experienced managers and assistant managers from nearby locations may serve as the training faculty, or management staff of the franchising firm may provide the leadership.

The large chain restaurants on the above list operate substantially as franchised operations. It has been estimated that only one in five franchised firms fail during the first five years of formation compared to four in five from independently operated ones. The main reasons for this difference are the financial investment required of the franchisee by the franchising firm, joint advertising, and aid in management provided by the franchisor. For example, McDonald's may require between $250,000 and $350,000 to be invested in such a new start-up.

Development and Site Requirements One of the first steps a prospective restaurateur should take, after identifying a location for the new eating establishment, is to check with the local zoning office to determine if the site meets local zoning requirements. Commercial zoning is required for such a business, and a new business owner should not commit funds to buying property or leasing a facility until this determination is made. Other pertinent development considerations might include checking with the local or county planning and economic development departments on current and future plans for the area [e.g., is the area targeted for community development improvements; are there future plans in the works for facade, street, and/or sidewalk improvements; are there zoning changes planned for the area (from commercial to industrial, etc.), are there plans being made for major traffic rerouting or street repairs, etc.]. Obviously, traffic rerouting or long-term closing of a service street may adversely affect the willingness or ability of clients to patronize the business.

Whether located in a central business district, along a commercial strip, in a shopping mall, or on a neighborhood boulevard, the restaurant site should have high visibility to attract customers. Ideally, the restaurant should be in a location where pedestrian and vehicle traffic is steady and constant, although some of the most exclusive and highly profitable restaurants can be found in locations of moderate visibility and traffic flow. These establishments are of high profile and long standing, attracting their customer base from years of quality five-star service. Since new restaurants must attract and build followings, a prime location is key to their success.

The ideal site would have easy access and exit. The parking lot, or nearby lots open to public parking, should be adequate to meet high customer density during lunch and dinner hours and heavier-than-normal customer traffic on weekends and holidays. The new owner of a fast-food restaurant may want to consider providing a drive-up window to service customers and to plan for the additional lot space requirement to include this feature. The outside physical appearance of the restaurant should be attractive and appealing to the eye. Signage, which is the first visual advertisement of the establishment to the public, should be eye catching in size and design. The design itself can signify to customers the type of establishment they are entering (quiet elegance, family dining, sporty, casual, etc.). The size, lighting, and inset of the sign should comply with local ordinances.

The design and layout of the facility must meet with local health and safety requirements, including fire, electrical, plumbing, and sanitation codes. Fire exits and occupancy limits must be in accordance with local and state regulations. The fire department should be contacted about the proper wiring, maximum crowd permitted, fire door markings, flame suppression system, venting, door locks, and emergency lighting (battery-operated exit signs, for example). The new business owner must obtain necessary building permits to make physical improvements inside and outside the facility. If the facility is leased by the owner, leasehold improvements must be specified in the lease agreement. Local health and safety inspectors will have to grant official approval that the above standards have been met and the facility is safe to house the business operation.

Inside table space should be adequate to handle the flow of traffic during moderate to heavy customer traffic conditions. Cleanliness of the facilities, including public restrooms, is a must. The food preparation area of a full-service restaurant is normally to the side or rear of the establishment, and is off-limits to other than employees, delivery persons, and inspectors. The serving area of a fast-food vendor is usually to the front of the establishment, with the kitchen, or cooking area, just behind it. Both the serving area and the kitchen should be clean and well ventilated so as to void offensive odors of burning grease and so on. The serving persons and cooks frequently wear bright (or white) uniforms or aprons so as to add to the look of cleanliness. These should be changed as needed to avoid appearances of staining or uncleanliness. Food handlers frequently wear a cap to avoid hair falling into the food being prepared or served.

Cost and Types of Assets Needed to Start the Business

Two sources of composite balance sheets for a large number of business firms include those published by Robert L. Morris Associates in the annual *Statement Studies* and by Dun & Bradstreet, Inc., in *Industry Norms and Key Business Ratios*. The former provides ratios for different sizes of firms, while the D & B source provides industry mean comparative statements plus some quartile ratios.

The amount of investment capital needed to open a restaurant depends on the size of the planned structure, location, ownership versus leasing of the building and equipment, and the general lavishness of the facility. The figure may run from $50,000 for a small neighborhood restaurant to more than $1,000,000.

The common-sized SIC 5812 percentage balance sheet as shown in the 1993 D & B source is as follows:

Assets		Debts and Net Worth	
Cash and near-cash	17.1%	Accounts payable	9.8%
Accounts receivable	4.2	Bank loans	.1
Notes receivable	.9	Notes payable	3.5
Inventory	7.4	Other current debts	16.7
Other current assets	6.2	Total current debts	30.1
Total current assets	35.8	Long-term debts	25.8
Fixed assets	41.5	Deferred credit	.2
Other noncurrent assets	22.7	Net worth	43.9
Total assets	100.0	Total debts and net worth	100.0
		Total net worth	$119,300

The cash includes such things as petty cash, demand deposits, negotiable order withdrawal (check drafting) accounts, and so forth. Since most restaurants accept major charge cards, the accounts receivable are the charge slips (or charges to institutional accounts such as hospitals or school clients) not yet processed or collected. Inventory includes investment in food stuffs and paper or plastic products supplies used for service. Other current assets include prepayments of interest, rent, taxes, and the like. Fixed assets include the investment in land, buildings, equipment, and so on (less depreciation). Other noncurrent assets are for things such as leases, leasehold improvements, trade names, goodwill, and other miscellaneous assets not above classified.

Most of the liability items are self-explanatory. Trade payables are for food items or supplies purchased. Other current debt includes such things as accrued wages, accrued payroll taxes, and other payables. Net worth as a percentage of total assets, or owners' equity, is normally somewhat smaller for small firms than for large ones. About 50% is average for most retailers, but small eating places have slightly thinner capital while drinking places tend to run about 55% in net worth.

In order to stretch limited capital and to reduce risk of asset loss, the beginning nonfranchised restaurant usually opens from leased facilities. If major renovations are needed, the leasehold may be made for 5 or 10 years with the leasehold improvement expenditure being amortized (i.e., expensed) over the life of the lease. Permission of the property owner should be obtained before making the needed renovations. Paving off-street parking areas and drive-up window lanes, if desired, are additional capital improvements. The grand opening (including such expenses as advertising, guest appearances, prizes, and labor for excessive numbers of employees) may run several thousand dollars. Working capital runs about 19% of annual sales in this industry, on average.

For a newly formed restaurant with a planned asset base of $100,000, some 35% to 40% of the assets would likely be allocated to tangible fixed items such as equipment and furnishings, another 35% to working capital (largely cash and inventories), and a lessor amount invested in leasehold and leasehold improvements.

A start-up firm is usually financed with the savings of the owner(s) and perhaps loans from family members. As inventories are bought and workers are hired, current debts run a portion of the asset accounts, perhaps 50% to 75% as great as the current assets. As the firm grows in size in terms of sales and assets, private investment sources include retained profits, bank loans, venture capital firms, small-business investment companies, and partners or other shareholders brought into the firm as owners. Public investment sources include the Small Business Administration and some local or regional development organizations.

Typical Business Ratios According to published figures by D & B, eating places (SIC 5812) in 1993 had mean sales of $1,031,000, gross profits of 52%, and after-tax net profit of 3.8%. With net worth averaging $119,000 and total assets of $271,700, the asset turnover for such a firm was about 3.4 times per year. The turnover ratio and profitability ratio at many chain restaurants have improved over the past few years, thanks substantially to the growing eating-out habits of young single adults and retired persons.

The Internal Revenue Service provides a breakdown of expenses for major SIC classifications for all firms in the category and for those earning a profit. So does the National Restaurant Association (NRA). The following is an expense breakdown by kind of restaurant reported for 1991 by NRA.

	Full Menu/ Table Service	Limited Menu/ Table Service	Limited Menu/ No Table Service	Cafeterias
Revenues (percent):				
Food sales	79.7	84.4	94.3	95.0
Beverage sales	18.1	13.9	5.2	3.1
Other	2.2	1.7	.5	1.9
Costs (percentage of revenues):				
Food items	27.6	30.0	31.6	33.8
Beverages	5.1	3.8	.6	1.2
Payroll	28.3	25.0	24.1	31.1
Employee benefits	4.5	3.2	2.8	4.3
Rent	4.9	5.5	6.5	4.1
Marketing	2.2	3.2	4.2	2.7
Utilities	2.8	3.0	3.3	2.3
Depreciation	2.5	2.4	2.3	2.5
Repairs/maintenance	1.9	1.7	1.7	1.5
Administrative and general	3.7	3.4	2.1	3.7
Interest	.9	.9	1.1	.7
Other	11.2	10.5	11.8	9.8
Total	95.6	92.6	92.1	97.7
Pretax profit	4.4	7.4	7.9	2.3

A review of the expense and pretax profit breakdown shows that limited menu restaurants tend to be somewhat more profitable than those that offer full menus or cafeterias.

In a successful restaurant, the food and supplies should not run more than about 28% to 33% of total revenues. Labor costs should be about 25% to 32%, and careful cost control is needed on many of the other items so as to preserve a fair profit margin.

For the typical restaurant, annual sales run about 1.5 to 3.5 times the size of assets, with the higher ratio generally applying to fast-food vendors. Asset turnovers have been increasing during recent years, suggesting more operations involved in leased facilities and more catering to high-volume, low-profit menu items.

Median ratios as reported by D & B for 1993 for SIC 5812 were as follows:

Solvency ratios:
Quick ratio	.6:1
Current ratio	1.2:1
Total debts to net worth	87.3%

Efficiency ratios:
Collection period	3.7 days
Sales to inventory	73.7 times
Assets to sales	28.5%

Profitability ratios:
Return on sales	3.3%
Return on net worth	21.2%

Legal Considerations A new business owner has many legal requirements to consider when starting a new enterprise. First there is the legal form of the business—will it be legally incorporated and registered with the state as a corporation, or will it operate as a sole proprietorship, a regular partnership, or a limited partnership? Within most states the secretary of state is the legally designated official to handle business registration and incorporation administrative matters. The state attorney general is responsible for prosecutory matters. The services of an experienced attorney should be retained to handle this and any other ongoing or periodic legal considerations pertaining to the business.

Licensing and registration of restaurants are required at both the state and local levels in many locations. One employee must often be certified by the department of public health under the management certification program. The firm must also register with the state's department of revenue if it plans to hire employees and sell at retail, including registering for unemployment compensation, before hiring employees. The state liquor control commission processes applications to sell liquor in many states. City councils or county officials may need to approve the issuance of a liquor license. Other local license requirements include inspection of facilities and operating permits. The municipal clerk (city or county) and municipal health departments should be contacted for their requirements. The local fire department controls safety inspections, such as the number of restrooms, fire exits, maximum crowds, and so forth. Information may be provided by trade associations and local chambers of commerce.

An appropriate tax planning and general accounting system should be designed by a knowledgeable accountant.

The prospective restaurateur should consult with a knowledgeable insurance agent on the appropriate insurance coverage for the new business, receiving competitive bids from at least two. A comprehensive insurance package for the new business might include the following, although resources might not permit the entire package:

1. Fire insurance: To cover damage to the premises, equipment and inventory loss caused by acts of humans or nature.

2. Liability insurance: To cover protecting the restaurant from financial loss due to claims of bodily injury or property damage that occur in connection with its operation.

3. Fidelity bonding: To cover employees handling cash receipts and other business funds, to guarantee against loss from embezzlement.

4. Crime coverage: To reimburse the business owner for losses due to robbery, burglary, vandalism, or employee pilfering.

5. Automobile coverage: For liability and comprehensive coverage of automobiles used for the business.

6. Worker's compensation: To cover injuries and loss of pay related to employee accidents on the job; mandatory in many states.

7. Business owner's life insurance: To cover loss to financial lenders in the event of the owner's death and/or provide funds for surviving partners to buy a decedent's interest in the firm.

8. Business interruption insurance: To compensate for revenues lost during a temporary halt in business caused by fire, theft, or illness.

9. Executive liability/decision-making insurance: To protect the business owner from personal financial ruin and to protect the business assets in the event of lawsuits being brought because of business decisions or actions.

Experience and
Training Required

An owner/operator must be knowledgeable in not only food preparation but in personnel hiring/firing/training, accounting, finance, cost control, advertising, and general management. Most restaurants are operated with a full-time manager, two full-time assistant managers, one or more full-time cooks, and several part-time persons who perform as assistant cooks, waiters/waitresses, and counter personnel.

The state or city requirement may mandate that at least one of the managers be certified as having completed a training program. For example, the Chicago City Wide College offers a food services sanitation program running for 10 weeks. The 25-hour course was $130.00 and offered 2.5 hours of college credit (in 1989).

The managers and assistant managers are usually experienced in operating a restaurant. After performing as assistant cook for several months, or having similar experience with other firms, such assistants may be promoted to cook. Other employees are usually trained on the job by experienced personnel. A weekly training session when the firm is not open for business is customary.

Key to Successful Management

Proper marketing is one of the most important factors that contributes to the success or failure of a restaurant business. A successful restaurant usually differentiates itself from the competition—emphasizing what is unique and desirable about its concept (type of food, menu, interior design, service, cost, entertainment) that will attract and keep customers.

Spot television commercials, radio ads, yellow page listings, and newspaper ads are all used to alert potential customers of services being offered.

Personnel and operating management are similarly important to the success of such an undertaking. Some of the areas of concern are:

1. Working capital. Experience dictates that a successful new enterprise will lose money the first year, with about 15% of the start-up capital being the average loss. Break-even may be reached the second year, with profits conceivably earned thereafter through conscientious cost control.

2. Advertising. Plan to stick to a designed image, be consistent and repetitive, and treat the expense as a fixed cost.

3. Employee training. Service people and counter help (cash register operators) represent a restaurant's front line of contact with the customer. They should be courteous, helpful, and diligent in providing timely service.

4. On-premise management. This is crucial. Owners and operators can expect to spend 10 to 14 hours daily in attending to decisions that are critical to the business and that cannot be delegated to another. Family members may share the load. Many restaurants close on Mondays so as to give management a break.

5. Cleanliness. This is probably the number one criterion by which patrons initially judge an establishment (i.e., absence of waste on tables and floor; absence of flies, roaches, and other pests; and cleanliness of uniforms worn by employees).

6. Portion control. The cost of goods sold needs to be maintained at a profitable level.

Information Sources Many sources of information are available on the eating/drinking types of businesses. This long list includes trade associations, magazines, government documents, investment services, and various directories. The prospective restaurant owner might wish to consult the periodic update of *Encyclopedia of Business Information Sources* by Gale Research, Inc., Detroit, Mich., for such data.

Catalog and Mail Order Houses

Business Types, Industry Characteristics and Prospects

Catalog and mail order firms have been assigned the SIC code designation of 5961 from the industry group SIC 596, nonstore retailers. On the date of the last business census for trade and service organizations, 1987 (which was published on a five-year cycle in 1990), some 60% of the firms operated as corporations, having mean annual sales of $3.9 million and employing 23 persons, on average. Some 5% operated as partnerships, employing 10 persons on average and having annual sales of $2.5 million. The single proprietorships were about 34% of the total number with average annual sales of $430,000 and an average of 3.6 paid employees in that base year. It would be necessary to adjust annual sales upward to account for the 4% to 5% annual inflation that occurred in the nation in the latter 1980s in order to estimate per-establishment sales in 1990 or later. In total, the mail order industry enjoyed a growth rate of about 10% yearly during the 1980s.

By 1991, according to *County Business Patterns* for the United States, for SIC 5961, some 7,444 such establishments operated, employing 148,473 persons and having an annual payroll of $2,826,947,000. This amounted to 20 persons, on average, per establishment, with an annual salary of about $19,040 per worker. Thus, catalog and mail order firms tend to grow to substantial size. Many, however, begin as a hobby in one's garage.

A majority (some 85%) of the mail order firms in 1987 had single units, while 15% had multiple units. Of the firms with multi-units, only three had 25 or more establishments. The firms with multi-units are usually incorporated.

The Bureau of the Census, in *Retail Trade—Industry Series*, listed about 40 lines of business items that were handled by mail order houses. Some 13 of these had product sales volumes that accounted for more than 10% of the total volume of such products sold at the retail level. These highly marketed products by mail order included the following:

Product Line	Percentage of Retail Sales	Product Line	Percentage of Retail Sales
Coins and metals	70.3	Audio/music equipment	12.7
Tobacco products	66.1	Drugs/health/beauty aids	12.5
Stamps and autographs	56.0	Kitchenware/home furnishings	12.4
Books/magazines/newspapers	29.6	Dry goods/curtains	12.2
Women's/girls' wear	26.1	Major appliances	11.7
Grocery and other	23.0	Auto tires/batteries	11.2
Men's/boys' apparel	13.6		

Comparable data were not found in the latest business census.

A survey was recently made, and the results published by Simmons Marketing Research Bureau, Inc., of the importance of ordering certain lines of merchandise by phone and mail. The results show the percentage of respondents who made purchases of each item during the year. A summary of the more important of such usage, based on the 1986 publication, is as follows:

Product Line	Percentage of Respondents	Product Line	Percentage of Respondents
Total making orders	29.9	Audiocassette tapes	3.4
Magazines	11.6	Other books	3.3
Needlecraft kits	7.9	Credit cards	3.2
Books: Bookclub orders	4.3	Trees/plants/seeds	3.1
Travel information	3.8	Other items	3.1
Records	3.4		
Average annual purchase	$125		

Direct marketing, such as telephone orders or mail orders solicited by mailouts or radio or TV ads or vending machine orders, accounted for about 14% of the $1.4 trillion retail sales in 1985, but some industry sources saw the possibility of mail order business growing to about one-third of total retail sales in the United States by the mid- to latter 1990s. A growth rate of about 10% in mail order business existed during the mid-1980s to mid-1990s. One of the prime reasons for the rapid growth in such mail order business has been the commitment of time by more working wives to the labor market. As of 1993, roughly 52% to 53% of workers were males while the balance were women. Mail order sales, that amounted to over $50 billion in the 1980s, were expanding by about 10% yearly. Some 40% of American men and 53% of American women buy certain items by mail. The typical mail order purchaser is a married person between the ages of 35 and 44 who has one child, according to one market survey.

The growth in mail order business has occurred despite the large numbers of shopping malls that have been developed in recent years, attempting to provide the convenience of one-stop shopping for busy shoppers. Some supermarkets have countered retail sales losses by broadening their inventory of offerings (florist shop, dry goods section, drugs/beauty aids section, etc.), and shopping malls have tended toward larger sizes. Some enterprising management groups for shopping malls attempt to make exit interviews with patrons leaving the mall to determine (1) some characteristics of the customers (age, sex, etc.), (2) where they are from, and (3) items they sought but did not find at the mall. They will thus be in better positions to modify new store additions to the mall that have a good chance of success.

Many large concerns have recently begun to market aggressively through direct marketing: Bloomingdales, for example, has gone to catalog sales in an effort to increase revenues. Montgomery Ward, conversely, dropped its mail order business after more than a century of experience in the endeavor, as losses continued in this activity for Wards (a division of Mobil Oil Company). Discount department stores (such as KMart, Wal-Mart, etc.), Sears, and other specialty stores had increased competition for products historically sold by mail order through Montgomery Ward (mail, telephone, store orders, etc.). Broyhill Furniture has likewise begun to market with mail order, bypassing retail furniture stores with a very substantial portion of overall corporate sales. A large share of PC and other electronic equipment is marketed through mail order catalogs.

The number of catalogs and offering circulars that are delivered by the federal postal service has been growing almost every year, with no end in sight. The rapid, and inexpensive, development of offering circulars with desktop publishing (see also the business profile for Desktop Publishing) is likely to increase the attempt at marketing directly many products and services. It has been estimated that about 8.5 billion catalogs were mailed to potential customers in a recent year. About 60% to 70% of households just ignore them. The average response rate is about 1% to 2%, and a firm that can target market its catalogs may be able to increase the response rate to 3%. In order to cut down on the lookers/casual shoppers who don't buy, Broyhill began to charge $10 for its colored catalog of offerings. Sears, JCPenney, and some of the other large mail order businesses have, at times, attempted to charge for their annual catalogs, but mail orderers are usually rewarded with future receipts of complimentary catalogs from the patronized firms. This mailing is classified as target marketing to recent past patrons.

Mail order business is generally profitable to the firms that undertake this method of distribution. The net profit margin, after taxes, was about 6.7% in 1984 for mail order businesses compared to 2.5% on store-type retail sales. However, many states are pressing for the collection of sales taxes by the companies that merchandise through the mail. Thus far, the Supreme Court has generally ruled that this collection process does not have to be done by a store operating from one state but selling/delivering to another state.

Trends in the future are likely to be mixed. Some firms will discontinue their mail order business as unprofitable. Others will flourish. It is likely that the mail order business, in total, will continue to grow by about 10% annually for the balance of the century. This may keep pressure on the selling price of store-displayed merchandise, leading to narrow profits by many of the store-displaying merchants. Spot ads on the national television networks reach an estimated 15 million persons, and this method of merchandising is likely to be continued in the future. Mailout brochures, catalogs, and offering circulars are likely to become thinner, slicker, and more sharply focused than in the recent past. Increasing postal rates eat into the profits of mail order firms, as such costs are one of the major expenses to many of the smaller mail order firms.

Market Opportunities in Various-Sized Communities

Some mail order types of businesses are begun as a hobby in the home, the garage, or the basement. It is a good idea for the owner to make sure that his or her business is properly zoned before undertaking an expansion. If there are employees, it is also necessary to obtain a business tax number from the secretary of state's office so as to withhold social security and federal and state withholding income tax from the gross pay of employees and to make such deposits on a timely basis into a depository bank.

Hobby-type manufacturing companies do often originate in small communities. As the business grows in size, the firm may franchise other firms to aid in the manufacture and/or distribution of the products. As the level of business increases beyond the scope of its initial housing, a nearby warehouse or store may be rented to carry on the expanded operation. In time, most such successful operations relocate to larger cities where transportation facilities are greater than those often serving small communities.

Speed in the receipt of orders, processing them for shipping, and transport of the items to their ultimate destination are paramount in the mail order business. Outages and back orders, while perhaps tolerated from time to time by patrons, may result in their seeking alternate suppliers of the desired items. Many of the mail orders are for impulse items, and if not shipped quickly from receipt of order, the request may be canceled.

The number of catalog and mail order firms in the United States totaled 5,871 in 1987 but had grown to 7,444 by 1991. Thus, one firm operated for about every 400,000 persons. As stated above, only about 1% to 2% of recipients of the ads respond as customers.

Franchising

Franchisors do not appear to be numerous in the catalog and mail order business.

Development and Site Requirements

Mail order businesses are sometimes begun as hobbies or weekend endeavors by a husband or wife from the home or garage. As goods are produced, they may be offered to friends. The line of merchandise is expanded, catalogs or offering circulars are printed, and these are mailed to friends. Thus a family-operated business grows into a full-time endeavor for one or more family members, and additional facilities and staffpersons must be added.

Many mail order businesses operate from a warehouse-type location, providing a bulk of the space for storage of inventory. Some space is needed for the office staff in (1) receiving telephone orders, (2) processing mail orders, and (3) handling sales returns, credits, billing, and the like. A significant amount of space, and several persons, may be needed to fill, crate, and ship orders received. A truck loading and unloading dock is imperative. The process should be handled smoothly, quickly, and with the minimum amount of wasted effort. It is important that the exact items ordered be shipped. When substitute or wrong items are shipped, it reflects on the ability, or perhaps honesty, of the firm's management. Some customers will tolerate mistakes and permit price adjustments or replacement product shipment (after a return), but the time delays may cause the client to look elsewhere for future items.

Some of the larger mail order businesses set up displays at several browsing locations across the nation but only accept orders to be filled from mail order inventory. Some clients like to browse, inspect the merchandise, and evaluate it in comparison to items sold by competing firms before ordering. Large ticket items are sometimes handled in this way, such as furniture, major appliances, valuable stamp or coin collections, guns, and the like.

As a mail order business grows in size, it should be able to keep track of inventory on hand and orders that are coming in. Efficient, prompt filling of orders (correctly) is the major key to building growth in sales. A computerized inventory control system, accounts receivable billing system, and listing and preparation of shipping labels for the clients to receive updates on new catalogs are imperative to a large mail order business. Lines of merchandise available for sale may be manufactured by subcontractors and mailed from their premises (after being marketed from the mail order business), and be billed from the mail order firm. Any complaints, returns and allowances, and so on, would be handled by the selling (mail order) organization.

Cost and Types of Assets Needed to Start a Business

Starting a business can be an expensive endeavor—or it might be begun as a mail order business with little capital. Consideration should be given to the needs for operating cash to pay for expenses until the firm reaches the break-even level, the amount needed for inventories, receivables, and housing costs such as a structure or improving a leasehold improvement.

Not all cash will be needed from the owner. Instead, some funds might be self-generating as the business expands. That is, the trade suppliers, accrued wages, and accrued taxes grow as the business expands. Banks and other institutions might lend funds to the firm, an auto or truck might be financed with a sales finance company, or a state lending agency might be a possible source.

Knowing the usual breakdown of assets and debts for similar types of business organizations is helpful to the business planner.

Two sources of data that provide survey-type, up-to-date common-sized income statement and balance sheet information on a large number of firms are the annually updated *Industry Norms and Key Business Ratios* by Dun & Bradstreet, Inc., and *Statement Studies*, updated annually by Robert L. Morris Associates. For mail order businesses in 1993, the balance sheet for the mean average-sized firm (D & B) and averages for the smallest (under $100,000 in assets) of four groups (RLM) are as follows:

	D & B	RLM
ASSETS		
Cash and near-cash	15.5%	10.6%
Accounts receivable	17.4	15.4
Notes receivable	.4	—
Inventories	39.1	42.2
Other current assets	6.2	3.6
Total current assets	78.6	71.7
Fixed assets	12.8	16.7
Other noncurrent assets	8.6	11.7
Total assets	100.0	100.0
DEBTS AND NET WORTH		
Accounts payable	19.5	22.6
Loans	4.7	13.6
Other current debts	14.1	9.9
Total current debts	38.3	46.1
Long-term debts	10.6	11.8
Deferred credit	.1	.3
Net worth	51.0	41.8
Total debts and net worth	100.0	100.0
Average assets (debts + net worth)	$374,000	$223,000

Sources: Reprinted with permission of Dun & Bradstreet, Inc.; and copyright Robert L. Morris Associates, 1992. In some instances, line items extracted from the RLM *Statement Studies* have been combined for the sake of comparability to the D & B data.

RLM cautions that the *Statement Studies* be regarded only as a general guideline and not as an absolute industry norm. This is due to limited samples within categories, the categorization of companies by their primary SIC number only, and different methods of operations by companies within the same industry. For these reasons, RLM recommends that the figures be used only as general guidelines in addition to other methods of financial analysis.

Several conclusions may be drawn from a comparison of the D & B and RLM common-sized balance sheets. The source of the RLM figures is bank data for its smallest category studied, firms with under $100,000 in assets in 1992. The D & B data are the averages of all surveyed firms for 1993. First of all, the RLM (small) firms use a lower ratio of total net worth than do the D & B (average) firms. Greater usage is often made of accounts payable and long-term debts by smaller than by larger firms.

Cash is significantly less at small firms, while accounts receivable and inventory values are greater compared to total assets at the smaller than the large firms. Thinly operated firms may be more reluctant to provide D & B with credit report information. The RLM data are taken from bank credit files while the D & B information comes from financial statements provided to it from its participating credit reporting companies. Thus, there is a tendency for the RLM firms in the sampling process to be somewhat smaller in size than the mean average of the D & B sample in each SIC grouping.

The *Almanac of Business and Industry Financial Ratios*, updated annually by Prentice-Hall, Inc., from corporate income tax return information filed with the IRS, provides an expense breakdown by size of firms. For the two smallest asset classes of firms in the Miscellaneous Retail Trade division, the ratios published in 1993 were as follows:

	Under $100,000	$100,000–$250,000
Cost of operations	55.9%	61.2%
Compensation of officers	4.5	6.0
Repairs	.4	.4
Bad debts	.2	.2
Rent on business property	6.0	3.5
Taxes (excluding federal tax)	2.5	2.4
Interest	.6	1.0
Depreciation/depletion/amortization	1.9	1.6
Advertising	1.7	1.5
Pension and benefits	.5	.7
Other expenses (wages, etc.)	21.0	18.7
Net before-tax profit	4.9	3.0

The firms in the mail order business typically have gross profit margins of about 40% to 45%. Direct marketing and transportation charges, as well as sales returns and allowances, are greater at mail order houses than at their counterpart, in-store retailing firms offering similar lines of products. Labor costs are somewhat less at mail order houses, and profit margins are about two times as great, industrywide. Rent and utilities are significantly less at the warehouse-type mail order houses than for the retail stores that operate from the high rent districts.

Typical Business Ratios   The use of typical business ratios from a group of similar firms or those computed from an industry-composite balance sheet or income statement are helpful in forecasting possible future (pro forma) financial statements for a business firm. These are frequently desired by financial lending institutions and other potential investors in the business concern. For mail order firms, certain key ratios in 1994, as provided by D & B, are as follows:

Solvency ratios:

Quick ratio (cash + accounts receivable/current debts)	.8:1
Current ratio (current assets/current debts)	2.3:1
Total liabilities to net worth (total debts/net worth)	65.5%

Efficiency ratios:

Collection period (accounts receivable/net credit sales × 365)	15.7 days
Sales to inventory (net sales/inventory)	8.1 times
Assets to sales (yearend assets/net sales)	30.9%

Profitability ratios:

Return on sales (net after-tax profit/net sales)	3.5%
Return on net worth (net after-tax profit/equity)	19.8%

Legal Considerations   The management of any concern should ascertain that it is operating legally. Charters of corporations are issued at the state level. Sales permits might be obtained at the state or local level. Zoning of property is usually done by cities and/or counties. Appropriate addresses might be obtained from the local chamber of commerce.

Several areas of activity in the mail order business require the aid of an attorney or an accountant. An attorney should be hired as an aid in drafting articles of copartnership or in drawing up and filing with the appropriate state office the articles of incorporation. An accountant is needed in designing a system of accounting, an inventory control system, and a billing and cash receipts system. The use of an office or personal computer, along with appropriate software packages, may aid the accomplishment of many of these tasks.

An attorney should be engaged for certain document preparation and review of legal contracts, land and/or building purchase, long-term leasing arrangements, franchise contracts, bankruptcy and liquidation proceedings, going public, buyouts, sellouts, and the like. The public accountant is usually somewhat knowledgeable in these areas, but when he or she suggests the aid of an attorney, one should be engaged.

The insurance package needed by a mail order business differs slightly from that by other types of trade companies. Fire insurance and perhaps insurance against other perils, such as storm-related roof damage followed by rains, winds, and so on, are of special importance in regards to the merchandise inventory, since this is the largest single asset of most mail order firms. If vehicles are owned by the firm, adequate liability insurance, as well as insurance on freight being carried, are of substantial importance. Workers' compensation insurance is required by most states, as is matching of OASDI and withholding of the proper amounts of federal and state income taxes and social security. Should merchandise display areas be available to the general public, adequate structure, merchandise, and liability insurance should be carried on the site and inventory. Fidelity insurance on persons handling large amounts of funds is suggested. Life insurance and health insurance are sometimes carried as fringe benefits to employees.

A clear understanding between the manufacturer and the mail order house (merchandiser) should be developed as to (1) warranty of product quality, returns, and allowances, (2) schedule of deliveries of sold merchandise, and (3) profit margin allowed the mail order, selling organization. A long-term selling agency contract may offer some protection against direct contact of the client by the manufacturer (rather than selling to the mail order business who then sells to the client). Clients sometimes sue the retailer (rather than the manufacturer) of goods, so carrying adequate insurance, as stated above, is recommended.

Experience and Training Required

Some mail order businesses begin as small manufacturing firms that are not adequate in size to justify a formal place of business, a workforce, and a marketing staff. As acceptance of the product increases, the founders go from part time to full time and additional workers are needed.

The workers should have training and experience in the jobs that they perform. Production workers should have normal production skills, such as artistic ability, machine operating ability, and so on. Salespersons should, ideally, have experience in advertising or direct selling. The full-time staff added to facilitate inventory control, billing, check or charge card processing, credits for returned merchandise, and so forth, should be experienced in accounting and in electronic data processing.

The founder/manager/owner should have general management skills in planning, organizing, staffing, supervising, and training personnel to do other functions of the business as it expands. Such skills may be learned by work experience or may be acquired by taking credit or noncredit courses at a nearby college or university. Small-business development centers frequently offer noncredit seminars in areas worthwhile to founders of small business concerns. The Small Business Administration offers numerous publications that are helpful to growth-minded business persons.

The manager/owner should have marketing skills or hire someone who is an effective direct marketer. The development of catalogs, offering circulars, and instructional packages for assembling mail order products is imperative in this line of business. Thus, the marketing manager should be accomplished in artistic drawing, mechanical drawing of illustrations, and other promotional techniques. In the mail order business, marketing of the product is about as important as the design and manufacture of the items to be sold. The development of a quality mailing list of prospective clients is time consuming, but it is often the key to good acceptance of the product by the catalog-receiving clients.

Keys to Successful Management

Three areas are probably of greatest concern to a mail order business. They involve (1) the development of items to be offered for sale, (2) ways for developing a growing, satisfied clientele of customers, and (3) developing appropriate techniques for expense control. Each of these areas will be addressed briefly.

1. The mail order house management must define its area of activities. Will items sold be only those manufactured in company-owned facilities, or will small, virtually unknown manufacturing firms be contacted to develop additional lines of products? When the latter is done by a medium- to large-sized mail order house, some firms limit the merchandise to be supplied by one firm to about one-fourth of the total. Thus, a burnout, temporary shortage of products or raw materials, or refusal to fulfill an order commitment for some other reason by one firm, will leave the mail order house with alternate suppliers of the items being offered for sale. Maintaining uniform quality control may be somewhat more difficult with multiple suppliers, but availability of supply at some prearranged price is usually increased.

2. Telephone order takers should be friendly and professional. Persons may be hired for about 150% to 200% of the minimum wage to handle order taking, but complaints should be taken by an experienced company employee. Friendly, prompt credit for items returned is necessary if sales growth is to continue. A sympathetic listener on the hot-line (toll-free complaint number) may be able to solve some of the problems. Many of the complaints may be that the wrong model has been mailed. The telephone operator should give the customer the option of returning the item, with the company suffering the additional transportation charges, or keeping the merchandise with some price adjustment. Thus the client is usually retained for future business.

The time that customers spend on hold should be made productive. It may be filled with pleasant background music or description of other lines of merchandise carried by the firm. Spot national news is used by some firms during waiting times.

3. Expenses should be controlled in a mail order business. Adequate expansion space should be provided for. Orderly arrangement of merchandise inventory so that ordered items can be located quickly is important to the efficiency and accuracy of order filling. Merchandise should be delivered within the promised time frame, such as 2 weeks or 30 days. Backorders for certain of the components of a set, or a portion of an order, may be tolerated by some clients but become a thorn to others. The use of the delivery system least expensive for quality handling of the merchandise is of substantial importance. Transportation firms and insurance companies should be asked to bid on this type of work, as in total the amount is substantial to a mail order store.

The cost of merchandise inventory, as well as quality control of the items, should be monitored by experienced merchandise personnel of the mail order business.

Direct merchandising is a large cost to the mail order firm, so attention should be directed toward determining the most effective way to sell items:

radio ads, spot TV commercials, direct mailing of offering circulars/catalogs to selected potential clients, full-line catalogs at a charge, and the like.

4. As the firm grows in size, the decisions must be made as to continuing to rent or buying facilities; whether to sell only through direct marketing or to open displays of merchandise for customer shopping and selection; whether to own a fleet of trucks or to use common carriers or the U.S. postal system for making deliveries; the optimum location of satellite merchandise warehouses in order to minimize delivery costs; and so on.

Information Sources

Several sources of information are helpful to the would-be business person in a mail order business or the owner that plans an expansion program. These include industry associations, reference books, directories of suppliers, periodicals, ratio studies, investment services, and government publications. A list of these sources is found in each update of *Encyclopedia of Business Information Sources*, by Gale Research, Inc., Detroit, Mich.

Real Estate Offices

Business Types,
Industry
Characteristics and
Prospects

Real estate offices have been assigned SIC Code 6531 (industry group 653). The broad area of SIC 653 includes real estate operators and lessors, except developers. These establishments primarily engage in renting, buying, selling, managing, and appraising real estate for others.

The Internal Revenue Service, Department of Commerce, and several other federal agencies use SIC 6531 as the designated code for real estate brokers, agents, and property management. While the nature of this type of concern is predominantly buying and selling of real estate as an agent for others, or simply bringing together the buyer and seller of real property, other functions are frequently undertaken. These include such things as locating financing, providing counseling advice to clients, and managing property for others for a fee.

The form of organization of a real estate firm may be as a single proprietorship, a partnership, or a corporation. In a very small community, a broker of real estate may operate from a home office or a small office centrally located. He or she may engage the services of one or more full- or part-time salespersons. There is the ease of organization of an unincorporated firm, and the owner has full control over its operation. A partnership is sometimes formed, bringing in another person with additional talents and funds. One partner should be a licensed broker. The second may be a salesperson or be engaged in managing real estate for others. Most modern-day real estate offices, however, are incorporated. In many states, the incorporation fee for a firm with capital of less than $100,000 is only a few hundred dollars, and a corporation does have limited liabilities (to the owners' personal assets) and continuity of existence should a shareholder (owner) die. It can also sell stocks and bonds and grow in size.

The number of persons engaged in real estate sales and management changes over the business cycle, following the fluctuations of housing starts. In 1980, when interest rates were high and housing sales were extremely slow, some 1.29 million new housing units were begun. The number increased to 1.8 million units in 1986. In the early 1990s, about 1.2 to 1.4 million housing starts was the annual range. Each year, about 3.5 million to 4.5 million units of used residential property change hands. During years of falling interest rates, more homes are sold, and real estate salespersons return to that job; but as rates rise and sales are slow, some salespersons leave that profession and seek other jobs. Not all of these transactions are handled by real estate dealers, of course, but a large percentage of them are. While a recent survey estimated that over 2 million persons were licensed to sell real estate, only about 900,000 persons were active participants in the field, and some 150,000 drop out each year due to disappointing income and other reasons.

Many brokerage firms in real estate do more than just show houses. They offer consulting to relocating professionals, introducing them to the new neighborhood, providing advice on schools, social and religious organizations, taxing districts, shopping centers, recreational sites, and the like. Handy reference maps and brochures have been prepared to highlight some of these areas in many communities. The brokerage firms attempt to match, as closely as possible, the desires of a client with the characteristics of property being offered for sale.

Substantial amounts of time may be spent by an enterprising selling agent before showing offered properties to a potential real estate client. The agent wants to obtain a good concept of the desires and dislikes of the client. It is best to work with both husband and wife, rather than only one of them, but this is not always possible, as a transferring husband or wife is frequently brought on a company visit to a possible site of changing employment. A part of the interview process may be an introduction to the community through the real estate brokerage firm. The selling agent needs a general guideline as to several things, such as the size of the home of interest, the number in the family, the number of bedrooms and bathrooms desired, the price range and financing needed, when possession is needed, any concerns about schools for the children, desires about a neighborhood (nearby shopping, churches, and recreation), and so on.

A real estate salesperson has two main jobs. One is selling real property to potential clients, but even before this can be done, the firm must attract a substantial listing of homes that can be offered for sale. The brokerage firm should develop a contract with an offering client, explaining the charge for the service. It is usually 6% to 7% of selling price on residential city property and perhaps 10% or more on farm or slow-moving commercial or industrial property. An attempt is made to match up the characteristics of property listed for sale with the desires of the potential purchasers. An offer is sometimes received from a potential client that is less than the offering price. This should be in writing, and most brokerage firms will ask the potential buyer to sign the designated form. The offer, if within the price range agreed upon by the owner, is transmitted to the owner. An acceptance or a counteroffer is sometimes made. When the two parties, buyer and seller, have reached a "ready, willing, and able" agreement, the buy/sell agreement should be drawn up by the real estate brokerage firm and signatures obtained by all concerned parties (both owner spouses and both buyer spouses, in most states). While the commission is usually paid by the seller in the transaction, buyers will sometimes hire agents/professionals to act on their behalf, to provide them service of a consulting nature, and so on.

Real estate brokers sometimes act as managers for real estate, especially for previous clients who may have located elsewhere. For this service, a monthly fee is usually assessed when the property is leased, often about 6% of revenues from rental plus reimbursement of out-of-pocket expenditures for maintenance, insurance, and taxes that are sometimes paid by the managing firm. A proper accounting of the revenues, fees and expenses, and funds transmitted to the property owners must be made. Some brokerage firms manage only larger properties, such as shopping centers or apartment buildings.

Many thrift institutions, especially savings and loan associations and savings banks, repossess homes on which the buyer is several months behind in making contractual mortgage payments. The homes may be fixed up (painted, worn appliances and carpets replaced, etc.) and offered for resale. Such offering is sometimes done by the staff of the institution, but it is many times done through multiple listing with nearby real estate brokerage firms.

The U.S. Department of Labor expects this job classification to continue to grow for the balance of the century, with brokers increasing by about 35% to 49% from 1986 to about the year 2000, or some 63,000 in 1986 to 94,000 by year 2000. The number of active salespersons in the industry is likely to grow from about 313,000 in mid-80s to perhaps 460,000 by the turn of the century.

Market Opportunities in Various-Sized Communities

Before starting a real estate firm, the owner(s) will have to develop a business plan. In developing a business plan, several important pieces of information will be noted, including whether or not the area could support the proposed venture, the existence of an unidentified market niche that may be exploited, the level of competition in the area, the customer base population, competitive pricing strategies, and a variety of other facets of the business that owners or managers need to know to develop a viable and profitable business.

Assistance in developing a business plan may be obtained from many sources—some at a cost, others free. A few sources available for assistance are the local chamber of commerce, banks, accounting firms, local and state government bodies such as city hall, the state department of commerce promotion, colleges (business management programs or small-business development centers), and libraries.

Not only should the broker develop a business plan for the firm, but the broker should ask that each agent hired to sell real estate draft a personal plan of his or her own. For example, this might include a goal of 18 listings per year, with at least 16 transactions handled during a year. If two years pass with less than 75% achievement, then perhaps the contract with the agent should be terminated. Each desk in the real estate office costs something like $15,000 per year to maintain; thus, a standard of minimum performance for each of the agents is necessary for the firm to stay in a healthy position.

Recent estimates indicate that over 2.1 million persons are licensed to sell real estate. This is one person per every 120 adult U.S. citizens, approximately. Only about 900,000 persons work in real estate as brokers, salespersons, appraisers, and managers, and some 150,000 leave the industry (as others are added) each year. A small community of 500 persons could, at most, support one real estate office consisting of a combination broker/office manager and one or two salespersons. Family turnover in most communities amounts to about 10% yearly, so if it is assumed that the above 500 persons constitute 200 residences, then a turnover rate of 10% is only 20 transactions. Should one-half of these be handled by a real estate firm, this is only 10 transactions per year for the office. Of course, the office staff might perform other functions, such as manage some rental property for absentee owners. Some offices also handle transactions in several cities, even extending beyond county lines—especially when farm and ranch properties are involved. A firm might very likely handle most of the real estate work for several nearby small communities.

Before developing a real estate office in a small city, an analysis should be made of such things as current level of competition, mobility of population into and out of the area, ability of homebuyers to obtain real estate financing through nearby financial institutions, and the like. Buying a partnership in a going concern, especially with someone nearing retirement age, may be a faster approach to building a clientele than beginning anew. While the 6% to 7% sales commissions may appear to offer unusually high financial rewards to real estate salespersons, only about 10% to 12% of such persons consistently earn above $50,000 yearly. More than half earn less than $20,000, which accounts for the large exodus from the ranks of salespersons each year. Subtract auto expenses from the compensation, and only about 75% to 80% of these figures is left.

Franchising   A real estate broker may wish to compare the merits of franchising with independent ownership. The franchising firm (parent) usually provides management consulting in the area of location and outlay of a firm, training of key personnel, bookkeeping tips, group advertising, logos, and so on. For this service, the franchisor receives some up-front fee plus some annual percentage of revenues. An additional assessment may be made for joint advertising, such as 1% or 2% of revenues.

Certainly the prospective franchisee should ascertain that the franchisor has complied with state and federal full-disclosure laws; check out the company's reputation and credit rating; determine the initial and ongoing cost of the franchise; ascertain the territory that is being offered and prospective future helps assured by the franchisor; determine the possibility of expanding the territory or selling the franchised operation to another; and ask a competent attorney to review the contract.

Some large franchisors in the real estate industry, including the mailing addresses, are as follows:

Better Homes and Gardens Real Estate Service
2000 Grand Avenue
Des Moines, IA 50312

Century 21 Real Estate Corporation
International Headquarters
P.O. Box 19564
Irvine, CA 92713

Electronic Realty Associates, Inc.
4900 College Boulevard
Overland Park, KS 66211

Gallery of Homes, Inc.
20 South Orange Avenue
Orlando, FL 32801

Realty World Corporation
12500 Fair Lakes Circle, Suite 300
Fairfax, VA 22033

RE/MAX International
P.O. Box 3907
Englewood, CO 80155

Development and Site Requirements In locating the business, consideration must be given to local zoning requirements. Many communities forbid, through zoning ordinances, the establishment of home-based businesses and the use and storage of noxious or dangerous chemicals. It is a good idea to check the local zoning ordinances prior to contracting to rent, lease, or buy a property to be operated as a real estate firm.

Several characteristics exist for a successful real estate office. A real estate office should be on a well-traveled street, be highly visible, and have an auspicious sign visible to the front and sides of the structure. Adequate parking should be provided off-street to accommodate employees and about an equal number of patrons. The structure should be neat and in good repair. Many such offices are located in large, older homes in areas of the city that have become commercialized with offices of medical doctors, dentists, attorneys, real estate, and the like.

The structure should have adequate working space inside with some rooms for privacy. A reception area is needed, where one or more receptionist/secretaries are located. The area might also contain a personal computer for doing certain types of work, such as correspondence, storage of information, retrieval of lists of offerings showing certain characteristics, spreadsheet analysis for real estate being managed or evaluated for a client, and so on. The broker needs a separate office, as he or she frequently meets with clients on a confidential basis. A master bedroom, with an adjacent bath, makes for a good combination office and small reception/lounge area. The formal dining room of the old home might be turned into the conference room, with a large table and chairs to accommodate 8 to 12 persons. Closings and other group meetings are held in such a room. Other rooms are needed for the salespersons. Several desks might be located in a single room, but at least one spare room is needed so that a salesperson may have some privacy with a client, as desired. Additional space is needed for storage. The kitchen might serve as a snack/recreation area. A three- or four-bedroom older home, with two or more baths, fills the bill nicely. Some older structures built more than 50 years ago also qualify for some tax credit for expenses in renovating them.

The conference room might do dual duty as a reading room, or library, as it is necessary in a real estate office to stay abreast of national trends and the economy, the state economy and changing real estate and contract laws, and the local economy and regulations bearing on real estate values and property use zoning. Subscriptions to several industry journals are helpful in such activities. At least one person must be a broker, passing the state-prescribed brokerage exam. Salespersons should be licensed by the state, which involves passing a real estate salesperson license exam on such areas as real estate principles, real estate law, mathematics of finance, land use control, and so forth.

The size of facility needed depends on several factors, such as the size of the city (or county) being served, the degree of competition, the expected size of the sales staff, types of properties to list and show (i.e., residential, income properties, farm properties, developments, etc.), requirements of a possible franchisor, expected need for growth, and so on. An equity investment of $100,000 would probably make a partial payment on an adequate structure, acquire needed office and EDP equipment, buy an auto for the broker (salespersons usually provide their own, often at their own expense), and leave some funds for working capital.

Cost and Types of Assets Needed to Start a Business

A real estate firm may be started on a small amount of capital, but this is usually dangerous. Some franchisors charge less than $10,000 and require different levels of other assets. First of all, about six to twelve months of losing money is typical for the start-up firm. The broker and the salespersons need some living expenses, so that some back-up capital is desirable. The average ongoing firm in the SIC 6531 classification had equity capital of about $138,000 and assets of about two times this level in 1993, according to surveys made by Dun & Bradstreet, Inc., in *Industry Norms and Key Business Ratios*. The averages for 1993 were as follows:

Assets		Debts and Net Worth	
Cash and near-cash	25.3%	Accounts payable	6.2%
Accounts receivable	13.9	Bank and other loans	5.5
Notes receivable	2.9	Other current debts	17.6
Inventory	1.2	Total current debts	29.3
Other current assets	10.8	Long-term debts	17.0
Total current assets	54.1	Deferred credit	.2
Fixed assets	26.5	Net worth	53.5
Other noncurrent assets	19.4	Total debt and net worth	100.0
Total assets	100.0%	Total debt and net worth (average firm)	$260,000

Certain of the larger of the above accounts will be reviewed briefly. The cash would be demand deposits or near-cash items, such as funds held in escrow accounts, negotiable order withdrawal accounts, or other interest-bearing temporary investments. Fixed assets refer to land, building(s) and office fixtures, and equipment owned. The other noncurrent assets would largely be for leaseholds, leasehold improvements, trade name, and other intangibles. Other current debts would be miscellaneous accruals for wages/commissions owed, taxes owed, interest payable, and the like. Long-term debts are usually installment notes on autos, equipment, or mortgages on real property.

Typical Business Ratios Let us first consider the typical income statement for a real estate brokerage firm. Revenues are primarily earned from commissions on the sale of property, although small amounts may be earned on consulting fees, appraisals of property, notary fees, finders fees, and interest on investments. The following were suggested by D & B as average (median) for 1985 to 1993, based on about 1,260 to 1,643 firms in these years:

	1985	1987	1993
Net sales and revenues	$394,169	$550,449	$621,484
Gross profits	45.0%	40.4%	46.2%
Net after-tax profits	9.1%	8.0%	7.7%

Each year the IRS provides information on all corporations with and without profits sorted by major SIC designation. These statistics are tabulated, by size of firm, by Prentice-Hall, Inc., in its *Almanac of Business and Industry Financial Ratios*. For the most recent year, 1993, the common-sized breakdown of expenses for the smallest two asset size categories of corporations in real estate, the following expenses as a percentage of revenue are shown for firms with reported profits:

	Below $100,000	$100,000–$250,000
Cost of operations	11.1	22.6
Compensation of officers	9.5	13.0
Repairs	.7	.6
Bad debts	1.1	—
Rent on business property	4.0	3.7
Taxes (excluding federal tax)	2.1	2.7
Interest	.9	2.4
Depreciation/depletion/amortization	1.4	2.0
Advertising	3.1	2.7
Pension and benefits	.8	1.9
Other expenses	55.1	41.5
Net before-tax profit	10.1	6.9

A major portion of the "other expenses" category goes for the payment of commissions to the salespersons. The brokers in the organization are usually the owners/managers, whose pay is covered under the "compensation of officers" account. However, in a small real estate office, the broker may also be the salesperson for farm or industrial property listings or may promote real estate listings.

Other key median financial ratios, constructed from balance sheets and income statements for real estate firms in 1993, were as follows, according to D & B:

Solvency ratios:

Quick ratio (cash + accounts receivable/current liabilities)   1.3:1

Current ratio (current assets/current liabilities)   2.0:1

Total debts to net worth (total debt/net worth)   55.7%

Efficiency ratios:

Collection period (accounts receivable/sales × 365)   23.6 days

Sales to inventories (net sales/inventory)   32.9 times

Assets to sales (total assets/annual sales)   37.4%

Profitability ratios:

Return on sales (net after-tax profit/net sales)   5.5%

Return on net worth (net after-tax profit/net worth)   17.4%

Legal Considerations   Many real estate offices are operated as single proprietorships or partnerships rather than as corporations. The franchised operations are often incorporated. The single proprietorship must maintain records of revenues and expenses and report these on Schedule C of the federal Form

1040 tax return. The partnership must file a partnership return, and each partner must recognize his or her proportionate share of profits on his or her respective Form 1040 tax return.

The corporation, whether a regular corporation or an S corporation that is taxed similarly to a partnership, must maintain separate records and file a corporate tax return. Single proprietors and partners are considered to be self-employed and must pay self-employment taxes (social security) equal to 15.3% of self-employment income (up to the base amount of about $61,200 in 1995). One-half of this self-employment tax is a business deduction. Owners/managers in a corporation are taxed just as are other employees. That is, they have social security, federal income taxes, and state income taxes withheld from their paychecks and deposited into an institutional depository account one or more times monthly. The aid of an experienced accountant may be needed in setting up a general accounting and tax planning system.

An attorney should be engaged to aid in incorporating a firm, in handling legal contracts, and in defending lawsuits. The closing of a real estate transaction, in most states, requires the use of a licensed attorney.

A professional insurance planner or agent should be engaged to outline a program of necessary insurance coverage. In general, this should include fire and extended coverage on real assets, liability insurance on automobiles, and workers' compensation insurance for job-related injuries to employees. Other types of insurance that might be desirable, if funds permit their purchase, include crime coverage, fidelity bond, life insurance on owners, health insurance on employees, and executive liability coverage against faulty decisions.

In most firms, the salespersons are independent agents to the firm and thus provide their own autos and deduct their self-employment expenses from their net commissions. The salesperson should have a written contract with the brokerage firm, specifying how he or she is to share in the commissions earned on each sale and the expenses that he/she is to pay. He/she may receive one-half of the commission earned on a sale. The balance goes to the firm to defray other expenses and as profit to the owner (broker). With multiple listing, the firm originally listing the property may receive a small share (such as 15%) of the ultimate sales commission (which amount will be divided equally between the listing person and his or her firm), with the balance going to the brokering firm, to be divided equally with the successful salesperson. Thus, agents are very defensive about a client to whom they first showed a property. Some firms have tried 100% commissions to the salespersons with an assessment of a fraction of revenues to go for expenses and management expenses by the broker, but this arrangement is not so popular as fractional commissions being paid to the salespersons.

Experience and Training Required

The broker (manager/owner) in a real estate firm should develop a policy of honesty and integrity and set a goal for remaining for the long run in the industry. Almost all states require that a broker be licensed with the state and be knowledgeable in several areas, such as real estate principles, law, contracts, mathematics, and management and have several years' experience as a real estate salesperson. Many states permit reciprocity, that is, for persons licensed in another state to sell, or broker, in their state, but many states in recent years have begun to impose more stringent educational and continuing education requirements on persons engaged either as a real estate salesperson or as a broker.

Most states require some formal college training of would-be real estate salespersons. Training in basic economics (macro- and micro-), financial mathematics, accounting, contract law, communications (speech and English), psychology, real estate principles, and real estate law are helpful to the dedicated real estate person. Many states are requiring annual continuing education in credit or noncredit workshops or relevant topics. Many very successful salespersons ultimately pass their own brokerage exam and set up their own office.

The selling staff should be instilled with a high degree of professionalism in their approach to the endeavor. Listings are solicited through personal acquaintances, advertising (newspaper, telephone directories, radio, spot TV ads, direct mailouts, solicitations of persons offering their own home for sale, and the like), and door-to-door canvassing. The homes to be shown (i.e., those for which the broker has a contract signed by the owners engaging such services) should be cataloged into similar groups, such as age, price range, number of bedrooms and bathrooms, size of lot, inner city versus urban versus rural property, and so on.

While the broker and one or two salespersons are usually present during most business hours, heavier showing of homes is often done on holidays, Saturdays, and Sundays. Open houses may be arranged for these days, with one or two salespersons available. Some salespersons prefer not to work on Sundays, but many are still able to sell $1 or $2 million in properties annually at other times by being aggressive. Salespersons are usually assigned to new shopping clients on a rotational basis, although repeat contacts are usually referred to the previous salesperson. A potential client, of course, may ask for a certain salesperson, or even the broker, but an experienced salesperson is usually assigned to do the showing of the listed properties thought to meet the needs of the client.

The salesperson should be a good listener, gathering data from the potential client that will be helpful in showing only properties with many characteristics desired by the client. Usually three or four properties will be shown, and one or two may be reshown to a client before a tentative offer is received from the client. Such an offer should be in writing.

It is important that a market sheet be developed on each property listed for sale. The sheet shows a general description of the property, a floor plan of land and structures, a photograph, and detailed information about the property. The salesperson, broker, or support staff completes these market sheets, which may be duplicated and distributed in large numbers at open houses of similar-type properties. Thus a client can narrow down his or her search of the listed properties by a review of the sheets.

Typical personnel and financial considerations of real estate firms include the following: hiring and training full-time salespersons, training/retraining and motivating the sales staff, promoting growth of listings and sales, controlling overhead, keeping up with changing trends in the national, state, and local economy, staying abreast of changes in local zoning and real estate ordinances, and earning an adequate profit on invested funds.

Keys to Successful Management   Helpful aids for operating a successful real estate firm are provided in many of the books and periodical sources shown in the next section. Experience, at least for the broker in the firm, is imperative. The following list of items should be considered as they are thought to be helpful in operating a real estate firm on a profitable basis:

1.   Develop a written business plan, including organization and plans for training and expanding staff.

2.   Develop a mission (or purpose) statement for each class of employee and for each independent selling agent.

3.   Decide on the scope of operation, such as city, county, state, or national.

4.   Evaluate the firm's strengths and weaknesses, attempting to develop short-term plans for overcoming the latter.

5.   Formulate assumptions helpful in forecasting revenues and operating expenses for about a year in advance, such as strength of the economy, probable housing starts nationally and regionally, in and out migration from the state of operation, highway building programs, pending zoning changes, demographic shifts regionally, and so on.

6.   Enumerate measurable objectives of the firm and for each of its principles [i.e., revenue and profits, earnings retention vs. payments, areas of operation (residence sales, income property sales, property management, etc.), duration of the firm, and so on].

7.   Develop a plan for communicating information from the broker/manager to the salespersons and support staff and back again to the broker, with weekly planning meetings often scheduled.

8.   Develop a growth strategy in the areas of endeavor of interest, such as the condominium market, open-house home showings, and possible integration with other business types [such as real estate ownership (i.e., limited partnerships), real estate management, insurance, or personal loan company].

9.   Create an action plan, outlining expected objectives and strategies to attain them and operative plans, such as 18 listings per year for each salesperson and 16 transactions.

10. Decide on the approach to making real estate appraisals, whether to be done in-house, by the financing institution, or by an independent certified appraiser.

11. Develop training workshops for the salespersons and support staff, covering company policy and changes in the industry.

12. Develop a fair profit-sharing (commission) arrangement for the salespersons and make sure that it is understood by new employees.

13. Develop a generous advertising program, probably amounting to 12% to 18% of revenues, with some institutional and some specific site ads to be included.

14. Review the business plan from time to time and update and amend it as appropriate.

15. Maintain a track record on the performance of agents; terminate the employment of those that don't normally reach the goals.

In order to build greater knowledge about national and regional housing areas, real estate brokers often participate in clubs or serve on city planning commissions. Thus they keep up with local zoning changes and make their positions known. In turn, they become better known and are often consulted as to opinions about city government and the like. With the shift in demographics for the next forty years toward an aging population, the trend is likely to be toward increased need of housing for the elderly. Separate bathrooms and bedrooms but person/family sharing of some living and dining areas seems to be a possible direction of real estate trends for the elderly. Some real estate firms specialize in one or a few types of offerings while others take whatever business comes along.

Information Sources — Many sources of information are helpful to one already in or planning to enter the real estate business. These include trade associations, books, periodicals, franchisors, ratio studies, investment advisory services, and government sources. A representative list of these appears in each update of *Encyclopedia of Business Information Sources*, by Gale Research, Inc., Detroit, Mich.

Hotels, Motels, and Tourist Courts

Business Types, Industry Characteristics and Prospects

Hotels and motels have been assigned SIC Code 7011. The broader industry group 701 includes auto courts, bed-and-breakfast inns, cabins and cottages, casino hotels, hostels, hotels, inns, motels, recreational hotels, resort hotels, seasonal hotels, ski lodges and resorts, tourist cabins, and tourist courts.

The lodging industry, SIC 7011, comprises primarily hotels, motels, and tourist courts. These types of operations have several characteristics in common but differ in appearance and location. All offer lodging to travelers. Most offer restaurant service within their own facilities or are near restaurants that are convenient to their facilities. Many offer swimming pools and other attractive features for entertaining their guests.

It has been estimated that 75% of Americans travel yearly. Some 109 million Americans take vacations, with 1.2 vacation trips per year with a duration of 6 days being average. About four 2- to 3-day trips per year are taken by families, on the average, usually on long weekends or holidays. These vacationers usually vary their routes from one year to the next, and smaller communities, especially those located on scenic routes on which several historical markers are located, are beginning to attract more tourists than in past decades. The falling value of the dollar internationally has made travel abroad more expensive, so many tourists are following the dictum "See America" on their vacation trips. Many of these travelers are beginning to explore smaller communities, quaint villages, and historical structures. Thus, more travelers should, in future years, seek out small tourist courts and bed-and-breakfast establishments near their planned routes of travel.

The expansion in the number of rooms for rent in the latter 1980s was excessive in certain portions of the hotel/motel industry, with the number of available rooms growing by about 10% yearly from 1986 to 1988 but with usage gaining only about 2% yearly. Bargain motels, especially, have been adding outlets. Motels with rate charges at the high end, say above $80 nightly for a double, have also been adding suites. Downtown hotels have been renovating, to some extent, and many are attempting to revitalize their restaurants and cater to a crowd of repeat patrons that live nearby. Some have been offering weekend discounts to city vacationers in order to fill the large number of rooms vacated by weekday business travelers.

Many of the motels are expanding nationally, while some of the larger hotel chains continue to expand internationally and into some fast-growing cities where they have not previously had facilities. Some of the older hotels have been sold for redesign as condominiums in states that permit the sale of condos.

Some of the investment advisory services in recent years have been moderately strong on this industry. However, 1986 tax changes eliminated the investment tax credit on equipment, stretched out the income tax guideline depreciation life of commercial buildings, and imposed somewhat stricter rules on offsetting noncash expenses (depreciation and depletion allowances, for example) against other income.

For the industry as a whole, the break-even level of occupancy was perhaps raised from 60% to about 70% as a result of these 1986–1987 income tax changes and by expansion. The 1987–1988 occupancy rate was around 65%, meaning that losses were being reported by this industry as a whole for several years. Still, expansion continues in certain cities. With recent upturns in the interest rates, future expansion will likely slow to a trickle other than for units on which work has already begun.

As forecasted, the recession that began in 1990 and rising gasoline prices during the Gulf War combined to produce an occupancy rate decline at U.S. hotels and motels of 7% and produced first quarter losses in 1991. By the first quarter of 1992, revenues gained 5% on occupancy increases of 2%. It was estimated that the lodging industry would be slow to recover in the 1990s due to the overbuilding of the latter 1980s.

Market Opportunities in Various-Sized Communities

Before starting a motel or hotel, the owner will need to develop a business plan. For this, several important pieces of information will be needed, including whether or not the area can support the proposed venture, the existence of an unidentified market niche that may be exploited, the level of competition in the area, the customer base population and the number of travelers that pass through, competitive pricing strategies, and a variety of other facets of the business that the owner or manager needs to know in order to develop a viable and profitable business.

Assistance in developing a business plan may be obtained from many sources—some at cost and others free. A few sources of assistance are the local chamber of commerce, banks, accounting firms, local and state government bodies such as city hall or the state department of tourism, college business management departments, or small-business development centers, libraries, and so on.

Large motels are often built in large cities with well-traveled airports. Motels are generally located with ready access to major interstate highways. Smaller tourist courts are likely to be located on state highways or in smaller cities than those justifying a major hotel or motel facility. Those communities that are too small to attract a hotel or motel may still provide lodging for travelers by offering such facilities in one or several bed-and-breakfast establishments.

Franchising   The industry in total has been adding to its space during the mid- and latter 1980s much more rapidly than the growth in the general population, thus driving the average occupancy rate downward by about ½% to 1% per year. Much of the growth has been expanded franchised operations by some of the mid-priced chains, such as Quality Inn and Days Inn. These expanding franchised motels often follow the principle of buy-build-sell-lease that was popularized by some of the national grocery chains in the 1950s and 1960s: Buy the land, build the building according to standard needs, operate it until a successful level of clientele is obtained, and sell it to a private owner/operator. A large percentage of Days Inn facilities are members of an affiliated group, generally benefiting from joint advertising, a national reservations system, similar layouts, and standardized facilities and attractions.

Several other large franchisors operate in the motel/hotel industry. The list includes Brutger Hospitality Group, Downtowner-Passport International Hotel Corp., Econo-Lodges of America, Inc., Family Inns of America, Ramada Inns Inc., and Scottish Inns. Some of these require as little as $25,000 investment for the first 100 rooms with additional charges for additional rooms. The minimum investment on some large hotels, however, might be as high as $5 or $10 million. In many instances, a 10% investment will buy into the group.

Before deciding to franchise an operation, information should be obtained from several franchisors. Certainly the franchisee would need to consider the operating territory promised, the aid in management, the benefit from joint advertising and tourist room reservation referrals, and the chance to sell or expand the operation. He or she would also need to consider the needed capital, the initial franchise fee, the periodic fee charge, and the contribution toward advertising. An experienced attorney should be used in evaluating a franchising contract before it is signed, and since some of the terms can be negotiated, this should be done before a contract is entered into.

Development and   In locating the business, either a hotel or motel, consideration must be
Site Requirements   given to local zoning requirements. A hotel might be located downtown, and its zoning would be commercial. Certain portions of the site might have to be reserved for off-street parking, setbacks, and the like. The height of the structure might be controlled by governmental jurisdiction.

A new motel is likely to be located at the entrance to a city or along a major highway. The property may be zoned as agricultural and need to be rezoned as commercial. This should be done before very much money is spent in the land purchase process or on plans for the business, but the deal might be assured by obtaining an option to buy the land at a stipulated price upon zoning change.

In order to maximize potential revenue, a hotel or motel should be strategically located to meet the needs of the customers sought. For the total lodging industry, about 40% of the revenues come from business travelers, about 25% from pleasure travelers, about 5.5% from government employees, about 25% from conference attendees, and the other 4.5% from miscellaneous personal travelers. Large hotels located near major airports and serving areas with large numbers of national firms may see close to twice the average percentage of income from business travelers. However, some aggressive hotel chains do extend their heavy bookings from week nights to weekends by promoting conventions. Motels, on the other hand, attract the bulk of their revenues from vacationing travelers. The motel's location should maximize its attractiveness to major clients sought. Some motels do promote overnight lodging for business travelers as well as for vacationers by locating between major airports and the downtown businesses, attracting a number of driving business persons that rent autos after arriving by air.

Franchised motels are purchased turnkey, as explained above. Some large chains follow the practice of utility companies in buying strategically located pieces of unimproved property years before they will be developed, when prices are perceived as being relatively low, and developing the land later.

Entire blocks of rundown city property are sometimes bought by an enterprising hotel chain, with development (hotel, parking, and some adjacent stores) being done over several years. While hotels do often provide parking for regular guests, this is usually done on a surcharge basis, with daily parking charges averaging 10% to 15% as much as the room rate. Parking is usually free (or a part of the total package) at motels.

High-rise hotels are usually attracted to large cities with nearby airports. Most cater primarily to business travelers during the week and attempt to book conventions or attract leisure-time travelers on the weekends. Some offer nearby or underground parking garages for patrons with autos, while others merely list public parking lots within walking distance of the facility.

Most hotels offer meeting rooms and convention halls in order to attract medium- or large-sized conventions. Some can handle conventions of over 1,000; but large conventions usually book facilities in several cooperating nearby hotels in downtown areas of very large cities. In the Midwest, Chicago and St. Louis are popular convention cities. In the South, Atlanta, New Orleans, Dallas, Houston, and San Antonio are popular convention cities. New York and Atlantic City are popular Eastern sites. Los Angeles, San Diego, and San Francisco are popular on the West Coast. Denver, Seattle, and other large cities and other regions attract some conventions, and it is not unusual for many of the better-run hotels to have booked conventions, allocating a certain large percentage of their rooms (at a preset reduced price) several years in advance of the expected event.

Motels cater to the traveling crowd and, accordingly, seek to locate near or on the well-traveled routes to major vacation attractions, such as the many Six Flags across the nation, Disney attractions, water attractions, and the like. Holiday Inns in some locations are somewhat of a combination hotel/motel, often being six to twelve floors in height and offering some convention rooms for meetings, balls, school dances, and other events. Some facilities cater to families with children, offering free or inexpensive rates to children that share rooms with parents, and offering swimming, arcades, and playground equipment for their paying guests. A few motels, such as Ramada, promote swimming pool membership to nearby citizens in some of their locations.

Tourist courts are usually smaller than motels, and many resemble rowhouses with a carport between them. They offer more privacy, in many cases, than do busy hotels or motels, but most are older and have smaller rooms. Most are single- or two-story and catch the late, spill-over crowd unable to obtain accommodations at their favorite motel chain. Prices are usually lower at tourist courts than at newly built motels, but the range of services offered at tourist courts is often limited. Some do have a separate restaurant, often located near the check-in office, and sometimes attracting more local guests than traveling guests. Tourist courts are often privately owned and family operated, whereas motels are usually one of several hundred facilities belonging to one of several dozen large chains.

Expansion of lodging facilities is usually done as entertainment complexes are added within a certain geographic region. Florida, Nevada, Colorado, and California were some of the rapidly expanding vacation states during the 1970s and 1980s. The north-central region appears to be undergoing a higher-than-normal rate of expansion in recent years.

Some rapidly growing motel chains (Days Inn, for example) avoid lavish spending on a fancy lobby and restaurant, but instead concentrate on the basics. Some motels have virtually eliminated the provision of meeting rooms. These merely concentrate on placing their funds and advertising into attempting to attract travelers rather than groups of persons (associations and seminars).

Large hotels should have one or more entrances where luggage and passengers can be discharged from taxis or their own vehicle. Motels, likewise, provide drive-in space for registering and then ask the auto owners to relocate their vehicles near their assigned rooms. Signs identifying the hotel and showing drivers where to exit major highway arteries leading to their parking lot entrances are very important, or patrons may build up resentment for the hotel/motel group and shun it in future travels.

Cost and Types of Assets Needed to Start a Business   Initial investment factors to consider include how much capital is required to operate the business until the break-even level is reached. The manager must consider the need for operating expenses as well as for equipping the facility.

Financing the hotel or motel could be with only owners' equity, but the corporate owner is likely to borrow up to about 75% of the total cost of the structure and furnishings on a long-term mortgage. Large life insurance companies, some savings institutions, and pension accounts are the normal lenders on this type of property.

The lodging industry as a whole had close to $32 billion of assets at yearend 1987. About 16% of this amount was in current assets (cash, notes and accounts receivable, inventories, and short-term investments) and about 17% in longer-term investments (largely stocks or as loans to subsidiary corporations). About 50% of total assets (net of accumulated depreciation) is structures and furnishings, while about 8% to 9% is invested into each of land and miscellaneous assets (largely intangibles of leases and leasehold improvements, trade names and trademarks, and corporate organization and start-up costs).

The lodging industry uses a significant amount of debt, with equity averaging about 30% of assets. Long-term debts amount to almost half of total assets, while current liabilities amount to about the same level as current assets. Miscellaneous debts, such as capitalization of net present value of leased facilities or intermediate-term credit loans, account for a significant amount of financing for the industry.

Each year Dun & Bradstreet, Inc., and Robert L. Morris Associates provide updated studies showing common-sized balance sheets for many different types of business firms. The D & B statement for 1993 in *Industry Norms and Key Business Ratios* provides the following breakdown of assets and liabilities for SIC 7011:

Assets		Debts and Net Worth	
Cash and near-cash	9.7%	Notes payable, short-term	2.8%
Trade receivables (net)	4.8	Bank and other notes payable	.1
Inventories	1.5	Trade payables	3.6
Other current assets	4.2	Income tax payable	—
Total current assets	20.2	Other current debts	11.7
Fixed assets (net)	49.7	Total current debts	18.2
Other noncurrent assets	30.1	Long-term debt	44.7
		Deferred credit	.2
Total assets	100.0	Net worth	36.9
Total assets (firm average)	$1.64M	Total debt and net worth	100.0

In addition to funds raised in the capital (stock and bond) markets, large life insurance companies and pension funds are very significant sources of funds for the lodging industry. Most such institutional funds are invested through the purchase of bonds or by making an over-the-counter, negotiated mortgage on facilities or through the extension of intermediate- or long-term notes, generally with quarterly repayment on principal and interest. Nevertheless, large aggressive pension funds have been placing close to one-half of net cash inflows into equities, and the shares of lodging industry giants are heavily held by pension accounts and mutual funds.

Prentice-Hall, Inc., annually reports a breakdown of expenses for different groups of businesses. In 1993, the expense breakdown for the two smallest asset-size classes (out of 12) of hotels and other lodging places with profits for the reporting year 1990 was as follows:

	Under $100,000	$100,000–$250,000
Cost of operations	14.7%	11.4%
Compensation of officers	7.4	14.9
Repairs	5.2	4.4
Bad debts	.6	—
Rent on business property	16.0	8.0
Taxes (excluding federal tax)	9.8	8.1
Interest	3.0	3.2
Depreciation/depletion/amortization	5.4	7.4
Advertising	.9	1.7
Pension and benefits	.1	1.7
Other expenses	43.4	54.4
Net before-tax profit	—	—

The "other expense" category includes salaries and wages other than to officers, payroll taxes, and miscellaneous expenses.

In this industry, assets usually turn over about one to three times each year, but quartile ratios are provided annually by D & B. For a recent year, selected median ratios were as follows for the SIC 7011 category:

Solvency ratios:

Quick ratio	.7:1
Current ratio	1.1:1
Debt to net worth	128%

Efficiency ratios:

Collection period	8.4 days
Sales to inventory	83.2 times
Assets to sales	141.8%

Profitability ratios:

| Return on sales | 6.5% |
| Return on net worth | 12.1% |

Despite cumulative losses to the industry from 1981 to 1986, it continued to expand nationally and internationally. By the early 1990s, the industry had generally turned profitable. There is some apparent growing shortage of workers in the industry, with the annual growth in employment (*U.S. Industrial Outlook* estimates) being about 2% to 3% during recent years. During these years, revenues for the industry have grown about 2.0% more rapidly than changes in the consumer price index.

Legal Considerations   Owners and managers of hotels and motels are subject to more legal constraints than their counterparts in most other types of businesses. Not only must legal consideration be given to such areas as form of organization, permits and licenses needed to construct and operate the facilities, and problems with employee management, but the owners are bound by law to provide a safe atmosphere for the registered guests. Thus, the aid of professionals in the areas of legal and accounting assistance is needed. Certainly an accounting firm is needed to develop a general accounting and cost control system and in income tax planning.

Fire and theft insurance are a must for hotels and motels. About 7,000 fires each year are reported in hotels and motels. At the very least, personal items may be destroyed and the patrons may have to be relocated (at hotel/motel expense) to a nearby lodging facility. On the other extreme, several lives may be lost with ensuing lawsuits by surviving relatives or business associates of the deceased.

In some instances, drunken employees have, with the use of a pass-key, entered a room and assaulted a paying guest. Courts almost uniformly find for the plaintiff and against the defendant, the latter being the owner of the establishment. Thus, control of keys is imperative in such a business. Other safety precautions, such as providing each room with a chain-lock, a deadbolt lock, and a regular key-driven lock will at least show the intent of management to offer safety to guests. Some large establishments have installed closed-circuit TV monitors in hallways and security guards that walk the hallways at regular intervals.

Some safety-minded hotel/motel managers have installed a microprocessor-based key control system that requires some voice or fingerprint identification of the person obtaining a certain pass-key. Thus a recorded worksheet of persons having the key during a given incident, or during recent days, can be maintained. This action may keep down inside robberies or other acts of crime by disgruntled ex-employees that may have duplicate keys. Regular rotation of locks on doors, though costing more money, may lead to greater levels of safety for registered patrons. Effective key control, then, is a very important legal consideration to such establishments.

Some clean-up crew persons must have master keys in order to gain admittance to rooms in order to change the linens, clean the bathrooms, straighten up the furniture, and vacuum the carpet. Most large hotels have designed master keys given only to certain key managers of the hotels, and sub-master keys, perhaps fitting all locks of guest rooms on a given floor, which might be assigned to the clean-up person on that group of rooms. Careful records should be kept on these keys, and they should be marked clearly, prohibiting duplication by unofficial persons.

Some motels have added a tag to keys seeking their return by negligent guests who leave with them, but a post office box address and no notation on the key as to the establishment or its address may avoid the possibility of a lost key being used by a dishonest finder to enter the room shown on the key.

Creditors usually mandate that property loss insurance be carried on the real assets. However, liability insurance, workers' compensation for job-related injuries, fidelity insurance on persons handling liquid assets, and liability and other coverage of vehicles should be carried by the prudent business person. As funds permit, life insurance on the owners and a group health insurance plan on workers might be added. A competent insurance planner might be engaged to develop a recommended insurance plan of coverage.

Experience and Training Required   In order to provide good services at a reasonable cost and to attract repeat patrons, the managers and employees of hotels and motels must be well-trained for their respective jobs.

Some large, expanding chains of hotels and motels have extensive training programs for newly hired management trainees. A few colleges and universities offer curricula in hotel and motel management. Unfortunately, most operating hotels and motels that have been in existence for years have very little formal training for employees. They often hire the best person available to head up a department and leave the training of the employees serving in that area up to the department head.

Thus, some employees are reasonably well-trained while others are left to their own initiatives in serving traveling clients. This approach often leads to disgruntled patrons who write (or telephone) with nasty remarks about the ill-mannered employees and the snafus that caused them long delays or led to overcharging.

Some hotel/motel chains have initiated a complaint form, or a telephone hotline, for permitting and encouraging guests to register their complaints. Such complaints should be taken seriously, with a return letter drafted by a hotel/motel manager showing he or she cares and has taken steps to ensure that such inadequacies are corrected in the future. The letter should be positive and solicit return visits from the disgruntled patron. In at least half the cases, according to surveys made, steaming off by patrons with some satisfaction gained by gentle telephone conversation or assurance letters will lead to return visits by the patrons. Less-than-satisfied travelers will not only refuse to return to that outlet, but some will warn close friends from such a visit.

Some aggressive marketers of motel space have hired guest relations officers to take care of complaints, or to train one or several assistants in the art. A staff of three handling this endeavor may require the revenues equivalent to two additional rooms per night, on average, but the approach may pay dividends of three to ten times this level in increased room occupancy from repeat, satisfied travelers, according to industry estimates.

Keys to Successful Management   The keys to successful management in the lodging industry are to know the wishes of your intended patrons and to provide quality service at a fair price. In this industry, the following are important:

1. Convenient location: To airports, major highways, major vacation attractions, restaurants, theatres, and so on.

2. Room comfort: Ease of access, cleanliness, adequate furnishings, comfortable mattress, adequate closet space, hot water in bathroom, bathroom fixtures that work properly, and so on.

3. Climate control: Adequate heating and air conditioning appliances.

4. Staff: Should be knowledgeable about company policy but attempt to make patrons' stays pleasant and joyful. An information booth with someone knowledgeable about city sites, complimentary maps, directions for guided tours, and the like is a helpful promotional approach.

5. Food quality: If prices are expensive, quality should be good. Food should be served promptly while hot. Sandwich bars may provide walk-in, stand-up, speedy service for patrons with little time to invest, especially during the noonday rush.

6. Food value: Motel/hotel guests expect to pay more for quality food than for service at a fast-food vendor. However, they expect larger portions of higher-quality items. Lack of food value, or poor service, is one of the chief complaints of disgruntled hotel patrons.

7. Swimming facilities: Only about 20% to 25% of patrons use the swimming facilities, even in hot weather. In cold weather, the ratio is even less. However, some vacationers—especially those with children—stop at a given location so that they may enjoy a short romp in the water before retiring. Pools should be clean, provide a lifeguard during normal hours of opening (such as 10:00 a.m. to 10:00 p.m.), and be readily accessible to assigned rooms.

8. Noise level: This should be kept to a minimum, or at least patrons should be given the choice of not being on a floor where an all-night high school party or something of similar noise level is being held or near the noisy elevator or icemaker, or should be permitted to relocate in a less noisy area of the facility. Otherwise, disgruntled patrons will not return.

9. Price versus value: Patrons are willing to pay for quality. Large rooms, or suites, lavishly furnished with large-screen TVs, cable TV channels, box office attractions, and the like are expected when the price is in the upper range. Lower-charging motels do not, nor are they expected to, provide such niceties for the standard charge.

Many budget hotels charge about $30 to $35 nightly, depending on their location (proximity to major attractions, ordinarily) or as much as 50% below the average daily rates. The average daily charge in recent years appears to be about $64.00 per night for two, but at least one-third of the hotels/motels probably charged $90 or above while a similar fraction charged $40 or below. Patrons expect less at the lower-priced motels, hotels, and tourist courts, but they all expect cleanliness and their needs for overnight lodging to be met.

Some hotels/motels attempt to increase their revenues by assessing a surcharge for telephone usage or by price gouging at the motel/hotel restaurant. The average patron does consume at least one meal at the facility, but the price should be fair for the quality of the food provided; otherwise, the patron will seek other accommodations on the next several trips. Some old-line hotels are beginning to make a comeback at providing quality food service for the home crowds, varying the menus, and advertising to local business persons and other patrons.

The initial key to success is to advertise and appeal to new patrons. A more important one, however, is to appeal to patrons and build repeat, satisfied visitors. Providing (unstamped) postcards with a photo of the facility in the rooms as a complimentary gift is an inexpensive way to advertise the lodging place to friends of satisfied travelers.

Information Sources   Information sources include associations for the industry, periodicals intended to serve the management, directories of suppliers of goods and services, business ratio sources, investment advisory services, and government documents. A typical list of these appears in each update of *Encyclopedia of Business Information Sources* by Gale Research, Inc., Detroit, Mich.

Beauty Salons

Business Types,
Industry
Characteristics and
Prospects

Beauty salons are categorized under SIC 7231. Beauty salons provide a wide range of services, including hair shampooing, cutting, styling, conditioning, permanents, waves, and coloring. Additional services may include wig fitting (along with cleaning and styling); application of hair extensions, hair weaving, or hair braiding; image consulting and fashion services that include makeup, facials and other skin treatments; exercise, massage, and tanning rooms; and manicures and pedicures. Barber shops (SIC 7240) and beauty salons sometimes operate as a combination (unisex salons), but their function as separate units is more common. According to statistics published by the Bureau of the Census, beauty salons are about 15 times as numerous as barber shops, with the latter declining in number most years.

There are three basic types of salons: specialty, full-service, and service and retail combination. Specialty salons offer specific services; for example, hair cuts exclusively. Full-service salons offer a full range of health and beauty services which might include wash and set, color, conditioning, permanents, cuts and so on. Service and retail combination salons offer the same services as specialty or full-service salons, in addition to lines of retail goods which might include hair care products, cosmetics, jewelry, nail care products, and in some instances, women's apparel.

Beauty salons are highly labor intensive. Industry innovations during recent years have made the job a bit more efficient, but have not led to a substantial amount of time savings for cosmetologists. Single proprietorships are usually owned by a licensed cosmetologist who may employ one or more additional persons. About 90% of beauty salon owners accept some hair-care clients even though they may employ four or more additional licensed cosmetologists or hair stylists.

The larger beauty salons are usually operated as a corporation and are franchised by one of more than a dozen holding companies that are active in this line. The one- or two-person salon may be operated from the basement or spare room of the owner's home, or from a storefront building along a commercial strip in a neighborhood area, and serve mostly neighborhood patrons. The larger salons (entailing six or more chairs) are usually located in busy shopping malls or strategically located strip centers.

Over the past 16 years, the beauty salon industry has expanded. In the years 1975 to 1990, growth in employees at beauty shops has been about 2.4% annually. The Bureau of Labor forecasts a 1.4% annual growth for the balance of the century. According to *County Business Patterns* for 1991 (the latest available in 1994), some 374,325 employees earning about $4,023 million were employed by 78,588 such establishments. Only 5,053 barber shops reported less than 5% that number of jobs, with earnings of about $208 million.

The largest single factor that has led to the continued growth in sales has been the growing number of women in the workforce. Many working women treat themselves on a regular basis (weekly or biweekly) to a salon visit for some type of personal care. Once this habit is formed, it is often continued by retired females. This is encouraging for continued industry growth since the overall participation of women in the American workforce is increasing. A Department of Labor taskforce report on child-care as a workforce issue stated that by the year 2000, 61.5% of women will be employed. By 1994, some 47% of the workforce was females and the balance males.

In the January 1990 edition of *Salon Biz*, several leaders of trade associations and manufacturing companies predicted that the next decade of the industry will offer increased opportunities for professionals in the field, with greater demands for hair care services, a surge in skin care services, and professional-use-only retail products.

The ethnic beauty industry (specifically African American) offers attractive opportunities for prospective entrepreneurs. According to the chairman of the American Health and Beauty Aids Institute (AHBAI) in his 1990s decade prediction, "The ethnic health and beauty aid industry (will be) embracing a new era . . . that meets the needs of an expanding $230 billion black consumer market . . . with a host of opportunities (for) the professional stylist."

The executive editor of *ShopTalk* magazine, a quarterly publication of Brainstorm Communications, Inc., estimates that 30% of revenues realized by American salons is provided by black consumers. The publication reports that black women frequent beauty salons on a more regular basis than their Caucasian counterparts, 16 times versus 10 times annually on average. Recent surveys on the frequency of usage of beauty salon services for the majority population suggest that about 11% of users go 2 to 4 times monthly. Another 16% go about once monthly, while about 33% use such facilities less than once a month.

Market Opportunities in Various-Sized Communities

In contrasting the number of beauty salon operators to total population in the United States, each beautician is available for service to about 300 females. About 65% of the shops have only one to four operators, and the remaining 35% employ five or more. A city of 30,000 people with an average per capita income should be able to support about 50 beauty operators. This could mean about a dozen shops with 3 to 5 operators in each. A very small community of 600 would probably provide average income to a single proprietor employing one full-time or two part-time assistants.

This industry makes heavy use of part-time trained operators, with close to 35% of total employed persons working part time. The average weekly time allotted is 30 hours, although about two out of three are full-time operators, with many working overtime hours in the evenings and on the weekend. This percentage of part-time personnel is about two times as heavy as the total in the entire service sector of the economy, as many of the part-time persons are college students who want only part-time work.

Average earnings per beautician (reported as salaries) was $10,750 in 1991 (according to the *County Business Patterns* source stated above). Tips probably average about a fourth of this figure. Many of the part-time employees make close to minimum wage, plus tips, while some of the more experienced operators are able to double this rate of earnings. Since 1985, wages and salaries have been growing by about 3% to 5% yearly in most industries in the United States.

Franchising   The investment breakdown for a large franchised beauty salon in terms of 1988 dollars, according to *Source Book of Franchise Opportunities*, published by Dow-Jones-Irwin, is about as follows:

Initial fee paid to the franchising firm	$7,000–$40,000
Additional cash investment	$5,000–$70,000
Periodic franchising charge (percentage of revenues)	0–5%
Additional advertising charge (percentage of revenues)	0–5%

The publication provides names and addresses of about 50 hairstyling salons that franchise, so inquiries should be made of them, along with visits and information gathered from nearby operating franchisors as to attributes and weaknesses apparent in such an undertaking.

Since the franchised beauty shops are almost always incorporated and are about two times the average size of shops in the industry, an outside bookkeeper (or accountant) should be retained rather than using employee time.

Development and Site Requirements   Clients patronize beauty salons for two primary reasons: service and convenience. If a salon's service is especially top quality, many clients will travel 5 to 15 miles to that salon. Prior to scouting locations for the ideal site, the prospective salon owner should review his or her marketing strategy. A marketing strategy, developed as part of a detailed business plan, identifies target markets and/or segments of a market. It outlines a business owner's method of identifying and contacting potential clients, as well as service features that will be emphasized. At the same time, the owner should review the location specifications as outlined in the business plan (please refer to Appendix C). These two items will be the blueprint for determining the ideal site location for the new business operation.

In selecting the site, the new salon owner needs to know the type of clientele he or she will try to attract—neighborhood or working class patrons, white-collar professionals and middle- to high-income patrons, upscale society matrons and socialites, or a combination. The owner of a salon who plans to cater to an upscale or white-collar professional market segment might consider locating in the central business district of a city or town, either in a prestigious office building, major hotel, or shopping mall, or along one of the district's well-traveled, high-density streets or avenues. Such locations will attract middle- and high-income clients who are employed in a city's downtown business district.

Construction of commercial retail shopping strips was on the upswing in the early 1990s in many locations, with most having one or more styling salons. Independent and franchised salon owners might consider such locations to draw clients from nearby and outlying areas. Another option is to locate along a neighborhood commercial boulevard or street to cater to local residents and clients from nearby and afar.

Once the location and site are identified, the salon owner should investigate:

1. Zoning laws: Is the area zoned for commercial establishments?

2. Stability: Is the area economically stable? Are there plans for area improvements or redevelopment? Is there an active local business association?

3. Government regulations: What are the specific local, state, and federal requirements and restrictions for salon enterprises? Beauty salons are subject to health inspections, Occupational Safety and Health Act (OSHA) standards, the Federal Trade Commission's industry trade regulation rules, and other state and federal laws. The state's department of professional regulation is responsible for licensing and testing of many professional and occupational groups, including cosmetologists. Local governments are responsible for site licensing. The local fire, sanitation, plumbing, and electrical usage regulations should be determined.

4. Signage regulations: Signage is the most obvious form of advertisement for a business. Are there local restrictions on size and type of signage displays?

5. Demographics: What is the population of the area, average age and income of residents, property values? Do the numbers indicate a sufficient population to sustain a salon operation?

6. Competition: How many existing salons are in the area? Can a new salon compete with the existing ones?

7. Traffic flow: Is the site located near a public transit line? Is the site easy to reach by public or private transportation? Is there plenty of automobile and pedestrian traffic, and is there sufficient off-street or street parking?

Next to location, the size of the salon facility is of prime importance. The size will be relative to the number of employees. For those salon owners just starting out with small operations (basic services provided by owner and perhaps one or two other hairstylists), a site's adaptability for expansion may not be especially important if the owner is renting (the owner could always move to a larger site). Principal factors to determine, however, would include: Is the site large enough to accommodate separate reception and client waiting areas, wash stations, color and chemical treatment areas, hairdryer stations, and perhaps separate areas or rooms for manicures and/or pedicures?

For the prospective owner who plans to purchase property or build a facility, expansion planning is quite important. What about special services that might be added at a later date—exercise room, tanning booths, massage room, retail station (professional products, cosmetics, etc.)—will the site be sufficient in size to allow for new revenue opportunities?

Because a salon's design and layout (both interior and exterior) will leave a lasting impression on first-time visitors, it is important to decide upon the particular image to be conveyed. Salon decorations and furnishings should be selected with an image in mind—contemporary, period, or antique; high-tech or art deco; bright or muted colors, and so on. Salon image also determines the layout—open stations versus private booths; open reception and waiting areas versus closed; separate wash, hair treatment, and dryer stations versus integrated.

A new owner might also consider investing in a refreshment and snack station for clients and employees; installing a television or entertainment unit for clients' viewing and listening pleasure; and decorating the salon with special accents ranging from mirrors, posters, and paintings to tropical plants to plush sofas, chairs, and coffee tables.

Cost and Types of Assets Needed to Start a Business The amount of capital needed to start a beauty salon operation depends upon the type of services to be provided, number of cosmetologists to be employed, type of facility (home-based, rental, purchased, newly constructed), site improvements (including plumbing, electrical, and heat ventilation installations), equipment, and interior/exterior design and layout.

An owner who operates out of his or her place of residence will require less capital for start-up than an owner who rents, purchases, or has a facility constructed. Unless the home-based operation requires major renovation to meet building code requirements, site improvement costs (including installations) should not be extremely high. With a rented or purchased facility, the capital investment is greater because of location, lease or mortgage costs, physical or structural improvement costs, and interior/exterior decorating.

The salon owner who opts to rent space should examine the most cost-efficient rental method, that is, fixed monthly rental fee or rental fee based on percentage of sales. [According to the National Cosmetology Association (NCA), salon building rental costs average 6.0% to 6.5% of anticipated gross income.] Salon owners can reduce capital expenditures if the owner of the rented facility provides the site improvements and interior/exterior decorating. If the salon owner must invest in site and design improvements (interior/exterior painting, plaster work, plumbing, electrical, and heating/ventilation/air conditioning installations), these costs can be negotiated to allow for amortization over the period of the lease under a leasehold improvements clause.

A prospective salon owner should give careful thought when considering purchasing property or building a salon. There are, of course, many benefits to purchasing a facility or building a salon, particularly in terms of taxes and rental fees (if the building is going to be multi-user). Whether purchasing or constructing a building, financing needs will be significant. The owner of a purchased facility must budget monthly mortgage and insurance payments in addition to standard operating costs. The salon owner who decides to have a new salon constructed from the ground up must contend with fee charges for the services of an architect and contractor and building expense charges in addition to start-up costs.

Major equipment investments for a beauty salon include: shampoo stations and chairs, styling stations and chairs, floor-model hairdryers, furnishings for clients' waiting area (chairs, coffee tables, lamps, magazine racks), storage cabinets for supplies, display cabinets for retail sale items (hair products, cosmetics, jewelry, etc.), basic trade appliances (blow-dryers, curling irons, hair clippers, and scissors), and supplies (hair products, protective gowns, combs and brushes, hair rollers, hairpins, etc.). According to the NCA, basic equipment needs depend on the selected decor and typically cost approximately $2,500 or more per cosmetologist. The largest start-up costs, NCA says, include air conditioning and heating, common work areas, work stations/chairs/tables, appliances, wallcovering/flooring, and ample electric facilities.

In terms of the salon's interior design and layout, costs will depend on the number of cosmetologists to be accommodated and the required square footage needed for each (typically 130 to 150 square feet per stylist), in addition to spacing requirements for the salon's common area.

A profile survey of salon owners by NCA reveals that most owners have ventured into business with at least $8,000 in capital. Again, the amount of capital depends on location, number of services, decor, quality of equipment, number of employees, and available cash to sustain the operation during the initial months of start-up.

The average asset and liability breakdown for a SIC 7231 organization in 1993, according to Dun & Bradstreet, Inc., in *Industry Norms and Key Business Ratios*, was as follows:

Assets		Debts and Net Worth	
Cash and near-cash	20.3%	Accounts payable	5.4%
Trade receivables (net)	8.4	Bank and other notes	4.6
Inventories	12.3	Other current debts	18.1
Other current assets	5.9	Total current debts	28.1
Total current assets	46.9	Long-term debts	15.3
Fixed assets (net)	35.9	Deferred credit	.2

Assets		Debts and Net Worth	
Intangibles and other noncurrent assets	17.2	Net worth	56.4
		Total debt and net worth	100.0
Total assets	100.0	Net worth	$45,705
Total assets	$81,038	Total debt and net worth	$81,038

The above, of course, is about average for a four- or five-operator establishment, and smaller amounts might be budgeted for a start-up facility. Fixed assets (largely equipment) are the single largest asset. Intangibles include such things as leasehold cost and leasehold improvements. Short-term notes payable are largely for regular borrowing from banks or amounts owed on installment notes due within 12 months for such things as equipment purchase or auto installment notes. Other current debts are largely payroll tax deductions and miscellaneous accruals.

Salon owners generally compensate employees on a commission basis, which could range from 40% to 50% of gross receipts (NCA estimates). Some chains (e.g., JCPenney) pay an hourly rate plus a bonus for efficiency. Owners must estimate salaries for themselves in addition to factoring in federal and state taxes for employees and self. In terms of operating expenses, much will depend again on location cost (lease/rent), decor, number and types of services, equipment costs, number of employees, taxes, fringe benefits, insurance costs, supplies, and utilities. Many of these items are important for estimating operating expenses because they are constant and tend to increase on a yearly basis.

According to information published in 1993 by Prentice-Hall for incorporated salons which had a profit in 1990, the expense breakdown for firms with assets as shown was about as follows for the general SIC 7200 designation (personal services firms):

	Under $100,000 Assets	$100,000–$250,000 Assets
Cost of operations	33.3%	26.5%
Compensation of officers	9.8	10.7
Repairs	.9	1.5
Bad debts	—	.1
Rent	6.8	6.3
Taxes (excluding federal)	3.9	3.8
Interest	.9	1.6
Depreciation/depletion/amortization	3.4	4.9
Advertising	1.4	1.9
Pension and benefits	.7	1.2
Other expenses (wages, etc.)	32.9	35.8
Net before-tax profit	6.0	5.7

Of the above items, labor costs are included in compensation of officers, pension and benefits, and other expenses. For most service firms, including hairstyling salons, labor costs and payroll taxes for officers and employees amount to about 50% to 60% of total revenues.

Obtaining financing for any new business can be difficult. The business owner must have up to 25% equity to invest in the business in some instances before a financial institution will give serious consideration to providing direct financing for start-up. The best advice for a prospective owner is to begin a disciplined savings program for the new business and develop a detailed business plan before approaching a financial lender. Many small business owners have started new businesses without assistance from financial lending institutions. In some cases these individuals have pooled their resources and relied upon assistance from family and friends.

In addition to family, friends, and financial lenders, a prospective owner might investigate the possibility of obtaining public financing from various federal, state, and local government programs. The Small Business Administration offers guaranteed loan financing programs for qualified prospective owners. Some economic development departments of local governments provide loan financing to qualified businesses.

The business promotion state agencies provide direct financing assistance to small businesses through a variety of lending programs. Small Business Micro Loan Program; Minority and Women Business Loan Program; and Community Development Assistance Program—Small Business Financing Fund are available in many states. Block Grant Business Loan Programs Financing Fund and Revolving Loan Fund are offered through some state agencies.

Any small business operating in or planning to locate in a given state is probably eligible for one or more of these loan programs. Owners' equity ranges from a low of 10% up to 30%. Bank participation ranges from 40% up to 80%. Some programs provide low-interest-rate loans which do not exceed 25% to 50% of the total business financing required. Some loan approvals are based on jobs to be created.

Typical Business Ratios   The IRS publishes very skimpy Schedule C information on single proprietorships, classified by major SIC codes (two and three digits). D & B and Robert L. Morris Associates publish composite balance sheets and key financial ratios, with annual updates, which are carried at most public, college, or university libraries and by small-business development centers. For a single proprietor with one part-time assistant in the early 1990s, the estimated revenues needed are about $30,000 to provide a fair labor compensation, cover other expenses, and leave an average return of 10% to 15% on owners' equity.

According to RLM's *Statement Studies* and trade publications, payroll runs about 45% to 46% of receipts for the large, franchised beauty salon. It is somewhat higher than this percentage for the large firms (revenues of

$100,000 to $200,000) and slightly lower for smaller operations (annual revenues below $50,000), due largely to high input of labor by the owner(s).

Charges for beauty salon services have generally kept pace with trends in inflation. The hairstylists (employees) usually receive a ratio of service revenues collected, with 40% to 50% being common. A bonus for earnings above some base level is customary in some of the corporate salons, such as 5% of revenues earned above a preset standard. Tips paid to individual stylists usually range from 10% to 20% of service charges and may total about one-fourth to one-third of the gross earnings of many operators. Gaining satisfied, repeat customers is the key toward earning a fair to high level of compensation for hairstylists.

Key financial ratios are published on about 800 industry lines annually by RLM and D & B. The following median key financial ratios for SIC 7231 (beauty shops) are provided from the 1993 issue of *Industry Norms and Key Business Ratios*, which is updated annually by D & B:

Solvency ratios:
Quick ratio	1.1:1
Current ratio	2.1:1
Total liabilities to net worth	51.0%

Efficiency ratios:
Collection period	27.0 days
Sales to inventories	39.2 times
Assets to sales	25.5%

Profitability ratios:
Return on sales	5.2%
Return on net worth	28.2%

Legal Considerations

A salon owner has many legal considerations to contemplate in starting the business. Will the salon be legally registered with the secretary of state's office as a corporation, partnership, or sole proprietorship? Approximately 27% of U.S. beauty salons operate as corporations, another 9% operate as partnerships, and the balance, or 64%, operate as sole proprietorships. The new owner should retain the services of an attorney in setting up the legal structure and in complying with state business registration and incorporation laws.

Retaining the services of an accountant or bookkeeper to establish and/or maintain the salon's financial records system is another legal consideration. There are specific IRS laws that business owners must be familiar with regarding business and employee tax contributions, workers' compensation, and unemployment insurance.

The locality in which the business will operate is responsible for issuing the business permit or license to operate. A prospective salon owner should contact the appropriate local or county government unit responsible for issuing business licenses, and in some areas that might be the local revenue department. Business licenses are usually renewable on an annual basis.

A knowledgeable insurance agent should be consulted on the appropriate insurance coverage for the salon. A comprehensive insurance package might include: fire, liability, fidelity bonding (for employees handling cash receipts and other business funds to guarantee against loss from embezzlement), crime and theft coverage, and workers' compensation. Additional coverage might include business owner's life insurance (to cover loss to financial lenders in the event of the owner's death and/or provide funds for surviving business partners to buy the other's interest in the business), and executive liability (to protect the owner from personal financial ruin and to protect the business assets in the event of a lawsuit).

Experience and Training Required

According to the state statutes in many states, any one or a combination of the following acts constitutes the practice of cosmetology when done for cosmetic or beautifying purposes and not for the treatment of disease or muscular or nervous disorders:

- Arranging, dressing, cutting, trimming, curling, weaving, cleaning, chemical restructuring, shaping, bleaching, coloring, or similar work upon the hair
- Any practice of epilation or depilation
- Any practice for the purpose of cleaning, massaging, or toning the skin of the scalp
- Beautifying, massaging, cleaning, or stimulating the skin of the human body, except the scalp, by the use of cosmetic preparations, antiseptics, tonics, lotions or creams, or any device electrical or otherwise
- Applying makeup or eyelashes, tinting eyelashes and eyebrows, lightening hair of the body, except the scalp, and removing superfluous hair from the body by the use of depilatories, waxing, or tweezers (but not including the services provided by an electrologist)

The state's department of professional regulation is the state agency that issues certification to become a registered cosmetologist. Requirements differ from state to state, so the appropriate state office should be contacted for exact requirements.

Cosmetology training schools, which must be licensed to provide this training, are sometimes independently operated. Others are operated through large high schools, community colleges, or four-year college or university programs. Some programs offer beautician services to the general public by trainee students at a fraction of the normal charge. A small portion of this revenue may go to the trainee, but generally the trainee works for tips, and the bulk of the revenue earned is used to help pay salaries of school instructors and/or operating expense.

In addition to formal training, the owner of a beauty salon and his or her employees should attend educational seminars and product and creative shows in order to keep abreast of the industry's latest trends, innovations, and techniques. Staff and owners should also study professional trade publications to stay on top of their profession, and join trade associations to foster and maintain contacts with others in the field.

The owner of a salon might also study business and management publications to obtain tips and recommendations on operating a successful business enterprise. The owner/operator needs skills in shop management, personnel, buying and servicing equipment, buying and selling beauty aids and supplies, accounting, and recordkeeping.

Business novices might consider enrolling in a self-employment training course sponsored by a nearby small-business development center or a Service Corps of Retired Executives (SCORE) chapter so as to learn the fundamental principles and techniques for owning and operating a business. A training course will aid the new salon owner in acquiring a general knowledge and a certain degree of expertise in management techniques, marketing, accounting, inventory control, taxes, and financial planning. Self-employment training courses offered by local community colleges, chambers of commerce, community organizations, and small-business development centers will cover these topics and provide assistance to the prospective business owner in developing a viable business plan.

Keys to Successful Management   Managing a salon is no different from managing any other business enterprise. The owner needs to have basic business organizational and management skills. New businesses often fail within the first five years of operation because of inadequate preparation of the business owner. Poor management has been cited as the number one reason for business failure. Inadequate financing is the second usual cause of business failure.

A salon's success can be measured in several ways. The three most often cited measures are profit, repeat clients, and name recognition. Measuring success strictly on the basis of profits can be deceiving. Some industry insiders say that a true measure of success is determined by the salon's market share rather than its profit. In other words, a salon might be turning a profit, but how much is it losing to its competitors in the service area? Is the salon meeting its full potential? Can it improve its competitive edge?

The most critical measure of success may very well be client loyalty, or the number of repeat clients. Without steady and repeat clients, a salon cannot produce profits or make a name for itself. It is only by providing clients with the type of services that they want that a salon can be assured of client loyalty.

While having a salon featured in a magazine or newspaper article does not generate cash in the register, such publicity does enhance the salon's reputation and image as an industry leader; and it can bring in new clients, which means increased profits.

One industry consultant with twenty years in the business has identified seven crucial errors salon owners make in business management. These seven "deadly" mistakes in salon management are:

1. Failure to research demographics when choosing the best possible salon location for the intended investment
2. Failure to plan enough start-up capital
3. Failure to hire the right employees
4. Failure to use professional products
5. Failure to write down job descriptions, pay arrangements, and job benefits
6. Failure to use a professional network of lawyers, accountants, and advertising firm
7. Failure to sell retail products for client home use

Whether starting out or building upon an established salon operation, smart marketing practices are essential for reaching and sustaining a steady client base. Because the salon owner wants to attract new clients, he or she should consistently employ promotional devices that are real attention grabbers—installing appealing outdoor signage and window displays, distributing flyers to passersby, discounting or offering special pricing during certain seasons or occasions of the year (Thanksgiving, Christmas, New Year's, Easter, senior prom, etc.). And don't forget the obvious, like listing the business in the business telephone directory and neighborhood business directory.

Some salons sponsor fashion shows independently or in cooperation with local designers. Others volunteer their services to groups and organizations staging charitable events. Salon owners also become active members in professional associations for networking and referral purposes. Radio advertising and published articles in trade magazines and newspapers are additional ways to promote the salon, as are television spots during prime viewing hours by women (afternoons or prime time in the evening) on local stations.

One of the keys to successful beauty shop operation is to give good, courteous service on a timely basis at a fair price. The general condition of the salon is also important; it should be comfortable for clients and immaculate from opening hours until closing. If possible, provide snacks and refreshments for clients. Remember the names of clients, appointment dates, and special events in their lives. This makes the client feel special and establishes a foundation upon which loyalty is built.

Cost containment and efficiency are important to any business owner, and in particular to the owner of a new business enterprise. For the beauty salon owner operating in this competitive field, it is important to look for new ways of increasing revenues while monitoring cash flow and product inventory and holding down costs. This is especially true for a sole proprietor who might find it rather difficult to generate enough profit from a one-person operation. One alternative for a sole owner/operator would be to engage a full or equal partner to share the costs and responsibilities of the salon business, in addition to sharing the profit. Another alternative for the owner/manager is to lease one or more chairs in the salon to outside hairstylists, thereby collecting additional income to help defray expenses without having to share the profits generated from the business.

As mentioned in other sections of this profile, the salon owner can offer additional services to clients in order to increase revenues and profits. A salon owner might start out offering manicures, pedicures, facials, cosmetics applications, and professional products retail sales. As the business grows, the owner might consider moving to a larger facility to install such client services as tanning booths, massage room, exercise room, or even a small clothing boutique area. An innovatively thinking owner can devise many ways to increase profits and provide his or her clients with the ultimate in beauty and personal care treatment.

Information Sources Many sources of information are available on the beauty shop industry. This long list includes trade associations, books and magazines, directories, financial ratios, investment advisory services, and government documents. A representative list appears in the periodic updates of *Encyclopedia of Business Information Sources*, by Gale Research, Inc., Detroit, Mich.

Building Cleaning and Maintenance Service Firms

Building cleaning and maintenance service firms have been assigned SIC code 7349 (industry group 734). Types of cleaning and maintenance services included under the classification are: acoustical tile cleaning, interior building cleaning, chimney cleaning, custodial services for schools, floor waxing, housekeeping, janitorial services, lighting maintenance (bulb replacement and cleaning), maid services, maintenance of buildings (except repairs), office cleaning, service station cleaning and degreasing, telephone booth cleaning and maintenance, venetian blind cleaning (office, plant, and residential), and window cleaning.

Individual companies or divisions of large building maintenance companies usually concentrate on either business maintenance or residential maintenance. Small firms in the industry usually operate as single proprietorships. As they grow in size, they more often incorporate than operate as a partnership. This limits the liability to the owners to their investments in the firms.

Factors affecting the business maintenance field include the fluctuating costs of supplies, the availability of inexpensive labor, competition, and regulatory issues. Time of operation also plays a major part in this type of operation. While a residential cleaning service will work usually during the daylight hours, a business cleaning and maintenance firm will work during the evening and/or night hours when most full-time workers are absent.

Most start-up firms find it difficult to compete effectively with larger, more-established firms. Since competition in this field is very fierce, profit margins can be minimal, and constant surveillance by the manager is required to keep costs down and productivity up to ensure profits for the company.

Firms may contract for three, six, or twelve months to provide a certain type of service to their clients. One safeguard, however, is to make sure that they can adjust prices upward to cover their own increasing operating costs. For example, as the minimum hourly wage increased by $0.45 in April 1990 and again in 1991, such firms needed to boost the pay to their blue-collar-type workers, who usually receive about 150% of minimum wage, on average. This would necessitate raising the prices that they charge for service in order to continue to operate profitably.

Outlook in the industry is for continued growth, although it is likely to be higher in some geographical areas than in others. According to a 1994 estimate by the Bureau of the Census in *U.S. Industrial Outlook*, employment growth in retail and service company maintenance, including hospital care, is likely to be at about 1.4% yearly during the near term. Growth rates in revenues may exceed this level, especially in health-care, educational, and residential establishments. The fast-growth firms with aggressive management frequently become targets for takeovers in mergers and acquisitions, with the asking price usually amounting to one year's total revenue (or perhaps six times the size of the firm's capital). The shareholders are customarily required to continue to manage the subsidiary corporation for the home office during a transition period of one to four or five years.

Market Opportunities in Various-Sized Communities

Before starting a cleaning service business, the owner should develop a business plan. In developing a business plan, several important pieces of information will be noted, including whether or not the area can support the proposed venture, the existence of an unidentified market niche that may be exploited, the level of competition in the area, the customer base population, competitive pricing strategies, and a variety of other facets of the business that owners or managers need to know to develop a viable and profitable business.

Assistance in developing these business plans may be obtained from many sources—some at cost, others free. A few sources available for assistance are the local chamber of commerce, banks, accounting firms, local and state government bodies such as city hall, the state agency designated to promote growth in commerce within the state, colleges (business management programs or small-business development centers), SCORE offices, and libraries.

A building service firm should have several large and diversified accounts in order to prove profitable and not be unduly susceptible to sales declines during a recession period. Such diversity may include cleaning and maintenance contracts for the local public schools, governmental buildings, hospitals, several office buildings, and a few plants. Firms that add home cleaning services should target community households that are average or above average in income level.

The fastest-growing segment of this type of business appears to be residential cleaning. Contacting local real estate firms, owners and managers of rental property, and individuals who attempt to sell their own dwellings are ways of adding new clients for carpet/drape/window cleaning, and so on. Shampooing of carpets is likely to decline in future years as new technological breakthroughs in dry cleaning gain in importance.

According to recent statistics, some 42,431 building maintenance firms operated in 1991, having 735,339 employees. Each had average earnings of $10,400. Some one-third of the workers were part-time. By late 1992, average weekly earnings of full-time workers were $277 for cleaners and $347 for cleaning supervisors.

A city with 20,000 in population is likely to have one or two building cleaning and maintenance establishments. One or two additional firms would provide single-unit residential and other residential cleaning. Hotels and motels are likely to employ their own staff. Smaller communities are likely to be served by such a firm located in a nearby city. However, this depends somewhat on the number of institutional accounts that can be served by a firm (i.e., schools, government buildings, and hospitals). Growth areas are preferred for new business formations over those with declining population bases, whether residential or commercial.

Franchising   Franchise opportunities exist and may offer an alternative entrepreneurial path to independent ownership. Franchising gives the entrepreneur an opportunity to use the mass buying power, training programs, specific territory, and name recognition factors of the parent franchise to build a profitable and viable business.

Most of the franchising firms provide training at their home office for key officers of franchisee businesses. Video cassettes may be provided that illustrate correct techniques for performing certain types of maintenance and cleaning assignments. Ongoing training should be provided by an enterprising firm in this industry, especially as new equipment or improved service products are acquired.

Several large franchising firms operate in the maid service and home cleaning/party servicing areas. Still others franchise operations in building cleaning and maintenance service. A representative list of the former, including the franchise fee, capital requirements, and training provided in the late 1980s, is as follows:

Name of Firm	Franchise Fee/Capital	Training
MAID SERVICE/HOME CLEANING/PARTY SERVICING		
Classy Maids USA	$9,000–15,000	1 week
Domesticaide, Inc.	15,000–25,000	1 week
The Maids International	7,500–11,500 + eq	Ongoing
Maids-on-Call	9,500–15,000	3 weeks
Merry Maids	15,000+15,000	1 week
Mini Maid Service	15,000–20,000	1 week
Servicemaster	Wide range of fees	3 weeks
Servpro Industries	Wide range of fees	1 month

Name of Firm	Franchise Fee/Capital	Training
MAINTENANCE/CLEANING/SANITATION SERVICE/SUPPLIES		
Chem-Mark International	$18,000	1 week +
Cleantech-Acoustic	19,700	Ongoing
Coustic-Glo International	9,759–25,000	2–3 days
Jani-King, Inc.	10,000–16,500	Ongoing
Lien Chemical	10,000 + 10,000	Ongoing
Mr. Maintenance	2,000–25,000	To 2 weeks
Mr. Rooter Corp.	3,500 +	To 2 weeks
Value Line Maintenance	23,000 +	1 week
Wash on Wheels	7,495–30,495	1 week +
Western Vinyl Repair	13,500–40,000	Ongoing

Development and Site Location

In locating the business, consideration must be given to local zoning requirements. Many communities forbid, through zoning ordinances, the establishment of home-based businesses and the use and storage of noxious or toxic chemicals. The building maintenance firm's inventory would stock these cleaning solvents as a matter of course. It is a good idea to check the local zoning ordinances prior to contracting to rent, lease, or buy a storefront property or to operate out of a residential unit.

Other considerations in locating the business are health requirements; physical size of the operation; storage space with proper ventilation and fire extinguishing systems in place; fire, electrical, and safety codes; expected traffic patterns; signage; and so on. Adequate parking for service vehicles and autos of workers and clients is essential.

The location of a cleaning service's headquarters building is not of primary concern because clients are usually contacted on their premises. The office area should be well maintained and orderly for clients that will frequently visit the home office for conferences. Additional space is needed for storing supplies and equipment; a dressing room for the workers should be provided; and a lounge area is practical where space allows.

Where the geographic area being serviced by a firm is substantial, several satellite locations for storing additional working equipment and supplies may prove profitable and efficient. Top-level managers would probably not staff the satellite operations; rather, a foreperson that supervises several crews of workers might maintain a small office with an answering machine so as to minimize office expense.

Cost and Types of Assets Needed to Start a Business

Initial investment factors to consider would include: How much capital is required to operate the business until the break-even point is reached? How much would be needed for wages, working capital, unforeseen expenses, and inventory? Developing a sound business plan would enable the entrepreneur to target these and other areas effectively.

Financing the business usually means a combination of personal, private, and public funding sources. A judicious combination of these three sources of funds and the incorporation of a sound business plan could make the difference between success and failure.

Personal investments are the source of funds or in-kind services available from the entrepreneur's personal life—family investment in time, money, labor, and use of the home as collateral to leverage a bank loan.

Private sources of funds include commercial lending institutions such as banks, savings and loan associations, life insurance companies, and finance companies. The key difference between private funding and public funding is in the source of the monies loaned. Private sources invest to make a monetary profit from the investment of others. Public sources are governmental agencies at the state level or the Small Business Administration that loan the money at relatively low rates of interest in order to bring the total packaged interest rate down to an attractive percentage so as to stimulate business development and make financing more accessible.

Many writeups are provided in industry literature about persons who have set up a small building maintenance firm with only about $2,000 or $4,000 in capital. Liabilities may stretch the total commitment to assets to about two times this level. For the average of these firms, however, there is roughly $90,000 in equity (net worth) and perhaps two times this level in assets. According to statistics published by Dun & Bradstreet, Inc., in *Industry Norms and Key Business Ratios*, the breakdown in assets and liabilities during recent years for the average firm in the SIC 7349 classification was:

Assets		Debts and Net Worth	
Cash and near-cash	17.5%	Accounts payable	8.2%
Accounts receivable	32.5	Bank loans	.3
Notes receivable	1.2	Other notes payable	5.6
Inventories	2.9	Other current debts	19.3
Other current assets	7.5	Total current debts	33.4
Total current assets	61.6	Long-term debts	13.9
Fixed assets	26.2	Deferred credit	.1
Other noncurrent assets	12.2	Net worth	52.6
Total assets	100.0	Total debts and net worth	100.0
Total assets	$175,000		

A few of the above terms will be explained. Near-cash refers to checking or savings accounts (liquid accounts). Other noncurrent assets generally refer to intangible assets such as leaseholds or leasehold improvements. Fixed assets are a mixture of land and buildings, cleaning equipment, and delivery equipment. Accounts payable are amounts owed to suppliers of inventories and equipment. Loans are amounts owed to suppliers of open market notes or equipment installment notes. Long-term debts include both equipment and mortgage notes.

A building maintenance service firm usually commits one-third of its total assets to accounts receivable, where monthly billing for service is customary, and the second-largest amount to investment into operating and transportation equipment. Most types of building maintenance service firms invest from 5% to 10% of each revenue dollar into materials and supplies; thus, the inventory figure for these firms is low. Wages payable and payroll taxes payable, which are included in "other current debts," usually constitute the largest source of short-term credit to this type of firm.

A typical building maintenance firm with assets of $100,000 and net worth of $50,000 should generate annual revenues of roughly $400,000. A breakdown of average revenues into percentages for the average of the SIC 7349 designation during recent years, according to published figures by D & B, is as follows:

Sales/revenues	$400,000
Gross profits (percent of revenues)	38.5
Net after-taxes profit (percent of revenues)	5.3

A review of the common-sized balance sheet for the D & B classification suggests that approximately 60% of the assets are current in nature, with the largest amount residing in receivables. Fixed tangible assets amount to 26% of the total, with most of this located in various types of cleaning equipment and transportation equipment. Miscellaneous other noncurrent assets are predominantly for leases or leasehold improvements. Self-generating credit, as a result of a buildup of current debts as current assets accumulate, amounts to about one-half of the current asset level. This type of firm uses little bank credit other than equipment notes or mortgage financing on real estate purchases. Since commitment to fixed assets is relatively small in this type of business, and the tax code permits an enterprise to expense up to $17,500 in long-term assets (in 1995) acquired each year, little depreciation is taken.

The assets are small in total compared to total revenues. Expense control is very important to such a venture. When the minimum wage rises, the firm must adequately adjust its charges on the maintenance contracts to offset rising wage costs. Thus, maintenance prices are often bid for periods of six months or one year as a maximum.

Many building service firms are started with a minimum of capital. Many are created from rented or leased quarters with some capital being spent on leasehold improvement and that cost amortized over about ten years (or the life of the lease). Other funds are spent for cleaning and transportation equipment. The salesperson often drives a company-owned vehicle while one or more panel trucks are usually available for hauling equipment and supplies to the contracted jobs.

In this type of business, it is important to determine the amount of direct labor (workers and forepersons, along with payroll taxes) involved, double it, and bid that amount on the contract. Expenses will usually be covered and leave from 5% to 8% as profits. Except for management's salaries, depreciation, rent, and utilities, other expenses in the firm are largely variable.

Typical Business Ratios   A comparison of actual operations with typical, industry-wide ratios is frequently helpful in making decisions as to service charge markup, amounts to allocate to certain expense categories, and a realistic profit expectation. Such ratios are also helpful in preparing projected financial statements.

The *Almanac of Business and Industry Financial Ratios,* updated annually by Prentice-Hall, Inc., from IRS-published data, provides expense breakdowns for corporations representative of major SIC groups. For the business services category, the following expense breakdown as a percentage of revenues was provided in 1993 for firms with under $100,000 in assets and for those with assets from $100,000 to $250,000:

	Under $100,000 Assets	$100,000–$250,000 Assets
Cost of operations	26.7%	36.1%
Compensation of officers	15.5	13.4
Repairs	.6	.7
Bad debts	.1	.3
Rent on business property	4.3	2.8
Taxes (excluding federal taxes)	3.2	3.9
Interest	.6	.9
Depreciation/depletion/amortization	1.8	2.6
Advertising	1.0	.9
Pension and benefits	1.5	2.3
Other expenses	36.6	35.9
Net before-tax profit	8.1	.3

For building service firms, D & B lists the following average key financial ratios during recent years:

Solvency ratios:

Quick ratio (cash + accounts receivable/current liabilities)	1.6:1
Current ratio (current assets/current liabilities)	2.1:1
Total debts to net worth	72%

Efficiency ratios:

Collection period (accounts receivable/sales × 365)	32.9 days
Sales to inventory (net sales/inventory)	102 times
Assets to sales (total assets/annual net sales)	22.3%

Profitability ratios:

Return on sales	3.8%
Return on net worth	22.5%

Many professional organizations are operated as a single proprietorship or as a partnership rather than as a corporation. A single operator of a house-cleaning business, for example, would only keep a record of receipts and expenses so that a Schedule C to the federal Form 1040 income tax return may be filed annually. A partnership must file a partnership information return with each partner recognizing on his or her own tax return one's proportionate share of net profits. Proprietors and partners are considered to be self-employed and must pay self-employment social security taxes (which were 15.3% of taxable income on the first $61,200 of base earnings in 1995). One-half of this amount is a business expense. A corporation, whether a regular or an S corporation, must file a corporate income tax return. The aid of an experienced accountant or attorney in tax planning and return preparation is recommended for someone not familiar with the federal income tax rules.

More than half of the service organizations file corporate C or S tax returns. The main reason for incorporation is a separation of personal assets and business assets for the firm. The S corporation must have fewer than 35 shareholders, all of whom must elect this tax treatment, and the filing status can only be changed with the prior consent of the IRS. In most states, incorporation of a small firm may be done for a few hundred dollars, so the decrease in risk is probably worth the additional cost and record keeping. Most corporations are chartered at state level. The corporation does have to file a separate tax return, although the S corporation does not pay taxes in its own name. Instead, the income is allocated to its shareholders as salaries and/or in proportion to stock ownership.

Every business firm that hires one or more persons on a regular basis must have a federal Employer Identification Number (E.I.N.) so that appropriate payroll taxes, state income taxes, and federal income taxes may be withheld from employees and paid into an appropriate depository financial institution.

Most local jurisdictions require that business operation licenses be applied for and renewed annually. Most municipal bodies have zoning requirements. Building cleaning firms are classified as commercial, although some are operated out of a home office in a residential district. Where crowds of persons are in attendance, fire codes as to restrooms and fire exits are in effect. Fire and safety inspections may be made periodically by the local fire and safety inspector.

Accounting and legal contracts should be reviewed and/or prepared by appropriate professional persons. An accounting or payroll system might be developed for a start-up firm. An attorney should be consulted about drawing up legal documents pertaining to the business.

As with most other businesses, adequate insurance coverage for real property, liability insurance on vehicles, and workers' compensation for job-related injuries (which is required in most states) is strongly suggested. Specialized insurance may be warranted in certain high-risk cases. Some types of insurance to consider include fidelity bonding, business interruption, executive liability, and decision-making insurance. An insurance planner might be consulted for necessary coverage.

Experience and Training Required

Training for management should cover the "how to" of the business, including general management, marketing, and financial and accounting functional areas. Attention should be given to the philosophy (i.e., growth-minded, risk-averse versus risk-taking, withdrawal versus reinvestment of profits) of the firm and "front office" administration in developing a business plan.

Management of a building service firm should have experience in this line of work, be aware of training materials available in written or video form useful in training forepersons and workers, and be promotional in nature. Many firms improve growth potential by having a marketing manager and an operations manager rather than attempting to assign one person to both areas. Another full-time office manager, perhaps a secretary/bookkeeper, is needed for handling messages, routine matters, collection of receivables, banking, and the like. The use of a personal computer in some accounting and expense tracking has grown in importance during recent years. In a small firm, the owner/manager may need all or most of these talents, but in a larger firm, specialists in these areas are often hired.

Forepersons and household workers should receive some training. Initial training involves some reading of instructional packages, video cassette reviews, and on-the-job training with an experienced worker. Ongoing training is often done in a monthly meeting, especially when new products and equipment are to be introduced. Most persons work in teams of two or three, with occasional spot checks by the supervisor or job foreperson. Since time is lost in transit, optimum scheduling might call for four to six houses in close proximity to be cleaned each day. The second day might concentrate the activity in another subdivision, and so on. The attempt is to obtain the maximum number of productive working hours and the minimum of transit hours out of the total payroll day. Workers are sometimes paid by the hour and sometimes by the job.

Providing only excellent service should be the motto. An attempt should be made to provide excellent service at a reasonable cost. Workers' potential should be developed to the fullest, meaning that employees paid by the hour should be encouraged to continue their formal and on-the-job education. It should be possible for employees to climb the ranks of the business to middle- or top-level management, operate satellite centers, or form a franchised firm of their own should the business continue to grow and prosper. Aggressive workers need the challenge of making decisions; being able to move up the corporate ladder and undertake different and more challenging jobs usually leads to less employee burnout (with job terminations) than being stuck in a nonpromotional position.

Keys to Successful Management

In order to be successful, the management of a building services firm must know its competition, have vision as to the markets that it can cultivate, promote a helpful atmosphere for both clients and workers, and strive for only profitable accounts.

Management in a building services firm should be able to gauge the approximate saturation point in a given market area. Markets should be developed where growth potential exists and where the firm has some price or other advantage. Effective labor and supplies cost control should be followed by the office staff and the field crew. The firm's operating objective should be to develop a good reputation in the industry for quality work at a fair price.

Spot radio ads, newspaper ads, listing in the yellow pages of the telephone directory, and direct contact (telephone or mailings) are the usual methods of advertising such services. Service vans often carry the company logo and a brief listing of services offered (often painted on the sides of the vehicle), along with a business telephone number. Billboards are used by some firms in the industry.

Owners/operators of building maintenance firms have to be aggressive and market their services to a wide range of clients, including government agencies, hospitals, chain retail stores, large offices of industrial plants, small and large service and retail clients, and individual households. A company might advertise to a variety of clients and offer daily services such as cleaning restrooms, floor/carpet maintenance, lighting replacement (as needed), dusting, and the like. Weekly cleaning service might include vacuuming drapes and venetian blinds, window cleaning, polishing floors, and carpet shampooing as needed.

Business maintenance contracts are intended to replace full-time building maintenance employees. Contracts may include a mixture of several types of accounts, such as industrial plants, offices within industrial plants, service offices, warehouses (night watchpersons), schools, hospitals, retail trade firms, and others. Management talent needed in this type of enterprise includes experience in sales, operations, and office/accounting/finance activities. The client usually benefits in two ways. A crew of three or four persons, after hours, is probably less costly than employing two persons on an 8-hour day. Moreover, the maintenance persons do not interrupt the daily routine of office work or manufacturing process in attempting to do their clean-up activities during regular business hours. The crews of workers are usually scheduled to work after the clients' normal business hours, such as from 5:30 to 9:30 or 10:00 p.m. on week nights, with major jobs scheduled for weekends. Residential cleaners usually work from about 9 a.m. to 3 or 3:30 p.m. on weekdays.

The largest single cost in a commercial maintenance firm is labor costs for workers and forepersons or supervisors. One rule of thumb often followed in the industry is to compute the estimated cost of direct labor of these workers, add about 11% to pay for social security and other payroll taxes, double the cost in order to cover other costs, and bid that amount. About 6% to 8% of sales will usually be left after covering management salaries, utilities and rent, insurance, depreciation, ad valorem taxes, miscellaneous expenses, and so on.

For a residential cleaning establishment, a crew of three persons is capable of cleaning several homes in a given neighborhood in a working day, devoting from 1 to 2 hours to each residence. One supervisor, using a van, may drop off, supervise, and relocate (after an hour or two) about three or four crews of laborers. Duties assigned to the working crew should be made such that the team members complete their assigned tasks about the same time. Charges for this type of service, again, might be roughly two times the expected out-of-pocket cost for direct labor and payroll taxes. In order to minimize transit time and transportation costs, a city might be divided into districts, with concentration of efforts made only on certain days of the week.

Information Sources Several sources of information are useful for improving the level of profitability of a building services firm or in learning more about the operation for someone not currently in this line of work. These include directories, handbooks of operating techniques, periodicals, trade associations, ratio studies, government documents, and investment services. A list of these for the business services industry appears in each updated issue of *Encyclopedia of Business Information Sources*, by Gale Research, Inc., Detroit, Mich.

Temporary Help Service Firms

Business Types, Industry Characteristics and Prospects

Suppliers of temporary help services have been assigned SIC code 7363, a part of the broader SIC code 736 for personnel supply services. Employment placement firms that seek to find jobs for enrollees on a permanent basis have SIC code 7361. The latter had about 12,750 firms with about 261,205 employees in 1991 and was paying out about $4,210 million in payroll at that time. Temporary help service firms numbered about 14,108, had some 1,230,355 employees in 1991 and had an annual payroll of about $16,986 million. By 1993, the industry had continued to grow and had an estimated 1,600,000 listed employees, making it one of the fastest-growing types of firms in the United States. One company alone, Manpower, boasts some 600,000 employees, or about the same as GM and IBM combined. Other large companies in the industry include Kelly Services, Viva Temps, and Contemporary. Some 20% of the jobs created since 1983 have been in temporary positions. The average size of each firm, in terms of listings, was about 85 in 1991, but growing.

The temporary help services firms are establishments primarily engaged in supplying temporary or continuing help on a contract or fee basis. The help supplied is always on the payroll of the supplying establishments but is under the direct or general supervision of the business to whom the help is furnished. Some areas of activity for temporary help include the following: employees leasing service, fashion model supply service, help supply service, labor pools, work power pools, modeling service, office help supply service, temporary help service, and usher service. In recent years, hospital office help service has been exploited by regional firms.

The temporary help service industry has been one of the fastest growing in the nation since about 1975. The passage of TEFRA (Tax Equity and Fiscal Responsibility Act) in the early 1980s accelerated this growth rate to about 30% to 35% yearly, although the rate of growth until the end of the century is expected to grow more slowly, with the emphasis on firm-supplied health care.

Temporary help service firms are most active in supplying four types of workers. The most numerous is office help (about 63% of the total), followed by industrial workers (about 15%), medical workers (about 11%), and technical workers (about 10%), according to recent surveys. One recent study seemed to support the fact that about 10% of the persons were professionally trained in accounting, engineering, systems analysis, law, controllership, or other top-level management areas. Such persons are usually between jobs, but some have suffered from burnout with one firm and prefer merely part-time work until a decision is made as to full-time employment with another firm.

The temporary help service firms themselves are merely offices where listings of workers and potential clients are maintained. The managers and other staff workers of such firms attempt to match the characteristics needed by the requesting firms with those of listed workers. Testing of listed workers, along with checking on references and providing some updating and training, are usually done by the enterprising managers of the temporary help service firms. Arrangements with nearby colleges and universities for courses of study, especially for workshops on the use of personal computers (word processing, spreadsheets, and database analysis, for example) are customary.

In many cases, the temporary help is priced at a level slightly above the going wage scale for permanent workers, but income from the requesting firms must pay not only the expenses of the worker but also the fringe benefits and the cost of the services of the temporary help service firm. For example, for each $100 spent in salaries by the temporary help service firms, another $43 is probably spent for the following: insurance and taxes ($11), hiring costs ($7), downtime ($10), and other out-of-pocket expenses ($15). Add to this a small profit margin of about 5% to 6%, and the charge should be about 150% of the wage rate paid to the workers.

Why do firms use temporary workers rather than permanent ones? Some have seasonal swings in their needs for workers (i.e., spring or Christmas selling rush, catalog mailings, etc.) and do not wish to fatten their permanent staff. Other reasons include planned absences of workers for vacation or maternity leave, or unplanned absences due to sickness of regular workers. Offices with about four or five regular workers are more likely to be clients than those with 10 or more, as work load might be more effectively shifted with a larger staff.

In this arrangement, temporary help service firms hire and place the workers, collect a stated fee for their performed duties, and then pay the temporaries their wages and fringe benefits. A knowledge of federal and state income tax laws on items to deduct and transmit to the taxing authorities, then, is needed. Most such workers are subject to payment of 7.65% of wages into OASDI, with matching by the employer (or temporary help service firm). Depending on the filing status and number of exemptions claimed, it might be necessary to withhold federal and state income taxes from the gross wages of the workers.

Some temporary help service firms are large in size, consisting of more than 100 offices in more than 50 different metropolitan locations. Some are smaller, however, and specialize in a limited geographic area and type of worker. Manpower and Kelly Services are two firms with a national reputation. It was estimated in early 1991 that some 131, or 5% of the total of such firms, had over 1,000 employees, according to Department of Commerce estimates in *County Business Patterns*.

Over the balance of the century, the fastest-growing segment of the population should be retired persons. Many of these persons who are still in good health become bored with retirement and prefer some part-time assignment with new experiences rather than the possible boredom of long-term employment. Their pension accounts during retirement are in place, so they are only seeking supplemental income and some interesting work assignments. The requesting firms are obtaining years of training and experience if needs and characteristics of workers can be matched adequately. Moreover, the requesting firm does not have to enroll such temporary workers (with fewer than 1,000 yearly hours of work) into its retirement plan. Thus, the overhead paid to the temporary help service firm is usually no greater than the fringe labor costs that are eliminated. Retired workers receiving Social Security retirement benefits can earn about $8,600 annually up to age 70 without losing Social Security, so many of such persons set this as the maximum level of income that they wish to earn during a given year. Payment of $8 or $10 an hour, however, would permit such a person to work between 800 and 1,000 hours annually or about 20 to 25 weeks on a full-time equivalent basis. Some retired persons go south during severe winter weather months and prefer employment during other time periods, such as normal vacation months by regular workers (i.e., June through August plus December).

It is estimated that the rapid rate of growth in the industry is likely to slacken, but may continue at about three times the overall growth rate in the national labor force. Some 2 million persons may be employed on a part-time basis by the year 2000. With the anticipated continued shrinkage in the unemployment rate in the nation over the next business cycle or two, a large platoon of potential part-time workers is likely to have increasing opportunities to earn supplemental income and to provide a vital contribution to the business community.

Market Opportunities in Various-Sized Communities

To be successful in a small community, the temporary help service firm would or should expect smaller hourly charges for workers than would be true in large urban areas. An attempt should be made to act as training and hiring agent for several of the large employers in the region, as well as making their services available to others and for listing of available persons wishing to be hired.

Before setting up a temporary help service firm, a survey should be made of the competition, including their location and office layout. The largest of the firms in this industry, Kelly Services and Manpower, usually concentrate on larger cities, but independent or regional firms frequently locate in small cities.

The suppliers of temporary help services that are attempting to establish national reputations would concentrate one or more offices in metropolitan areas. A city of 20,000 population should be able to support a moderate office in this endeavor. Or such an office might serve several business communities within a radius of about 20 miles, making up about this population. As stated previously, offices with four to five office workers are potentially greater users of such temporary office workers than are offices of larger size. Areas with several hospitals, clinics, medical office complexes, and the like are potential users of temporary medically trained nurses and aides that prefer part-time to full-time employment.

Persons that list with temporary help service firms are usually from three walks of life. Retired persons aged 55 to 70 frequently desire part-time employment to avoid boredom or to gain supplemental income. Mothers of small children sometimes desire part-time employment to earn supplemental family income and to build their own retirement fund through social security and/or IRAs. Some persons who lose their jobs for miscellaneous reasons elect to list with a temporary help service firm in order to appraise the field for permanent employment. Conversely, some business firms, prefer to use the facilities of such a firm in screening and training their prospective employees, hiring workers on a temporary basis for a time and then offering them a permanent job. When this technique is followed, some fee is normally paid to the supplying firm to compensate it for screening and training endeavors. This technique is most often done by firms that relocate from one area to another and have not established their own human resource management staff in the area. Nevertheless, most listed part-time persons are not available on a full-time basis but rather prefer part-time employment.

Franchising   Franchising opportunities exist and may offer an alternate entrepreneurial path to sole ownership. Franchising gives the entrepreneur an opportunity to use the mass buying power, training programs, specific territory, and name recognition factors of the parent franchise in order to build a profitable and viable business. Owners of the help service firms receive some training tips from the franchisers and then train their own listed workers.

Most of the franchising firms provide training at their home office for key officers of franchisee businesses. Video cassettes and other teaching aids are provided that illustrate correct operational and management skills. Ongoing training should be provided by an enterprising firm in this industry, especially as new office equipment is installed or new training programs for clients are introduced.

Several large franchising firms operate in the temporary or permanent and temporary help service industry. A list of these, including the name of the firm, its city and state of home office, and the minimum investment requirement, is provided. Since the figures are subject to change, the interested reader should contact the home office for up-to-date information and a prospectus on its operation.

Name of Firm	Location of Home Office	Minimum Investment
AAA Employment Franchise, Inc.	St. Petersburg, Fla.	$10,000–$30,000
ADIA Personnel Services	Menlo Park, Calif.	70,000–75,000
Bailey Employment System	Monroe, Conn.	40,000
Baker & Baker Employment	Athens, Tenn.	10,000
Bryant Bureau	Sarasota, Fla.	40,000–80,000
Career Employment Services	Westbury, N.Y.	15,000
Careers USA	Philadelphia, Pa.	125,000–155,000
Cosmopolitan Care Corp.	New York, N.Y.	50,000
Demo Specialists, Inc.	Rockwall, Tex.	5,000+
Employers Overload Co.	Minneapolis, Minn.	30,000
Engineering Corp. of America	Seattle, Wash.	25,000
Express Services, Inc.	Oklahoma City, Okla.	12,000
Manpower, Inc.	Milwaukee, Wisc.	50,000
Norrell Corp.	Atlanta, Ga.	50,000–80,000
The Olsten Corp.	Westbury, N.Y.	40,000–50,000
Remedy Temporaries	San Juan Capistrano, Calif.	35,000
Staff Builders	Lake Success, N.Y.	100,000
Temps & Co.	Atlanta, Ga.	60,000–95,000
Temp Force	Atlanta, Ga.	60,000+
Today's Temporary	Dallas, Tex.	60,000–100,000
Western Temporary Service	Walnut Creek, Calif.	2,500–10,000
Uniforce Temp Personnel	New Hyde Park, N.Y.	45,000–55,000

Someone interested in a franchised operation should probably check out competitive terms and costs with two or more firms that franchise in their area before making a decision.

Development and Site Requirements

In locating the business, consideration must be given to local zoning requirements. Many communities forbid, through zoning ordinances, the establishment of home-based businesses and the use of streets for parking a large number of autos. It is wise to check the local zoning ordinances prior to contracting to rent, lease, or buy a property or to operate out of a residential unit.

A supplier of temporary help services is likely to be located in a commercial office building. Working space for its own office personnel (i.e., office manager/training person, receptionist/telephone operator, and accountant) would be needed. A conference room for testing or training new or experienced persons who wish to have their skills upgraded is desirable. The conference room could double as a library where job manuals and job descriptions of usual clients are available for study by prospective temporary workers.

Some nearby parking space for prospective hiring firms and temporary workers is needed, although many of the repeat orders and worker placements could be handled by telephone once relationships have been developed.

An occasional visit by the employment firm's office manager to the work places of the temporaries may be useful in keeping down possible problems. The day-to-day, on-the-job supervision of the temporaries, of course, must be left to the regular staff persons of the companies using their services. However, developing a feel for the atmosphere and the types of persons that would fit into such an environment would aid in assigning certain persons to a particular job.

Nearness to a community college, business training school, or the like might be helpful in providing inexpensive training on the state of the art in certain types of work assignments, especially office skills.

The second largest line of workers seems to be medical assistants, although some temporary help service firms list persons with a wide range of marketable skills. The temporary help service firm might pay the expenses of training the listed person, but the contractual arrangement might be for a portion of such costs to be repaid to the firm unless the person lists as a temporary for a certain minimum time period, such as six months.

Cost and Types of Assets Needed to Start a Business

Initial investment factors to consider would include: How much capital is required to operate the business until the break-even point is reached? How much would be needed for wages, working capital, unforeseen expenses, and inventories? Developing a sound business plan would enable the entrepreneur to target these and other areas effectively.

Financing the business usually means a combination of personal, private, and public funding sources. A judicious combination of these three sources of funds and the incorporation of a sound business plan could make the difference between success and failure.

For 1993, Dun & Bradstreet, Inc., in *Industry Norms and Key Business Ratios*, lists 499 firms in the SIC 7363 classification. The mean breakdown of assets and liabilities is provided below as a guide. This would, of course, vary somewhat for a given firm, depending on whether it operates out of owned facilities or leased office space. The following is considered average in the industry.

Assets		Debts and Net Worth	
Cash and near-cash	18.5%	Accounts payable	8.0%
Accounts receivable	50.3	Bank loans	.6
Notes receivable	.8	Other notes payable	8.4
Inventory	.8	Other current debts	23.9
Other current assets	6.9	Total current debts	40.9
Total current assets	77.3	Long-term debts	10.5
Fixed assets	13.0	Deferred credit	.2
Other noncurrent assets	9.7	Net worth	48.4
Total assets	100.0	Total debts and net worth	100.0
Total assets	$424,000		

Of the above items, cash would consist largely of demand deposit accounts or near-cash items such as negotiable order withdrawal (NOW) or money-market investments. Accounts receivable would be billings made to the hiring firms of the temporaries.

Other current assets would be for such things as prepayment of insurance (i.e., workers' compensation, health insurance, professional insurance, fidelity insurance, and the like). Fixed assets would largely be for office equipment. Other noncurrent assets would be investments into leasehold and leasehold improvements, and the like, for rented facilities. A well-established firm might own the facilities out of which it operates, but most would operate from rented office space until becoming well-established in a given metropolitan area.

Accounts payable would be for such things as office supplies, amounts owed on owned vehicles, billings for workshop attendances, billings for training manuals, and so on. Amounts owed to banks or other financial institutions would be for installment payments on personal computers or other office equipment, amounts owed on autos or other equipment purchased on intermediate payment terms, and the like. The largest liability would be for wages payable and taxes withheld from the gross pay of the temporary employees. Net worth in the industry averages about one-half of total assets needed.

Roughly $500 in assets is needed for each temporary person listed with the firm, but close to half of this can be obtained from debts. Thus, a person with $25,000 wanting to start such a firm might be able to support $50,000 in assets and $300,000 in annual billings (roughly a 6 : 1 ratio is average in the industry) and have a staff of three office workers and perhaps 80 to 100 temporaries listed for a wide range of occupations.

The breakdown of income statement data for an average-sized firm in this industry might be about as follows:

Revenues (billings and miscellaneous)	$2,790,000
Gross profits (percent of revenues)	23.5
Net after-tax profits (percent of revenues)	3.6

Typical Business Ratios The IRS publishes a breakdown of expenses for corporations. This information is picked up by Prentice-Hall, Inc., each year in the *Almanac of Business and Industry Financial Ratios*. From the 1993 edition, the expense breakdown for the broad industry group business services (except advertising) as provided for the smallest two asset-size categories of firms was as follows:

	Under $100,000 Assets	$100,000–$250,000 Assets
Cost of operations	9.9%	16.9%
Compensation of officers	6.8	—
Repairs	3.2	3.1

continued

	Under $100,000 Assets	$100,000–$250,000 Assets
Bad debts	—	—
Rent on business property	10.0	7.7
Taxes (excluding federal tax)	3.7	7.4
Interest	1.6	—
Depreciation/depletion/amortization	2.0	3.3
Advertising	.5	1.5
Pension and benefits	—	7.0
Other expenses	54.4	48.0
Net before-tax profit	8.1	5.1

Since the above is a mixture of several subclassifications of business firms, including temporary help service firms, the exact breakdown of expenses may not apply. The average temporary help service firm doubles the rate that it expects to pay its employees in the bidding process. The additional funds are needed to cover other operating expenses, including payroll taxes for the temporary help employees, their fringe benefits, and so on, and to leave about a 4% to 6% profit to the firm.

Knowledge about solvency ratios, efficiency ratios, and profitability ratios in a given line of business is helpful in reaching decisions about pursuing a given type of business or in making forecasts of pro forma statements and cash budgets. For the suppliers of temporary help services, the following ratios are about average:

Solvency ratios:

Quick ratio (cash + accounts receivable/current liabilities)   1.7:1

Current ratio (current assets/current liabilities)   1.8:1

Total debts to net worth (total debts/net worth)   99.5%

Efficiency ratios:

Collection period (accounts receivable/sales × 365)   38.3 days

Sales to inventories (net sales/inventories)   91.5 times

Assets to sales (total assets/net sales)   16.7%

Profitability ratios:

Return on sales (net after-tax income/sales)   2.2%

Return on net worth (net after-tax income/net worth)   27.8%

An analysis of the above suggests that net worth approximately equals accounts receivable for such a going concern. With the collection period running about 38 days, or about one-tenth of a year, net worth needs to be about 12% of expected annual billings. Thus, a net worth of $50,000 should support annual billings of about $500,000. This might be equivalent to some 50 temporary workers, each earning on average about two-thirds of $500,000/50 or $6,667. National averages run only about one-half this level, but the more efficient firms would strive for workers that are available for one-third to one-half of normal working days in order to keep down training costs and other operating overhead.

Legal Considerations

The aid of an accounting firm or a legal firm should be sought in certain types of events. The services of an accounting firm would be useful in deciding whether to operate as a single proprietorship, a partnership, or a corporation. Due to the chances of being sued by the place of employment or a third party, a corporate form of organization offers a greater sense of security to the owners of such a firm. Carrying adequate workers' compensation and other insurance on the staff of workers is also important.

Long-term contracts should be developed with the aid of an attorney. Needless to say, the aid of an attorney should be sought when suing or being sued by a third party.

The firm should be appropriately licensed. The location of the firm would be in a commercially zoned area. Fire codes could be a factor, and might dictate the number of persons permitted on the premises at any one time. Emergency exits and number and location of restrooms should comply with health and safety standards.

Knowledge about state and federal income tax withholdings and transmission of funds and appropriate filings of schedules is imperative for such a labor-intensive type of organization.

Developing a form that protects the temporary help service firm from substantial loss of investment when temporaries take full-time jobs or become trained and move to another temporary employment firm is needed. An attorney should be used in drafting the wording of such a contract.

Experience and Training Required

Training for management should cover the "how to" of the business, including general management, marketing, and financial and accounting functional areas. Attention should be given to the philosophy of business, involving such areas as being expansion minded, avoiding legal and business risks, and so on. The needed training in these areas might be obtained through college credit in appropriate courses at nearby colleges or universities or through taking the "nuts and bolts" courses offered by regional small-business development centers.

The permanent staff of a supplier of temporary help services would probably number three or more. An office manager/owner should have adequate capital but should also have knowledge about the temporary help needs of the business community. Clients can be developed, with patience and hard work, but having personal acquaintances with a few personnel officers in a given city would be a definite bonus to such a fledgling firm.

The office manager might also participate heavily in designing training sessions for the listed temporaries. A receptionist/telephone operator/secretary is also needed. The third person should be trained in payroll accounting, but might spend some hours in training the temporaries in the use of personal computer spreadsheets, databases, and graphics.

The decision would have to be made as to the types of temporaries to list and promote. This might be allocated as follows: office workers, with heavy emphasis on personal computer skills featuring state-of-the-art word-processing knowledge (perhaps 60% of total listings), blue-collar laborers (10%), machine operators (10%), medical support staff persons (10%), and others (professionals, etc.) (10%).

The temporary help service firm would maintain an inventory listing of such persons, by skills and attributes, and attempt to match them with requesting business firms. Ideally, at least two or three days of lead time for matching potential supply persons to their jobs would be needed, but unscheduled absences of workers and certain near-term deadlines do not often cooperate. Listed workers should know that they would sometimes be asked to be available to move to a new job with only an hour or two of advance warning. When this is done, the hiring business firm should realize that a less-than-ideal fit and less than the normal amount of briefing has been done by the temporary help placement firm.

Most temporary help service firms do attempt to offer suggestions to their listed persons as to how to upgrade their skills, how to dress, and peculiar likes and dislikes of their supervisors on their temporary assignments.

Not only do the workers expect their regular wages, but many expect or appreciate special recognition. This might be in the form of annual Christmas bonuses (often a percentage of profits allocated on the basis of earnings during the year), other awards, vacation trips, or other gifts. Time off, such as a week of paid vacation for a person who works more than 1,000 hours during a given year, might be appropriate.

Keys to Successful Management The owners/managers of a supplier of temporary help services should have office management training. Ideally, the persons would be familiar with the general needs of the business, industrial, and health communities in which they intend to operate. Certain steps thought to be helpful in developing such a successful operation include the following:

1. Develop a clientele of participating firms. Offices with four to six full-time employees would be sought for office workers.

2. Develop a listing of industrial firms that have substantial seasonal swings in sales or production. Those that sometimes acquire large subcontracts or contracts from other large firms or the Department of Defense are prime candidates for needing temporary employees.

3. Develop a liaison with the health-care facilities in the area, and inquire as to their stance on hiring temporaries, along with their usual needs (practical nurses, registered nurses, nurse's aides, blue-collar cleaning personnel, etc.).

4. Advertise for the listing of potential part-time employees with desired characteristics. This is likely to include retired persons, housewives with small children, and miscellaneous persons between full-time job assignments.

5. Develop a well-designed, but relatively inexpensive, training program for the listed persons.

6. Attempt to match up the desired traits and skills of sought-after persons with those available.

7. Set a fair price for the services of those placed on the job. This will likely be from 150% to 200% of the going wage for such entry-level persons on a full-time equivalency basis. But remember that billings have to pay fringe benefits as well as the operating costs to the temporary help service firm. On a long-term or intermediate-term basis, a slight reduction in the normal billings might be appropriate.

8. Attempt to stay abreast of changes in office skills needed/desired by the requesting organizations. Attempt to offer, through firm or college facility workshops, skill-updating seminars.

9. Act as an intermediary between the requesting firms and the temporary employees, attempting to assign those persons likely to be acceptable to the former.

10. Develop a good liaison with the temporary workers by giving them proper recognition of bonuses, gifts, or vacation days for above-average performances.

Information Sources Several types of information are useful to the manager/owner of a temporary help service firm. These include associations, books and directories, periodicals, financial ratio studies, investment services, and government services. A representative list of these is provided in the periodic updates of *Encyclopedia of Business Information Sources*, by Gale Research, Inc., Detroit, Mich.

Nursing Care Facilities

The federal agencies designate three different SIC codes to nursing and personal care facilities. SIC 8051 is for skilled nursing care facilities. Intermediate-care facilities have been assigned SIC code 8052, while nursing and personal care facilities (not elsewhere classified) have been assigned SIC code 8059 from the SIC group 805.

The 8059 category includes establishments engaged in providing some nursing and/or health-related care to patients who do not require the degree of care and treatment that a skilled or intermediate-care facility is designed to provide. Patients in these facilities, because of their mental or physical condition, require some nursing care, including the administering of medications and treatments or the supervision of self-administered medications in accordance with a physician's orders. Establishments primarily engaged in providing day-to-day personal care without supervision of the delivery of health services prescribed by a physician are classified as SIC code 8361.

The elderly population in the nation is the fastest-growing age segment. In 1994, there were about 31 million elderly persons (above the age of 65) living in the United States. By the year 2000, there should be about 35 million elderly. Since the retired elderly have different needs in housing, generally, than do the working families, much more national attention must be directed toward retirement centers and villages and long-term nursing care facilities.

The older segment of working adults is typically between ages 55 and 64. Some persons work beyond that time, of course, and base OASDI retirement benefits will be phased in for older persons near the turn of the century. By about 2022, a person will need to be 67 (rather than the current 65) in order to receive such base OASDI benefits. Otherwise, they are reduced by 6.67% yearly for each year below this age. Also, such benefits will increase for those that retire beyond this base age.

Persons below about age 65 do not usually require as much health care as do older adults, but their needs approximately double for each five years of age beyond about age 65. Thus, an 80-year-old needs about eight times as much assistance as a 65-year-old person. Those within ages 65 to 74 are often able to care for themselves, but many appreciate some hot meal service and health-maintenance service. Those aged 75 to 84 need these types of services plus standby medical care service. Those even older require specialized-service living facilities, as a general rule.

In 1987, the Department of Commerce identified some 9,482 establishments in the SIC 8051 designation and 3,933 in the SIC 8052 designation. By 1991, the total of SIC 805 firms had increased to 19,598 with an average size of employment of about 80. The pay per employee was slightly above $19,000 yearly at the SIC 8052 establishments and about 10% higher at the skilled nursing care facilities (SIC 8051). By 1992, registered nurses (RNs) were earning almost $36,000 yearly, according to a *Wall Street Journal* article (Jan. 19, 1994), licensed practical nurses (LPNs) were earning almost $23,000 on average, and nurse's aides were earning almost $16,000. The latter category was growing more rapidly than the former two due to shortages of RNs and LPNs in many locations. The level of salaries varies widely from one city to another and is higher in large cities such as New York, Los Angeles, and Chicago than in smaller cities such as St. Louis or Dallas.

The duties of RNs, LPNs, and aides differ. The RNs monitor patients' health, keep medical charts, dress wounds, and administer drugs. The LPNs do the same duties but must be directly supervised by a physician or an RN. The aides change beds, move patients, and bathe and feed patients, as a general rule.

Skilled nursing care facilities (SIC 8051) tend to pay out a larger percentage of their total revenues as salaries/wages (33.5%) than do their counterpart (SIC 8052). In 1987, some 5% were single proprietorships, 9% were partnerships, and the balance were corporations. The average size of their employment was 84 persons.

Nursing and personal care facilities (SIC 8052) often have more revenues than do the SIC 8051 facilities, but only about 19% of the revenues are used to defray the cost of payroll. About 16% of these in 1987 were single proprietorships, 9% were partnerships, and 76% were corporations. Some wings of their establishments are operated more like condominiums than as nursing homes, and some cater to elite patrons by building in plush apartments and many amenities. On average, they staff only about half as many persons as do SIC 8051.

The number of persons attracted to nursing homes has been growing during the latter twentieth century. For example, in 1980 (the census), some 0.63% of the population resided in nursing homes. The percentage was slightly higher by the 1990 census. Moreover, the percentage of the total population in age groups beyond the normal retirement age should be increasing, as shown by the following statistics on aging (in thousands):

Population Age	1990	2000 (est.)	Yearly Change (percent)
65–69	10,006	9,110	−.9
70–74	8,048	8,582	+.6
75–79	6,224	7,242	+1.5
80–84	4,060	4,965	+2.0
85 and over	3,461	5,136	+4.0

Of the above, the 85 and over age group should be about 14% of those beyond the age of 65 by the year 2000. And since the above-65 age group is the most rapidly growing group (due to population demographics and extended mortalities for U.S. citizens), the need for increasing such nursing and personal care facilities is apparent.

In 1987, it was estimated that those facilities that were oriented to caring for Medicare patients usually priced their care between $15,000 and $18,000 yearly per patient. Even those operated at a break-even level by municipalities charged $65 to $75 daily or upward for rooms of double occupancy. Those that provided care for private patients often charged from two to three times this rate. An alternative, of course, is home nursing care, where costs run about 15% to 40% as much as hospital costs and where routine skilled nursing care might run about one-third as much as in the hospital. Many nurses provide evening home care on a moonlighting basis to patients able to afford it. The cost of such care has been growing about 3% yearly above the general consumer price index (CPI) changes.

Several problems are seen on the horizon as far as providing health and personal care are concerned. There is a rising shortage of nurses, and the number of student nurses enrolled in college programs declined over the 1980s (due to low salaries in the profession, a falling number of high school graduates, and other reasons). Some hospitals and other facilities that hire nurses have attempted to fill this shortage by overtime assignments for the nursing staff, hiring temporary nurses, or employing nurses from foreign countries. The American Medical Association (AMA) favors training registered care technologists to assist in the nursing industry, but the American Nurses Association (ANA) fears this might lead to compromises in the quality of the care provided.

The OASDHI has undertaken a very large financial responsibility by attempting to provide Medicare and Medicaid to those that qualify. In the early 1990s, over 33 million persons were enrolled for Medicare with about 10% of these being disabled. Some 97% were considered to be elderly (above 65 years of age). In 1992, there were close to 25,000 providers of Medicare service in the nation, including hospitals, skilled nursing care facilities, home health agencies, independent labs, dialysis facilities, and other providers.

The Part A Medicare provides hospital insurance that pays in-patient hospital care, which is limited to 100% of the cost for 60 days, less the deductible of between $500 and $600; the Part B supplement requires a copayment. Ultimately, the patient must pay everything when Medicare payments are exhausted. More often than not, the patients are transferred from the hospital to skilled nursing care facilities (or back home with home health care visits two or three times weekly by assigned nurses). Many of these persons must be cared for around the clock by relatives or live-in maids.

Before Medicare will pay for the skilled nursing care facility charges, the liquid assets of the covered person must be below some maximum level (i.e., about $2,500 in 1990). The person is allowed to have a prepaid burial policy and a home that are exempt from this ceiling. Where more assets are available, the insured must first exhaust his or her own funds before the costs are covered by Medicare. Then the OASDHI program pays (up to its ceiling) the costs for up to 12 months. If the person remains in the nursing home beyond this point, the person's home is sold and the proceeds applied against the charges. For this reason, many of the elderly prefer to remain in their home as long as possible and only transfer to skilled nursing care facilities when health is failing or death is approaching.

More private insurance plans to cover needed health care for the elderly are needed by a majority of the U.S. population. The American Association of Retired Persons (AARP) has developed a supplemental benefit plan that pays $50 or $75 in cash daily to aid in deferring such costs. This may be marginally adequate for intermediate-care facilities, but certainly it is grossly inadequate for hospital care, which often runs over $300 daily.

The outlook in the industry can be forecast with a high degree of accuracy. The demand will continue to accelerate; there is likely to be a decline in federal reimbursements (or more patients must pay themselves); the facilities will grow in size through expansions and consolidations, being operated in a more businesslike manner; and there will likely continue to be growing disenchantment with regulation at both the federal and state levels. If the recent trends continue in the growth of chains (predominantly through mergers and acquisitions), anti-trust laws are likely to be applied to this type of service. However, anti-trust laws are usually not applied where state regulation is in place, so monitoring is likely (licensing, inspection, required reporting, and the like) in some states, with little required in others.

Federal legislation was introduced in 1993 that would attempt to reduce the rate of growth in charges for health care, which had been growing in the 1970s and 1980s by about two times the general CPI increase. But 1993 witnessed a slowdown in the growth in prices of health care to about 6%, due partially to health policies requiring a higher fraction of copayment by the patient; to holding the line on what Medicare will pay for many types of services; and to reducing the number of tests given by many of the health providers. Also, there was a growing trend toward treating more patients as outpatients (in the hospital for about 24 hours for certain types of surgery, then home for recovery) and using more nurse's aides with lower pay levels in some cases to perform routine tasks.

Close to 33 million Americans are estimated to be without health insurance. The Clinton health-care bill, though failing in 1994, aimed at providing basic coverage to this group. Part-time workers are usually not provided such care by their employers. Many retired singles are also not covered, except by the limited coverage of Medicare.

Market Opportunities in Various-Sized Communities

Nursing care facilities are sometimes operated by not-for-profit groups and sometimes by profit-making firms. The potential owner(s) of such a home should make a business plan that attempts to forecast the degree of competition and level of unmet demand for such facilities over the next few years. Thus, some idea as to the appropriate size of the facility, its likely level of revenues, the rates that potential clients would be able to pay, and other information might be obtained in the market analysis for such a firm.

Important demographic information about competing firms, their charges, and the potential for clients might be obtained from a number of sources. The local chamber of commerce, public or university libraries (especially in the government documents section), banks, accounting firms, not-for-profit groups, small-business development centers, government agencies (city, county, or state), and private research institutions might provide important demographic data at little or no cost.

There are benefits and drawbacks associated with locating nursing and personal care facilities in small communities. First of all, the cost of living is lower in such locations, and the ratio of elderly to total population is greater. However, there is a tendency for the wage scale to be lower in such facilities, and many of them have a shortage of trained medical staff—both physicians and registered nurses.

A better choice of location would likely be a small city near a large metropolitan area. It is doubtful that one small city would have enough aged citizens seeking such living arrangements. The location of one or more facilities to serve several small cities, however, might be a viable alternative. In future years, it is likely that reduction in payments of the Medicare program will dictate that the cost of facilities, as well as the availability of staff personnel, will be strong locational factors for newly designed nursing and personal care facilities.

Development and Site Requirements

Of primary concern to the potential owner of a nursing or personal care facility is zoning and licensing. The location should also be such that it will be acceptable to its potential clientele. Many children of nursing home residents want to visit them several times weekly, so a location within about 20 or 25 miles of a large city or on a busily traveled thoroughfare is important.

Since the charges made to private clients are usually two times as great as those paid by social security (Medicare) clients, studies should be made of the demographics of an area before additional health-care facilities are built. Nursing and personal care facilities are oftentimes a combination of retirement home with some available nursing care. Special-services health-care facilities are sometimes added later.

Most persons who enter a nursing and personal care facility do so at the insistence of some near relatives. Thus, there is a tendency for them to locate in small cities near larger ones, or perhaps in the outskirts of large metropolitan areas. Many of the patrons have living relatives (other than a spouse) within about a 5- to 15-mile radius of the nursing home.

The average demand for the facilities is about 60 beds per 1,000 in the population over age 65. Nebraska, South Dakota, and several other states have a ratio about 150% of this level, while it runs much lower in Florida and New Mexico. Of all facilities planned, about half have less than 50 beds and the others have more. Only 5% have over 200 beds, so this type of facility tends to be intermediate in size.

The facilities tend to use more LPNs than RNs. This is likely caused by the wage difference, as well as a shortage of RNs. Turnover rate of employees is also a problem to nursing care facilities, with turnover being greatest for those with 50 to 300 beds. This is probably due to their being located in or near large urban areas where better employment opportunities are available than in rural areas where jobs are often scarce. In fact, many hospitals in small communities were being closed due to insufficient funds generated in the latter 1980s and early 1990s, and some medical staff were available for hire in such locations.

The patrons of many nursing homes are largely transient. About half of the patrons stay for about 60 days before going to another nursing home or returning to their own residence. The other half stay an average of 130 days. Those who expire while at a nursing home have generally been there somewhat longer than three years.

Most persons residing in nursing homes tend to be past 75 years of age. In 1977, one survey indicated that the median age was 81. Fifteen of each 1,000 persons aged 65 to 74 were in nursing and personal care homes, 68 of each 1,000 persons aged 75 to 84, and 216 of each 1,000 persons aged 85 or more. Nursing home residents are expected to increase by about 2.0% yearly over the 1978 to 2003 period, according to the survey and estimate. Should these ratios continue to hold, the number of patients at such facilities should grow by about 10% yearly due to the demographics of the U.S. population. Employment in such establishments grew at almost a 5% rate in the 1975 to 1990 period, but such growth rate is expected to be about 2.9% yearly for the following 15 years—about two times the overall growth in population.

Thus, the number of persons within these age categories in a given location, and the present facilities serving them, would be the prime factors surveyed in locating or expanding such facilities in a given location. The ability to obtain an appropriate license and the state's reputation for fairness in inspection of the facilities would be other factors. There is some attempt to draw a mix of private patients and Medicare patients, and those facilities with an eye toward attracting a majority (say 60% or more) of private patients usually build more plush facilities than those that expect to attract the lower-paying Medicare patients.

Nursing homes and personal care facilities have a tendency to be multi-level but not unusually tall structures. First of all, the installation of elevators is expensive, and some zoning commissions are reluctant to permit the erection of such facilities more than about five stories in height. Many are about three stories in height: a basement, a ground-level floor, and a second-story floor. One or more elevators are usually installed in such buildings, especially if federal funds have been used in their installation, so that handicapped patrons may have access to the facilities. Moreover, fire escapes are less of a problem in low structures, and the structures are viewed by prospective clients as being safer than are the exceedingly tall structures.

Many of the nursing homes and personal care facilities have special-project rooms in the basement, such as laundry, small commercial businesses, and recreation rooms. Offices tend to be near the entrance of the ground-level floor. Patients tend to be located in wings off the first- and second-level floors. The kitchen, more often than not, is located centrally in the facility. Some build a few small eating rooms adjacent to the main dining room that might be shared by the patrons and their visitors, who dine as paying guests from time to time.

Some facilities are located near major highway arteries so as to attract passing motorists who might have relatives that would be potential clients of the facility. Working adults, for example, might perceive the establishment as being appropriate for an aging parent, aunt, or uncle.

Cost and Types of Assets Needed to Start a Business

The potential developer of a nursing care facility must estimate with some degree of accuracy the amount of funds needed for operating the facility. Funds are needed for operating cash, receivables, inventory of equipment, linens, gowns, and so on. Substantial amounts of funds are invested into land and structures, often owned but sometimes leased and renovated.

Funds are available from several sources to finance assets of such a firm. The equity owner(s) often provide about 40% of total needs, while the balance comes from a mixture of short-term debts (about 27% of total assets) in the form of trade payables, wages payable, taxes payable, and so on. Long-term mortgage debt might be obtained from financial institutions. Still other long-term debt arrangements might be possible through some state lending program.

Dun & Bradstreet, Inc., annually prepares *Industry Norms and Key Business Ratios* on about 800 lines of business. Three of these fall into the assisted living and nursing care facilities area. These are SIC categories 8051 (skilled nursing care facilities), 8052 (intermediate-care facilities), and 8059 (other personal care facilities). Common-sized statements, published by D & B in 1994, are shown for these three categories:

	SIC 8051	SIC 8052	SIC 8059
ASSETS			
Cash and near-cash	10.0%	11.2%	10.8%
Accounts and notes receivable	22.6	15.9	23.0
Inventory	.7	.9	.7
Other current assets	6.9	8.1	7.1
Total current assets	40.2	36.1	41.6
Fixed assets	37.1	40.2	32.4
Other noncurrent assets	22.7	23.7	26.0
Total assets	100.0	100.0	100.0
Average total assets (thousands)	$2,527	$1,327	$1,542
DEBTS AND NET WORTH			
Accounts payable	8.9%	6.0%	8.4%
Bank and other notes payable	2.8	2.8	2.6
Other current debts	16.2	17.0	16.8
Total current debts	27.9	25.8	27.8
Long-term debts	38.3	35.8	32.7
Deferred credit	.7	.6	1.2
Net worth	33.1	37.8	38.3
Total debts and net worth	100.0	100.0	100.0

Most of the above accounts are self-explanatory, but a few of them will be described briefly. Other current assets include prepayments such as taxes, insurance, magazine or organization subscriptions and memberships, prepaid services, and the like. Other noncurrent assets include intangible assets, long-term investment in other facilities, and so on. Long-term debts are usually in the nature of mortgages on real property, installment notes on equipment, or amounts owed on revenue bonds issued by a municipality to aid in the construction of the facility. The Federal Housing Administration is involved in financing for many of these types of institutions, although the FHA merely insures the mortgages, and funds are provided by private financial institutions.

Typical Business Ratios

Key financial and business ratios are of two types. One type is merely a breakdown of operating expenses as a percentage of sales or revenues; the second type is industrywide ratios computed from composite balance sheet and income statement data.

Each year, the IRS provides a breakdown of operating expenses and key ratios for most major SIC designations for corporations that file corporate income tax returns. Prentice-Hall, Inc., in *Almanac of Business and Industry Financial Ratios*, provides this information for about 12 asset size classifications. For two of the smaller classes of nursing and personal care facilities, the following appeared in the 1993 edition:

	$250,000–$500,000 Assets	$500,000–$1,000,000 Assets
Cost of operations	48.4%	31.6%
Compensation of officers	1.2	2.9
Repairs	1.6	.8
Bad debts	1.1	—
Rent on business property	—	7.2
Taxes (excluding federal tax)	7.3	6.5
Interest	1.8	1.3
Depreciation/depletion/amortization	2.7	1.6
Advertising	.2	.3
Pension and benefits	2.2	1.7
Other expenses	35.8	41.5
Net before-tax profit	—	4.6

The largest two expense categories for the nursing homes are the cost of operations (food, utilities, assignable labor) and the other expenses category, which is largely payroll and payroll taxes. Rent, ad valorem taxes, unemployment taxes, and compensation of officers are the other large expense categories.

Beginning with the 1991 recession, Medicare and many private insurers became much slower in remitting for charges. Accounts receivable built up, and many of the health-care providers had to resort to a buildup of debt and some reduction in equity.

Key business ratios are sometimes helpful in making forecasts of projected financial statements or comparing actual ones to industry benchmarks. D & B provides such ratios for about 800 lines of business and includes the upper quartile figure (the 25th percentile), the median (the 50th percentile), and the lower quartile (the 75th percentile) in its array of comparative firms. For the SIC categories of 8051, 8052, and 8059, the following median ratios are shown for the 1994 study, but other ratios may be obtained by the interested person from the D & B source.

	SIC 8051	SIC 8052	SIC 8059
Solvency ratios:			
Quick ratio (quick assets/current debts)	1.1:1	1.1:1	1.2:1
Current ratio (current assets/current debts)	1.5:1	1.5:1	1.6:1
Total debts to net worth (percent)	138.5	101.8	111.9
Efficiency ratios:			
Collection period (days)	31.8	25.9	28.7
Sales to inventories (times)	195.7	179.8	184.3
Assets to sales (percent)	68.7	70.1	64.8
Profitability ratios:			
Return on sales (percent)	3.4	3.5	3.9
Return on net worth (percent)	13.9	11.7	11.4

Some of the above are operated as not-for-profit corporations, so the usage of median ratios may be somewhat deceiving as to actual returns achieved for the profit-making group. The large, expanding firms in health care attempt to earn a reasonable profit for their shareholders. About 25% of the firms earn 30% yearly (or more) on their equity ownership, so this type of business venture does offer potential profits for those that are well managed. Another 25% (approximately) operate at break-even or loss levels.

Legal Considerations Nursing and personal care facilities must be appropriately licensed at the state level. A federal tax employer identification number (FEIN) must be obtained by all firms with a payroll to employees.

Nursing homes and personal care facilities probably have a greater need for legal aid than do the average type of trade or service organization. It is important to design a cost control and bill-tracking accounting system so that appropriate clients will be billed for the services that they receive.

Certain of the contracts (such as mandatory meals to be paid for) are drawn providing certain flexibility (choices) to the clients. Some states mandate that up-front billing be limited and that contracts not exceed a certain period of time, such as two or three months. The aid of an accountant would be helpful in these negotiating endeavors.

Knowledge about state and federal regulations, as well as possible changes in Medicare requirements and the like, is needed by the managers of the nursing care facility. Certainly the owners should carry property insurance, liability insurance on persons injured on the premises, and professional liability insurance for employees. Most states mandate that workers' compensation be carried on employees for on-the-job injuries. The fringe benefits most often afforded employees are paid vacation days, sick days, and health-care insurance. Certainly these benefits, as well as potential insurance carriers, should be reviewed by a competent attorney.

Legal contracts must be drawn up and reviewed in a number of areas. Appropriate licensing requires certain legal applications to be filed. Periodic inspections of facilities lead to legal implications for the facility or its owners, and these should be monitored by a competent and knowledgeable attorney.

Local commissions usually set and enforce fire codes (the number of persons that may be in a given facility, such as a meeting hall or a dining facility), the number of bathrooms and fire escape exits, and the like. These must be investigated before the facility is designed and built. The engineer for the building should be aware of these and comply with building codes.

Experience and Training Required Nursing homes and personal care facilities need a diversity of management. Fewer than 25% of them operate as single proprietorships or partnerships. The larger ones are incorporated, and many own multiple facilities in several locations. Top-level management must have strengths in general management, marketing, and financial areas. Public relations with employees, clients, and regulatory authorities are important. Building a good reputation (through word of mouth) is needed to keep down room vacancies and to reduce the problems of excessive inspections and so forth.

A well-run nursing care facility has an adequate staff of nurses, orderlies, and other employees. Most have a dietitian and several food handlers. The office workers should have experience in similar types of operations or be trained to handle processing of patients, insurance (private company and Medicare), billing, out-patient billing, and so on. It is important that services be billed and tracked to appropriate patients, or such revenues might be irretrievably lost to the firm. Trained specialists are usually hired, if available, to head up each of these areas, and then they provide assistants on-the-job training. The most efficient of this type of firm have one full-time equivalent employee for about every eight patients, while the ratio might run one to three for the less efficient ones.

For patients who need nursing care, it is probably more efficient to assign about 15 patients to each nurse on a primary basis. She or he would get to know the patients well. The second-shift nurse (late afternoon/evening shift) would be assigned primary nursing duty to another group of patients (but see others not really assigned to her as demand arises). Thus they get to know their patients well, building a better liaison of trust, and usually get better cooperation from the orderlies and other personnel. Medical doctors (or at least medical care technicians) are usually on call but may not be physically located at the nursing and personal care facility.

The nurses try to involve the patients in group activities such as television, quiet gatherings, singing, visiting ministers with sermons, and the like. It helps to pass the time and to keep down boredom. Also, it creates a more friendly atmosphere to permit visitors at most times of the day, say from 9 a.m. to about 9 p.m., rather than creating very restrictive visiting hours. Thus, close relatives (working children of aging parents, for example) can run by for a few minutes on their way to or from work. For this reason, location near a busy highway will sometimes attract persons from a greater distance than otherwise.

Keys to Management Success   Several areas must be considered in designing and operating a nursing and personal care facility. The following are listed as suggested areas for investigation:

1. Demographic studies into potential unmet demand should be made, along with those already available, with ranges of facilities and prices, before a new facility is built.

2. A forecast should be made as to the probable mix between private patients (and their required standard of living and ability to pay for same) and those covered by Medicare. The mix should be considered in designing the facility.

3. It will be necessary to advertise the facility through a number of sources. This will probably include local chambers of commerce, not-for-profit organizations popular with the aged, and word of mouth. Some such establishments advertise on radio and television. Knowing what patrons want and trying to provide these services go a long way toward advertising the facility through word of mouth.

4. The primary goal of the nursing and personal care facility should be to attract and keep satisfied clients. Knowledge about managing insurance accounts and collecting for services provided is important, but patients should be made to feel wanted and not guilty. Moreover, some relatives have a feeling of guilt for the abandonment of their aged relatives to a nursing home. Where possible, this feeling should be overcome or downplayed.

5. Patient-centered and patient-care management should be practiced. This means that care must be taken in designing admitting practices, care planning, charting of the patients, billing procedures, bookkeeping, cost accounting, cost reporting, and document preparation.

6. The successful nursing and personal care facility emphasizes quality care. Its staff persons are sensitive to patients' needs, cleanliness (rooms, bathrooms, dining rooms, and the like), attractive dress for themselves and encouraged for the patients, the absence of offensive odors, a few small rooms where guests may meet with their patient/relatives, and so on.

7. Effective cost control and tracking of expenses (with billing to appropriate clients) are all-important, as unbilled expenses reduce revenues and the ability of the establishment to operate on a profitable level.

8. Since some turnover of clients occurs, some program of advertising should be in place. The ads should provide facts, and such brochures might be distributed as mailers to selected potential clients. Nearby retiring persons (often making the newspaper) would be one possible listing source. Posting the notices in local churches, visitors' centers, and offices of chambers of commerce might be appropriate in some locations.

Information Sources   Several sources of information are useful to the management or potential management for nursing or personal care facilities. These include directories, periodicals, trade associations, ratio studies, investment advisory services, and government documents. A selected list of these is provided in each update of *Encyclopedia of Business Information Sources* by Gale Research, Inc., Detroit, Mich.

Management and Business Consulting Firms

Consulting firms are assigned SIC codes 8742 and 8748. SIC 8742 is essentially for establishments primarily engaged in furnishing operating counsel and assistance to managements of private, nonprofit, and public organizations. Their activities are varied and include strategic and organizational planning; financial planning and budgeting; marketing objectives and policies; information systems planning, evaluation, and selection; human resource policies; practices planning; and production scheduling and control planning. SIC 8748 refers to establishments primarily engaged in furnishing miscellaneous business consulting services.

In 1993, according to *U.S. Industrial Outlook*, there were about 635,000 persons employed by consulting firms in the nation. Many of the consulting firms are large, with the top seven firms each having over 1,000 persons that devote their time to consulting work. These are, in order of size, Andersen Consulting (Chicago), Coopers & Lybrand (New York), McKinsey (New York), Booz Allen & Hamilton (New York), Gemini Consulting (New Jersey), CSC Consulting (Massachusetts), and Boston Consulting Group (Boston). Still, some 40% of consultants are self-employed. Many of the smaller firms have from one to four employees, but the few dozen that operate with regional or national scope often employ more than 100 persons scattered among various offices located in large cities. Andersen Consulting in 1993 was the largest operating consulting firm, earning almost $3 billion and having a 53%, three-year growth in such revenues worldwide. The firm boasted some 22,500 consultants, many M.B.A.-degreed persons with some accounting training.

A consultant is an individual who receives any form of remuneration from another party in exchange for advice and expert opinion. Primary research (interviews) and secondary research (data analysis) provide the factual basis for a consultant's expert opinion. The final result is usually a written or oral presentation made to the client. At this time specific recommendations are offered to remedy the problem situation. Consultants work extensively in information systems, cost reduction, strategy development, and reengineering of products.

The consulting trade literature suggests some general recommendations and cautions for beginning a consulting firm. Primarily, do not go into business alone, as close to 90% of such firms fail in less than two years. Should a person initiate a firm alone, about six to twelve months of operating funds (enough to cover insurance, rent, taxes, general overhead, etc.) for the business should be available to maintain operations to the point of breaking even. A consulting firm may be begun on a part-time basis until a clientele base can be built. A well-focused field, such as pension planning, tax planning, estate planning, engineering, product marketing, or plant management, should be targeted. Larger firms, with more specialty staff persons, may diversify into broader categories. Business firms primarily use consultants during periods of strong business and profits, often discontinuing their work during periods of tight profits. Thus, it is important for a consulting firm to build a good reputation when business is brisk.

It is possible for a consultant to achieve personal and financial success in any technical or professional field such as business management, education, and government. Within each broad field, individuals practice their expertise in specific subcategories such as financial management, time and motion study, career counseling, or computer system design. The key to success in consulting is the ability to specialize and develop your image as an expert in your field. Recommendations from satisfied clients are the core of any consultant's sustained growth. Thus one is not faced with reestablishing credibility.

The area of consulting has taken on greater importance in the world of commerce in the 1990s than previously, especially in European and Asian industrial countries. The first world conference by the consulting industry was held in Europe in May 1987. Employment in the field increased dramatically from the mid-1980s to 1993. Revenues grew by upward of 5% yearly, on about a 2% increase in employment. This period was generally one of deregulation and global competition, so it is likely to be followed by several years of shakeout (weaker firms going out of business) and acquisitions and mergers.

Consultants are often brought in to analyze situations from an objective, unbiased viewpoint. Management and staff members will often more easily accept recommendations when suggested by an outsider. Consultants play an important role in service and support functions such as accounting and legal matters. Hiring additional personnel for a company is more expensive than using consultants for specific short-term projects. And consultants are needed at all levels of government, in business, social, family, and educational situations. The field is very fertile, indeed.

The trend in the latter 1980s and early 1990s was toward large public accountancy firms acquiring specialty consulting firms. Electronic data processing (EDP) companies have also been acquiring consulting firms as subdivisions. More recently, large advertising firms have followed their lead. Many people gravitating toward the industry have been either retiring or fired corporate executives. For example, the acquisition of one firm by another usually frees up some staff persons of both firms. Many of these people find their way into the consulting ranks. In the United States alone, employment gained more than 25% from 1985 to 1987. The Department of Labor does not expect this phenomenal rate of advancement to continue, but some successful firms have been able to go from a few dozen to a few hundred employees in a period of two to three years.

Market Opportunities in Various-Sized Communities

To be successful in a small community, the consultant would or should expect smaller fees and would need to cultivate the small number of growing business owners in the region. As stated previously, many consulting enterprises start and go out of business within a two-year period due to insufficient revenue generation. A retired person, without excessive risk, may begin to operate such a firm out of his or her home or a shared office and should acquire professional insurance to safeguard against resource-taking lawsuits. A pension might provide livelihood expenses and permit the person to develop the entrepreneurship.

Before setting up a consulting office, a survey should be made of the competitors, including their location and office layout. The major types of firms that provide services in the consulting arena include a few large consulting firms such as McKinsey & Company and Arthur D. Little that usually concentrate their resources in large cities; the management consulting division of the Big Six or Eight public accounting firms (Arthur Andersen is the largest in terms of consulting revenues); general consulting firms; specialist consulting firms; small consulting firms; and sole practitioners (often part-time consultants).

In order to market your services, first determine exactly what you plan to accomplish and what specific services you offer. Carefully define your business objectives and set short- and long-term goals. Once you establish your priorities, concentrate on those relationships that will best further your aims. Find those people, business groups, or professional associations that need your ideas or services.

Keep finding those groups. It's like mowing the grass. It's a job that needs to be done over and over again for as long as you own the lawn, or business. Some professionals advertise their services. Should you? Advertising may lack a certain degree of professionalism and credibility. Several other avenues of promotion are traditionally successful for consultants.

The first of these avenues is to pursue every opportunity to speak before audiences that are likely to contain good prospects for you. You will find that audiences generally fall into one of two groups: cross-disciplinary and specialized groups. Both offer excellent potential for finding new clients. Lectures will provide you with a modest honorarium. However, more important than the fee is the public relations value of your appearance. If your lecture is properly promoted, you will find new clients looking you up for weeks and months afterwards.

The second method used by successful consultants is that of gaining media exposure. Newspapers, magazines, newsletters, radio and television talk shows all have an insatiable appetite for new information or old information with a new angle. There is a high degree of interdependency between the information providers and the information disseminators in our society. You as an expert can, should, and must take advantage of it.

Volunteer to write an article or regular column about your specialty for an appropriate publication. Once your article appears, be sure to have reprints made for promotional use. Send them to business associates, clients, and prospective clients. Another positioning device is the presentation of a technical paper or results of a survey you conducted. Offer your services for radio, TV talk show, or workshop panels. Be a moderator or discussion leader. This exposure continues to reinforce your position as a known expert in your field.

On a national basis, one consultant exists for about every 4,000 persons. Even in small communities, local or regional chapters of SCORE (Service Corps of Retired Executives) or ACE (Active Corporate Executives), sponsored by the Small Business Administration, may provide opportunities to meet groups of business persons willing to hire a consultant.

Development and Site Requirements In starting a consulting firm, some attention should be given to the physical location of the headquarters, base of operation, office, or whatever. Increasingly, consulting firms are operating out of the home as "home-based businesses." This can be very tricky, as many communities do not allow home-based businesses located within a residential area. Before "hanging out your shingle," check the local zoning ordinances. In general, the consultant operates mostly at the client's site rather than in an office environment. Since this is the case, a modest office setup is the norm. Vehicular or pedestrian traffic is not a prime concern, but good quality work and a strong reputation are.

A consultant wishing to work with another person, perhaps someone with complementary strengths, would likely seek a small suite of offices in a commercial building. For example, a retired middle- or top-level corporate executive with an M.B.A. might form a consulting firm with a retired industrial engineer. Each would want his or her own private office for meeting prospective clients and for doing routine analytical work. A part-time or full-time person would probably be hired to handle the secretarial, bookkeeping, and other office chores. A conference room, restroom, and coffee area are nice additions. A modest four-room office suite, located in a commercial building, is a good site.

Consulting firms do not encounter large groups of persons frequenting their business, so location, traffic patterns, visibility, and signage are not very important. Instead, a major part of the work is initiated on the premises of the clients. However, occasional visits from several staff persons of a client firm might necessitate the use of a conference room. Metered or nearby lot parking for a few autos, thus, are important.

While the owners or managers of commercial office space usually require that a one- or two-year lease be signed, a growing business usually has little difficulty in negotiating for more space within the same building.

Assistants could always use the conference room for working space when not needed for infrequent meetings.

Cost and Types of Assets Needed to Start a Business

Because of the wide range of consultants and their fields of expertise, it is difficult to give a specific dollar amount needed to begin a consulting business. Let it suffice to say that one should be able to begin with a minimal capital investment of $10,000 to $25,000. This nominal amount takes into account rental fees and utility costs. The IRS permits home office deductions from revenues generated, and it makes sense to keep your costs down. Office equipment, desks, filing cabinets, an electronic typewriter, and stationery are all necessary. Do not hire full-time office help until your income warrants the expense. An answering machine and a fax are valuable assets. A personal computer to help one organize and store data is certainly a consideration, but wait until you see if your operation is sufficiently viable to justify renting or purchasing such an item. Invest a few hundred dollars to print a professional brochure describing your complete services. It should be personal and written in such a way as to encourage potential clients to contact you. A good brochure will pay for itself many times over.

Knowing the asset, debt, and capital breakdown of a large number of firms in an area of planned business activity is helpful in developing lists of resources and projected financial statements. The two sources of widely used data for such work include Robert L. Morris Associates' *Statement Studies* and the annual study by Dun & Bradstreet, Inc., of 800 lines of business, *Industry Norms and Key Business Ratios*. The following balance sheet breakdown, in percentages, is about average in the management and business consulting services industry:

Assets		Debts and Net Worth	
Cash and near-cash	25%	Accounts payable	11%
Accounts receivable	33	Bank loans	1
Notes receivable	2	Other notes payable	5
Inventory	2	Other current debts	18
Other current assets	8		
Total current assets	70	Total current debts	35
Fixed assets	19	Long-term debts	9
Other noncurrent assets	11	Net worth	56
Total assets	100	Total debts and net worth	100
Average total assets	$225,000	Average total net worth	$125,000

The average-sized consulting firm has about $750,000 in revenues, a 46% gross profit margin, and a 7.3% net profit margin, after taxes. About half the revenues go for salaries and the balance to cover other expenses of operation, including fringe benefits.

Setting up a consulting office entails some advance planning. For instance, an accountant, bank loan officer, or account executive at a brokerage firm might be consulted. Some will provide free advice to a business shopper in hopes of obtaining reciprocal business at a later date. Decisions need to be made about:

- Locating and enrolling clients
- The form of business organization (sole proprietorship, partnership, corporation, etc.)
- The scope of the operation (how wide a field of potential clients)
- Hiring temporary, part-time, or full-time help
- The wisdom of proceeding alone versus combining efforts with others who have similar aspirations

The methods of financing a start-up consulting firm can vary from a single source to a multi-tiered financing structure. In general, most start-up consulting firms do not need massive inventory, accounting systems, or buildings; therefore, the initial need for a lot of capital does not exist. A consulting firm may realistically start on a very low budget requiring only an identified expertise on the part of the consultant and a client base.

In the cases where financing the start-up becomes an issue, several avenues should be explored. First, the consultant could finance the entire start-up cost from savings or personal equity. Second, the start-up may be financed through a collaboration of personal equity (maybe a home equity loan), bank financing, public (governmental) funds, or a combination of the three.

Typical Business Ratios Key business ratios in the areas of solvency, efficiency, and profitability are sometimes helpful in developing financial statements or evaluating a firm's strengths and weaknesses.

Solvency ratios:	
Quick ratio (cash + accounts receivable/current debts)	1.8:1
Current ratio (current assets/current debts)	2.0:1
Total debts to net worth	66%
Efficiency ratios:	
Collection period (accounts receivable/sales × 365)	49 days
Sales to inventory (net sales/inventory)	35 times
Assets to sales (total assets/annual net sales)	32%
Profitability ratios:	
Return on sales (net after-tax profit/annual net sales)	5.5%
Return on net worth (net after-tax profit/net worth)	22.8%

The Internal Revenue Service does not provide a separate breakdown for expenses for the consultant classification. However, the firm is operated much like a small or intermediate-size accounting firm, and the breakdown of those expenses might serve a useful purpose as a guide to one planning a consultant business. These are about as follows:

	Percentage of Revenues	Important Factors
Cost of operations	19–16	Rises with size.
Compensation of officers	20–25	Mix influences.
Repairs	0–2	
Bad debts	0–2	
Rent on business property	4–8	Owns vs. leases.
Taxes (excluding federal taxes)	4–5	Owns vs. leases.
Interest	1–2	Type/amount of debt.
Depreciation/depletion/amortization	3–4	Newness of assets.
Advertising	.1–.5	Philosophy.
Pension and benefits	3–5	Owner's wishes.
Other expenses	38–50	Number of employees.
Net before-tax profit	2–8	Profit margin.

Of the above expense categories, the two largest are for compensation of officers and other expenses. The latter category includes wages and salaries paid to other than corporate officers, payroll expenses, and miscellaneous business expenses.

There appears to be little economy of scale in the consulting firm business. However, the hourly charges are usually higher for large consulting firms operated in large cities than those made by smaller firms. Such hourly billings normally fall in the range of $50 to $200 per hour of time input by the lead consultant, with lower rates for time of assistants. Extra billings are not ordinarily made for secretarial time or out-of-pocket office expenses. Mileage may be billed for auto travel, as well as billings for motels and meals for necessary overnight, out-of-town travel.

Legal Considerations

Many professional consultant organizations are operated as a single proprietorship or as a partnership rather than as a corporation. A single person with a consulting business would only be required to keep a record of receipts and expenses so that a Schedule C to the Form 1040 federal income tax return may be filed annually with the IRS.

Partnerships must file an informational tax return, providing a statement to each partner as to his or her share of deductible interest, property taxes, charitable contributions, and self-employment income. Each partner must then recognize this income on his or her own income tax return.

More than half of the business service organizations file corporate C or corporate S tax returns. The main reason for incorporation is a separation of personal assets and business assets for the firm. The S corporation must have fewer than 35 shareholders, all of whom must elect this tax treatment, and the filing status can only be changed with the prior consent of the IRS. In most states, incorporation of a small firm may be done for a few hundred dollars, so the decrease in risk is probably worth the additional cost. The corporation does have to file a separate business return. Although the S corporation does not pay taxes in its own name, the income (after officers' salaries and other expenses) is allocated to its shareholders on a proportionate ownership basis, and they must report the income. Most corporations are chartered at the state level.

Every business firm that hires one or more persons on a regular basis must have a federal employer identification number (FEIN) so that appropriate payroll taxes, state income taxes, and federal income taxes may be withheld from employees and paid into an appropriate depository financial institution.

Most local jurisdictions require that business operation licenses be applied for and renewed annually. Most municipal bodies have zoning requirements. Consulting firms are classified as commercial, although some are operated out of a home office in a residential district. Where crowds of persons are in attendance, fire codes as to restrooms and fire exits are in effect. Fire and safety inspections may be made periodically by the local fire and safety inspector.

Accounting and legal contracts should be reviewed and/or prepared by appropriate professional persons. The development of an accounting or payroll system might be developed for a start-up firm. An attorney should be consulted about drawing up legal documents pertaining to the business. An architect or engineer might be engaged for certain aspects of consulting.

As with most other businesses, adequate insurance coverage is strongly suggested. Specialized insurance may be warranted in certain cases. Some types of insurance to consider are: fire and casualty insurance on real property, liability insurance on the premises and on vehicles, workers' compensation, fidelity bonding, business interruption insurance, and executive liability and decision-making insurance.

Experience and Training Required

The manager/owner of a consulting firm should ideally have several types of skills and abilities. These include diagnostic skill, the ability to determine objectives and to apply logic and intuition to the challenge. The prospective consultant should be able to use imagination and conceptual skills to create viable answers to problems. Communication skills, sales and marketing abilities, and general management talents are needed. The potential consultant should have one or more areas of general expertise that are in demand by paying clients.

Persons managing or supervising groups of consultants should have expertise in their field of activity, experience, leadership qualities, perspective (open-mindedness), and good interpersonal skills for relationships with the client's staff. The supervisor of the project needs to be a generalist in order to see the broad picture, but specialists are sometimes brought in where a certain few problem areas exist.

Most large consulting firms expect their staff to work at least 50 hours weekly, with some of this time in workshop training sessions. Some minimum, such as 6 or 7 hours of work per day, should be billable to clients. Turnover is about 15% yearly, with many persons giving up their jobs in order to begin their own privately run consulting firms.

A consultant should have recognized expertise in some line of work that can be sold to firms in a similar profession. A potential consultant might consider going with another consulting firm for a few years in order to gather experience. If he or she proves to be successful, valuable experience can be gained.

Things to consider in working for another firm include:

- Gauging the climate, culture, and environment of the firm
- Realizing that taking a job with another firm means starting over, regardless of the years of experience
- Evaluating the reputation the firm has with its clients
- Determining the reason for hiring (e.g., rapid turnover of employees, expanding, etc.)
- Evaluating the financial condition of the firm
- Appraising personal tolerance to risk and depletion of personal savings
- Determining the complementary skills of a potential partner

Before entering the consulting business, the professional person should make a realistic evaluation of his or her own strengths and match them up with generic needs in several areas of consulting, such as general management consulting, sales training consulting, human resources development, executive search, financial advisement, engineering consulting, account audits, and so forth. Newspaper advertisements might be reviewed in large, regional newspapers, such as *The Wall Street Journal*, in order to determine the ease of obtaining employment before quitting one's current job to seek another in consulting. Shortage of professional workers in a region suggests a high likelihood of success for a consultant in that area.

Besides having the necessary skills and experience to offer to others, the successful consultant must also possess certain personal attributes. These would include empathy, inner security, high ethical standards, tact, and marketing ability. Empathy relates to how effectively you can put yourself in your client's shoes. Inner security means you can work without the need of a boss to motivate you. High ethical standards is self-explanatory. In today's business climate, ethics are too often shunted aside for the realization of "the bottom line." As a consultant you must retain a very high degree of ethical standards even in the face of adversity and the potential of loss of the immediate contract. Tact will work to your benefit in building up and maintaining a client base.

Keys to
Management
Success

Several considerations should be kept in mind before you decide to go into business as a consultant. Your field of expertise must be specialized enough within a broad framework to encourage individuals and business firms to seek your help. You must have the skills, experience, and credentials in your chosen field to qualify as a paid consultant. In some instances, certain licenses or state certification are required before you can establish a practice. Ensure that there will be enough demand for your service to enable you to support yourself and a family over the long term. Ensure that there is a real growth potential for your expertise.

In order to be successful, a management consulting firm must have a viable service, develop an effective marketing strategy for the service, and develop an efficient cost control system.

The consultant must determine the area of activity he or she wishes to pursue. This may fall into one or more of the following:

- Pure strategy advisor
- Management audit (done by accounting and other firms)
- Traditional management consulting, usually done in the traditional functional areas of business (i.e., manufacturing, research and development, selling, financial, etc.)
- Human resource management (hiring and training full-time employees for the firm to be more expert in its endeavors)
- Specialized services, such as financial, merger making, and so on

Usual selling techniques, or approaches, include direct contact with known business persons, mailings to firms that could possibly use the services, participation in regional association programs and seminars, guest lecturing to possible clients, and so on. An aggressive approach must generally be followed for a start-up firm.

Some advisors suggest that one day a week be devoted to marketing the consultant firm through personal contacts, donated work to worthwhile civic organizations, writing/publishing, seminar or association participation, and similar activities.

The consulting staff must be able to prepare and present an effective proposal, showing background, objectives, work plan, staff needs, proposed budget, and so on. Not all of these proposals will result in a contract with the intended client, of course, but it is usually an effective type of advertising.

A consulting firm must earn the respect of its clients and strive for a long-term reputation of doing quality work at a fair price. It is often better to review the range of answers, showing the likely consequences of each plan adopted by the client, than to promote only one solution.

Effective cost controls need to be in place in order to keep the total expenses within the allotted budget.

Generally, the benefits to the client must be at least two times the cost of the consulting in order for the contract to appear to be worthwhile. This might be a short-range target.

Most successful firms attempt to build in training programs for the employees of the client's firm so that they may recognize and solve similar problems in the future.

The process of consulting usually involves numerous approaches, including providing information to clients, supplying solutions to problems, diagnosing a situation and making comments, supplying recommendations, assisting in implementing action in the client's firm, helping build a consensus regarding direction to take by the client, providing education to the client's staff, and improving the organizational effectiveness of the overall operation. While the last two tasks appear to eliminate potential (future) work from this client, they are the strategic areas that will most often earn an outstanding reputation for the consulting firm and result in its promotion, by word of mouth, to other clients.

Professional literature in the field generally suggests that a consulting firm start on a small scale. That is, a sole proprietorship should probably begin the business on a part-time basis, perhaps sharing an office with another professional person, while still employed at his or her regular job. As revenues and clients increase enough to support the owner and another office worker (such as a combination secretary/bookkeeper), it might be prudent to set up a separate office in a commercial building. Visibility and signs are not critical to developing and attracting clients, but forging a reputation in the community is crucial.

In marketing the product, a plan should be developed and personal calls or mail should be utilized to target clients. An alternate approach is to offer seminars, give speeches, attend association meetings, or do volunteer work in the area in order to meet and attract potential clients.

Before a contract is granted by a hiring firm, the consulting firm and its staff should prepare a proposal. Included should be the background of the problem, the objectives of the endeavors, the details of the work plan, the staff required, and an estimated budget. Details of the plan would usually be open for negotiation between the client and the employed consultants.

Information Sources An ongoing consulting firm, or someone contemplating the development of one, should have access to certain types of information. These include such things as handbooks and manuals, trade associations, periodicals, ratio studies, government documents, and so on. A representative list should be obtained from the periodic update of *Encyclopedia of Business Information Sources*, Gale Research, Inc., Detroit, Mich., which is housed in many public and college libraries.

PART III
Cases in Small-Business Financing

Little Egypt Travel Agency

In late 1994, Ms. Jane Mason and Mr. Ed Monroe were in the process of forming a travel agency. Ms. Mason was certified to sell airline tickets, while Mr. Monroe had served on the city council for several years in their city of Little Egypt. Ms. Mason had been employed by a manufacturing firm of about 1,500 employees for more than 10 years and had handled the travel reservations for staff of the firm. The management was planning to phase out their office work of handling the reservations and, should an agency be formed by her and an associate, had promised that the $200,000 in annual flight arrangements would be placed with the firm for at least a year, and possibly longer, should business dealings continue smoothly between them.

Only one other travel agency operated in the city of about 6,500 population, and none other within about a 30-mile radius of the city. An analysis of business and individual travelers suggested that another travel agency should be supportable. Airlines and other tours usually paid from about 7% to 11% of ticket sales. Ms. Mason felt that about 10% would be average. An analysis of the probable level of business attainable by the two partners/owners (or officers if a corporation should be formed) was as follows, with the salaries account reflecting withdrawals of the two partners plus two other employees. Net profits, net of any tax burden, would be retained in the firm for expansion purposes.

Four-Year Income Statement Forecast
Little Egypt Travel Agency

	Year 1	Year 2	Year 3	Year 4
Sales ($145 per ticket)	$1,153,620	$1,289,340	$1,583,400	$1,764,360
Less cost of tickets (90%)	1,038,258	1,160,406	1,425,060	1,587,924
Net billings	$ 115,362	$ 128,934	$ 158,340	$ 176,436
Estimated expenses:				
Salaries (fixed)	61,800	65,000	69,000	71,000
Rent (9% billings)	10,383	11,604	14,251	15,879
Insurance (fixed)	2,500	2,500	2,500	2,500

	Year 1	Year 2	Year 3	Year 4
Advertising (8% billings)	9,229	10,315	12,667	14,115
Payroll taxes	7,416	7,800	8,280	8,520
Telephone ($400 per month)	4,800	4,800	4,800	4,800
Utilities ($250 per month)	3,000	3,000	3,000	3,000
Miscellaneous office expenses	4,940	4,940	4,940	4,940
Total expenses	$ 104,068	$ 109,959	$ 119,438	$ 124,754
Net before-tax profit	11,294	18,975	38,902	51,682

One of the first assignments undertaken by the two principals to be involved with the company was to develop for further study a list of provisions of the articles for a partnership. If the firm were incorporated in Illinois, about the same points should be covered in the bylaws for the firm, Mr. Monroe believed. The first draft of the partnership articles is as follows:

Provisions of the Articles of Copartnership
Little Egypt Travel Agency

I. The name of the firm shall be LITTLE EGYPT TRAVEL AGENCY.

II. The objectives or goals for the firm shall be to provide services of booking reservations and putting together travel packages for individuals, firms, and groups for travel in the United States and abroad.

III. The commencement of business shall be upon the signing of all agreements herein and renting suitable space for the agency. The partnership shall be dissolved upon mutual agreement or upon the death or incapacity of either partner.

IV. Each partner shall contribute initially the sum of $25,000 in cash. Up to $2,000 in office equipment may be substituted for cash if usable to the firm and if agreed upon by the other partner. The capital to be maintained, with annual adjustment, shall not fall below this level for either principal.

V. Additional advances of funds from the principals to the firm shall be on a short-term basis, for as long as needed by the firm, and shall bear an interest rate equal to the prime rate plus 1 percent.

VI. All deposit accounts and checking accounts shall be held by the Little Egypt National Bank, state of Illinois. Two signatures shall be required, from the two partners or one partner and the office manager to be hired to work in the firm.

VII. Each partner shall receive initial withdrawals of $400 weekly from the firm. Additional withdrawals, if permitted by the other partner, are to bear an interest rate equal to the prime rate plus 1 percent, and are repayable upon demand (or as mutually agreed by the two partners). This is subject to annual inflation adjustments.

VIII. Profits in excess of withdrawals shall be reinvested in the firm for purposes of financing growth in working capital, except as mutually agreed upon by the partners, or for possible payment of federal income taxes.

---

continued

IX. Each principal is expected to contribute not less than 40 hours and not more than 50 hours weekly to the operation of the firm, with the parties alternating weekends of duty (Fridays and Saturdays). In general, the hours of operation are from 8:30 a.m. to 5:30 p.m. on weekdays and to 2 p.m. on Saturday. The firm is closed on Sunday.

X. Debt contracted in the name of the firm shall be made only with the mutual consent of both partners, and each shall sign notes payable.

XI. The firm shall purchase term life insurance for each partner, conjointly payable to the firm and a beneficiary of said principal, in an amount equal to the capital of each, and shall be used as partial payment for a buyout by a surviving partner in the event of the untimely death of one of them.

XII. The value of the firm, in the event of a buyout/sellout, shall be not less than 1 and not more than 1.5 times the net billings of the previous year, with the exact amount and admission of another partner to be negotiated by the parties involved.

XIII. An office manager and a part-time employee/bookkeeper shall be hired to aid in carrying on day-to-day operations of the firm. As bookings increase, one or two additional salespersons are to be added. Hiring/firing of employees is to be conjointly determined by the company's principals (or delegated to the office manager).

XIV. Amendments to the forestated articles of copartnership shall be made only with the mutual consent of all principals involved.

x_____/_____x
(Signatures of Partners)

NOTARY SEAL AND SIGNATURE   _____

_____   _____
(Signature of Notary)   (Signatures of witnesses)

ASSIGNMENTS

1. Study the articles of copartnership, and comment on their need or need for change at this time.

2. In the event that the two partners should decide to incorporate, develop a set of corporate bylaws that would embrace a majority of the listed points, plus other relevant ones.

3. Contrast the given forecasts of activity for the first four years of operation with financial ratios on the retail travel agency industry. Comment on those forecasts as to reasonableness. Refer to the ratios of Dun & Bradstreet, Inc., or Robert L. Morris Associates.

4. Prepare forecasted balance sheets (from industry benchmarks and the given forecasted income statement) for the firm.

5. Develop a break-even point and chart for the firm.

6. Develop an organization chart for the firm.

B and B Property Management and Real Estate Sales, Inc.

The B and B real estate company had come into existence some two years earlier, being formed as a partnership. It had resulted from the pooling of interest by Mr. I. M. Brown and Mr. P. C. Benning, located in the two small cities of Thus and So, about 10 miles apart in southern Illinois. At the time of their merging, each was the only real estate firm in its respective community. They had also handled the writing of property insurance for two or three independent carriers, but competition was intensifying in that area to the extent that they phased out that type of operation so as to concentrate their efforts on real estate. Each separate firm had been operated by the principal (Brown or Benning) holding a brokers license in the state of Illinois, with two other salespersons each. Each firm had an additional office worker who was a combined receptionist, secretary, and bookkeeper. With the staff of four, each was able to operate with about three million to four million dollars in annual sales and to manage a portfolio of rental property owned by absentee holders.

As compensation for their services, the single proprietorships received 7% in sales commission on city property sales, 10% on the sale of farm property, 8% on the sale of commercial or industrial property, and a 7% management fee on rental property, in addition to reimbursement for out-of-pocket cash expenses on managed properties. This level of compensation was about average in the area. Each of the individually owned firms employed at least one salesperson of each sex, and sometimes two, that concentrated on residential property sales. The broker himself handled the sale of farm or industrial property. The commercial property listings were sometimes shown by one of the salespersons. The approach usually followed was to match the sex of the salesperson to that of the potential buyer, as far as possible. If a husband and wife were inspecting the property, the salesperson might be of either sex.

Compensation to the salespersons were in line with that paid in the industry. Each person who made a sale was paid one-half of the commission earned. The salespersons had to provide their own auto and cover the expenses of operating the vehicle. This was written up in their contract of employment so that the costs incurred could be expensed for tax purposes. Other amounts went to the firm to pay office salaries, other office expenses, and as compensation to the brokers, who were involved in directing the operation of their respective firms.

The two proprietorships were pooled as B and B Property Management and Real Estate Sales, Inc., of Thus and So, Ill. It was decided to continue to operate the firm in the two offices for another year and, if profits permitted, to locate just to the outskirts of the largest of the two cities on the highway that linked the cities of Thus and So. By the end of the third quarter after the combination, two salespersons in So had resigned their jobs, electing retirement rather than to continue to sell real estate. Steps were immediately taken to buy and renovate a large, auspicious home in a desirable location on the outskirts of Thus. The price of $70,000 was paid for the property, that included two acres of land, and it was rezoned from residential to light commercial. Another $15,000 was spent in the renovation program. A local savings association had made a 5-year loan at a 10% rate for $50,000, and the balance was financed from assets of the partnership. Combined asset and liability and net worth items are reflected below:

B and B Property Management and Real Estate Sales, Inc.
Balance Sheet (year end)

Assets		Debts and Net Worth	
Cash and near-cash	$49,452	Accounts payable	$42,004
Accounts receivable	68,220	Mortgage loan, current	10,000
Notes receivable	10,724	Notes payable (auto)	6,256
Inventory	8,937	Other current debts	33,365
Other current assets	23,534	Total current debts	91,625
Total current assets	160,867	Long-term debts:	
Fixed assets	140,000	Mortgage, noncurrent	40,000
Other noncurrent assets	51,432	Other long-term debts	33,961
Total assets	352,299	Deferred credit	1,192
		Net worth	185,521
		Total debts and net worth	352,299

Properties were sold totaling $12,525,000 during the previous year. Gross profits on the transactions amounted to $115,000 while an additional $24,200 was earned on the management of real estate for others. Interest earned on NOW accounts amounted to $3,675. This level of income, after paying commissions to salespersons and other operating expenses, left the two broker/partners with $61,200 in profits (with equal division of profits) for the year's operations. Each were married with two teenaged children still in high school. Neither had significant amounts of income other than from the operation of B and B.

Mr. Brown and Mr. Benning were in the process of incorporating the firm. They had already received their charter of incorporation, which authorized the sale of up to 200,000 common shares, each with a par value of $5. They had each received $90,000 in stock for their share in the firm a few days earlier, and $5,521 had been earned in profits since that time. They were unsure as to the items that should be included in the set of bylaws, but believed that the following would reflect their joint wishes:

B and B Property Management and Real Estate Sales, Inc.
Bylaws and Operating Policies

1. The purpose of the firm shall be for the sale of listed real estate and the management of properties for others.

2. The name of the firm shall be B and B Property Management and Real Estate Sales, Inc.

3. The firm is to continue the operation of a partnership that had previously held its assets.

4. The initial capital stock issued to the two founders shall be in equal amounts, but this might be changed at a later date by their mutual consent. Shares shall not be sold to third parties other than immediate family members of the founders without the mutual consent of all shareholders.

5. Borrowings from financial institutions must have the signature of both principals in the firm, one operating as chairman of the board and the other as operations president. Checks drafted for amounts in excess of $500 must have dual signatures.

6. The brokers/principals of the firm will have initial salaries of $1,000 monthly. Commissions payable to them will amount to 10% of the commissions earned on a listed property and 30% of the commissions collected on their own sales. Net income after defraying expenses will go to build up retained profits.

7. Concurrence of both brokers/principals will be needed for new hires or discharges, major change in activities, loans other than accounts payable or miscellaneous accruals, and infrequent business dealings. Their attorney shall be called in to mediate any major differences and shall have the deciding vote in breaking a deadlock.

8. Life insurance in the amount of $100,000 shall be carried by the firm on the life of each principal, with one-half payable to the beneficiary of the insured and one-half to the firm. Since this exceeds the limit permitted by the IRS, a portion of the premiums may be taxable to the respective insured.

X_____

X_____   X_____

Signature of Notary   Signatures of Principals

Seal

The B and B firm had been incorporated for only a month, but time was growing short as to filing for S corporation status if the owners elected to do so.

ASSIGNMENTS

1. You have been hired as a financial consultant to analyze the given bylaws and comment on their pitfalls and strengths.

2. Determine whether it is in the best interest of the current owners to form an S or C corporation, and suggest an appropriate division of the stock among family members, employees, etc.

3. Develop a workable plan for (a) selling more stock of the firm for expansion purposes and (b) bringing in other shareholders in the event that other local real estate sales firms in neighboring cities are acquired.

4. Develop an organization chart, a break-even chart, and a set of job descriptions for employees in the firm.

Southern Building Company, Inc.

The Southern Building Company, Inc. (SBC), of Beaumont, Tex. has been incorporated since 1962 and has been an intermittent borrower from the Texas National Bank since 1975. The firm had repaid its bank loan satisfactorily in the past, but as the bank credit officer was analyzing the account in June 1995, he noted that the balance of the loan had expanded to an alarming size. He also noted that the most recent income statement reported a net loss of $23,000. Although the loan was partially secured, the credit officer felt that he should analyze the statements, obtain a current credit report, and watch the account closely in order to catch other adverse factors that might further degrade the collectibility of the account.

No change has occurred in stock ownership of SBC since 1984, when one of the stockholders/officers sold his interest to an incoming officer. The three officers, president, secretary-treasurer, and vice-president, are the only stockholders. The president, Mr. Jack Johnson, age 56, had been in the construction business since 1948, although he was employed by others until 1962. The secretary-treasurer, Mr. Frank McBain, age 61, was engaged in the auto business for about 30 years before he sold his distributorship to become an officer in the construction firm. He still maintains some outside activities. The vice-president, Mr. Sam Jones, had had 9 years of experience in the insurance agency field before joining the firm in 1989 at the age of 31.

The firm has been engaged as a commercial and residential contractor around Gulf South cities. Its contracts are often received through competitive bids with developers of shopping center malls or new housing subdivisions located in Texas and Louisiana Gulf South cities. Some of the work with commercial property owners (large life insurance and pension funds, predominantly) is obtained on a cost-plus basis so that the firm receives payment every 15 days for the work which has been completed, plus 10% profit above total costs. A 10% retainer is held in escrow until the job is completed and accepted by a team of inspectors for the controlling municipality and the owning firm.

The number of employees of the firm varies with the amount of work, but is usually between 25 and 50. The company owns its own equipment, which is in good repair, and leases additional equipment as needed. The company owns its own warehouse of approximately 14,000 square feet, in which it stores some equipment not in use and inventory items for its various jobs. It also owns office space in one end of the warehouse.

Although three of the four most recent balance sheets indicate small cash balances, Exhibit 4 discloses that the average cash balance for the years 1987 through 1992 was rather substantial. The repayment of accounts payable at the end of a month often reduced the month-end cash balance far below the monthly average. In addition to the regular demand deposit account, the firm maintains a payroll account with a balance of from $7,500 to $25,000 and a profit-sharing retirement plan account which averages about $10,000. The former was started in 1980 while the latter was inaugurated in 1982. The bank considers the account to be profitable, and does not wish to precipitate any action that would endanger the loss of the customer.

The accounts receivable of the firm fluctuate rather widely over a period of time. The bank desires to have the bank loan secured with receivables equal to at least 125% of the amount of the note. As the pledged accounts are collected, the amount would be repaid on the bank loan. When the customer needs additional funds, he would pledge additional accounts, and a credit would be given to his drawing account.

Investments in machinery and equipment during the past 3 years were slightly less than the amount of the depreciation allowance. The investments consisted of shares of stock in two local country clubs, where actual or prospective clients are sometimes entertained.

The loan record of the firm is presented in Exhibit 2. During 1991, the outstanding 30-day loan averaged about $125,000. During much of 1992–1993, the loan balance was below $25,000. In the second half of 1994, the loan balance began to rise and reached a high point of $562,500 on February 28, 1995. From the end of November 1994 until May 1995, the collateral was barely adequate to cover the account by 100%. The bank recently suffered losses on loans to other contractors, and although it wishes to keep the account, it wants to guard against any loss in the event that the company gets into financial difficulty.

An analysis of the income statements (see Exhibit 3) for the years ended February 28, 1994 and 1995, indicated some alarming features. Although sales doubled during the period, gross profits remained the same. Operating expenses during the period, and other expenses, remained so high that the company operated at a net loss of $23,000 in the latter year, compared with a net after-tax profit of $50,000 during the preceding year. This loss occurred despite the fact that the officers' salaries had been reduced by $45,000 and no income tax liability had been incurred.

Although the account had been a profitable one for years, the bank loan officer has grown concerned over recent events. He is not sure whether the loan limit should be reduced, whether more collateral should be demanded, or whether to watch the account and hope that the situation would be improved within the near future. A study of ratios and trends, he feels, might pinpoint the growing problems of weakness and permit early corrective action.

ASSIGNMENTS

1. With the use of ratio analysis, evaluate the financial progress (or lack of it) achieved by the firm during the past few years. Use industry and company trend analysis.

2. What action should the bank credit loan officer recommend?

3. Assume that some type of corrective action is recommended by the bank credit committee. Compose a letter to the president of the firm disclosing the action and suggesting remedies.

EXHIBIT 1. Balance Sheets for Years Ended

	2/1992	2/1993	2/1994	2/1995
ASSETS				
Cash	$ 4,429	$194,768	$ 5,321	$ 15,019
Accounts receivable	1,119,297	255,980	714,110	1,024,656
Inventory	23,652	19,761	525	—
Prepaid items	29,624	41,994	29,723	32,050
Total current assets	1,177,002	512,503	749,679	1,071,725
Land and buildings	27,495	27,495	27,495	27,495
Machinery/fixtures, net	259,383	222,845	220,963	200,330
Investments	7,562	8,588	8,588	10,962
Due from officers and employees	3,604	2,772	—	11,286
Cash value of insurance	13,625	20,250	42,790	57,250
Miscellaneous assets	719	1,094	—	—
Total assets	1,489,390	795,547	1,049,515	1,379,048
DEBTS AND CAPITAL				
Notes payable, bank	125,000	24,463	123,174	562,500
Notes payable, other	20,970	—	—	46,518
Accounts payable	439,123	130,233	289,526	276,612
Accrued debts and taxes	238,856	136,071	185,993	101,824
Income taxes payable	43,179	68,651	—	—
Due to officers	20,000	—	—	—
Total current debts	887,128	359,418	598,693	987,454
Deferred liabilities	10,834	—	—	—
Deferred credits	326,381	118,761	95,228	63,134
Capital stock	125,000	125,000	125,000	125,000
Paid-in capital above par	16,032	16,032	16,032	16,032
Retained earnings	124,015	176,336	214,562	187,428
Total capital	265,047	317,368	355,594	328,460
Total debts and capital	1,489,390	795,547	1,049,515	1,379,048

EXHIBIT 2. Loan Balance and Security Pledged

Date	Loan Balance	Receivables Balance	Other Collateral
2/28/92	$135,834	$341,871	None
5/31/92	12,709	284,074	None
5/31/92–11/30/92	—	—	None
5/31/93	19,030	—	Equipment chattel
8/31/93	14,274	212,835	
11/30/93	9,516	212,835	
2/29/94	79,758	158,481	
5/31/94	145,625	96,641	Retainers receivable
8/31/94	531,250	428,229	Retainers receivable
11/30/94	532,250	365,055	Retainers receivable
2/28/95	562,500	335,511	Retainers receivable
5/31/95	525,000	277,604	Retainers receivable

EXHIBIT 3. Income Statements for Years Ended

	2/1992	2/1993	2/1994	2/1995
Completed contracts	$5,085,484	$5,705,161	$3,732,913	$7,065,689
Less: Job costs	4,448,806	4,903,908	3,262,855	6,587,906
Gross income	$ 636,678	$ 801,253	$ 470,058	$ 477,783
Operating expenses:				
Salaries/bonuses: Officers	NA	NA	110,590	65,500
Salaries/bonuses: Other	NA	NA	178,151	212,718
Bad debts	NA	NA	3,896	—
Depreciation	NA	NA	88,134	95,804
Pension plan payments	NA	NA	10,793	—
Taxes and licenses	NA	NA	15,256	13,072
Other expenses	NA	NA	135,082	169,689
Total operating expenses	$ 609,710	$ 763,583	$ 541,902	$ 556,783
Net income	$ 26,970	$ 37,670	$ (71,844)	$ (79,000)
Plus: Other income	66,705	75,725	151,877	76,188
Less: Other deductions	9,479	4,590	3,086	(24,323)
Less: Income taxes	43,179	68,651	26,554	—
Net income to retained earnings	$ 41,017	$ 40,154	$ 50,393	$ (27,135)

EXHIBIT 4. Average Demand Deposit Balances

	Monthly Averages		Annual Average
	High	Low	
1991	$ 68,641	$17,756	$ 39,543
1992	242,809	28,140	128,226
1993	272,533	35,291	127,794
1994	154,482	26,644	58,064
1995:			
January		$28,384	
February		78,256	
March		31,493	
April		40,032	
May		77,079	

EXHIBIT 5. Dun & Bradstreet Credit Report Requested

The local D & B office informed our bank loan officer that no recent credit report was available on the firm, and that we had been sent the most recent one compiled about two years before. The *Reference Book* published by D & B six times per year still listed the firm as having a "Fair" credit rating.

Van's B & B Stopover

Van and Vivian Smith, retired for two months and traveling through the Midwest, stopped over at a nice scenic bed and breakfast lodge near a major tourist attraction in southern Missouri. While the one-acre grounds and the five-bedroom home of about 40 years of age was comfortable, it was not lavish. The couple really stayed at the site due to no vacancy at the nearby Holiday Inn.

The lady who greeted them was sad due to the recent death of her husband of 60 years. The lady herself was about 77 years of age, and her husband had been 81. She was being pressed to sell the property and to relocate with one of her older children, a widowed daughter aged 58 who still worked but planned to retire in about four more years.

A "For Sale by Owner" sign graced the property. Van and Vivian had little interest in being tied down to such a venture so soon after retirement, but their 60-day driving vacation trip grew weary on them, and they decided to revisit the B & B. They were greeted by the same sad lady, a Sady Hawkins, and shown to an upstairs bedroom. The home appeared to have a combination den and bedroom on the ground level, along with a great room where guests were greeted, plus a kitchen/dining area. The five bedrooms on the second floor each had their own bathrooms, a feature not always present in B & B locations.

While the rent for a double at the Holiday Inn would have been $60 per night, the B & B priced its room, with clean linen and a continental breakfast, at $45 for a couple. The price was reasonable, but the Smiths, for the second time, were the only patrons. Van commented on the absence of other guests, and he was told that the owner did not believe in advertising, other than having a sign displayed near the major highway that bordered the entrance to the site. "I'm an old lady and just don't like to be bothered with the noise of children," she said.

"How much for the property?" asked Van.

"She's worth more as a home than as a commercial business, young man," the answer came, "but I'd let her go at our cost of 10 years ago, plus some major improvements to the parking lots. In total, I'd need $75,000 for the property."

"Cash or credit?" Van asked.

"Well, let's see. I was thinking about cash, but I might take a third down and the balance over five years. After all, I'm not so young anymore, and I would need the value of the property to meet possible health-care costs as I grow even older. I'd give you a low rate of interest of 6% per year, with monthly payments."

"We'll stay here an extra night and let you know in two days," Van promised. In their driving tour, intending to locate a place to live away from the Chicago congestion and noise, the Smiths had decided that a little occupation of their time might prolong their lives. Thus, they were now giving serious consideration to the purchase and operation of the B & B.

Van spent more than two hours in inspecting the property. Except for the need of a paint job inside and outside of the property, and the need to replace the downstairs carpets and have the upstairs ones cleaned, he could find no major flaws with the structure. Such upkeep would run about $3,000. Nothing in his discussion with Mrs. Hawkins had concerned the furnishings, but he assumed that they would go with the deal. When asked, she replied, "Well, I'd want the things from my own bedrooms, and a few personal items, pictures and things, from the downstairs. The balance of the furnishings can go with the home."

"We have a two-bedroom condominium with some living room furnishings, so that is fine," he acknowledged. "I'll make a few estimates of possible revenues and expenses and give you our reply at breakfast tomorrow," Van promised. As an afterthought, he asked, "Oh, would you happen to have an estimate of your taxes, insurance, and utility costs on the business?"

"You are serious, aren't you, young man?" the owner replied. "As a matter of fact, I was reviewing those figures just this week. I have my gas and electric on an equal-payment plan. They are now running $175 monthly. Water and trash are $30 monthly combined. The telephone is $30 local plus long-distance calls. My last ad valorem tax bill was for $1,200. I don't have any hired help, but after all expenses and depreciation, my net income on the property is so low that I have no self-employment or income taxes. Is there anything else I could tell you?" she asked.

"I suppose not," Van stated, planning to rough out the possible revenues and expenses if they could achieve a 60% occupancy rate yearround; run variable breakfast costs at 10% of rent; keep other variable costs to 10% of revenues; and manage on the same fixed costs as currently. He and his wife could manage the facility alone, or he might invite a divorced niece to live behind the facility in a mobile home and share in the work. Such an arrangement would permit the Smiths some time away from the venture on vacation trips and the like, and the venture would give them some income and productive usage of their time. Mrs. Smith had in mind to install a small gift counter, investing $2,000 in equipment and inventories, within the great room of the facility.

Van thought that he might use his own conversion van and advertise airport pickup and delivery to the major attraction centers in the area for overnight patrons. Well, it was an idea worth exploring, anyway. Van knew that he would have a long night of number crunching before reaching a "buy decision."

ASSIGNMENTS

1. Determine the monthly payment to amortize a $50,000 loan at 6% yearly for 60 months.

2. Develop projected balance sheets and income statements for the first three years of operation. Assume 40%, 50%, and 60% occupancy rates yearly, respectively, and the same nightly rates as currently charged.

3. Assuming that the niece-assistant is provided with living space and food in the B & B and paid $5 hourly for an average of 20 hours per week for 50 weeks per year, estimate her labor cost.

4. Suggest ways for advertising the availability of the bed and breakfast inn.

The S & S Fruit Farm, Inc.

The S & S Fruit Farm, Inc., was formed in 1992 upon the early retirement at age 56 of Roberto Sanchez, a Southern Illinois University agriculture teacher. He had 30 years of service in the system, plus two years of military service which he had bought in at the time of his retirement. His monthly retirement income, reduced by 24% due to early retirement, came to about $3,000. His wife was opposed to the purchase of the 80-acre fruit farm to the south of their major city, and she continued to teach in a nearby public school.

Mr. Sanchez brought in his older brother as a junior stockholder. Loupi Sanchez, aged 60 at the time of the formation of the venture, took early retirement from a State of Illinois job on highway construction and maintenance. His retirement, with 35 years of service, including five buy-in years at a reduced rate, gave him about $3,600 monthly retirement income. Loupi's wife, an agrarian at heart, was thrilled at the thought of rediscovering a country life.

The 80-acre tract was sold at auction by the savings association that held the foreclosed mortgage on the property. The Sanchez brothers bid on the property at $1 over the outstanding mortgage plus accrued ad valorem taxes. Their investment was $20,000 in cash and the assumption at 7.5% interest of a $60,000 mortgage with 20 years left to be repaid. The available equipment was rusty and hardly usable, but with an additional $30,000 to be invested by Roberto and Loupi on a 2 to 1 basis, the brothers felt that they could spend about half of this amount on some used, auctioned farm equipment in good repair and have enough money left to develop the fruit farm. Loupi was well versed in equipment operation and repair, inasmuch as his lifelong job had been with earth-moving equipment.

For their investment into the property, $30,000 by Roberto and $20,000 by Loupi, the stock was assigned in a 60–40 ratio. Before she would go along with the venture, Louisa Sanchez, wife of Roberto, insisted that a buyout agreement be signed by Loupi and his wife upon the possible death of Roberto. While Loupi and his spouse somewhat scoffed at the idea, they agreed to the proposition with the price to be 60% of book value of the assets in the firm, less one-half of the debts assumed to belong to Roberto and his spouse. Term life insurance was carried on his life, with the premiums being paid by his brother, Loupi.

Two structures were located on the premises. One was adequate, needing a moderate amount of repair, for Loupi and his wife; while the second was more of a commercial building for storing equipment and supplies. The residence was located to the front of the fruit farm, bordering on a gravel road, while the second was near the fields to be cultivated.

At the time of purchase, some 20 acres of the farm was in peach and apple trees. Some of them were recoverable, while about half would need to be replaced with three-year-old trees. This was quickly done by the Sanchez brothers, and some two years later, the replacement peach trees were beginning to yield small crops. The red and golden delicious apple transplants would begin to bear in another year or two. As money supply grew short, more capital contributions were made by the brothers. To date, an added $15,000 had been made by Roberto and $10,000 by Loupi, with the money largely being used for buying berry plants and bushes and replacing and adding fruit trees. At the current time, only $1,200 remained in the corporate cash account: receivables and short-term debt were nill; and supplies on hand amounted to about $3,600. Equipment cost, two years earlier, had amounted to $21,000 and was now being carried at 60% of that level. No attempt was made to increase the value of the farm from growth of trees, but their costs were capitalized.

A two-acre stock pond was located on the upper slope of the farm. It had a good field of drainage and seldom witnessed water level droppage of more than a foot or two from its normal depth of about 15 feet. The pond was mainly used to provide irrigation to a patch of strawberries and one of blueberry bushes that had been added to the farm.

The Sanchez brothers knew that pick-your-own fruit was popular in the area, so they began, after acquiring the farm, to set out 24 acres of strawberries and a similar plot of blueberry plants. Thus, when in full production, the farm would have about 24 acres each in strawberries, blueberries, and tree fruit (roughly 10 acres of peach trees, 4 of plum and cherry trees, and 10 of red and golden delicious apples). Thus, the harvest season would run from early May on the strawberries to late September on the apples. The remaining two acres of tillable soil were devoted to a pumpkin patch. All in all, the Sanchez brothers were pleased with their accomplishments during the first three years of their operation.

Then tragedy struck. Roberto did not die, but he had a stroke which left him speechless and paralyzed on his right side. Fortunately, the life insurance policy contained a premium waiver clause on the insured, such that the renewal premium would be waived by the insurance firm upon the disability of the insured until such time as the insured was certified to return to work. This was a help, as Loupi found himself in the position of having to hire outside help to fill in the schedule of work previously done by Roberto. An elderly nursery worker and his wife agreed to move into one end of the renovated equipment barn and work yearround for rent, utilities, and $600 monthly, putting in short days during certain months and regular days during seasons of high demand. While the Sanchez couple did not socialize with the elderly couple, they did appreciate their help in organizing activities on the fruit farm, with both being engaged with the pick-your-own patrons. Several teenagers were hired at minimum wages during the height of the harvest season, with three used during the four weeks of strawberry picking; two employed during the eight weeks of early, midseason, and late-season picking of the blueberries; and two on hand during the peach and plum harvest in August and the apple harvest during September. All the students were half time at minimum wage and received no fringe benefits.

Gross revenues from the strawberries came to about $3,000 per acre; blueberry harvest was just getting started and would average about $1,000 per acre in year 1 but grow by $1,000 per acre per year for the next three years before leveling out. The peach and apple trees, sometimes adversely affected by late frosts, generally provided about $2,500 per acre of producing trees. The peach, plum, and cherry trees were expected to be at full production by year 6, but only at one-third and two-thirds production in years 4 and 5, respectively. Apple tree production would take about two years longer at about these same rates. At the current time, only half of these orchards were in production. The pumpkins were largely used as give-away prizes to patrons of the pick-your-own fruit.

The pick-your-own fruit was offered at about 65% of retail price so as to shift the cost of labor harvest largely to the buyers. The nearby cities provided a steady stream of patrons for the farm produce gathering projects. No. 1 fruit could probably be sold at $10 to $12 per bushel, locally, depending on the regional harvest level.

In addition to the nursery caretakers' monthly stipend of $600 and the wages of the part-time workers from May 1 through September 30 of each year, Roberto and Loupi were each receiving $1,500 monthly as their remuneration. Loupi's wife largely headed up the collection station activity of cash-and-carry sales during the May to September months and earned 1.5 times minimum wage for her 50-hour-per-week activity.

The used equipment was depreciated over 5 years with the straight-line depreciation method. Variable costs ran about 10% of revenues, and fixed costs other than labor amounted to $6,000 yearly.

ASSIGNMENTS

You and a friend have been engaged as a Small Business Institute team to provide counseling to the client, the S & S Fruit Farm, Inc. Specifically, you are asked to do the following:

1. Estimate the balance sheet from the above facts.
2. Prepare an estimated income statement, with breakdowns of expected revenues and expenses, for the next three years.

3. Comment on the insurance arrangement and make any other suggestions felt to be in the best interest of the Sanchez family. You may assume that the firm is currently operating as an S corporation.

4. Develop a plan of promotion for the firm as its harvest increases in size due to the plants growing to maturity.

The United Wholesale Durable Goods Firm, Inc.

The financial officer of the United Wholesale Durable Goods Firm, Inc., Mr. Knight, was trying to determine the probable borrowing needs for his company in early 1994 for the current year. His assistant had prepared a cash budget by quarters for 1994, but the financial officer believed that it should be recast by months showing the appropriate tax prepayments required under the latest Tax Revision Act. Under TRA, corporations were required to pay, by the middle of the fourth, sixth, ninth, and twelfth months, one quarter of the estimated tax burden for the year. Any unpaid amount could be deferred to the first and second quarters of the following year, not to exceed 10% of the total tax burden. Any deficiency carried the penalty rate equal to the borrowing rate of the U.S. Treasury Department (running about 7% in 1994). Deficiencies above the allowable deferment carried a penalty of 25% of taxes owed.

The firm was a closely held, family-owned and -operated corporation. During its 41-year history, it had been run by the grandfather (still the chairman of the board) and his eldest son (now president of the firm). The 16-year-old son of the president, Mark United, was expected to become active in the firm upon his graduation from college. In total, some 16 members of the family owned stock in the firm, but the chairman of the board owned 31%, the president owned 20%, and other board members and officers of the firm owned 25%. The balance was spread among 10 other family members, with none holding more than 5%. The family shareholders usually just returned their voting proxies and permitted the board to cast them for reelection of their chosen candidates. The nine members of the board were elected annually for 1-year terms and generally comprised seven shareholders, one bank officer, and one attorney. Input from the latter two were desirable on certain financial or legal matters.

The firm stocked a line of consumer durable goods that are largely considered to be necessity items. Sales did not vary more than 2% or 3% over the business cycle, but neither was there any pronounced growth in sales in real terms. For the past five years, monthly sales from January to December had averaged 7.5%, 7.5%, 10%, 12%, 15%; 10%, 8%, 6%, 6%, 6%, 6%, and 6%, respectively. While a base stock of inventory was carried for popular items, buying during one month was about equal to expected cost of goods sold the following month. Items were bought on terms of net 30 days and carried an average profit markup of 20% based on sales. Selling, delivery, and administrative expenses were largely fixed, averaging 15% of sales. Noncash items amounted to 3% of sales.

The yearend 1993 balance sheet for the firm appears in Exhibit 1. The company in recent years had followed the policy of paying out 80% of earnings as dividends, inasmuch as many of the shareholders depended on dividends for meeting their living expenses. The management of the firm had given some thought to buying back a portion of the shares and possibly even going public, but the board chairman was not in favor of losing control of the firm.

The financial officer had assigned his assistant the job of preparing a cash receipts and disbursements schedule, by quarters, to determine the probable borrowing needs of the company during the next fiscal year. After careful study of the cash budget, the financial officer became convinced that it might not be detailed adequately to correctly reflect the need for bank borrowing to finance inventory and receivables. He also felt that the estimate of state income taxes (6%) and federal income taxes (34%) might slightly overstate the probable tax liability of the firm. At the very least, he asked his assistant to research such liability and to recast the statements on a monthly basis for all of 1994.

The bank officer, in talking with the financial officer's assistant, wondered if it would not be possible for the firm to avoid payment of corporate taxes if the firm were to obtain shareholder approval to be taxed as an S corporation rather than as a C corporation. This was discussed at the January board meeting, but no decision had been made at the point of attempting to recast the cash budget on a monthly basis for 1994.

ASSIGNMENTS

1. As assistant to the treasurer and financial officer in the firm, make a comparison of the total tax burden to the firm and family members, assuming that all are in the 28% marginal tax bracket, if electing C or S corporate status. The four family members employed by the firm withdrew a total of $180,000 in salary plus their share of dividends in 1994, with the board chairman and president each receiving $60,000 and two junior officers earning $30,000 each.

2. Develop the monthly cash flow statement as requested by the financial officer of the firm.

3. Develop a pro forma income statement and balance sheet for 1994 for the firm.

4. Comment on the wisdom of following such an 80% dividend payout policy and borrowing heavily from the bank. Suggest viable alternatives.

EXHIBIT 1. United Wholesale Durable Goods Firm, Inc.
Balance Sheet as of December 31, 1993

	Amount (thousands)
ASSETS	
Cash and near-cash	$ 250
Accounts receivable	600
Inventories	2,000
Other current assets	150
Total current assets	3,000
Fixed assets, net of depreciation	2,000
Total assets	5,000
DEBTS AND NET WORTH	
Accounts payable (1-month purchases)	600
Other current debts (about constant)	200
Bank loan (prime rate + 1%)	550
Total current debts	1,350
Capital stock	3,000
Retained earnings	650
Total debts and net worth	5,000

EXHIBIT 2. United Wholesale Durable Goods Firm, Inc.
Cash Flow Budget for 1994
(Thousands)

	Quarter 1	Quarter 2	Quarter 3	Quarter 4
Cash receipts	$2,100	$3,700	$2,400	$1,800
Cash disbursements:				
Purchases of merchandise	2,000	2,960	1,600	1,440
Taxes (federal and state income tax)	50	50	50	50
Other cash disbursements	300	300	300	300
Dividends	60	60	60	60
Total disbursements	2,410	3,370	2,010	1,850
Beginning cash balance	250	100	100	110
Plus: Cash receipts	2,100	3,700	2,400	1,800
Cash available	2,350	3,800	2,500	1,910
Less: Cash needed	2,410	3,370	2,010	1,850
Difference (+/−)	(60)	430	490	60
Current bank loan	550	710	380	0
Minimum cash balance	100	100	100	100
Surplus (needed) funds	(710)	(380)	10	(40)*

*Less amount of interest on the bank loan for the year.

St. Louis Oriental Restaurant, Inc.

The downtown St. Louis Oriental Restaurant, Inc., was formed in late 1990 about two blocks from the St. Louis Mall (that was housed in the Old Railroad Depot) in order to provide lunches and fine dinner meals to people that worked, shopped, or traveled in that section of the city. While three other restaurants would be located within a block of the planned location, none of them concentrated on Oriental foods as a specialty. In fact, the founder of the firm thought that only three or four fine Oriental restaurants operated in all of the greater St. Louis area, that extended across five counties of Missouri.

Fine restaurants usually do not cater to the breakfast crowd, but the firm planned to open at 10:30 a.m. and to remain open until 9:00 p.m. Patrons would not be seated after 8:30 p.m., the doors would be locked at 9:00, and patrons would generally be urged to depart not later than 9:30. Drinks would only be served with meals, as adequate bar service appeared to exist near the planned location.

Instead of buying a building, a suitable one with some adjacent parking was obtained on a 10-year lease. Space was available for adding a drive-up window, and a public parking lot across the street from the location contributed to the rapid growth in sales for the establishment. Its founder, Mr. Kevin Choy, born of a Korean father and an American mother, set some management goals and objectives for the firm upon its formation as a single proprietorship. These included the following:

1. Targeting annual growth in sales of at least 15%.

2. Targeting a rise in the profit margin (which was 4% of sales in 1991) of ½% each year for the first five years of operation before becoming constant.

3. Insisting on quality of food served, but limiting the portion sizes so that food costs would not exceed 30% of the prices charged for the items on the menu.

4. Carefully restricting the cost of labor to 25% to 26% of revenues.

5. Retaining one-half of earned profits in the firm for expansion or debt reduction.

6. Promoting specials so as to have reasonably level sales of 8% to 9% of annual totals in a given month. The higher figure would likely be reached during May, July, November, and December, as Mother's Day, Independence Day fireworks shows, the Thanksgiving holidays, and Christmas shoppers generally caused business to rise in those months. Volume of customers was likely to rise by about 10% to 15% yearly, and prices were expected to accelerate upward by 5% due to inflationary pressures.

The Oriental Restaurant was opened for business in late 1990 with a net worth of $65,000—which represented a bulk of the assets owned or controlled by the founder/manager of the firm. Growth was almost instantaneous for the firm, due to expansion of the mall and good crowds that enjoyed fine Oriental foods prepared by the crew of Oriental cooks and served by Oriental waitresses. Infusions of capital totaled $15,000 in 1991 with another $30,000 in 1992 in the form of preferred stock sold to the father of the owner of the small corporate firm.

While the restaurant had operated as a single proprietorship for one year, an unfortunate incident of alleged food poisoning and the defense in court caused the owner to reconsider and to incorporate the firm in early 1992. The suit was settled out of court for $5,000. The owner felt all along that it was just a nuisance suit with little grounds for allegations; however, in order to stifle illwill and loss of patronage, the suit was settled. The plaintiffs (husband and wife) agreed to drop the case for such a settlement. The firm immediately increased its liability insurance coverage to provide for such a contingency in the future, along with property insurance and workers' compensation coverage.

The size of the work crew in the Oriental Restaurant averaged about nine at any point in time, but since the restaurant was open about 80 hours weekly, some eight full-time workers, plus its owner and manager, were usually on hand at any one point in time. The owner handled the buying of wholesale food items, made cash deposits daily, promoted business growth, and supervised the general management of the firm. An assistant manager was hired for each of the early and late shifts, with the two alternating on weekends so as to average 40 hours per week. The two assistant managers (who served as ushers when needed) each earned $1,200 monthly (in 1992). The four cooks, with two or three on duty at any point in time, were each being paid $5.00 hourly and $7.50 for overtime above 40 hours weekly. The waitresses worked for 70% of minimum wage and were expected to earn the balance from tips (about average in the industry). To them, tips usually ran about equal to wages paid. One busboy during the early shift and another for the late shift handled table cleanup and dishwashing, being paid $4.40 hourly. A receptionist/cash register operator was on duty at all times, and the two persons that filled this position also rotated weekends on and off duty. These persons received a flat $200 weekly for their work in the firm. Part-time help was sometimes added if larger-than-average crowds of patrons were expected. The part-time workers did not receive health benefits payments, sick days, or two weeks of paid vacation time as did the regular full-time workers, and the part-timers received minimum wages.

After leasing to the firm for three years, the owner of the leased property decided to sell the facility. When approached in late 1993 about buying the property, the restaurant owner contacted a nearby savings and loan association that agreed to lend up to 75% of the value of the facility. In 1994, some $65,000 was borrowed, with a commitment for additional funds to add a drive-up window facility. By the end of 1994, the balance owed on the note was $81,000. The firm was paying interest at ½% over the prime rate plus $1,000 monthly against the principal of the mortgage loan.

The assets in building-owned restaurants are predominantly long-term assets. The cost of the structure, improvements in parking facilities, and investments into kitchen equipment, dining tables, chairs, and other fixtures and equipment often amount to 70% to 75% of the total assets. The businesses usually accept cash or major credit cards, discounting the charge slips on a weekly basis at 1.5% of their face amount. Few bad debts are incurred, as the validity of each credit customer is checked out before the charge slip is accepted. Long-term mortgage debt and owners' equity also run about 65% to 75% in a restaurant. Such figures for the St. Louis Oriental Restaurant are reflected on the following balance sheets.

St. Louis Oriental Restaurant, Inc.
Comparative Yearend Balance Sheets

	1993	1994
ASSETS		
Cash and near-cash	$ 35,385	$ 49,918
Accounts receivable	9,011	12,836
Notes receivable (employees')	2,418	3,328
Inventory	15,824	23,137
Other current assets	11,429	16,322
Total current assets	74,067	105,541
Fixed assets	78,022	116,792
Other noncurrent assets (structure and two lots)	67,692	94,606
Total assets	219,781	316,939

	1993	1994
DEBTS AND NET WORTH		
Accounts payable	18,022	26,623
Equipment loans	1,539	2,377
Notes payable (bank)	9,011	12,519
Other current debts	32,527	48,016
Total current debts	61,099	89,535
Long-term mortgage (10-year)	58,000	81,000
Deferred credit	440	630
Net worth:		
Preferred stock (7%)	—	30,000
Common stock ($10 par)	80,000	80,000
Retained earnings	20,241	35,774
Total debts and net worth	219,780	316,939

Key Profit and Loss for 1993 and 1994 Data

Net sales	$646,412	$705,092
Net profit after 15% taxes		28,556
		20,241

ASSIGNMENTS

1. Estimate the amount of wages for the firm in the current year and expected in the following year, assuming a 15% growth rate in volume and a 5% increase in prices.

2. Using the percentage of assets to sales method, prepare pro forma statements for the firm for the next two years (income statements, balance sheets, and sources and uses of funds).

3. Prepare monthly cash flow statements for quarter 1 of 1995 and quarterly cash flow statements for the last three quarters. Indicate how this will impact on needs for bank borrowing. Make and state needed assumptions. Use industry breakdowns as needed.

Buy-Low Mail Order Gift Shop

The Buy-Low Mail Order Gift Shop was planned to begin operations in early 1995, just on the fringes of a retirement village in southern Illinois. At the time of the gift shop's formation, the community would have about 500 resident families, some two-member and a few one-member families. Plans for the retirement village called for adding about 200 families yearly to the facility of family-owned homes, multi-unit structures (duplexes and fourplexes), and three-story condominium or apartment structures for the next five years, when the village would approximately fill its allotted space. The developers had a waiting list of interested resident members, so they felt sure that the goals for the planned membership in the retirement village would be met. While the two founders of the gift shop felt that it would probably lose money for the first six months, due to the lack of reputation in the community and the lack of customer traffic, both felt that the firm could be profitable by the end of the second year and that profits could be increased thereafter by aggressive buying and selling and rigorous expense control.

Mr. Beaumont, who had a degree in marketing management from a leading Illinois university, and Mr. Money, skilled in accounting and financial management, each invested $20,000 in the venture. Both had jobs at the present time. Mr. Money was keeping the books and providing management consulting to about 20 clients. His time was undercommitted, however, as he spent only 20 to 25 hours weekly on the tasks. Mr. Beaumont had an assistantship and was enrolled in two graduate marketing courses at a nearby university. He was spending only about 30 to 35 hours weekly on the tasks, and both felt that they could commit at least 20 hours weekly to the development and management of the gift shop. It was their plan to hire one middle-aged lady to run the shop during periods when neither of the owners could be present. By the time that the shop reached satisfactory size, their outside activities could be curtailed so that full-time attention could be devoted to the operation of the gift shop. If they were successful in its operation, they felt compelled to begin a wholesale and franchised licensing of other gift shops in other retirement villages in the Midwest.

Since the firm would be paying for its own utilities, Mr. Money was able to negotiate a very favorable leasing contract with the developer of the retirement village. He was to pay the sum of $4,000 yearly during the first and second years of the five-year lease. The rent would be $4,500 yearly during years 3 and 4 and then move to $400 monthly thereafter. The two founders had an option to renew the lease for a similar period of time at $400 monthly thereafter. The space was to be sandwiched between space allocated to a real estate sales office and a credit union catering to accounts of residents in the community. Both managers in the gift shop felt that high customer traffic would be generated in this location. Each felt that the shop would have outgrown its facilities by the end of the fifth year.

Plans formulated initially called for the investment of $20,000 by each of the two founders. Additional amounts of permanent capital needed would be borrowed on a term loan basis. Certain amounts of short-term liabilities would be self-generating. That is, as payroll was made, tax withholdings would be held by the firm for a few weeks before being deposited. Some merchandise could be bought on terms of 1%/10 days, net 30 days, while other lines could be bought on terms of 3%/10, net 30. This would average a 2% discount, if paid within the discount period. Mr. Money had investigated their potential borrowing ability from a local commercial bank, that would handle their NOW account, and was promised a working capital loan, in reasonable amounts, at a rate of 1% above the prime loan rate, with quarterly rate adjustments. Three-year term credit would run 1 percentage point above the 90-day renewable loan rate. In early 1995, the prime rate was running 7% but was expected to rise by a point or two over the next two years.

Mr. Money felt that it was reasonable to assume that first-year sales would approximately equal the investment capital in the firm. The sales would probably double the next year, increase by one-half in year 3, by one-third in year 4, by one-fourth in year 5, and so on. Growth in the firm would be financed by withdrawal of slim salaries by the two managers during the first two years of operations. Once they gave full time to the venture, however, their salaries would have to be increased. Each of the two managers intended to withdraw $500 monthly from the firm to supplement their income, and they planned to hire a retired lady on a fill-in basis for about the same salary. Social security payments would probably push the total allocated to the wage expense account to the approximate amount of $18,750 in years 1 and 2. After that time, another salesperson might have to be added, probably at $5 hourly. Certainly by the fourth year, at least one of the managers would need to be full time in the operation. The other might head up the wholesale/franchise portion of the business, if it were developed.

Since the primary clientele of the gift shop would be residents of the community, and most received retirement checks the first of the month, it was decided by the two owners that charge accounts, to be paid by the fifth of the month after purchase, would be permitted to retirement village residents only. Checks on local banks would be accepted, with adequate identification by the makers, and Visa, MasterCard, and Discovery cards would be accepted for payment of purchases. Total cost of credit, including a 3% discount to cash customers and the cost of discounting the charge slips, would likely run about 3% of total sales.

The two prospective owners of the firm were not sure whether to operate the firm as a partnership or as a small corporation. Neither had they decided whether a regular or an S corporation would prove advantageous. The financial management specialist, Mr. Money, had developed a realistic forecast of sales, expenses, income statement, and balance sheet items for the first four years of operations. These forecasts, shown in Exhibits 1 through 3, are only for Buy-Low Mail Order Gift Shop and do not reflect any possible increase in revenues due to a wholesale and franchised operation for shops.

Exhibit 1 reflects an analysis of the projected sales for the firm and the projected cost of labor. Other expense projections for the first four years of operation are shown in the income statement projections, Exhibit 2. Pro forma balance sheets are shown in Exhibit 3.

EXHIBIT 1. Buy-Low Mail Order Gift Shop
Sales and Labor Cost Projections

	Year 1	Year 2	Year 3	Year 4
Number of families (average)	500	700	900	1,100
Customers per week (percent)	10	15	18	20
Number of customers per week	50	105	162	220
Average purchase	$15	$15.50	$15.90	$16.40
Sales per week (average)	$750	$1,628	$2,576	$3,608
Sales per year (50 weeks)	$37,500	$81,400	$128,800	$180,400
Number of employees	3	3	4	4
Hours per week (average)	25	25	25	25
Total hours	75	75	100	100
Wage rate per hour	$5	$5	$5	$5
Total wages per week	$375	$375	$500	$500
Total wages per year	$18,750	$18,750	$25,000	$25,000

EXHIBIT 2. Buy-Low Mail Order Gift Shop
Projected Income Statements

	Year 1	Year 2	Year 3	Year 4
Sales	$37,500	$81,400	$128,800	$180,400
Less: Returns and discounts (average 4%)	1,500	3,256	5,152	7,216
Net sales	36,000	78,144	123,648	173,184
Inventory, initial	5,625	5,175	11,193	17,788
Plus: Net purchases (reduced by 5% returns and 2% discounts)	16,453	35,588	56,555	79,107
Less: Ending inventory	5,175	11,193	17,788	24,881
Cost of goods sold	16,903	29,570	49,960	72,014
Gross profits	19,097	48,574	73, 688	101,170
Operating expenses:				
Freight-in	329	712	1,131	1,582
Advertising	2,000	1,200	1,200	1,300
Wages	18,750	18,750	25,000	25,000
Payroll taxes	1,875	1,875	2,500	2,500
Utilities	1,725	1,869	2,000	2,100
Insurance	2,000	2,000	2,100	2,400
Other, including rent	4,600	4,624	4,643	4,725
Total operating expenses	31,279	31,030	38,574	39,607
Net profits (losses)	(12,182)	17,544	35,114	61,563*

*A portion might be withdrawn at the owners' discretion.

EXHIBIT 3. Buy-Low Mail Order Gift Shop
Projected Yearend Balance Sheets

	Year 1	Year 2	Year 3	Year 4
Cash or near-cash (NOW)	$ 8,743	$19,496	$44,658	$ 96,883*
Accounts receivable (5 months sales)	1,500	3,300	5,200	7,200
Inventory (from Exhibit 2)	5,175	11,193	17,788	24,881
Store supplies	400	400	450	500
Store fixtures, net	10,000	9,600	9,200	8,800
Other assets	2,000	2,500	3,000	3,500
Total assets	$27,818	$45,087	$80,296	$141,764
Accounts payable (1 month's purchases)	1,400	3,000	4,700	6,600
Other debts (accruals, etc.)	400	400	450	450
Capital stock	40,000	40,000	40,000	40,000
Retained profits (losses)	(13,982)	1,687	35,146	94,714
Total debts and equity	$27,818	$45,087	$80,296	$141,764

*Some cash available for withdrawal by owners (for salaries, to pay taxes, or to invest in the wholesale/franchising operation).

ASSIGNMENTS

1. Study the given information carefully, along with the Business Profile on Catalog Mail Order Firms, and comment on the reasonableness of the plans formulated by Mr. Money and Mr. Beaumont. Develop a marketing strategy for the firm, using Appendix C.

2. Develop a detailed business plan for the proposed firm, including sections on goals, organization (chart), duties of each employee, guidelines for marketing, management, financing decisions, employee benefits, and so on.

3. Develop a plan and strategy for undertaking the addition of a wholesale/franchised operation in year 3 or 4, assuming that the given forecasts of revenues, expenses, and profits are substantially on target. Refer to the Business Profile on Franchising for additional information.

4. Suggest possible problem areas likely to be encountered when promoting a franchised operation for other similar shops.

Green Acres Landscape and Garden Center, Inc.

The Green Acres Landscape and Garden Center, Inc., had been in operation for more than 10 years. It was formed in response to growing need for landscaping and grounds services in and around retirement villages. The company was not so large as to list its securities on one of the major exchanges, but middle-management executives in the four-state firm were encouraged to buy shares in the venture. The company usually invested little in real estate. Instead, it leased space within or adjacent to a retirement village being built and handled the landscaping of the single-unit dwellings and around the multi-family dwellings within the village. It continued to offer monthly services of caring for the lawn and the plants, removal of snow and ice from driveways and walkways, and so forth, during all months of the year. The charge for the landscape work ran from about $1,000 to upwards of $3,000 per dwelling but averaged about 5% of the investment in the lot and structure. In 1994, the firm was charging a flat $20 monthly for its care of plants and snow removal on a yearly contract basis on a single-unit dwelling with average vegetation. On larger lots, or with those more heavily planted, the charges ran higher.

The decision in 1994 was whether or not to expand the facility to another recently developed retirement village in southeastern Missouri. The firm was currently serving Arkansas, Missouri, Illinois, and Indiana. Two middle-management officers of the parent firm usually relocated to the new venture, one handling the landscaping and the other the land care. After the village was 80% filled, which usually occurred within about six to eight years of its formation, the landscape specialist moved to another location while the manager of the grounds remained to supervise the work on established lawns and so on. Plants used in the landscaping were not grown from cuttings but were instead bought from nearby nurseries, when available, or hauled in from a more distant location as needed. The plant specialists knew, however, that plant survival rate was usually best when the plants were fresh and had been established on a regional root base rather than transported several hundred miles to a different climate.

The corporate treasurer had determined that the recent cost of debt was about 10%, on a pretax basis. Its capital structure usually ran about 40% long-term debt and 60% common equity. The cost of the latter in 1994 was estimated to be 12% after taxes. Dividend payout ran about 40%, and the firm targeted a return of 15% on common equity in its new investment plans, pricing policy, and so on. Thus, book equity was increasing about 9% per year. The tax rate to the combined firm was 34%. Limited trading of the over-the-counter common shares was for about two times book value per share.

The firm usually bid against several competitors for the major contracts with the developers of retirement villages for the right to lease space in or adjacent to the villages. Builders of family-owned residences, of course, had a choice of Green Acres or other nurseries for landscaping or yardwork and snow removal, but the firm often received 80% of the separate residences and virtually all of the developers' contracts for site servicing due to its volume buying and competitive pricing.

The plants were usually bought in large volumes from nearby nurseries, so if regional nurseries missed out on the primary contracts, they were usually contacted as providers of plants for the jobs. Plants were bought in wholesale lots, relocated to the plant store within the retirement village, heeled out, and planted into their permanent location during the early spring and late fall months. Virtually all the planting took place in March through May and again in October through December. The three winter months were devoted largely to plant care (guarding against damage by rodents and freezing) and driveway and walkway clearing of snow and ice, and the severely hot summer months to frequent watering, hedge clipping, grass cutting, sidewalk grass edging, and so on. Vacations for the employees were rotated at periods of demand slackness in their related specialty. The firm usually ran a staff of four full-time persons and about four to eight part-time manual laborers. The landscape specialist primarily designed the planting job and supervised its completion. The lawncare specialist supervised a crew of four to six manual workers. The nurseryperson spent his or her time in buying and caring for the plants. The office worker served as a combination receptionist, secretary, and bookkeeper. One of the managers in the firm and the nurseryperson worked as superintendents on jobs of planting and extended plant and lawn care, respectively. Part-time or full-time manual laborers were usually available in ample supply at about 150% of minimum wage.

The firm usually followed a definite expense program in its operation. Plant costs ran 55% of their selling price at retail; labor costs ran 20%; payroll taxes and fringe benefits (such as vacation days, sick days, workers' compensation, etc.) ran 20% of labor cost; utilities (primarily water) ran 1% of sales; advertising costs were budgeted at 2% of sales; and other costs ran 8% of sales. Thus, pre-interest and pretax profit margins were targeted at 10% of revenues. On the maintenance program, the formula was somewhat different, but the same 10% of revenues was targeted as income prior to interest payments.

When a new retail nursery and plant store was located in a newly designed retirement village, its chosen location was to the front of the village. It frequently leased two or three lots for a minimum period of five years with a view toward returning one of the lots to the developer once the major portion of the planting had been completed. A cement structure adequate to house the office, a small reception area, and a retail selling area, usually about 1,200 square feet, was built. Plants were enclosed with eight-foot-high chain-link fencing, but several sliding gates permitted easy access for unloading and loading of plants from or to trucks. Parking spaces were provided to the front of the structure and plant area. The company owned several pieces of power equipment at each location, but in total, it committed about 80% of assets to working capital (largely inventory), another 10% to leasehold and leasehold improvements (with average lives of 10 years), and the balance to equipment with an average life of 10 years. The firm took straight-line writeoffs on its amortization and depreciation schedule. Current debts, with no implicit cost, ran one-third of total assets, and permanent debt and equity capital accounted for the balance (in a 4 to 6 ratio).

In order to encourage prompt payment by the contract companies (for the landscaping jobs) and by the monthly paying contract customers for lawn care and grounds maintenance, the firm offered terms of 2%/7 days EOM, net/30 days, and charged a 1.5% monthly interest assessment for payments received after 30 days. The monthly maintenance was terminated after a period of two months' delinquency, and a tax lien was placed on the property for the amounts owed. The tax lien, plus accrued interest and legal costs, had to be paid off before a renewal maintenance contract was reinstated. In the past, the firm had used the tax lien very infrequently, as the threat of this was usually adequate to solicit payment. The firm did, however, retain the services of a regional attorney for such usage as required. On balance, the discounts taken were about in line with the interest charged to the late-paying clients.

On a given project, it was not unusual to lose money the first year but to make it up in years 2 through 5. After the fifth year, the firm was largely doing lawn care and site maintenance work with a reduced crew of workers. The trick was to downsize the firm so as to keep labor costs to the target percentage of revenues.

Estimates of revenues from the proposed retirement village called for $250,000 in year 1; $350,000 in year 2; $375,000 in year 3; $400,000 in year 4; $300,000 in year 5; and $250,000 each year thereafter. As earth-moving equipment (largely for planting) was no longer needed at one location, it was moved to another retirement village in an expansion stage. Initial capital called for an investment of $120,000, with $48,000 in long-term debt and $72,000 in equity. About this level of assets would be maintained for 8 years and then reduced by 25% for continuing lawn and site maintenance work.

ASSIGNMENTS

1. Determine the weighted average cost of capital for Green Acres.

2. Determine a schedule of probable cash flows for 10 years.

3. Determine the approximate payback for the expansion plan.

4. Determine the average after-tax return on the average asset investment for the proposed expansion and on book equity for years 1 through 8.

5. Apply the weighted average cost of capital as the discount factor to the cash outflows/inflows of the project to determine the profitability index, assuming sale at book value at the end of the tenth year.

6. Determine the internal rate of return promised on the venture. What decisions would you recommend on the proposal?

Atlanta Wholesale Furnishings, Inc.

During the summer of 1994, two young men in Atlanta, dissatisfied with their jobs as furniture salesmen with a leading furniture store in that city, were seriously considering the possibility of opening their own discount furniture business. Mr. Joe Hamilton and Mr. Jim Mizelle had six and eight years of experience in selling, while Joe had been assistant to the buyer of certain lines of high-priced furniture as the need arose. Each were selling about $750,000 in furniture yearly, receiving a drawing account (for weekly withdrawals of $400) against commissions of 4% of actual sales. A great deal of their sales volume came from repeat customers and from referral customers who asked for them by name when coming into the furniture store. Not only did they each enjoy considerable customer loyalty, but the majority of their customers were wealthy people who bought the more expensive lines of furniture and related items. Because of the nature of their clientele and the nature of their sales approach, about 60% of their sales volume was in special-order items that were not part of the store's regular inventory. This percentage might have been even higher had they been freed from the store management's understandable policy of encouraging sales of merchandise already in stock.

Aside from their dissatisfaction with their compensation, the two felt that the store management's policies were hindering their sales potential by requiring them to concentrate a part of their time in selling the store's lower-priced furniture lines.

Mr. Hamilton and Mr. Mizelle determined that by liquidating or borrowing against their investments, life insurance policies, and the like, they could raise only $50,000 on their own. They also had families that were willing to invest $50,000 in 8% cumulative preferred stock in their venture; but both were somewhat reluctant to invest funds of relatives in a new start-up that might or might not meet with success. In order to conserve expenses, they decided that for the present, they would share a two-bedroom apartment (both were seriously dating but neither were married), Mr. Mizelle would retain his selling job where currently employed, and Mr. Hamilton would begin the new venture. Once sales had risen to a level to support the added employee, Mr. Mizelle would resign his position with his current employer. Their immediate problem was to determine the feasibility of a business of their own and to determine the capital necessary to start it. They also wished to put together a list of potential suppliers of medium- and high-priced furnishings and a list of potential clients on which they could call.

Mr. Hamilton and Mr. Mizelle envisioned a small, high-quality furniture store that would attempt to reach only the wealthier portions of the market and that would do largely custom-order business. The two men intended to serve as the entire sales force for the firm, with Mr. Hamilton devoting full time and Mr. Mizelle devoting half time (when not working at his current job). They would, of course, need to hire one office worker to care for telephone calls, referrals, and minor bookkeeping. The retired aunt of Mr. Mizelle promised to see to the duties, not to exceed 30 hours weekly, at a price of $600 monthly. This would permit her to continue to draw her full OASDI check, and it would give her a higher standard of living. The two principals in the operation owned a ¾-ton truck and a stretched van between them and felt that these would be adequate for making most deliveries. When larger pieces of furniture had to be delivered, a rental van could be obtained at a price of $20 daily plus mileage charge.

The customary markup in quality furniture was 50% of selling price. Some lines carried even higher prices. The two founders, however, wished to offer their lines of furnishings as discount furniture, however, and planned to discount usual selling prices by 20%. On average, a gross profit margin of 40% was targeted on their operation.

A suitable building, which would be available on January 1, 1995, was located at a monthly rental of $1,500. Capital improvements of $20,000 would be necessary, and the leasehold would be signed for 10 years. The renovation would require 60 days until completion. In the meantime, furniture could be ordered for delivery once the store was suitable for usage. Mr. Hamilton planned to resign his position on the first of the year, traveling to New York City and Dallas in order to arrange for shipments of certain furniture lines. He also planned to obtain a wide range of catalogs of items that could be ordered from elite furniture makers. Since housing starts were reasonably slow, due to uncertain interest rate levels, furniture makers were more than willing to sell on extended credit terms. Three such companies had approached Mr. Hamilton about placing some lines of their merchandise on consignment with the planned new store. This seemed to be a good arrangement to the prospective owners, as they would avoid tying up their money in the inventory until after it was sold.

It was Mr. Mizelle's belief that furniture could be sold on terms of 90 days same as cash. That is, one-fourth would be payable at the point of sale and one-fourth each at 30, 60, and 90 days after the date of delivery. The special-order items required about 60 days' order time, so the second of the payments would be received about 90 days after the initial downpayment. The customers, of course, might buy floor items, charging them to their major credit cards as an alternative. These charge slips were discounted at 1.5% of their face amounts, but bad debt losses were nil when using them, so long as only viable charge cards were taken.

Sales of furniture follow a strong seasonal and cyclical pattern. Strong sales of new homes encourage the buyers to acquire some new furnishings, especially wall decoration items, living room, and formal dining room sets. The den, kitchen, and bedrooms are furnished or refurnished more on a utility basis as needed. Monthly sales during January through April are each about 5% of annual totals; sales from May through September are about half of annual sales; while the balance (30%) is about evenly distributed over the last quarter of the year.

Expenses of the operation would include the monthly rent of $1,500; utilities (heat, power, water, telephone) averaging $300 monthly; miscellaneous expenses of $500 monthly; and salaries to the three employees. Mr. Mizelle, on a part-time basis, planned to withdraw $600 per month. The receptionist would also be paid $600 monthly. Mr. Hamilton planned to pay himself $1,500 monthly until the business was financially healthy, and then he and Mr. Mizelle (as a full-time partner) would each draw $3,000 monthly, each planning to marry at that time.

A local bank offered a credit line of 50% of the value of receivables, on a pledge basis, at a rate of 12%. The bank also offered a personal loan to the two men in the amount of $15,000 each (unsecured) at a similar rate. Their vehicles were clear of debt, and these were each worth about $10,000 and would become company assets.

The assets of the planned firm would consist of approximately the following:

- Cash: A two-week supply (1/24 of annual sales)
- Accounts receivable: 60 days average age
- Inventory: Anticipated turnover of four times yearly
- Other current items: Miscellaneous accruals of $2,000
- Leasehold improvements: $20,000 for renovating the store
- Other: Office equipment, vehicles, etc., at cost/value of $10,000, $20,000, and $40,000, respectively.

Recurring expenses, not previously enumerated, were estimated to run $500 monthly for advertising, $200 for janitorial expenses, $200 for postage and other office expenses, $400 for insurance (including workers' compensation, liability insurance, and property coverage), payroll taxes (10% of payroll), and $200 for miscellaneous expenses.

Mr. Hamilton and Mr. Mizelle believed that monthly sales in year 1 might average $40,000 in slow months (January through April), $80,000 in May through September, and $240,000 during the fourth quarter, but with additional 10% closeout price specials. Since the store would not officially be opening until early March 1995, the first year would have only 10 months of sales. Sales growth was expected to be one-fourth in year 2, one-fifth in year 3, one-sixth in year 4, and so on, until it came in line with inflation levels. Prices would then be adjusted to approximate cost-of-living changes. As the level of sales increased, the duo expected to add one or two selling persons to the staff and perhaps one or two hourly paid delivery persons on a part-time basis (probably two afternoons per week plus Saturdays).

In order to minimize risks to them, they decided to incorporate the firm. The cost of incorporating their small firm was estimated not to exceed $300, including legal expenses. They also planned to file for S corporate treatment with the IRS so as to minimize taxes.

ASSIGNMENTS

1. Develop a business plan for Mr. Hamilton and Mr. Mizelle, including forecasts of asset needs, sources of capital, sales projections, expense projections, break-even analysis, and so on.

2. Recommend a course of action for Mr. Hamilton and Mr. Mizelle.

Consumer Durable Goods Franchisers, Inc.

Consumer Durable Goods Franchisers, Inc., a wholesaler of furnishings and household electronic equipment, had been selling its products to the Jones Discount House for the past four years. The wholesale supplier offered terms of 2/10, n/60 in an attempt to encourage prompt payment of invoices. Other suppliers in the immediate geographical area offered similar terms. The account of the Jones Discount House and numerous other accounts had recently become about 30 days slow in their remittance for trade purchases. The credit officer of the firm had become concerned about the slowness of some of these accounts and pondered the possible alternatives for correcting the situation. He did not wish to take any action that might precipitate the loss of accounts, but he believed that some action should be planned before the problem became even more acute, involving the need to hire a collection agency for collecting on some of the accounts.

As a starting point, Mr. Brown, the credit officer of the wholesale consumer durable goods supply firm, made a study of the fixed and variable components of his firm's expenses. He wished to determine the profitability of each of the accounts in terms of providing net profits and in terms of absorbing a fraction of the company's fixed overhead. Since the company had excess capacity, the loss of an account would result in the aggregate loss of fixed expense coverage and net profits. Mr. Brown determined that at the current level of sales, fixed expenses totaled $1,800,000 per year. Variable expenses totaled 65% of sales; and net income before cash discounts, interest, or income taxes averaged 10% of sales.

During the past two years, the firm had been forced to borrow from its commercial bank in order to finance the buildup of the slow-paying accounts receivable. The company was currently paying an interest rate of 10% on the credit granted on pledged accounts receivable, and was asked to maintain a compensatory balance of 15% of the desired line of credit.

Mr. Brown had appealed to his slow-paying customers for discount or prompt payment, but he had been informed by some of the delinquents that they had been unsuccessful in their attempts to borrow from local banks. One of the customers went so far as to say: "If you are not willing to grant us 90 days of credit, we are confident that some other makers of furniture will be willing to do so." Mr. Brown believed that several of the other slow-paying customers were in similar situations, so he felt that pressing too severely for prompt payment might cause some to turn to other suppliers.

During the past twelve months, the average monthly order from the Jones account had amounted to $6,000. Approximately 25 other accounts had monthly purchases ranging from $3,000 to $16,000 and were following a pattern of payment similar to the Jones Discount House. Whatever course of action was settled upon would be applied to all of the accounts and not just to the Jones Discount House, as the integrity of the supplier needed to be preserved.

Before reaching a definite conclusion as to the course of action to recommend to the board of directors of the concern, Mr. Brown wished to find answers to several questions, thereby strengthening his defensive position with the board at the next meeting.

ASSIGNMENTS

1. What annual contribution does the account of the Jones Discount House make toward fixed expenses?

2. How much annual profit does the account produce, including the cost of providing merchandise, financing cost, and the like?

3. Assuming that enforcement of the regular terms or granting credit only on COD terms to the 25 slow-paying accounts would result in the loss of half of the accounts but the prompt servicing of the remainder, what course of action would seem more desirable from a profit and loss standpoint?

4. Suggest a course of action to be taken by a credit officer in minimizing slow and delinquent accounts and bad debt losses during a period of recession in its industry or the nation.

Ables and Ables Consulting, Inc.

Mr. Ken Ables and Ms. Delores Ables, his unwed twin sister, had each been employed by public accounting firms for eight years. Each had been promoted to chief auditor for their respective firms, but neither felt that he or she was in line for becoming a partner in the firms. Each was making in the low $40,000 range in salary, having been hired in his or her mid-twenties and having received pay raises once each year. Each lived rather frugally, and between them they had more than $100,000 to invest in a small accounting or consulting firm. Each consulted his or her recent past account principals and discovered that several would give their business to the new firm rather than remaining with the previous one. Advertising cards would be mailed to professional acquaintances and personal friends once the firm had been established.

The firm was initiated on July 1, 1993. Both partners had remained with their respective firms through May of that year, giving themselves substantial overtime from doing audits and tax returns for corporate and partnership clients. They knew that it would probably take about six to nine months before the firm would reach a break-even level. It was their plan to hire an office manager the first year. It would be necessary to add a junior executive, they both believed, in year 2. As revenues increased and as the clientele became larger in size, it would be desirable to add even more staffpersons. The two principals, who decided to form a professional corporation for liability and other reasons, would elect the S corporate tax treatment so as to minimize federal income taxes. Moreover, it would be possible to expense a greater part of the payroll taxes and fringe benefits than if operating as a partnership.

The Ableses sought a location intermediate in distance from the two communities that they planned to serve. Thus they would be within about a 20-mile radius of expected clients. This was important so as to minimize their own travel time and that of their clients. A busy consultant in the region usually charged about $60 to $75 per hour for the time billed. It was desirable to bill not less than 6 hours per day to clients if expenses were to be covered, adequate compensation was to be paid to the consulting partners, and any profits were to be left as a return on capital. It was decided that the initial charge would be $60 hourly, but the clients were to be told that this was introductory and the hourly billing rate would likely advance by about $5 per hour each year thereafter. At this rate, each accountant or consultant might generate about $60 × 30 hours × 50 weeks = $90,000 in annual revenues. Junior partners serving on an assignment billed at lesser rates, such as $30 to $40 hourly customarily. The work of secretarial staff was not billed separately. Neither was the cost of office materials, if used in moderate amounts. However, only a dozen copies of the final report were presented to the client. If more copies were needed, it was at an extra printing charge.

It was decided that a large, four-bedroom house with ample parking, located on the highway intermediate between the two cities, would be leased for the office space. The living room would be used as the outer office/reception area for the secretary/bookkeeper/receptionist. Each consultant would have a separate bedroom to be used as an office. The extra room would be used as a study, conference room, or storage space until needed by other consultants being added in the third and subsequent years of operations. The den would be the normal conference room/library, and the kitchen would be used as a snack area. The two bathrooms would be assigned one each to gentlemen and ladies.

The actual income statements for the first 18 months of operation and projected for year 3 are shown below:

Ables and Ables Consulting, Inc.
Actual and Projected Income Statements

	Second-Half 1993	1994	1995 (projected)
Revenues billed	$105,635	$221,255	$279,220
Expenses:			
Compensation of officers	31,691	66,377	83,766
Cost of operations	16,479	34,516	20,383
Wages expense	11,092	29,592	50,260
Continuing education cost	3,000	4,500	7,500
Lease rental expense	10,615	10,615	10,615
Taxes	4,859	10,178	12,286
Depreciation	7,360	8,408	9,493
Liability insurance	3,908	7,523	11,169
Pension and benefits	2,641	5,531	12,565
Tax service books	1,250	1,400	1,800
Interest expense (autos, etc.)	1,650	1,650	3,071
Professional dues	1,067	1,991	2,792
Repair expenses	739	1,549	2,396
Donations	800	1,250	2,250
Advertising expense	898	1,328	1,089
Bad debt expense	211	443	838
Miscellaneous expenses	264	553	698
Total expenses	$98,524	$187,404	$232,971

	Second-Half 1993	1994	1995 (projected)
Net profits	7,111	33,851	46,249
Dividend withdrawals (taxes)	2,489	9,562	11,812
Reinvested capital	4,622	24,289	34,437

In year 1, a secretary was hired at an annual wage of $11,092. A staff assistant was hired in year 2, and another was planned in year 3 at a beginning salary of $18,500. Wage increase increments would be made yearly to the experienced persons, averaging about 3% to 5% above the rate of inflation.

Initially, some $45,000 would be invested in fixed assets, such as furniture and fixtures, leasehold improvements, and partial payment on two autos for use by the principals in visiting their clients. The furniture would be depreciated at 10% yearly, the autos over 5 years, and the leasehold improvements over the life of the lease, 5 years. About $12,000 in office equipment would be acquired, which would have an estimated life of 3 years. The balance of the funds would be held in cash until needed for operating expenses. A NOW account was opened which promised to pay 3% interest, so idle funds would be earning a small rate.

Following are the balance sheets at the beginning of business, yearend 1993, and yearend 1994.

Ables and Ables Consulting, Inc.
Balance Sheets

	Initial	Yearend 1993	Yearend 1994
ASSETS			
Cash	$ 41,127	$ 32,462	$ 38,764
Accounts receivable	—	22,828	38,840
Other (prepayments)	—	10,608	13,000
Total current assets	41,127	70,898	90,604
Long-term assets:			
Fixed assets	45,926	40,155	53,117
Office equipment	12,947	11,320	14,147
Total assets	100,000	117,373	157,868
DEBTS AND NET WORTH			
Accounts payable	—	4,262	4,109
Dividends payable	—	2,489	9,562
Wages payable	—	—	3,986
Total current debts	—	6,751	17,657
Installment notes, long-term		6,000	11,300
Total debts	—	12,751	28,957
Common stock ($10 par)	100,000	100,000	100,000
Retained earnings	—	4,622	28,911
Total debts and equity	100,000	117,373	157,868

By the end of the second year, the Ables felt that they had a good grasp of the monthly billings. By month and by quarter, they ran about the following percentages of annual totals:

January	14.80	February	14.80	March	14.80
April	11.20	May	5.95	June	5.95
Quarter 3	14.75	Quarter 4	17.75	Total	100.00

The costs were accumulated, with some progress billing, so that on average 70% of billings were collected in the month of billings; 20% the following month; and 10% the second month after billing a client.

ASSIGNMENTS

1. As the newly hired junior executive in the firm, you have been asked to prepare a cash flow statement by month for the first six months and by quarter for the last two quarters of year 3. Make any needed assumptions, but state them.

2. Prepare a pro forma balance sheet as of December 31, 1995, that ties together the previous balance sheet and the cash budget.

3. Suggest more appropriate employment of idle funds.

Complete Office Help

Mrs. Joan Boudet, principal of the Complete Office Help service firm of Midtown, Ill., was in a quandary as to whether to borrow funds and expand her sole proprietorship or to sell the business for the equivalent of one year of revenues and seek employment in office-type work.

The current management had operated the small firm for two years, having bought the firm, its list of customers, and about $5,000 in office equipment at a price of $15,000 some two years before. Assets in the firm, when acquired, were a telephone switching station adequate to handle 15 lines, one computer work station, a typewriter, two desks and chairs, and a copy machine. While the equipment was still functional, its trade-in value was only about 75% of undepreciated amount. Some $10,000 in personal savings and a $6,000 bank loan were invested into the firm, giving it start-up assets of $16,000. The loan was repayable out of revenues generated by the firm equal to $250 monthly on principal plus interest of $\frac{2}{3}$% monthly. Business assets were pledged as collateral for the loan.

The owner, plus a half-time hourly paid person, took care of the phone-answering business. The employee was paid $5 hourly. A great deal of slack time was available, so contract typing was promoted. The jobs were mostly term papers for Illinois State University students, legal briefs for local attorneys, and book manuscripts for college and university professors.

The monthly answering service charge had ranged from $40 to $100 monthly at the time of acquisition, but this was soon changed to a minimum of $75 monthly with additional charges of $3 each for more than two incoming calls daily per client. By the end of the first year of operations, some $3,000 of equipment upgrade was needed, and the number of answering clients had been increased to 27, with an average of $80 assessed each, payable on a monthly basis. With the current equipment, only three additional telephone lines could be handled, but these 30 lines were about all that two persons could handle on a reasonably timely and efficient basis. The phone upgrade cost $3,000.

As the reputation of the office grew, the volume of manuscript typing work also increased so that the owner (full-time) and three half-time persons were needed to handle the volume of work. Only base wages of $6

317

hourly were being paid to the part-time typing workers. The typing charge rates were set at about two times the average direct salary being paid to the typist. The part-time persons generally typed straight manuscripts, while the owner attempted to cost the more complicated tables and graphs at $25 hourly. She also handled the legal briefs and charged the attorneys that hourly rate. Two additional computer centers and a faster copy machine were acquired at a total investment of $5,500.

Rent and utilities were running at a flat $400 monthly. One more year existed on the present rental lease. Insurance, including workers' compensation insurance, was about $100 monthly. Payroll taxes were running 12% of payroll. Equipment was depreciated over a 4-year life using straight-line depreciation. Some pick-up and delivery of manuscripts were being made, at an average monthly cost of $75. Postage and the use of fax machine and telephone were running about $150 monthly. Other variable costs ran about 10% of revenues.

Mrs. Boudet had received some inquiries from her other clients about providing them with pretrained temporary help at a charge rate of $10 hourly. Trainable help, on a part-time basis, could be hired at $6.50 hourly, plus payroll taxes and workers' compensation that were paid by the firm. This potential expansion would require another computer center and software library costing $10,000. Another $10,000 in working capital would be needed.

The business owner estimated that about half a day of her time would be involved with training a person for a job. She would not pay the worker for this time, but neither would her time invested be recoverable directly. It was estimated that from 40 to 80 hours of temporary help would be used for each job. She planned to charge $10 hourly and pay her workers $6.50, leaving the other $3.50 hourly for covering overhead and her time.

Mrs. Boudet had called her loan officer at the bank for an appointment to discuss her situation, when out of the blue a competitor offered to buy out her business, as it now existed, for a price of $50,000. This was about equivalent to the current annual billings for telephone answering services and contract typing. She decided to pursue the bank interview and see what developed before making a decision whether to continue the firm or to accept the offer.

The bank loan officer asked that she take the two-page form used for LowDoc, Bank-SBA loan participations, complete it, and return with it in two days. The interest rate on the loan, if approved, would be at the prime rate plus 2.75%, repayable over a period of 36 months for the $20,000 loan. When asked about security, Mrs. Boudet believed that the equity in her home could be pledged as collateral for the loan.

ASSIGNMENTS

1. From the information provided, complete the Bank-SBA participation loan form.

2. Prepare estimated financial statements for the second page of the form.

3. Contrast the merits of expanding the firm into the allied area of temporary help service and selling it for $50,000.

Sleepy Grove Nursing Village

Mr. Jason Brown, owner of Sleepy Grove Nursing Village of St. Louis, Mo., was reviewing the cost of operations. The nursing home had been making a reasonable profit since its beginning in 1975 but had not made the 10% pretax return that Mr. Brown expected on all of his investments. While reviewing the various costs of operations, Mr. Brown noted that the cost of laundry service had been in excess of $31,000 for the prior year. Thinking that this figure was quite high for a 150-bed nursing home, Mr. Brown decided to investigate the possibility of installing a laundry in the nursing home, thus avoiding the cost of the contract laundry service. Mr. Ray Williams, administrator of Sleepy Grove, was assigned the task of gathering cost data on each method. Only through a thorough analysis of cost could the relative advantage of one method be determined.

Before the cost of each method could be found, Mr. Williams had to determine the quantity of linen that was being used in the home. It was determined that the home had been operating at approximately 96% of capacity since its establishment. Even though there was a waiting list of patients to be admitted, some beds were always vacant due to deaths and transfers to various hospitals. It was determined that each patient used about 5 pounds of linen per day, or 35 pounds per week. From a review of the records of the contracting laundry, the amount of linen used by each patient was found to be as follows:

Item	Quantity per Week	Cost per Item
Sheets	4	$.28
Pillowcases	3	.16
Patients' gowns	2	.18
Towels, bath-size	7	.14
Towels, hand-size	7	.10
Washcloths	7	.06

The nursing home had been contracting laundry since it opened in 1975. The service had been provided on a year-to-year contract basis. The rates had been increased two years earlier, and it was believed that they would remain stable for at least two more years. Because of the probability of stable laundry rates and capacity occupancy in the nursing home, it was believed that the total cost of the service would remain stable over the coming few years.

Mr. Williams believed that there was sufficient area in the existing building to accommodate a small laundry facility. A representative of Universal Laundry Machinery Industries advised Mr. Williams that in order to process the approximate 5 pounds of laundry per patient-day, it would be necessary to purchase several pieces of industrial-sized laundry equipment. The machinery should be depreciated over a period of 10 years for tax purposes and would have no scrap value at that time. The following equipment would be needed:

Item	Cost
42- × 36-inch washer, end-loading, motor drive, automatic control	$9,500
42-inch solid curb extractor and motor	6,700
37- × 42-inch drying tumbler and motor	1,940
110-inch flatwork ironer, gas-heated	7,560

The laundry machinery representative stated that this machinery would be warranted for 90 days against defect. For the fee of $72 per month, extended warranties could be acquired. Soaps, detergents, disinfectants, and so forth would average $180 monthly.

Engineering data on the equipment provided the following utility requirements for 40-hour work weeks, 52 weeks per year:

Water	3,000 cubic feet
Natural gas	39,000 cubic feet
Electricity	282 kilowatt-hours

Mr. Wilson obtained the following utilities rate schedule from the local providers of the services:

Water	$1.50 per thousand cubic feet
Natural gas	$1.30 per thousand cubic feet
Electricity	$.06 per kilowatt-hour of usage

In addition to the cost of establishing a laundry, there would be the cost of buying linens. Under the arrangement with the local linen service, linens were provided as part of the service. The linen requirements and cost for a 150-bed nursing home were estimated as follows:

Item	Quantity (dozens)	Price per Dozen
Sheets	35	$40.00
Pillowcases	15	9.60
Patients' gowns	40	27.00
Towels, bath-size	30	10.50
Towels, hand-size	40	4.40
Washcloths	30	2.40

Such a supply should be sufficient for the needs of the nursing home for at least two years. The typical life of nursing home linen items is two years. The linens should be included in the cost of operating the laundry.

Two employees would be employed in working a 40-hour week in the laundry room, amounting to about $1,280 per month.

ASSIGNMENTS

1. As the assistant to Mr. Williams, make the analysis. Estimate the discounted cash flow rate of return on the proposed investment in the laundry room project.

Globe Garment Sewing Center, Inc.

On June 8, 1994, Mr. John Nolan, president of the Globe Garment Sewing Center, Inc., of Chicago, Ill., was comparing the differences between two financial proposals extended by Mr. George Sloan, representative of ABC Factoring, Inc. The first proposal was to sell outright accounts receivable to ABC, and the other was to borrow from ABC by a pledge of accounts receivable.

Globe had been formed in 1984 with initial capital of $200,000, and sales of products by the company had grown from $775,000 in the first year to $2,600,000 by 1993. The 15 largest stockholders of the firm, that combined held 51% of the voting shares, were opposed to the issuance of more stock for the financing of working capital needs, especially since the stock had not recovered from its lofty heights of the run-up in price in August 1993. The stock, unfortunately, had taken a nosedive from $29 per share to about $12. It had only recovered to $16 by early 1994, and the major shareholders considered it to be severely underpriced.

The company operated at a $24,000 loss in 1990, but by 1991 to 1993, profits had risen to these more substantial levels:

Year	Sales	After-Tax Profits
1990	$ 775,000	$(24,000)
1991	1,185,000	23,200
1992	2,135,000	43,100
1993	2,600,040	70,740

Unfortunately, as sales continued to rise, so did the need for working capital to finance growing inventories and accounts receivable. Even with close cost control of raw materials and work in process, and selling on a job-order basis, needs for working capital continued to mount.

Some working capital funds were provided by making purchases from suppliers that gave credit terms. Terms of 1%/10 days, net/30 or 60 days were customary. Some offered a discount of 2% if paid within 10 days of purchase. These were taken by the sewing center, as the rates seemed to be higher than other credit costs.

Terms on the factored accounts receivable called for selling any and all accounts rated by Dun & Bradstreet, Inc., as "High," "Good," or "Fair," and pledging (on a recourse basis) accounts rated as "Limited." The cost of such pledges would be 2.5% of those sold. Interest would be assessed at the annual rate of 15% and based on the credit terms plus 10 days. Since the sales were on terms of 1%/10 days, net/30 days, the cost would be assessed on 40 days. Any discounts taken, of course, would go to the factoring firm, but they would be approximately offset by the interest charged the Sewing Center. A reserve of 5% of the accounts sold would be maintained by ABC to take care of possible returns and allowances. Such reserve would be paid to Globe as it exceeded 5% of the accounts held for collection. The factoring of the accounts would free up the equivalent one-half account collection person, with payroll costs of $8,000 annually.

As an alternative to the selling of accounts receivable (or factoring), the ABC Factoring Company stood ready to lend up to 80% on the "High"-, "Good"-, and "Fair"-rated accounts but would not accept "Limited" accounts as their collection problems were too severe. As Globe continued to collect on these accounts, there would be no savings from freed labor. Moreover, the average loss on bad debts of 1% on "High," "Good," and "Fair" accounts would have to continue to be borne by Globe. The 3% loss on the limited accounts, of course, would apply to Globe no matter which of the two arrangements were undertaken. The cost of the accounts receivable loan was to be on a daily basis, stated as $1/24$% per day. Moreover, Globe would have to undertake a quarterly audit of its accounts receivable account at an annual cost of $1,200 in order to satisfy ABC as to its creditworthiness and validity.

After the interview with the ABC financial representative, Mr. Nolan expressed his desire to give the matter his consideration for a few days before reopening discussion on the matter. He knew that his accounts receivable had grown to about $400,000 (on average), approximately evenly divided between accounts with D & B ratings of "High," "Good," "Fair," and "Limited." He assigned his assistant the job of making the necessary computations that would suggest the appropriate course of action to be taken.

ASSIGNMENTS

1. Compute the implicit cost of trade credit when terms are as follows: 1%/10, net 30; 1%/10, net 60; 2%/10, net 60.

2. Develop an economical course of action regarding the paying of the above trade accounts on a discount versus prompt basis.

3. Determine the annualized cost of funds provided by ABC Factoring through the pledge of accounts receivable, including other relevant costs.

4. Determine the annualized cost of funds provided by ABC Factoring through the factoring arrangement, also including savings and extra costs incurred.

5. Determine the cost/savings difference on an annual basis of borrowing versus factoring of the accounts receivable, assuming that they continue to average about $400,000 at any one point in time.

Lyles Clothing Stores, Inc.

In March 1994, Mr. Stephen P. Lyles, president of Lyles Clothing Stores, Inc., was considering an expansion of his firm into new product lines. This expansion was considered by him to be mandatory if his firm was to stay in competition in the industry. Mr. Lyles and his colleagues were now faced with the problem of raising new funds for the expansion. Historically, Lyles Clothing had maintained a simple common stock structure and relied mainly on internal funds and common stock sales to raise the funds needed to add capacity to existing product lines. However, Lyles's management had indicated that it was willing to consider any of the five following sources of financing for the new product expansion: (1) internal financing, (2) common shares, (3) preferred stock, (4) bond financing, or (5) term loan financing.

Lyles Clothing Stores, Inc., was formed as a corporation in 1978, with Mr. Lyles and three of his associates contributing the necessary capital. Mr. Lyles owned majority interest in the corporation at its outset, and it was still a closely held corporation in 1994, with Mr. Lyles holding 56% of the stock and the other 44% being held by company employees. Moreover, certain of the key employees had begun to grumble that they were not afforded some profit-sharing bonus plan or stock purchase plan at a bargain price.

Lyles Clothing was incorporated in Brownsville, Tex., a popular location for clothing manufacturers, since cheap Mexican labor could be used to keep production costs low. The firm originally manufactured work clothes, which were marketed in bargain basements of large department stores and Army-Navy stores throughout the South. Two company salespersons were hired to represent the firm in this area, one based in Dallas, the other in Atlanta. Recently, Mr. Lyles had been approached by a promoter for a factory outlet syndicate in Chicago about opening a small wholesale center for everyone in that location. At such a location, the first item was usually sold at retail price. The second item of similar price carried a discount of 50%. Thus, the goods were usually bringing about 75% of retail price. Such an operation would involve the investment of about

$250,000 in terms of leasehold improvements, inventory stocking, and the need for other working capital. Some 20% of this amount might be self-generating, so that the firm would be investing about $200,000 of its own funds. If this expansion route were added, Lyles would attempt to locate five such centers, in areas not directly competing with other outlets for their garments, and invest about $1 million in the venture.

In 1979, Lyles Clothing expanded its line of goods to include overalls, and some large chain stores such as Dixie Stores, Inc., began to carry the product. At that time, Mr. Lyles hired three more salespersons to open up markets for products in other parts of the United States. This raised the number of salespersons employed by the firm to five. These persons were provided offices and were based in Dallas, Atlanta, New York, Chicago, and Phoenix, and were to cover territories in Texas, the Southeast, the East Coast, the Midwest, and New Mexico and Arizona, respectively. Every salesperson was successful, and all were still employed by Lyles in early 1994, though two were approaching retirement age.

Because of sound management and an intelligent expansion program, sales increased steadily from $4 million in 1978 to $34 million in 1993, with declines only in the recession years of 1980 and 1990. A new sales record was projected for the year ending December 31, 1994, with net earnings as a percentage of sales reaching 4.85%. Even though Lyles Clothing was in good financial condition and still experiencing sales growth, management felt that the new product expansion was necessary so that the firm could continue to grow and remain in competition with other firms in the industry.

Garment firms had begun to be more competitive in pricing permanent press clothing. Lyles also wished to invest in the process and to begin making permanent press jeans and overalls, walking shorts, overcoat shells, small tents, and the like. However, this product diversification was not meant to be an end in itself but was to be used by management to create a new company image which, they hoped, would eliminate the market's tendency to consider Lyles Clothing as a manufacturer of only work clothes and would act as a stepping-stone to more sophisticated clothing lines, such as dress slacks and suits, denim suits, and the like.

In order to finance the proposed expansion and develop the new company image, management predicted that $5 million would be needed for the following investment outflows: (1) increasing the labor force and hiring a young and aggressive marketing and production manager; (2) opening up an office in the Empire State Building in New York, at the heart of the clothing industry; (3) financing a national advertising program; (4) buying the necessary machinery and equipment that would be needed for undertaking the permanent press process; and (5) investing in the additional material inventory that would be needed. Investment in outlet stores would add another $1 million in needed capital. The firm's management believed that building manufacturing additions would not be necessary since there was already enough floor space available to absorb the expansion.

Financing of temporary current assets was not a problem, and management would consider various sources of funds for financing the permanent current and fixed assets of the new investment after an analysis of the relative merits and cost of each was obtained. The cost would be compared to the expected rate of return of the new investment of about 10.0% after taxes. This was arrived at by taking the cost of 20% targeted short-term credit of 8%, on average; the cost of 20% planned long-term debt of 10%; and the approximate cost of 60% equity of 13%. The weighted average cost appeared to be about 9.6% to 9.9%, but due to market fluctuations, Mr. Lyles thought that they might as well raise this to 10% as the hurdle rate for new expansion plans in order to be on the safe side.

The market price of short-term borrowing and long-term debt was easy to determine, but the cost of equity was not so easy. Several finance textbooks argued that the market cost of capital was influenced by the risk-free rate of borrowing (the Treasury bill rate), the risk-premium rate on common stock (which was thought to vary from 6% to 9% over the stock cycle), and the relative price volatility, or beta, of the stock in question. Since the stock was not actively traded, Mr. Lyles believed that the average beta for traded textile stocks, about 1.25% of the movements in the Standard & Poors average of 500 stocks, might be used as a proxy. Since stock prices were moderately priced in 1994, he felt that the 7% risk premium would be in order. The T-bill rate had been about 4.2% in recent months, so this seemed to provide a cost of the company's equity as follows:

$$K = RFR + RP(beta) = .042 + (.07)(1.25) = .042 + .0875 = .1295$$

A review of the net income and book value for the company indicated that the firm had earned about 11%, after taxes, on the 100% equity firm. He had once approached an investment banker about selling some stock but was discouraged when told it would go for less than book value per share at that time. He thus felt that the use of some tax benefit from debt issues might be in order. The company was currently paying federal income taxes at the rate of 34%, with 2% the average state income tax rate. Thus, the firm appeared to be forgoing the tax shield on interest of about 36% when debt was used rather than common or preferred stock.

Mr. Lyles realized that depreciation and retained earnings were a main source of funds in the industry, and he himself had used this source in the past. Retained earnings cost had been estimated to be high, perhaps 13% less the 15% or 28% tax bracket of the firm's shareholders. The firm also had a source of $3 million to $4 million on which it was earning 5% to 6%, fully taxable. This was the buildup of Treasury notes in anticipation of an expansion program. Moreover, several closely held firms with excess liquidity had recently been charged with excess retention of earnings and had to pay a penalty tax of 30%. This Mr. Lyles wished to avoid.

The company, during recent years, had distributed a $.50 cash dividend on each share of common stock. The book value was about $14 per share, so this yield (on book) was only about 3.5%. The company had been reinvesting the other 7.0% to 8.0% return on book equity in expansion assets. Some large holders of stock, however, had begun to grumble that the firm should not retain the earnings only to hold them in low-yielding Treasuries.

Mr. Lyles was especially concerned about the use of common stock to finance the expansion because he would have to buy 83,000 of the 320,000 additional shares of stock needed to raise the $5 million (if they were sold at book value) in order to maintain his controlling interest in the firm. As an alternative, the stock might be made available to the shareholders, at 95% of book value per share. Some thought had been given to paying managers in the firm a total bonus equivalent to 10% of pretax profits but payable into a supplemental pension plan with common shares of the firm. Each such employee who enrolled in the plan would also be permitted to shelter an additional 5% of his or her income, not to exceed $9,000 yearly. Mr. Lyles was not sure how much money this would bring in, so, for the present, he felt that more dependable sources might be determined.

If a rights issue were made to old holders, it would have to be priced so as to sell, but Mr. Lyles just did not believe that the stock should be sold at less than book value per share. Based on the first-of-the-year equity, the company in 1993 had earned $2,034,869/$19,517,500 = 10.43%. Book value per share at the end of the year would be $21,571,369/1,600,000 shares = $13.48, and discounting this by 10% to 15% as a minimum would cause the stock to sell for about $12 on a rights basis. The growth in earnings per share had averaged at least 10% in most years, and with the 3.5% dividend yield on book equity, Mr. Lyles believed that it should bring at least the book value if offered in the marketplace, even after a 10% underwriting charge as suggested by one investment banker.

An issue of preferred stock was considered by management to be an alternative method of financing, but they also noted that the use of preferred stock in the industry had declined since 1950 for other than convertible preferred issues used in acquiring other firms. These were often priced so as to yield about 75% as much as regular preferred shares but were convertible into common shares at a 10% premium above their going price at point of issue. Underwriting cost on preferred shares was about 4% of issue size for amounts of $4 million to $6 million. Market yields were similar to those of bonds for a given company.

Lyles Clothing has an A credit rating with Dun & Bradstreet, which the president of the firm thought would probably equate to an Aa rating by one of the bond rating services if the issue were in moderate amounts, say from $5 million to $10 million, and carried sinking fund contributions over the life of a 15-year bond issue. The cost to the firm would likely be about 10%, after paying an underwriting cost of 2%, and yield the investors about 9.8%. Convertible bonds, at a 15% conversion premium above book value per share, might be sold with a 7.0% yield, but Mr. Lyles felt that this potentially carried some dilution of voting control when/if the bonds were converted. The underwriting cost would also be 2%, and the bonds would be callable at 108% of face amount.

Mr. Lyles had heard that expansion financing was sometimes obtainable from a financial institution Small Business Administration loan, but he had not pursued the exact terms. He had approached one life insurance company that had expressed an interest in making a term loan, repayable quarterly from years 3 through 7 of the issue and carrying an interest rate of 9.5%. This was about intermediate between the short-term loan rate of 8.0% and the 10% cost of bond funds, so Mr. Lyles thought it might be a viable alternative. There would be no underwriting cost of the loan, but an annual audit of the records would be required (estimated to cost $5,000 yearly) with statements and audit report provided to the lender.

As an aid in preparing some cost and benefit comparisons from the various types of approaches to obtaining the $5 million or $6 million in expansion funds, the treasurer of the firm provided Mr. Lyles's assistant with the most recent financial statements for the firm. These are provided in Exhibits 1 and 2.

Exhibit 1. Lyles Clothing Stores, Inc.
Balance Sheet for December 31, 1993

ASSETS

Current assets:		
Cash and NOW accounts		$ 4,358,469
Short-term Treasury bills		4,000,000
Accounts receivable	$ 1,864,000	
Less: Reserve for bad debts	150,000	1,714,000
Accrued interest receivable		25,000
Inventories:		
Raw materials	$ 1,450,000	
Work in process	1,090,000	
Finished goods	2,270,000	4,810,000
Prepaid expenses		630,000
Total current assets		$15,537,469
Fixed assets:		
Land		380,000
Factory building	$ 2,000,000	
Less: Allowance for depreciation	800,000	1,200,000
Machinery and equipment	$10,500,000	
Less: Allowance for depreciation	3,000,000	7,500,000
Delivery equipment	$ 120,000	
Less: Allowance for depreciation	60,000	60,000
Office equipment	$ 100,000	
Less: Allowance for depreciation	45,000	55,000
Total fixed assets		$ 9,195,000
Total assets		$24,732,469

Current debts:	
Accounts payable	$ 1,784,000
Accrued wages	360,000
Accrued expenses	665,000
Accrued taxes	318,770
Total current debts	$ 3,127,770
Deferred credits:	
Rent received in advance	33,330
Stockholders' equity:	
Common stock ($10 par)	16,000,000
Capital surplus	1,500,000
Earned surplus	4,071,369
Total shareholders' equity	$21,571,369
Total debts and equity	$24,732,469

Exhibit 2. Lyles Clothing Stores, Inc.
Income Statement, Year Ending December 31, 1993

Gross sales	$34,670,000	
Less: Returns and allowances	690,000	
Net sales	$33,980,000	
Cost of goods sold:		
Finished goods inventory, Jan. 1	$ 1,580,000	
Cost of goods manufactured	21,255,000	
Goods available for sale	$22,835,000	
Less: Finished goods inventory, Dec. 31	2,270,000	
Cost of goods sold		20,565,000
Gross profit on sales		$13,415,000
Other income:		
Rental income	$ 167,670	
Interest income	337,500	
Purchase discounts	61,000	566,170
Selling and administrative expenses:		
Depreciation:		
Delivery equipment	$ 20,000	
Office equipment	5,000	
Bad debts	236,000	
Other selling expenses	5,510,000	
Other administrative expenses	4,930,000	10,701,000
Interest expense		45,000
Net before-tax profit		$ 3,235,170
Less: Provision for federal/state taxes		1,200,301
Net after-tax profit		$ 2,034,869
Less: Dividends declared		800,000
To retained earnings (earned surplus)		$ 1,234,869

ASSIGNMENTS

1. As the assistant to Mr. Lyles, prepare an estimate of the cost of capital and discount factor for evaluating expansion projects.

2. Compare the proposed capital structure to that of its industry, garment manufacturing.

3. Analyze the strengths and weaknesses of using various types of expansion vehicles (i.e., rights issue, bonds, etc.).

4. Assuming a $5 million annual expansion program for the next five years, develop sequential financial plans to arrive at the proposed capitalization structure of 20%/20%/60%.

Shoney's Restaurant, Inc.

The Shoney's Restaurant, Inc., of Midtown, USA, had been in operation for slightly under five years. The closest other Shoney's restaurant was located in a town some 18 miles distant. Shoney's restaurants, while privately owned, are franchised from the parent organization. This accounts for the largely similar layouts, menus, uniforms, and services provided by the franchised firms. As typical in other franchised operations, Shoney's has an up-front franchise fee and assesses a periodic percentage of sales to defray continuing management fees and joint advertising.

The Midtown Shoney's was owned and operated by three college-trained individuals, Mr. Frank Myers, Mr. Fred Myers, and Mr. Ted Jeffreys. Frank and Fred Myers, brothers in their early 30s, held degrees in marketing and small business management, respectively, from a regional university. They rotated as comanagers of the firm. Mr. Jeffreys had a degree in financial management from the same school, and he was chief accountant and treasurer of the organization.

The typical Shoney's restaurant is built on a site with adequate parking space, good visibility, and a heavy traffic flow past the location. About a week prior to the grand opening, the employees have been hired and are trained by Shoney's management and sometimes by a team of experienced Shoney's managers from a nearby establishment, with about 65 employees being average for any given Shoney's location. The employees are hired to do different jobs in the establishment. Assistant managers often seat clients and oversee the overall operation of the establishment. Two or more cooks are busily engaged at all open hours in the kitchen. One or two employees are used as cleanup persons, that act as buspersons and load the dishwasher or wash the utensils by hand. Waitresses offer full restaurant service to the clients, although many Shoney's locations have a self-service breakfast bar and salad bar that is located centrally among the dining tables. The breakfast bar may be available from about 7:00 a.m. to noon, with the salad bar replacing it until about 8:00 or 9:00 p.m. on weekdays and perhaps an hour or two later on weekends and holidays. About 13 to 17 waitresses/waiters work each shift, with most of them being part time for

15 to 20 hours per week. Many are senior high school or college students that work part time in the evenings or on the weekend shifts. The establishments, unlike some restaurants, are usually open seven days a week and are also open on holidays. One cashier usually manages the checkout cash register and, in busy times, might be assisted by another person.

The pay scale is different for the employees. The manager and assistant managers are usually full-time persons, receiving some fringe benefits in addition to their weekly or monthly salary. The cleanup crew and kitchen help (cooks and cook's helpers) are paid hourly, while the waitresses/waiters are paid 60% of minimum wage and are expected to earn a similar amount from tips provided by patrons. The franchised chain encourages the employees to be courteous to its customers, to promote repeat business, and to serve fresh food in a wide array of offerings. After the initial opening, new employees are trained by those with substantial experience in the firm. They also have a nightly review of all Shoney's rules and procedures during their first week on the job. Shoney's promotes workers from within. That is, they might move from busperson to assistant cook to cook; or from waitress to cashier to assistant manager; and so forth. Thus, most Shoney's restaurants are successful from a labor relations and financial standpoint.

There is wide variability in the size of crowds of patrons at Shoney's restaurants. The busiest days are on weekends, especially during brunch on Sundays. At this time, the restaurant may be working some 35 of its 65 to 70 employees, and patrons are sometimes waiting for half an hour before being seated. On university weekend special events (parents' day, football games, and the like) business is likewise booming. Discounts or specials are sometimes run on slow days, such as Tuesdays and Wednesdays, in order to spread the load of once-or-twice-a-week customers.

The Midtown Shoney's had been successful from the beginning, although it suffered a small loss in its first year of operation. Quarterly sales during its first five years of operation averaged as follows: year 1 (partial year), $187,300; year 2, $301,856; year 3, $432,740; year 4, $480,576; and year 5, $545,988. Growth in sales was expected to continue in future years due to a sustained advertising program, daily specials, coupons and senior citizen discounts (for persons 60 or older), and banquet facilities for group sizes up to about 30.

The breakdown of assets and debts and equity in the establishment ran about as follows:

Assets		Debts and Equity	
Cash	16%	Accounts payable	12%
Inventory	12	Other current debt	16
Accounts receivable*	2	Long-term debt	28
Other current assets	5	Owners' equity	44
Equipment	35		
Leasehold and leasehold improvements	30		

*Mainly charge slips.

Midtown Shoney's offered about 45 items on the breakfast bar. The buffet bar was offered after noon, but more than half of the patrons ordered from the menu rather than using the buffet bar after about 1:00 p.m. Senior citizens provided about 20% of total business to this Shoney's, and their repeat business was especially solicited. Competition within a few blocks of the outlet included a Ponderosa, a Rax restaurant, a Kentucky Fried Chicken, and a Long John Silver. Several other specialized food restaurants, such as Pizza Hut and McDonalds, were nearby.

The managers and assistant managers rotated between the breakfast, lunch, and dinner shifts with the three owner/managers rotating weekends. One job of the manager/assistant manager was to ascertain that there were adequate inventories of fresh foods and vegetables and that items being offered as specials were in long supply. An adequate supply of dishes, silver, napkins, and so on was the responsibility of the manager or assistant manager, who also handled customer complaints that arose. The cashier was expected to be courteous to the exiting customers, always asking if the service and food were satisfactory and enjoyable, and so forth.

Sales at the Midtown Shoney's varied widely from month to month. December and January were the slowest two months, with sales running about half the average rate. February and November sales accounted for about 6% of annual totals, while March and April were about average (i.e., 8.3% to 9%). Sales during the other months ran from 9.5% to 11% of annual totals, with August being the heaviest month of sales. This could be attributed to the heavy back-to-college traffic of parents bringing their students and stopping at Shoney's for a meal while in the city.

The following formula for monthly expenses existed for the Midtown Shoney's Restaurant. Rent was $2,000 monthly plus 2% of sales; utilities ran about $1,000 fixed plus 2% of sales; salaries were $35,000 fixed plus 26% of sales; purchases were variable at 40% of sales; advertising (including the franchise fee) ran 5% of sales; and insurance and maintenance were fixed at $150 and $200 monthly, respectively.

Net profits on the Midtown Shoney's were modest, and the abilities of the three owners were underutilized. It was their belief that the addition of five billboards around highways entering Midtown would direct heavier customer flow to the establishment. Moreover, investigation indicated that the Shoney's restaurant located in the adjacent city could be bought at a realistic price. Some cash was available through the current business, and the three owners each had an additional $30,000 that could be invested in an expansion. Moreover, if the second location were acquired, both could be advertised on the same billboards.

It was anticipated that billboards would be placed about ten miles from each of the Shoney's, facing the flow of traffic, on each major highway. Five billboards would be needed to cover the approaches of major highways to the two cities. Billboards of America agreed to redo the billboard every year for the next 5 years. A 5-year loan to pay for the purchase of the billboards and their maintenance was available at a local bank. It was anticipated that 175 additional customers per year would be drawn to each of the Shoney's restaurants as a result of billboard advertising. Payout of the 5-year project was projected at three years.

The second, and more expensive, capital investment proposed was the buyout of the nearby Shoney's in the adjacent city. While the level of activity there was currently only about one-third the level at the Midtown location, the creation of a nearby regional shopping mall had the potential to increase business by 100% to 150%, perhaps in years 2 through 4 after the proposed year of purchase.

It was anticipated that the only change in personnel at the nearby Shoney's restaurant would be the addition of one of the Myers brothers full time and the treasurer on a part-time basis. This would not displace any of the current workers, as the part-time accountant at that location, one of the current owners, would be retiring and moving to a southwestern state.

It was anticipated that asset turnover at the nearby Shoney's restaurant would occur about three times in the second year after acquisition. The asking price (by the current three owners of the nearby restaurant) was $300,000, but Mr. Jeffreys, the Midtown Shoney's treasurer, felt that it could be bought at that price, payable with 25% down and 25% at the end of 12 months, 24 months, and 36 months with no interest-carrying cost. The parent organization voiced no opposition to transferring the franchise from one set of owners to another.

Forecasted income and expense items on the proposed acquisition are as shown in Exhibit 1. After the fourth year of operation, sales were expected to gain about 10% yearly for four additional years and then to move parallel to inflationary pressures. Prices of items sold in 1995 and later years were expected to be raised adequately to offset increases in costs due to rising minimum wage scale and so forth.

Exhibit 1. Projected Statement of Revenues and Expenses

	Year 1	Year 2	Year 3	Year 4
Sales	$574,375	$796,604	$1,065,480	$1,361,162
Fixed expenses:				
Depreciation	16,000	16,000	16,000	16,000
Amortization	14,000	14,000	14,000	14,000
Salaries	50,000	62,000	72,000	82,000
Rent	24,000	24,000	24,000	24,000
Insurance	4,000	4,000	4,000	4,000
Utilities	24,000	24,000	24,000	24,000
Maintenance	5,000	5,000	5,000	5,000
Total fixed expenses	$137,000	$149,000	$ 159,000	$ 169,000
Variable expenses:				
Salaries	149,698	208,964	277,024	353,900
Taxes	17,238	24,110	31,964	40,834
Rent	11,492	16,014	21,310	27,224
Utilities	11,492	16,014	21,310	27,224

	Year 1	Year 2	Year 3	Year 4
Variable expenses:				
Advertising	28,730	40,186	53,274	68,058
Total variable expenses	$218,650	$305,288	$ 404,882	$ 517,240
Total expenses	$355,650	$454,288	$ 563,882	$ 686,240
Cost of products	229,840	321,484	426,192	544,460
Total costs	$585,490	$775,772	$ 990,074	$1,230,700
Estimated pretax profits	$(11,115)	$ 20,832	$ 75,406	$ 130,462

ASSIGNMENTS

1. Estimate the potential value of the nearby Shoney's.

2. Comment on the ability, or lack of it, of the owners of Midtown Shoney's to make installment payments on the acquisition.

3. Should the firm undertake the use of billboards? Why or why not? What is their indicated investment cost?

4. Suggest risks inherent in a franchised operation that are not present in an individually owned firm.

Capital Janitorial Services, Inc.

In May 1993, Ms. Davis, Mr. Early, and Mr. Forrest of Center, Tex., were considering the acquisition of the common stock of Capital Janitorial Services, Inc., from the sole shareholder, Mr. Arant. Since the shares were not actively traded, the problem arose of determining a fair evaluation for the stock. The three prospective owners also needed to decide whether they would gain a tax advantage by electing to operate as an S corporation or whether such an election was advisable. Since the three buyers did not have enough cash to handle the transaction, an installment purchase plan would have to be developed which was satisfactory to the buyers and the seller.

During the past 20 years, janitorial service businesses had been formed in most cities large enough to support them. A city such as Center, with about 200,000 population and having moderate amounts of commercial and industrial businesses, would not profitably support more than three or four midsized janitorial services. Moreover, several such firms had failed for lack of business during recent years. The city had three other firms in addition to Capital Janitorial.

Capital Janitorial Services was first organized in 1988 by Mr. Early, the sales manager of the present company. He operated the firm as a sole proprietorship for about 18 months but found it extremely hard to supervise the operations activities and to build up the clientele. Consequently, after operating the firm for more than a year at a loss, he sold his interest in the firm to three individuals, Mr. Arant, Mr. Bartel, and Ms. Cole, who incorporated the firm at that time. Mr. Early continued with the firm as sales manager. The owners were not active in the management of the firm other than making an occasional visit to the business and serving on the board of directors (which met quarterly). As the revenue and labor force grew in size, an operations manager was added so that Mr. Early could devote full time to sales expansion, customer problems, and general clerical and accounting work. Ms. Davis joined the firm as operations manager late in 1989, and with two managers, an active sales manager, and an operations manager, revenues and profits began to rise. Mr. Forrest was added as office manager two years later.

The manager worked a 50-hour week for a flat salary. The crew supervisors were hourly paid employees, while the janitorial workers were paid by the job. In early 1993, each of the two managers were receiving $2,000 monthly salary plus total bonuses of 20% of the profits. Each of their salaries were scheduled to advance to $2,200 a month and their total bonuses to increase to 25% in July 1993. No additional changes were planned for the future. The full-time office manager and crew supervisors received about $1,400 each per month, and the janitorial workers (mostly moonlighting from 5:00 p.m. to about 9:00 or 10:00 p.m.) received about $100 weekly (being paid at $5.00 per hour), largely being blue-collar workers or part-time working students.

From incorporation in 1990 to March 1993, Mr. Arant, Mr. Bartel, and Ms. Cole were the shareholders in the company. Mr. Arant owned 40% of the shares, Ms. Cole owned 40% of the shares, and Mr. Bartel owned the balance. Late in March 1993, Ms. Cole and Mr. Bartel sold their shares to Mr. Arant at an aggregate price of $120,000. Mr. Arant had other business interests and indicated a willingness to sell his shares of stock to Ms. Davis and Mr. Early. Mr. Arant offered to sell the shares for an immediate cash payment of $24,000 plus a monthly payment of $2,400 from February 1994 through July 2003. Mr. Arant agreed to retire the remaining bank loan out of the downpayment so that the aggregate asking price of the stock was $288,000.

Ms. Davis and Mr. Early were undecided as to whether the asking price was generous or excessive. The market value of the fixed assets was about $12,000 above their book values, so that the adjusted net worth of the firm was about $100,000, including net profits generated subsequent to the March 31, 1993, balance sheet date. During the fourth quarter of the 1992–93 year, monthly revenues were about $70,000. Ms. Davis believed that total annual revenues would increase by about $100,000 per year for the next five years. Profits were expected to increase slightly more rapidly than sales since a portion was fixed in nature. The rate of growth in revenue was expected to be only about $50,000 per year subsequent to 1999. The firm was earning profits of about $44,000 annually before payment of the bonuses to the sales and operations managers. As additional 1% of revenues could be saved by terminating the accounting service contract with Mr. Bartel (who charged 2% of revenue) and employing a part-time accountant. Other economies could probably reduce expenses by an additional percentage point.

Ms. Davis believed the offer to be attractive. Mr. Arant's share of the profits would amount to approximately $2,400 per month if he retained ownership of the stock. In addition, 40% of the initial cash payment would be used to retire the bank loan. Since repayment was not scheduled to begin until six months after the transfer of ownership, the downpayment would, in reality, be an advance payment of Mr. Arant's share of profits for about six or eight months. On the other hand, the debt incurred by the three proposed shareholders, or by the firm, created a substantial risk in the event that profits declined. Another problem was how to divide the buyout if it were consummated. Should the office manager have an equal share? What of the current bonus contract in force to the sales and operations managers? Should/would the bonuses continue with the new firm?

Mr. Arant had already expressed his desire that the transaction be considered as an installment purchase of the stock so that any gain on the shares would be taxed as a long-term capital gain. Ms. Davis, Mr. Early, and Mr. Forrest, however, were desirous of expensing some of the purchase price of the securities if this could be done legally. Should the shares be purchased by Ms. Davis, Mr. Early, and Mr. Forrest with personal funds, the corporation would be taxed on its income at the normal and sur-tax rate. The shareholders would then have to pay personal taxes on their own taxable income. Each had four exemptions and about $10,000 in deductions, not considering any interest cost of the buyout. None of them had income other than from salary and bonuses from the janitorial business.

As an alternative, Ms. Davis, Mr. Early, and Mr. Forrest could each receive some shares of stock in the corporation for the downpayment, with the firm acquiring the remainder on an installment debt basis. The interest would then be an expense to the firm. If Mr. Arant were willing to draw up an agreement guaranteeing not to start a competing firm in the same city for a definite time period, such as five years, the amount paid for the stock in excess of its fair value could be capitalized and amortized for tax purposes over the cease-and-desist period. If the latter were done, this excess would be taxable to Mr. Arant as ordinary income. Personal assets of Ms. Davis, Mr. Early, and Mr. Forrest consisted of mortgaged homes, household furnishings, and small amounts of liquid savings.

For the next ten years, assuming that the business was acquired, Ms. Davis, Mr. Early, and Mr. Forrest planned to continue to draw their basic salaries from the firm. The bonuses and retained earnings would be used to retire the stock acquisition debt and to build up the company's assets. If the three shareholders wished, they could elect to operate as an S corporation which permitted the shareholders to be taxed on their proportionate share of profits instead of the firm being taxed as a corporation. This would eliminate the double taxation on distributed profits. If this was done, the tax burden equivalent to the owners would have to be pulled from the firm to satisfy the taxes owed.

The potential investors were not sure of the value of the firm. They believed that recent historical profits should be capitalized by about 12% and that the three-year average growth in profits might justify an additional 1% capitalization rate. Since the payments were to be made from periodic profits, Ms. Davis did not believe that a present value analysis was appropriate. However, she did wish to determine what amount of the

$288,000 asking price to consider as purchase price and what amount to consider as interest expense. Since Mr. Arant's tax bracket was 28%, they believed that he would cooperate in setting the value of the firm and the implied interest, within reasonable limits, so as to total the $288,000. Bank term loans were currently going at about 10%.

Ms. Davis, Mr. Early, and Mr. Forrest realized that Mr. Arant would desire a reply to his installment sales offer within a few weeks. If the offer did not appear attractive, a counteroffer could be made. Mr. Arant, however, did not appear overly anxious to dispose of the firm, so Ms. Davis, Mr. Early, and Mr. Forrest were not in much of a bargaining position.

ASSIGNMENTS

1. Redesign the organization chart in Exhibit 1 to reflect its proposed ownership and incorporation.

2. Comment on the tax implications of the proposed sale.

3. Project the financial statements for the next five years, including quarterly cash flow statements for years 1 and 2 after the potential acquisition.

4. Evaluate the pricing of the firm and the imputed interest on the installment purchase contract offered by Mr. Arant.

Exhibit 1. Organization Chart
Capital Janitorial Services, Inc.

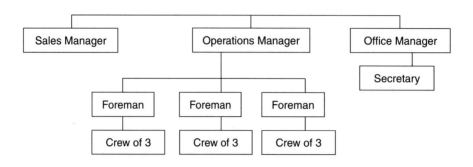

Exhibit 2. Comparative Statements of Revenue and Expenses for Year Ending June 30
Capital Janitorial Services, Inc.

	1990	1991	1992	Mar. 31, 1993 (9 months)
Services rendered	$174,884	$342,752	$571,300	$526,576
Expenses:				
Supervisory salaries	25,652	19,472	58,654	58,678
Janitorial salaries*	83,190	166,560	275,860	267,634
Supplies used	8,490	17,522	35,358	37,280
Direct costs	288	918	728	1,000
Overhead (see Exhibit 3)	90,792	119,080	165,636	151,052
Total expenses	$208,412	$323,552	$536,236	$515,644
Net before-tax profit (loss)	(33,528)	19,200	35,064	10,932

*Includes the salaries and bonuses paid to the sales and operations managers, forepersons, and crew supervisors (10% wage premium).

Exhibit 3. Schedule of Overhead for Year Ending June 30
Capital Janitorial Services, Inc.

	1990	1991	1992	Mar. 31, 1993 (9 months)
Advertising	—	$ 224	$ 704	$ 296
Amortization of leasehold improvements	$ 162	584	560	592
Bad debts	400	940	332	90
Bank charges	86	240	430	306
Breakage expenses	440	504	90	472
Commissions	7,038	536	—	8,044
Depreciation:				
Automotive equipment	2,832	4,262	7,252	4,728*
Furniture/fixtures	240	360	412	380
Janitorial equipment	2,406	6,946	9,860	7,340
Employees' expense allowance	3,266	2,112	960	—*
Insurance (including workers' compensation)	3,436	6,676	10,368	10,552
Interest	288	456	24	712
Laundry	336	784	776	1,350
Legal and accounting	4,568	4,748	7,752	15,570
Mileage allowance	10,688	11,540	9,876	6,144*
Miscellaneous (supplies, etc.)	2,032	2,060	2,636	2,546
Office expenses (supplies)	3,072	1,848	4,824	3,558
Office salaries: Manager and secretary	26,736	34,796	49,280	36,860
Payroll taxes	8,916	12,478	24,532	21,888
Rent	3,384	4,030	4,752	4,066
Rental (equipment)	—	232	100	62
Repairs	680	456	1,200	2,260
Taxes and licenses	364	500	1,564	968
Telephone/telegraph	3,200	5,640	7,192	4,456
Travel (to meetings)	—	1,048	740	544
Truck expenses	4,718	7,962	13,992	11,728
Uniform expenses	584	738	1,108	232
Utilities (water/heat provided)	—	76	20	788
Warehouse operation	920	6,304	4,300	4,520
Total	$90,792	$119,080	$165,636	$151,052

*Autos and vans were acquired, and travel mileage was largely phased out to certain types of employees.

Exhibit 4. Balance Sheet as of Mar. 31, 1993
Capital Janitorial Services, Inc.

			Amount	Percent
ASSETS				
Current assets:				
Cash			$ 12,328	
Accounts receivable, trade			78,006	
Inventory—supplies			12,694	
Inventory—uniforms			508	
Total current assets			$104,376	74.7
Fixed assets:	*Cost*	*Accumulated Depreciation*	*Net Amount*	
Automotive equipment	$24,492	$10,068	$14,424	
Furniture and fixtures	5,056	1,412	3,644	
Janitorial equipment	40,888	26,952	13,936	
Total fixed assets	$70,436	$38,432	$32,004	22.9
Other assets:				
Accounts receivable, other			1,772	
Leasehold improvements			196	
Meter deposits			480	
Total other assets			$ 2,448	1.8
Deferred charges (prepaid taxes and licenses)			844	.6
Total assets			$139,672	100.0
LIABILITIES AND CAPITAL				
Current liabilities:				
Accounts payable, trade			$ 3,980	
Notes payable, bank			9,400	
Due to affiliates			1,340	
Due to officers			5,960	
Taxes payable and accrued			11,640	
Payroll taxes withheld/payable			2,148	
Accrued insurance			17,108	
Accrued salaries and wages			12,616	
Total current liabilities			$ 64,192	46.0
Capital:				
Capital stock ($10 par)			48,000	
Retained earnings			27,480	
Total capital			$ 75,480	54.0
Total liabilities and capital			$139,672	100.0

Bibliography

Almanac of Business and Industry Financial Ratios. Prentice-Hall Inc., Englewood Cliffs, N.J.

Encyclopedia of Business Information Sources. Gale Research, Inc., Detroit.

Industry Norms and Key Business Ratios. Dun & Bradstreet, Inc., New York, 1993–94.

Statement Studies. Robert L. Morris Associates, Philadelphia, 1993, 1994.

U.S. Department of Commerce, *Business Census, Retailing.* Government Printing Office, Washington, D.C., 1992.

U.S. Department of Commerce, *Business Census, Service.* Government Printing Office, Washington, D.C., 1992.

U.S. Department of Commerce, *County Business Patterns.* Government Printing Office, Washington, D.C., 1993.

U.S. Department of Commerce, *U.S. Industrial Outlook.* Government Printing Office, Washington, D.C., 1993 and 1994.

U.S. Department of the Treasury, *IRS Statistics of Income (Proprietorship, Partnership, and Corporation),* selected. Government Printing Office, Washington, D.C.

Appendix A
Present Value Tables

Table 1. Present Value of 1 Factors

Years (N)	1%	2%	4%	6%	8%	10%	12%	14%	15%	16%
1	0.990	0.980	0.962	0.943	0.926	0.909	0.893	0.877	0.870	0.862
2	1.970	1.942	1.886	1.833	1.783	1.736	1.690	1.647	1.626	1.605
3	2.941	2.884	2.775	2.673	2.577	2.487	2.402	2.322	2.283	2.246
4	3.902	3.808	3.630	3.465	3.312	3.170	3.037	2.914	2.855	2.798
5	4.853	4.713	4.452	4.212	3.993	3.791	3.605	3.433	3.352	3.274
6	5.795	5.601	5.242	4.917	4.623	4.355	4.111	3.889	3.784	3.685
7	6.728	6.472	6.002	5.582	5.206	4.868	4.564	4.288	4.160	4.039
8	7.652	7.325	6.733	6.210	5.747	5.335	4.968	4.639	4.487	4.344
9	8.566	8.162	7.435	6.802	6.247	5.759	5.328	4.946	4.772	4.607
10	9.471	8.983	8.111	7.360	6.710	6.145	5.650	5.216	5.019	4.833
11	10.368	9.787	8.760	7.887	7.139	6.495	5.988	5.453	5.234	5.029
12	11.255	10.575	9.385	8.384	7.536	6.814	6.194	5.660	5.421	5.197
13	12.134	11.343	9.986	8.853	7.904	7.103	6.424	5.842	5.583	5.342
14	13.004	12.106	10.563	9.295	8.244	7.367	6.628	6.002	5.724	5.468
15	13.865	12.849	11.118	9.712	8.559	7.606	6.811	6.142	5.847	5.575
16	14.718	13.578	11.652	10.106	8.851	7.824	6.974	6.265	5.954	5.669
17	15.562	14.292	12.166	10.477	9.122	8.022	7.120	6.373	6.047	5.749
18	16.398	14.992	12.659	10.828	9.372	8.201	7.250	6.467	6.128	5.818
19	17.226	15.678	13.134	11.158	9.604	8.365	7.366	6.550	6.198	5.877
20	18.046	16.351	13.590	11.470	9.818	8.514	7.469	6.623	6.259	5.929
21	18.857	17.011	14.029	11.764	10.017	8.649	7.562	6.687	6.312	5.973
22	19.660	17.658	14.451	12.042	10.201	8.772	7.645	6.743	6.359	6.011
23	20.456	18.292	14.857	12.303	10.371	8.883	7.718	6.792	6.399	6.044
24	21.243	18.914	15.247	12.550	10.529	8.985	7.784	6.835	6.434	6.073
25	22.023	19.523	15.622	12.783	10.675	9.077	7.843	6.873	6.464	6.097
26	22.795	20.121	15.983	13.003	10.810	9.161	7.896	6.906	6.491	6.118
27	23.560	20.707	16.330	13.211	10.935	9.237	7.943	6.935	6.514	6.136
28	24.316	21.281	16.663	13.406	11.051	9.307	7.984	6.961	6.534	6.152
29	25.066	21.844	16.984	13.591	11.158	9.370	8.022	6.983	6.551	6.166
30	25.808	22.396	17.292	13.765	11.258	9.427	8.055	7.003	6.566	6.177
40	32.835	27.355	19.793	15.046	11.925	9.779	8.244	7.105	6.642	6.234
50	39.196	31.424	21.482	15.762	12.234	9.915	8.304	7.133	6.661	6.246

Table 2. Present Value of 1 per Period Factors

Years (N)	1%	2%	4%	6%	8%	10%	12%	14%	15%	16%
1	0.990	0.980	0.962	0.943	0.926	0.909	0.893	0.877	0.870	0.862
2	1.970	1.942	1.886	1.833	1.783	1.736	1.690	1.647	1.626	1.605
3	2.941	2.884	2.775	2.673	2.577	2.487	2.402	2.322	2.283	2.246
4	3.902	3.808	3.630	3.465	3.312	3.170	3.037	2.914	2.855	2.798
5	4.853	4.713	4.452	4.212	3.993	3.791	3.605	3.433	3.352	3.274
6	5.795	5.601	5.242	4.917	4.623	4.355	4.111	3.889	3.784	3.685
7	6.728	6.472	6.002	5.582	5.206	4.868	4.564	4.288	4.160	4.039
8	7.652	7.325	6.733	6.210	5.747	5.335	4.968	4.639	4.487	4.344
9	8.566	8.162	7.435	6.802	6.247	5.759	5.328	4.946	4.772	4.607
10	9.471	8.983	8.111	7.360	6.710	6.145	5.650	5.216	5.019	4.833
11	10.368	9.787	8.760	7.887	7.139	6.495	5.988	5.453	5.234	5.029
12	11.255	10.575	9.385	8.384	7.536	6.814	6.194	5.660	5.421	5.197
13	12.134	11.343	9.986	8.853	7.904	7.103	6.424	5.842	5.583	5.342
14	13.004	12.106	10.563	9.295	8.244	7.367	6.628	6.002	5.724	5.468
15	13.865	12.849	11.118	9.712	8.559	7.606	6.811	6.142	5.847	5.575
16	14.718	13.578	11.652	10.106	8.851	7.824	6.974	6.265	5.954	5.669
17	15.562	14.292	12.166	10.477	9.122	8.022	7.120	6.373	6.047	5.749
18	16.398	14.992	12.659	10.828	9.372	8.201	7.250	6.467	6.128	5.818
19	17.226	15.678	13.134	11.158	9.604	8.365	7.366	6.550	6.198	5.877
20	18.046	16.351	13.590	11.470	9.818	8.514	7.469	6.623	6.259	5.929
21	18.857	17.011	14.029	11.764	10.017	8.649	7.562	6.687	6.312	5.973
22	19.660	17.658	14.451	12.042	10.201	8.772	7.645	6.743	6.359	6.011
23	20.456	18.292	14.857	12.303	10.371	8.883	7.718	6.792	6.399	6.044
24	21.243	18.914	15.247	12.550	10.529	8.985	7.784	6.835	6.434	6.073
25	22.023	19.523	15.622	12.783	10.675	9.077	7.843	6.873	6.464	6.097
26	22.795	20.121	15.983	13.003	10.810	9.161	7.896	6.906	6.491	6.118
27	23.560	20.707	16.330	13.211	10.935	9.237	7.943	6.935	6.514	6.136
28	24.316	21.281	16.663	13.406	11.051	9.307	7.984	6.961	6.534	6.152
29	25.066	21.844	16.984	13.591	11.158	9.370	8.022	6.983	6.551	6.166
30	25.808	22.396	17.292	13.765	11.258	9.427	8.055	7.003	6.566	6.177
40	32.835	27.355	19.793	15.046	11.925	9.779	8.244	7.105	6.642	6.234
50	39.196	31.424	21.482	15.762	12.234	9.915	8.304	7.133	6.661	6.246

Appendix B
Current Federal
Income Tax Rules

What to File

Single Proprietor. Ordinarily must file Form 1040 (long form), including a Schedule C for business income and expenses.

Partnership. Must file a partnership information return; each partner shows respective share of profit/loss on Form 1040, Schedule C.

Principal of S Corporation. Firm must file return; owners must report their proportionate share of income, whether distributed or not.

Self-Employment Tax Rates

Year	Base for OASDI	Base for Medicare	Total Rate
1994	$60,600	Unlimited	15.3%
1995	$61,200	Unlimited	15.3%
1996+	CPI adjusted	Unlimited	15.3%

Income Deferrals

Cost of firm-provided term insurance on employees in excess of $50,000 in coverage is taxable income to the employee.

Some firms have a 401(k) deferral plan. Employees can shelter up to 20% of income (with an upper limit of about $9,000); and the firm can contribute additional amounts, with the total not to exceed $30,000 yearly.

Self-employed persons may shelter under a Keogh Plan up to 25% of taxable income, not to exceed $30,000 yearly.

Auto Expense Deduction

This expense may be claimed at a rate of $0.29 per mile or actual expenses for business mileage. Straight-line depreciation over a 5-year life is used for an auto. The firm may take an immediate equipment writeoff of $10,000 yearly in 1987 through 1992 and $17,500 in later years in lieu of capitalizing and depreciating.

Retirement Income Treatment

Those born in 1938 or earlier use a base age of 65. Those born later see the base age gradually moving to 67 (by the year 2022). In 1993 and 1994, if taxable income exceeded $25,000 and $32,000 for single and joint returns, respectively, then up to 50% of such OASDI income was subject to taxes. If taxable income exceeded $34,000 and $44,000, then 85% was subject to taxes.

Distribution of Deferral Accounts

To avoid a 10% tax penalty, deferrals should be begun from age 59.5 to 70.5, and deferrals are usually withdrawn over the estimated remaining life of the subject.

Other Payroll Taxes

State Income and Federal Unemployment Taxes.

State Workers' Compensation. (Bought from a casualty insurance company.) Rates vary by state and job classification.

Payroll Records

A firm employing one or more persons must have a federal employer identification number (FEIN); must receive a W–4 Form from each employee to be filed with the personnel department; and must deduct appropriate amounts for OASDHI and federal and state income taxes. Payroll taxes must be deposited on a timely basis with a depository bank, usually by the ninth of each month following payroll deductions.

Appendix C
Business Plan Outline

Introduction: Purpose statement or cover letter

SECTION I

The Business

- Business description
- Target market
- Market analysis
- The competition
- Marketing strategy

Management

- Business organization/form of business
- Management/personnel
- Insurance
- Supplies/professional services
- Licenses and permits

Location/Building Description

- Site description
- Building
- Equipment

SECTION II

Financials

- Financial plan (balance sheets/income statements), historical and projected
- Sources and uses of funds statement
- Monthly operating expenses worksheet
- Personal financial statement

Index